D1496366

THE I TATTI
RENAISSANCE LIBRARY

James Hankins, General Editor

MANETTI

ON HUMAN WORTH AND EXCELLENCE

ITRL 85

GIANNOZZO MANETTI
◆ ◆ ◆
ON HUMAN WORTH AND EXCELLENCE

EDITED AND TRANSLATED BY

BRIAN P. COPENHAVER

THE I TATTI RENAISSANCE LIBRARY
HARVARD UNIVERSITY PRESS
CAMBRIDGE, MASSACHUSETTS
LONDON, ENGLAND
2018

Series design by Dean Bornstein

Library of Congress Cataloging-in-Publication Data

Names: Manetti, Giannozzo, 1396–1459, author. | Copenhaver, Brian P.,
editor, translator. | Container of (expression): Manetti, Giannozzo, 1396–1459.
De dignitate et excellentia hominis. | Container of (expression): Manetti,
Giannozzo, 1396–1459. De dignitate et excellentia hominis. English.
Title: On human worth and excellence / edited and translated by
Brian P. Copenhaver.
Other titles: I Tatti Renaissance library ; 85.
Description: Cambridge, Massachusetts : Harvard University Press, 2019. |
Series: I Tatti Renaissance library ; 85 | Includes bibliographical references
and index. | Text in Latin with English translation on facing pages ;
introduction and notes in English.
Identifiers: LCCN 2017047325 | ISBN 9780674984585 (alk. paper)
Subjects: LCSH: Human beings. | Manetti, Giannozzo, 1396–1459.
De dignitate et excellentia hominis. | Dignity — Religious aspects —
Christianity. | Theological anthropology — Christianity.
Classification: LCC BD450 .M26813 2018 | DDC 128 — dc23
LC record available at https://lccn.loc.gov/2017047325

Contents

ॐ§?ॐ

Introduction

※※※

1. Mortified for Glory

Antonio da Barga, from a village north of Lucca and probably still in his teens, took vows as an Olivetan monk in 1414. He chose a branch of the Benedictine Order that was also young—just a century old. The founder—San Bernardo Tolomei—was learned and ascetic: he named his Congregation of Monte Oliveto for the hill outside Jerusalem where on the night before Jesus died, he suffered "in agony . . . and his sweat was as it were great drops of blood." In 1430 Antonio became prior of an Olivetan house in Florence, soon rising to an office that sent him on inspection tours throughout Italy and elsewhere. His visits gave him access to people and records that informed his *Chronicle of Monte Oliveto*, unfinished when he died in 1452.

The *Chronicle* can be read in a modern edition, as can only one other work by Antonio: his *Book on Mankind's Worth (Dignitas) and the Excellence of Human Life*, the first product of Renaissance Italy to name *dignitas* as its subject. Like the *Chronicle*, this text is unfinished, but much shorter, only fourteen pages when printed, and unoriginal as well: the first fourth simply copies (silently) from Peter Lombard's *Sentences*. It was the next section, about half as long, that started the Quattrocento conversation about *dignitas* with advice on how to approach this topic.[1]

Since the end of the eighteenth century, modern thinkers have traced their own ideas about human dignity not to Antonio, who was in no way modern, but to Giovanni Pico della Mirandola and his *Oration* of 1486. Readers have been misled by an early editor who—after Pico's death—gave this work a title unknown to its author, *Oration on the Dignity of Man*, supplying the speech with a

false identity. *Dignitas* occurs only twice in this text of 7,400 words and not to name a property of human beings.[2]

Pico gave the speech no title and never let it be printed. When his nephew Gianfrancesco published it after he died, the nephew explained that the speech had come to embarrass his uncle — just as his uncle's message embarrassed him. The *Oration* declares that humans must exit this world in order to become angels. Gianfrancesco — like his hero, Savonarola — would have approved had his uncle said no more, and if his words could have been taken metaphorically, as a pious call to asceticism. But Pico wanted to turn humans into angels with Jewish magic.[3]

Angels also figured in the evidence when Antonio da Barga sketched a case for human *dignitas*. Chanting the Psalms every day, he had learned that God made mankind "a little lower than the angels." "The angels are above us now," he wrote, but "they will be our equals in the future" — a future of heavenly bliss, earned by penitence and prayer. But conventional Christian piety was not Pico's project in the *Oration*, which urges people to use magic and Kabbalah. Since Pico's directive — to learn the ecstasies of Kabbalah and escape the body — makes no demands on human *dignitas*, he barely mentions the word and shows no interest in what it might mean.[4]

Dignitas, however, along with *excellentia*, was plainly on Antonio's mind when he gave advice about writing a book on those topics:

> In the book and in your conclusions you should repeat this often: Be aware of your rank (*dignitas*), you human; the heavens have been prepared for you, and you must not sink down. . . .

> Also, you should say this about man's worth (*dignitas*) — namely, about the soul's immortality. . . .

Also, you should say this about man's worth (*dignitas*) — in particular, about the making of man and the handsomeness of his parts that Lactantius writes about.

Also, Jerome says this about man's worth (*dignitas*): great is the worth (*dignitas*) of souls so that from the moment of birth each one has an angel appointed to watch over it. . . .

Also, about man's worth (*dignitas*): angels have their assignments . . . to watch over humans and instruct them. . . .

And although man's excellence (*excellentia*) makes him incomparably more outstanding than other created things, . . . yet there will be twelve blessings in which he himself, wholly human, will abound forever. . . .[5]

All but the last of these telegraphic directions come from a list that takes less than two pages to describe what should go into a treatment of human *dignitas* and *excellentia*. The list — seventeen brief items — is the second part of Antonio's text, following long selections from the book that had educated theologians in the Latin West since the twelfth century, Peter Lombard's *Sentences*, never mentioned by Antonio. In the third section of his little work — almost two-thirds of the whole — the monk spins a long excursus from his vision of twelve heavenly blessings to come. Almost everything he writes comes from the Bible and Peter Lombard. A single mention of Cicero merely names a famous person, but citing Lactantius just once was consequential, alluding to a treatise *On God's Workmanship* that would soon catch Giannozzo Manetti's eye.[6]

The human beings that Lactantius and Antonio call handsome live on earth in bodies that have not yet died. From Antonio's perspective, this esteem for an attractive physical frame is remarkable, considering what Peter Lombard had asked: "Why was the

soul joined to a body since it would seem to have higher standing had it remained bodiless?" Antonio copied Peter's question along with two answers: either God moves in mysterious ways; or he has used the wonder of body/soul union to teach humans how an eternal home for the elect can be a kingdom of spirits that admits no earthly bodies.[7]

The bodies most of interest to Peter and Antonio will be raised above earth and glorified: agile, beautiful, healthy, youthful, knowing no pain or other sadness — these are the transfigured bodies that humans will enjoy in heaven. Mortal bodies, unglorified, draw only two positive comments from Antonio: their handsomeness is praiseworthy, and their erect stature reflects the soul's aspirations by looking up toward heaven. Otherwise, he discusses the body of flesh and bone mainly to puzzle over its junction with the soul. The glorified body, by contrast, fills paragraph after paragraph as he catalogs its twelve blessings along with six other joys and the three levels of heaven where such bodies will dwell for all eternity.[8]

As Antonio composed his instructions, in the weeks before Easter of 1447, he felt the weight of his body — "weakened and worn out by many fasts, vigils and observances of the *Rule*." Lent was still the season, once described by a famous preacher of his Order as "kept with fasts and by tormenting our flesh, standing for the present age in which we must share in Christ's sufferings by mortifying our bodies," until Easter comes with new life. The preacher and Antonio knew how Paul had comforted the Corinthians, who were "always bearing about in the body the dying of the Lord Jesus so that the life also of Jesus might be made manifest in the body." This "dying" in the Authorized Version is *nekrôsis* in Greek, *mortificatio* in the Vulgate: literally, the act of Christ's dying, which the faithful must embody. Human mortifications in Lent repeat the divine mortification, while anticipating joys that Easter and resurrection will soon bring.[9]

Antonio probably wrote within days of Laetare Sunday, which follows the Thursday that marks the middle of Lent. The name of that Sunday, in a penitential season, tells Christians to rejoice, with Lent more than half gone and Easter closer than ever. Preachers in monasteries, where life itself was a liturgy, marked the ritual calendar with sermons on Laetare Sunday about the glorified body — giving reasons to rejoice in a time of mortification. As Easter approached in 1447, Antonio was prior of a monastery in Naples, where his responsibilities made him think all the more about these sacred rhythms of liturgy and about all his monastic experience — experience that explains why the glorified body dominates his instructions about *dignitas*.[10]

Antonio addressed his advice to Bartolomeo Facio, a scholar assigned by the Genoese to represent them at the court of King Alfonso of Aragon, Sicily and — since 1442 — Naples. Generosity to scholars like Facio was one reason why contemporaries called Alfonso "magnanimous." But when Antonio wrote to Facio, in terms of endearment, it was a dead pope, not a living king, that he was thinking about.[11]

Antonio tells Facio about "a little book in splendid language" on "human misery and man's vileness" by "a man called Innocent, once Supreme Pontiff of the Roman Church," adding that the pope — Innocent III — had "promised to write a companion volume . . . *On the Worth and Excellence of Human Life*." But duty prevented Innocent from keeping his promise, and Prior Antonio now finds himself in the same plight, "fettered by all these obligations." He asks Facio to do the job instead. Praising him as "skilled in the art of oratory," the monk calls on his friend to bring "Ciceronian eloquence" to the task. Then he spells out his recommendations — "not finished, just a bit of a brief sketch with various headings and distinctions."[12]

The phrase "headings and distinctions" describes seventeen items in the second part of Antonio's text, an outline of just two

pages preceding the long digression on the glorified body and following the material from Peter Lombard's *Sentences*. These pages started the process that Manetti would complete with a very different treatment of *dignitas* and *excellentia*.[13]

In an age saturated with religion, Manetti impressed his contemporaries as being remarkably serious and pious—for a layman active in the world. Living apart from the world by Saint Benedict's *Rule*, Antonio saw things differently—notably the issue of human worth and excellence. The outline that he sent to Facio attributes *dignitas* to a rational, immortal, and unbodily soul that accounts for mankind's superiority to other earthly creatures and for human dominion over them, also for parity with angels and likeness to God. Nothing about human activity, creativity, effort, energy, or ingenuity comes into the monk's reckoning.

But his beloved son in Christ, Facio, also lived in the world—living very much like Manetti. Born before 1410, Facio was younger than Manetti by ten years or so but quicker to apply himself to the classics; he left La Spezia for Guarino's famous school in Verona around the time when Manetti began similar lessons in Florence. By 1436, while tutoring and polishing his Latin with compositions on history, language, and society, he had also found government work in Genoa. In 1443 the Republic sent him to Naples as ambassador to King Alfonso's court. Manetti, first assigned to Naples in the same year, joined the royal retinue along with Facio—the more engaged of the two in learned society and its polemics. Lorenzo Valla was writing his vicious *Antidote to Facio* before the envoy was called to Rome in 1448 by Pope Nicholas V's election.

After 1447, as Antonio was preparing his outline, both Facio and Manetti were clients of Nicholas and of Alfonso as well. The Jubilee of 1450 in Rome gave Facio the occasion to present something new to the pope, who (like Alfonso) had already received his essay *On Happiness in Life*, which—by the author's own account—

overlaps with his new offering *On Human Excellence and Superiority*. During the same period, Facio was working on the most memorable product of his scholarship, *The Deeds of Alfonso, First King of Naples*, completed in 1457, the year of his death in Alfonso's city.[14]

Facio's short statement on *excellentia* and *praestantia*, about seven thousand words, made little stir. One reader was Manetti, who shared two patrons with him, but the essay was seldom copied and was printed only once. The lone edition of 1611 carries a mistaken dedication to Pius II, who became pope after Facio died. Another mistake, attributing the papal treatise on human misery to Innocent IV—who reigned thirty years after its author, Innocent III—may be Facio's, though the fourth Innocent, from an eminent Genoese family, should have been known to him. Except in Genoa, however, the third Innocent was the more famous: his tirade on human misery—finished before he became pope—survives in hundreds of manuscripts.[15]

Facio marketed his gift to Pope Nicholas as breaking ground on an understudied topic. As of 1366, in fact, Petrarch had discovered no attempt at all to answer Pope Innocent III. It was that pontiff—or Cardinal Lotario dei Segni, as he still was in 1195—who set the terms of the Quattrocento debate with his unkept promise to "describe the *dignitas* of human nature," after first dealing with mankind's *miseria* and *vilitas*. So when Facio found his topic, delivered to him by a monk, a key antithesis had already been established: *dignitas* versus *vilitas* and *miseria*. Although the title he (or an editor) picked—*De excellentia et praestantia*—does not mention *dignitas*, the word appears a dozen times in the text, as in the phrase *hominis dignitas*.[16]

After arguing that God made humans because of his own infinite goodness, Facio raises a "deeper" question about their *dignitas*, asking "what gifts God gave man and also which ones other animals lack, . . . since mankind's whole distinction (*praestantia*) lies in these gifts." The best divine endowment of all is the immortal

soul that makes humans resemble God. Although some pagans understood the soul's special nature, Christian authorities come first for Facio, who also presents his own arguments for immortality from metaphysics, natural instinct, and divine justice: the prose is stylish but the mood no less medieval than Antonio's. Cicero comes up only once amid dozens of references to Aquinas, Aristotle, the *Book of Causes*, Chrysostom, Gregory the Great, Jerome, Lactantius, "the distinguished Master of the *Sentences*," but especially Augustine and the Bible.[17]

One theme that holds Facio's attention goes back to the eleventh century and farther: the architecture of the soul's resemblance to God as originally analyzed by Augustine. Triads of faculties like mind, will, and memory reflect the whole Trinity, not just Christ's human nature. This likeness to God proves mankind's superiority to the rest of earthly creation, a rank confirmed by the ministrations of angels in heaven, who guard every human soul from birth and give the holiest people special help. Further evidence of mankind's primacy comes from miracles worked by prophets and saints and from sacramental and judicial powers granted to priests and popes. God gave his best gift, however, when his only Son took on "this lowly mortal body."[18]

Although man's physical stature is exceptional — an erect body towering over every earthbound beast, a beautiful form to match the soul's excellence and house its powers of reason and speech — it is the mind, not the body, that enables humans "to build cities, design shelter and clothing, establish laws, observe the turning heavens and motions of the cycling stars, devise medicine and so many more arts and sciences." Even here, however, where Facio turns briefly to human agency in this life, what makes the action possible is a defect of bodies — the elemental structure of material things that are "broken up and taken apart so that people can use them." Humans who destroy some material things in order to make others have bodies made of the same destructible matter —

bodies doomed to decay except that immortal souls preserve them. Bodies themselves, as apart from souls, remain filthy and vile until God purges their corruption at the end of time.[19]

Facio notices God's many gifts to man "in this troubled and mortal life," before the Last Judgment, but he pays little attention to them before hurrying on to the afterlife and its transcendent delights. His earlier book about "life's happiness" had focused on passing pleasures that "last scarcely a generation," whereas heaven's bliss is perpetual and shows "human worth (*dignitas*) far more fully." Although the blessings to come are impossible to observe and hard to grasp, Facio spends a third of his essay on them—less attention than Antonio gave, though he is no less captivated by the afterlife. Some details of the blessings reflect Antonio's outline, but some do not, and Facio names a new source—Thomas Aquinas.[20]

The beatific vision heads Facio's list of blessings, but he cannot decide whether "we shall look on the divine majesty with the spirit's eyes rather than the body's." In either case, bodies in heaven will surely be glorified—brighter, quicker, finer than any flesh and immune to all pain and disturbance. The body's glorification repairs flaws of the flesh that Facio, Antonio, and their ancestors had all suffered: joys of the glorified body heal physical and moral lesions in the old Adam.[21]

Facio took his bearings on the glorified body—and other evidence for human *dignitas*—from Antonio, and Manetti learned from them both. He too ends his account of *dignitas* and *excellentia* in realms of celestial bliss, but he finds glorification less important, giving it only 5 percent of his text, to close four books on many more subjects than Facio and Antonio had covered. That Manetti knew Facio's essay on *dignitas* is certain, because he praises it in presenting his book to Alfonso; that he also had Antonio's outline is more than likely, though he never mentions it.[22]

Manetti's book was ready by the end of 1452, while he was still representing Florence abroad, as he had done since 1437: his busi-

est diplomatic service began in 1443 in Naples and ended ten years later in Rome, after several missions to both cities. When he began work on *dignitas* is uncertain, but he recalls accepting the task from Alfonso in conversations at Torre del Greco near Naples. Three of his assignments after 1443 were to Alfonso's court—the last in 1451. In 1452 the coronation of Emperor Frederick III called him to Rome, stalling his progress on the book. He finished it back home in Tuscany, while on administrative duty in the Mugello. By then relations with his city had gone bad, forcing him to leave Florence in 1454 for Rome and patronage from Nicholas.

When Nicholas died in 1455, Manetti turned to Alfonso in Naples, before Manetti himself died in 1459 at the age of sixty-three, after writing the pope's biography, working on a *Life* of Alfonso and dedicating a little work to him about earthquakes, like the one that struck Naples in December of 1456. Weightier projects from the 1450s were translations from Greek and Hebrew. Although his colleague Facio allowed that such writings "attract and amuse readers with novel material," innovation did little for Manetti's reputation.[23]

Nicholas encouraged Manetti to take on the Bible. Since Jerome's was the last Latin New Testament made from Greek, the version that Manetti started around 1453 was an epochal novelty, which almost no one noticed: the same for his translations of all three of Aristotle's ethical works, prepared in the same period. Since so few Christians—even in Rome—had access to teachers of Hebrew, since they had no lexical or grammatical guides to that language in Latin, since even scholars as serious as Leonardo Bruni discouraged the study of the sacred tongue, Manetti—facing such obstacles—probably had to start learning Hebrew well before he finished his Psalter in 1458, along with an *Apologeticus* to explain and defend his choices.[24] Manetti's motives for translating the Psalms were apologetic in a different sense as well: he hoped that a better version would help convert the Jews and confute their

attacks on Christian scholars. He left a separate work *Against Jews and Gentiles* unfinished.[25]

The experience with biblical literature and Aristotle's philosophy that Manetti gained by translating Greek and Hebrew texts came mostly too late to inform his work on *dignitas*, but earlier historical and biographical studies—including a *History of Pistoia* and *Lives* of Boccaccio, Dante, Petrarch, Seneca and Socrates—acquainted him with brilliant people whose glorious stories surely helped him decide that *dignitas* and *excellentia* are indeed features of the human condition.[26]

2. Manetti's Dignitas: Body

Human glory was far from Lotario dei Segni's thoughts when he reviled mankind in the late twelfth century. The first two parts of his book denounce misery in this present life, leaving the next for a third part.

Starting with the matter that humans are made of, in conception, development, and birth, then throughout life from infancy to senility—both rich and poor, both servant and master, married and celibate, godly and wicked—Lotario shows how all are loaded down by dread, failure, filth, frustration, noise, pain, shock, sickness, terror, toil, torture, and the fear of death. On top of these physical and psychological horrors, the second book piles sins—and punishments for sins—of ambition, arrogance, boasting, bribery, corruption, deceit, desire, drunkenness, gluttony, greed, lust, perversion, pride, and waste. The third book shows what happens to sinners whose bodies rot in the ground and go unglorified after Judgment Day, when anguish, despair, futility, remorse, and tribulation will compound and aggravate the torment of Hell's black flames.[27]

Lotario's contempt for his own kind is relentless, intensified by mannered prose: if there were a Library of Loathing stocked with

attacks on the human species, and if its masterpieces were ranked, the cardinal's book would make the top ten. Manetti found its lurid music unforgettable: "he goes on endlessly about . . . the human body—the nakedness, the lice, the spit, piss, shit, fleeting time, old age, the different pains that mortals suffer." The summary is sordid and exactly right, as any chapter of *De miseria* will show, like this one about conception, prompted by a question from Job:

> "Who can cleanse what has been conceived from unclean seed?" . . . Who does not know that copulation, even in marriage, never happens with flesh entirely free of the itch, never without lust boiling over, without the rank stench of the wanton? By this the seeds conceived are dirtied, infected and defiled, and the soul that later flows in from them picks up the stain of sin, the blemish of guilt and the filth of wickedness, just as liquid is tainted when poured from a tainted vessel after being polluted by touching the pollution.[28]

Manetti conveys the full force of Lotario's harangue, unlike Antonio or Facio. Both Antonio and Facio framed their statements as responses to a pope, but with no complaints about the writer or the writing about *miseria*: their aim was just to supply a missing response about *dignitas*. Manetti was more ambitious. He mentions Innocent III only after making his own positive case— and at much greater length than his predecessors, filling three books. Only at that point, having already established "the astonishing value (*dignitas*) of human nature and mankind's unbelievable excellence (*excellentia*)," he adds a fourth book to rebut the pope and other defamers of mankind. Although he finds the pope's arguments "trifling, childish and quite remote from pontifical and apostolic seriousness," he gives them enough attention to make the last book the longest of the four.[29]

The first three books praise the body, the soul, and the body/ soul composite. The least original, in one way, is the first: more than half of it comes — with comments and full attribution — from Cicero's *On the Nature of the Gods* and Lactantius' *On God's Workmanship*. In other ways, however, this part of Manetti's project is strikingly original — not only in contrast to Lotario's revulsion for the body but also in light of the earlier reactions to him by Antonio and Facio. Even Facio — a layman, not a monk — thinks of the "lowly mortal body" as destructible, diseased, filthy, vile, and corrupted by its matter.[30]

Manetti's attitude is different. Humans have bodies "worthier and more wonderful" than those of other animals. Their "grand and godlike" structure exhibits "so exact a plan and . . . such great ingenuity" that God's providential design is plain to see in them. Their many features of "worth (*dignitas*) and excellence (*excellentia*)" manifest God's wish to make the body a "fitting vessel for the rational soul." The Creator made the body for the soul, in other words, not the reverse, but the physical result of his "most perfect plan" is in itself a great good and a wonder.[31]

To show God's purposes in the human body, Manetti begins — in a traditional way — with Adam's creation from the soil. But to interpret the first man's earthy name (*Adam, homo, humanus, humus, anthrôpos*), he turns not to Christian exegesis but to philology and poetry. A show of classicism — Latin etymology dressed up with Greek, Hebrew, and a little pagan verse — is the prelude to a bolder departure from the advice that Facio had taken from a monk. Manetti gives most of his first book to two witnesses who have discovered God's providence in the body, and the first is Cicero, a heathen.[32]

Writing *On the Nature of the Gods*, Cicero at one point makes a Stoic case — against the Epicureans — for the government of the universe as divine and providential, arguing from the nature of divinity itself, from the order of the universe and from structures

and functions of celestial and terrestrial nature, especially the living human body. Manetti reproduces most of what Cicero says about the body, as he moves down from the mouth through the throat to the major organs below, stopping at the intestines. He describes bodily processes, mainly breathing and blood flow, and structures, mainly bones and sinews, that extend through the whole anatomy. A key observation is that God has put the head, with its organs of sense, at the top of an erect body.[33]

Manetti's second witness is a book *On God's Workmanship*, whose author was known to him as a Christian from a later and much larger work on *Elements of Divinity*. While still a convert who had not fully declared himself, Lactantius wrote the earlier work to praise the Creator without yet naming him as the Christian God. Lactantius — the "Christian Cicero" to his admirers — found the master's various accounts of the body "thin and scanty," though they certainly impressed Manetti. Like Cicero's study of Roman religion, *De opificio* makes a case for providence, but a narrower one, focused on human anatomy, physiology, and psychology. The topics picked out by Manetti are erect stature, the head and its contents, the hands, thorax, respiratory, digestive, reproductive and other internal organs, the anatomy of speech, the soul, and the mind.[34]

When Cicero's description of the internal organs reached the intestines, he broke it off, but the complexity and functionality of the plumbing fascinate Lactantius. He sees the apparatus of excretion as yet another triumph of providential design: his attitude is not at all squeamish and nothing like the hysteria about "dirt and defilement" that Manetti would find in Lotario's book. Actually, the anatomical detail embarrassed Lactantius less than Manetti, who skips the seminal and urinary apparatus before dropping a larger section of *De opificio* on the uterus, conception, and embryonic development.[35]

But Manetti's excerpt from Lactantius is almost twice the size of his selection from Cicero. Where Cicero finds the body's architecture skillful and well designed, Lactantius points out that its symmetry and perfection are also *visible*—a perceptible, external beauty that failed to impress Cicero. By identifying the body's appearance, paired with its functionality, as providential, Lactantius gave Manetti reasons—Christian reasons—to praise the human arts of painting and sculpture as expressions of divine beauty. More emphatically than Cicero, Lactantius also takes the structure of the body to prove human superiority to other animals.

"After recounting what two inspired people—both glories of the Latin language—did not hesitate to say about the human body," Manetti turns next to "what scientists (*phisici*) have thought about the same topics." Although he names Aristotle, Avicenna, Galen, and other authorities on natural philosophy in this final part of his first book, the erudition comes mostly secondhand, from an unnamed *medicus*, Mondino de Luzzi, whose *Anatomy* had been standard reading since the early fourteenth century. From this comprehensive mapping of the body, Manetti took information not supplied by Lactantius or Cicero. Since Mondino defends anatomy by insisting that the body's value makes it worth studying, his interests coincide with Manetti's. Confirming traditional praise of the body as "worthier and more wonderful than in other living things," Manetti compiles evidence of human superiority from the body's structure, its power over other living bodies, and its lack of superfluous parts.[36]

The many parts and their whole fabric are "truly a wonder, . . . constructed with a certain intricate and exact artifice," including "the testicles and private parts: the great skill that produced and arranged them for procreation would be hard to explain." Having gone this far with Mondino's exposition, Manetti skims over the rest—internal anatomy, the major thoracic and intestinal organs,

and the reproductive system, perhaps because his selection from Lactantius had dealt with them. Maybe he thought that too much information would make his first book too long.[37]

Before closing, Manetti shifts to larger features of design: the whole body as a microcosm, its proportions reflected in Noah's plans for the ark, and Augustine's musings on the human face, wondering at its conspicuous display of similarity (in the species) balanced by dissimilarity (among persons). At a glance, while recognizing each other as human, people can also tell one another apart, and what they observe is "as good for practical needs as for looks."[38]

"If we see these vessels for our souls . . . as wonders so great," Manetti asks, "what shall we say about the soul itself?" The soul is his next topic, and this first book needs to end. But one more paragraph about "funeral rites . . . held with dutiful piety" delays the closing. Why bury the body after working so hard to praise it? No doubt Manetti foresaw how his fourth and final book would end, as Facio and Antonio ended theirs, with dead bodies resurrected and glorified.[39]

3. Manetti's Dignitas: Soul and Body

To show how steep a climb he faces in his second book, Manetti points out that Cicero and Lactantius, his main authorities on the body, found the soul more difficult. Beginning cautiously with terminology — asking whether *anima* or *animus* is the right word — he looks for a definition or description to address the obvious question: what is a human soul?[40]

Answers from pagans come first, only to be rejected — except Aristotle's: he had refuted his materialist predecessors in a work dedicated to the soul, where, dealing in definitions, he spoke more clearly (so Manetti thought) than Plato with his myths and metaphors. According to Manetti — though not all philosophers agreed

with him—Aristotle showed the soul to be "rational, immortal and indestructible," lacking only creation *ex nihilo* (incompatible with an eternal world) for a "perfectly correct and complete definition of the soul as the human body's immortal and indestructible form, capable of reason and intelligence and created by God from nothing." Since even Aristotle's account is incomplete, however, Manetti looks next to Moses and the Bible: only there will he find the core of an optimist Christian anthropology.[41]

Without the Bible story of Genesis, Manetti's story about *dignitas* would be utterly different, but the main lesson of creation *ex nihilo* is the Creator's power, not human excellence. In fact, the basis of Manetti's anthropology is immortality, seen as the feature of the soul in which humans most resemble God. Not power or wisdom or knowledge but eternity makes people truly like God. And since this likeness is divine, the nature of the human soul proves the superiority of human nature. Hence, to confirm mankind's excellence, what must be demonstrated is immortality, as Manetti (echoing Facio) does with arguments from posterity, instinct, and justice. Without hope for an afterlife, mankind's habitual concern for posterity would be pointless, not at all providential. Likewise futile would be the instinctive wish to live forever—as evident to Augustine as it was to Cicero. But divine justice excludes such absurdities from the human condition.[42]

To describe how humans resemble the Creator, the simple words of Scripture say that he made them "in our image, after our likeness." But what theologians saw in those words was far from simple, requiring ingenious distinctions. Since the triune God, as apart from the second person of the Trinity, has no body, it cannot be the body—finite and defective—in which humans are like the Godhead as a whole. To find a locus of resemblance, some interpreters looked for the Trinity's unseen *likeness* in the soul—the nonbodily part of the human composite—while others praised God's *image* in humans as more distinctive, claiming

that an animal might be like a human but still lack the human image.

If Manetti brought anything of his own to this old dispute, it may have been to parse the Hebrew grammar of "our image" and "our likeness." Assuming that he had enough Hebrew at the time, he could have known that although *Elohim* — the Creator's name at this point in the creation story — has a plural ending, it can take singular verbs. When God creates Adam, however, the name goes with plural words: hence "our image" and "our likeness" in the Authorized Version. Commentators long before Manetti had explained the plural *Elohim* as trinitarian, but not to link the divine name with the human soul.[43]

Manetti mentions no interpreter of these issues later than the ninth century, though he knew Peter Lombard, who used all five of the Christian authorities whom he cites — Ambrose, Augustine, John of Damascus, Gregory the Great, and Remigius of Auxerre — and whose salient thoughts had been digested for him by Antonio and Facio. These experts show that pagans were wrong about the soul, even though some heathens assumed they were immortal when they decided to kill themselves.[44]

Having proved the soul's eternal existence, Manetti proceeds to its powers of intellect, memory, and will as described by Augustine: intellect to acquire knowledge, memory to store and recall it, and will to decide action on what the soul knows. Intellectual achievement is Manetti's focus: first, "the great deeds and remarkable devices that people have thought up and invented" to improve technology and the fine arts; next, mankind's accomplishments in poetry, history, rhetoric, law, philosophy, medicine, astrology, and theology. Theologians have bragged "that their own minds are like God's," Manetti notes, and he accepts their achievement as support for his case. Some official theology was more restrained, however, giving divine grace or illumination credit for man's intellectual kinship with God.[45]

Manetti's enthusiasm peaks when he praises art and technology. Relying on his own experience in Florence, he names Giotto, Ghiberti, and Brunelleschi alongside antiquity's most renowned painters, sculptors, and architects. But what excites him most is shipbuilding—crucial for the commerce that made his city rich.

Before reviewing the roster of ancient artists—the painter Apelles, the sculptor Praxiteles, the architect Phidon of Athens, and others—Manetti starts with adventure, technology, and "Jason's endowment of genius." He cites (from Cicero) some lines from Accius about a peasant who had never seen a ship before sighting the Argos: the great vessel "groaning on the deep" left him "completely terrified." The elder Pliny—a more sophisticated critic known to Manetti—disliked ships for different reasons: he despised the person who made the first sails, "as if dying on land were not good enough; . . . what curse would be enough for this inventor is hard to know." A huge ship was enough to frighten the peasant, but it was innovation itself that the Roman sage found risky: navigational invention was particularly hateful for bringing foreigners to Italy.[46]

Manetti—no intransigent traditionalist like Pliny—cheers the Argonauts for crossing "dreadful surges of the savage deep fearlessly and undaunted." He also admires the argonauts of his own day. "This technology (*artificium*) of sailing has grown so much," he boasts, "bit by bit through many ages up to our own day, that progress (*procedere*) has been miraculous." One advance in material culture invites another—technical invention promotes territorial discovery, and vice versa. Modern sailors make "daily trips on the British and icy Ocean," he brags, and "recently they have also tried to penetrate almost into deepest Moor Land, beyond the former limits of navigation, where—so I've heard—many islands, inhabited and cultivated but completely unknown up to now, have been discovered."[47]

What Manetti sees in the technology and art of his time — what makes a vocabulary of progress useful to him — is the cumulative achievement of effort over time, which proves to him the excellence of human thinking. After praising the mind so energetically, he has little to add about the soul's other faculties of memory and will — though his next book will return to the will as the engine of human action, guided by understanding.[48]

About halfway through that third book — on the body/soul composite — Manetti sums up: "humankind is immensely powerful and well endowed, seeing that humans can use all created things as they will, also commanding them by their own might and having dominion." This affirmation of *voluntas, imperium,* and *dominium* ties Book 3 into Books 1 and 2 — which the third often repeats. The body stands erect, once again, now as the subject of pictorial art: "the immortal gods were painted in temples . . . only as human just because that form stands so much taller and higher." We also hear again about "discoveries and inventions" that have come "from that special, singular shrewdness of human thinking."[49]

Despite the repetitions, Manetti presents the body/soul union as a distinct topic, but he does little to develop it. Declaring that "composition is a miracle of God Almighty," he leaves the mystery unsolved. The wonder is that God could join components "so far apart and so contrary," but what this amounts to — beyond the polarities of material/immaterial, destructible/indestructible, and mortal/immortal — remains unsaid. He makes no move to examine these antitheses, let alone understand them. He was no philosopher, and he wrote long before Descartes moved philosophy toward a more explicit dualism.[50]

This third book on the difficult topic of body/soul union is Manetti's least coherent statement about *dignitas.* Some parts of it are more impressive, however, even novel: a definition of humanity, a theology of incarnation, sensory and sexual pleasure as God's design, and a theory of human roles.

After defining the soul in the previous book, Manetti now needs a suitable account of the composite. But he cannot find it in ancient pagan texts. Calling man a social or civic animal silently concedes mortality: such descriptions are blind to God's image in man. The more common definition—rational animal—is better, since rationality is mental, hence immaterial and at least eligible for immortality. But the full definition, as Cicero took it from the Stoics, puts humans in the genus *animal*, marked by two differences, *rationale* and also *mortale*, because the gods, like humans, are *animalia* ("living things") yet immortal. Students of logic in the universities found this problem in their textbooks, dangling from Porphyry's Tree: "on Porphyry's view, both we and the gods are rational, but the mortal added to us separates us from them."[51]

Manetti's task was to subtract mortality from a better definition, but near the end of Book 3 he takes a different turn—an abrupt detour, in fact, from optimism about human excellence. A human who "has been given such status that he visibly dominates and commands all of creation" will be prone to "envy, pride, indignation, ambition, lust for domination and other such disorders of the soul." Scorn makes such a person "so angry that he pursues his detractors zealously and to the death." "Thinking about this again and again," says Manetti, "and wishing to give a novel description and definition of the human, I have shown—correctly, in my view—that this is an animal given to anger." *Animal indignabundum*: with an unusual adjective, Manetti constructs a surprising definition, perhaps drawing on his political experience.[52]

Indignation is sinful, a type of anger, and Manetti never doubts that humans are sinners. But sin is fungible in the economy of salvation. "Had our first parents not sinned at all," he maintains, "Christ would still have come down to earth." God's purpose would not have been to redeem humans but to honor them with "the inconceivable glory and astonishing honor of lowering himself

to take on this human flesh." Since Augustine first discussed the issue, theologians had disagreed about it, as Manetti realizes.[53]

In fact, as things worked out in Eden, the first parents fell "headlong into the Devil's traps and snares; they "truly damned themselves forever, along with the race that they were to propagate." Adam and Eve committed the *original sin*, thereby spoiling the *original justice* installed in them by God. This "clear knowledge of the true good, beyond the natural gifts of understanding, memory and will," shows that stupidity and sin are not natural or essential in humans—not part of the definition. Hence, when Manetti claims that "God wanted to offer unending happiness" to humans, the offer extends to life on earth, in the body, as part of the original situation—until the parents of us all "provoked God to a universal punishment for humankind."[54]

Nonetheless, even "after the detestable lapse of that pair," the artifice of the "skilled Craftsman" has also

> granted nearly limitless pleasure, picking and choosing it from creatures of every type, though the human would also fall into vice because the virtue that God planned for man always clashes with a pleasure, like an enemy in one's home. Through each of the senses—sight, hearing, smell, taste and touch—the pleasures and delights enjoyed by humans are certainly stronger, surer and more abundant than those had by other animals.

In traditional virtue ethics (not identified as Aristotelian by Manetti) vices cluster around virtues as extremes bracketing means. Vices—especially vices of sense—lurk where the path of virtue leads. It is dangerous, but also beneficial, that the five human senses bring more kinds of pleasure, enjoyed more intensely, than pleasures had by other animals. This sensory advantage, like God's other gifts to man, is providential. And "for sexual pleasures" the advantage is even plainer. Instructed by Cicero and Lactantius,

Manetti concludes that pleasure is maximized in humans because of God's plan, and, by the same design, that the pleasure most enjoyed is sexual. The purpose of sex might be either natural and biological, to propagate the species, or ethical and ascetic, to provide an irresistible delight for the saintly to resist.[55]

These comments on pleasure show God equipping man with "the maximum of beauty, wit, wisdom, riches and resources," preparing Manetti's readers for his next effort, "to examine what role (*officium*) he has conferred" on humans. The *officium* or *officia* selected is, or are, more Cicero's than Aristotle's and—despite the terminology—closer to *De finibus* than to *De officiis*.

Tacit acceptance of a theory/practice antithesis complicates Manetti's presentation, which shares Cicero's preference for action (*actio*) and practical wisdom (*prudentia*) over contemplation (*contemplatio*) and theoretical wisdom (*sapientia*). Nothing in Aristotle quite matches what Cicero writes in *De finibus* about understanding and acting. Where the Greek philosopher reasons from functions (*erga*, or *officia* in Latin) of human labor and the human body to some global human function, he identifies it as "the soul's activity in accord with reason (*energeia kata logon*)," so that *logos* or reason (*ratio*), not understanding (*nous* or *intelligentia*), guides the soul's action. This rational activity is a single *ergon* for Aristotle. But Manetti's *intelligendi et agendi munus* is binary—the understanding and acting that is nonetheless man's one and only *officium*. Since the *actio* in question is more than a synonym for *intelligentia*, however, the theory/practice divide persists.[56]

Manetti has now described humans and has found a special role for them. Convinced that "man's power is great, his reason upright and his strength amazing," he concludes

> that his role is equally upright, honest and singular: he has the ability to manage and the knowledge to govern the world that was made on his account, in particular each thing that

we see existing on this earthly globe, and he could by no means achieve all this unless he could do it all by acting and understanding.

Finally, after God had made man "so beautiful, intelligent and wise, so wealthy, worthy and mighty, and finally so happy and so blessed," the only gift that could improve the human condition was God's own incarnation, something of "astonishing value (*dignitas*)" enjoyed not even by angels.[57]

4. Manetti's Dignitas: *Terms of Debate*

Manetti's last book turns from informing an audience to defeating opponents—from persuasion to polemic. He denounces a picture of human life so bleak that death seems better, and he retraces ground explored by the three previous books. His opponents include many pagans, several biblical and Christian authorities, and a pope: Innocent III. To block assaults from those three quarters on three targets—body, soul, and the body/soul composite—he gives his fourth book more structure than the third, despite two disruptions: the three-part format breaks up his reply to Innocent, the main adversary; and this final book ends with a topic, the glorified body, too loosely attached to the previous books.

Those books "have brought together everything I found relevant to that special worth (*dignitas*) and singular excellence (*excellentia*) of man." If Manetti has made his case for human happiness, no one will be able to counter it since "something known to be the best of all would live in some kind of constant, perpetual misery." The ultimate guarantee is Christian theodicy grounded in Scripture, which testifies that "God created everything to be very good," making mankind not only "the very best but also—to put it this way—better than the very best." Superlatives come easily to Manetti, and the abstract hyperbole reassures him—though not

enough to dispense with the many concrete details in this longest of his four books.[58]

In the end, his royal patron will have his guarantee of "the worth (*dignitas*) of man's body and how admirable it is, next how exalted the loftiness of his soul and then besides how splendid the excellence (*excellentia*) of the human composed of those two parts." At the lexical level, most of this extravagance is clear enough. *Excellentia*, paired with *dignitas*, is as empty and adaptable as "excellence" in English: a short entry in the *Oxford Latin Dictionary* lists only "superiority" and "'pre-eminence" as English equivalents of the cognate "excellence." But the longer entry on *dignitas* gives more than a dozen alternatives to that word's English cousin: "distinction," "esteem," "excellence," "fitness," "importance," "honor" "position," "rank," "standing," "status," "suitability," "worthiness," and "visual impressiveness."[59]

Since the range of *dignitas* is wide, choosing an English equivalent could never be simple. And understanding Manetti's use of the word is harder. A text from Quattrocento Italy that talks about *dignitas* inevitably brings to mind the speech by Pico della Mirandola (previously mentioned) that was called *de dignitate* by mistake. The mistake eventually led Pico's admirers to interpret the *Oration* as promoting a concept that Kant called *Würde*. Since the Enlightenment, the Kantian concept, now "dignity" in English, has been enormously productive — and just as controversial — in law, moral philosophy, politics, and theology. Whenever "dignity" enters the conversation in such arenas, its post-Kantian burden comes with it. Seen by modern eyes in a Renaissance work of moral philosophy, *dignitas* rendered as "dignity" bears the same load, aggravated by anachronism.

Whatever Manetti meant by *dignitas*, it cannot have been the *Würde* in Kant's theory of value, long since absorbed into assumptions about "dignity" in modern times. To simplify: human dignity

in current moral usage is *universal*, in that all people have it just by being human; *inalienable*, because they cannot lose it, even voluntarily; *unquantified*, unable to increase, decrease, or be measured; and *absolute*, not reliant on or relative to anyone or anything outside the individual person. Since this cluster of constraints on "dignity" did not operate until the end of the eighteenth century, the English transliteration of *dignitas* is a mismatch for Manetti's Latin word. He never says what he means by it, however, and makes no effort to distinguish it from *excellentia*, *praestantia*, and other words that he groups with it. In general, his *dignitas* is rank, status, value, and/or worth—more or less as Cicero used this common Latin word, but not as "dignity," *dignità*, *dignité*, *Würde*, and so on came to be used after Kant.[60]

Although Manetti never defines or describes *dignitas*, other lexical issues interest him. He calls attention to technical terms from medicine, philosophy, and theology; he has strong views about translating biblical Hebrew and Greek; and he wonders whether *anima* or *animus* is the right word for a soul.[61] Interpretations of *imago* and *similitudo* are especially prominent—not of *excellentia* or *dignitas*, however, despite their importance for him.[62] It helps that he is very fond of pleonasms: one favorite is *dignitas et excellentia*; another is *praestantia et dignitas*. These conjunctions suggest that the worth or value indicated is the (non-Kantian) transactional kind that confers or confirms rank or status.[63]

But Manetti never tells us this. Since he gives no definition or description of *dignitas*, he cannot make an argument like the following, where D stands for dignity, and X, Y, and Z are features of D:

p^0 → X, Y, and Z belong to D;
p^1 → whatever has X, Y, and Z has D;
p^2 → <u>humans have X, Y, and Z;</u>
c → therefore, humans have D.

He often asserts the conclusion (c) of this argument, he states the minor premise (p^2) even more often, and sometimes he suggests the major premise (p^1); but for D he supplies no definitional, descriptive, or analytic statement like p^0. Hence, since he provides no conceptual clarity about D — a thematic concept for his book — he can make no argument that requires a clear concept of D. If *dignitas, excellentia,* and *praestantia* can all be said of humans, what value does *dignitas* add? Manetti has nothing to say.

Does the silence matter? Incontrovertibly, Manetti's book (unlike Pico's speech) is about *dignitas,* and he certainly thinks that humans have it. Need we know more — if what he has in mind, generally speaking, is rank, status, value, and/or worth? The worry is that *dignitas* already had two pedigrees when he learned the word — one ancient and Roman, the other medieval and Christian — and they were not congruent.

Half the recorded uses of *dignitas* in classical Latin come from texts by Cicero, including philosophical works favored by Manetti. In high-minded tones, Marcus the philosopher theorized about the word, but theory never hobbled Tully the politician, who used it just as he pleased — sometimes in slogans for electioneering. Cheapened by Roman politics, *dignitas* still always expressed value, but its core was pragmatic and political, with allowances for social, moral, rhetorical, and aesthetic needs. Status, office, rank, and socio-economic resources were often in play. The values in question were usually human, belonging to a single person. But groups of humans (the state, an audience) as well as nonhuman things (the universe, a building, a speech) could also have *dignitas,* whether they were natural (a tree) or artificial (a temple).

But when judgments were aesthetic, not all humans could have *dignitas,* which in that case was gendered: a handsome man's *dignitas* was *venustas* in a woman. When the stakes were political, male *dignitas* required *otium,* the serene leisure that excluded all women

and children and most men too—all the enslaved and almost all others, who, even if they were citizens, could not afford the civic involvement that Cicero expected of the sage. The few free adult males who could pay the price for *dignitas* might lose it and then regain it: it was transitory, circumstantial, and not inalienable. Its features are hard to pin down: bodily or nonbodily, external or internal, material or immaterial, physical or psychological, visible or invisible? It depended on the situation.[64]

Did a sordid past in Roman politics take *dignitas* off the table for some early Christian speakers of Latin? The word never occurs in the Latin New Testament, which uses many words like it—abstract nouns ending in -*itas*—especially in the Epistles. Hence, in the Bible's distinctly Christian part, *dignitas* has no pedigree at all, and very little in the older books. Since Scripture is nearly a blank slate for *dignitas*, the first Christians could make of it what they would—departing from classical usage. That something would be made of it was likely, since the word was so common in Latin. A familiar statement (not mentioning *dignitas*) from the opening of the Bible turned out to be formative: "let us make man in our image, after our likeness."[65]

By the year 1100 or so—about ninety years before Cardinal Lotario declaimed about misery—the place of *dignitas* had been secure in the medieval lexicon for some centuries. An anonymous text of that era, *De humanae conditionis dignitate et miseria*, resembles other Christian treatments of the topic in its grim asceticism, though with refinements on distinguishing the divine image in man from the likeness. The image is "worthier" (*dignior*) because an animal may resemble a human by likeness while "none but another human has the image of a human." To enact the divine image, one does now "what God does eternally" by nonbodily acts of remembering, understanding, and loving the best of all the best, which is God. Those three psychic exercises "will express the *digni-*

tas of your creation," a state so elevated that its glory is incomprehensible.

The unspeakable glory is real, if ethereal, and the incarnate God has stored it up for sinners striving to be righteous. Meanwhile, vainglory and foolish joy are traps to be avoided by shunning the world's "parade of *dignitates*" and attending to "the miseries of the present life." Life is a shaky bridge over the chasm of Hell. Having exalted the divine in man's spirit, the anonymous writer bewails the body's condition at the end of life in language meant to disgust and horrify. In death the flesh will be "stinking and pitiful, consumed by rot and worms." Crawling into every portal of the senses, they will stuff the throat and belly to make "the body's whole frame melt away in rot."[66]

The stage has been set for Cardinal Lotario, who wrote a script for someone like Manetti to refute. Lotario also planned to "describe the *dignitas* of human nature, humbling the exalted in the present work, then in the next one exalting the humble." Since no exaltation ever came, only abasement, *dignitas* was left to be known indirectly and negatively by what excludes it from abased humanity: *miseria* and *vilitas*. *Dignitas* is eliminated, so Lotario implies, because humans are wretched and worthless. To rescue *dignitas*, Manetti needs to restore value and excellence to mankind. This *dignitas* is the worth conferred by rank and status, because immortality makes humans like God and thus better than other creatures: there is little more to say about Manetti's *dignitas* — except to repeat that it is not the usual Anglophone "dignity."[67]

5. Manetti's Dignitas: *Polemic*

By always using "Innocent III," a pope's name, for the author of a book written when Innocent was still Cardinal Lotario, Manetti gave his main opponent papal standing. Accordingly, he claimed to

be "restrained . . . by the reverence due to a supreme pontiff." But the Italian words behind his Latin—

> . . . *vieta*
> *la reverenza de le somme chiavi*—

were spat by Dante at another pope, Nicholas III, as the poet railed at Nicholas in Hell. So what we hear from Manetti about Innocent is not just "some few honest rebuttals of his sayings." Dismissing a pope's thoughts as lightweight and immature is hardly reverential. Neither Antonio da Barga nor Facio had actually attacked His Holiness: what made Manetti so aggressive is intriguing but unknown; perhaps, since Valla's *Donation* was even more belligerent and already circulating, Manetti thought that he could take a smaller risk to support Alfonso against the papacy.[68]

Before first engaging Innocent, Manetti addresses others who thought the body "naked and defenseless in its natural state—so frail, so feeble and such a ruin." These include pagan and biblical authorities, none given as much attention as the pope, who traced the human body's worthlessness to its origin from mud and slime. To these complaints Innocent "adds many more such accusations, full of disgrace and dishonor and loaded with blame, but to avoid going on too long, I am skipping them," says Manetti, and then he moves on to the soul—but not to Innocent, who did not vilify the soul. Those who did were pagans claiming that it would perish with the body, that like the body it was diseased and that transmigration into other bodies was its only route to immortality.[69]

One way for Christians to understand death is that the body dies when abandoned by the soul, which can sustain life—if not the body's life—on its own. Not just the body's reliance on the soul but also each person's lifetime in a body give special significance to the body/soul composite—which may be why Manetti's indictment focuses on slanders against the whole person. In order to attack them later, he piles up anecdotes illustrating the perverse

heathen view that life's miseries make death a positive good—that "to end it was better." Even the long-suffering Job, regretting his birth, asks "why did you bring me out of your belly? Would that I had been eaten up and no eye would see me."[70]

Ambrose too, "a very holy and learned man, had no hesitations about dealing separately with death as a good" in order to argue that the body's demise brings eternal life, not death, to the just. Commenting on Job, Ambrose describes three kinds of death. The first comes to the soul from sin, the second is mystical death, and the third ends the body's life. Just as the first is always bad, the second—when the soul dies to sin through baptism—is always good. The third kind is mixed: "most should fear what the good see as just because it finishes everyone while delighting few. The fault lies not in death, however, but in our weakness." Citing additional evidence from Job and Ecclesiastes, Ambrose provides Manetti with an extreme statement—though not lurid like Lotario's—of the Christian asceticism that he aims to refute: it was too harsh even for Augustine, who insisted that "the death of the body, the soul's parting from the body, is not good for anyone."[71]

Innocent is the closing witness against the whole person's *dignitas*. "Starting with the first instant of birth and continuing to the final moment, he crams a lot in. From all this I have chosen only what is more memorable," says Manetti, selecting the pope's rage at the newborn who "wail and howl with noises of pain and complaint to express our nature's real true misery." Then, having assembled testimony from all his opponents, he rejects it piece by piece.[72]

Once again, pagan assaults on the body come first, for Manetti to deflect by arguing that the body's flaws are not in God's plan or human nature: instead, it was "from falling into sin that Adam got every weakness of his body, all its afflictions and any remaining disadvantages." Even so—an opponent might say—whatever the source of the infirmity, the body is, in fact, infirm and seems so

naturally. Manetti concedes that a "law of death . . . threatens all human bodies from the time of birth," only to counter that "more kinds of pleasure than distress rule this ordinary, everyday life" because nature supplies remedies for pain, making most people happier with life's joys than they are anguished by its griefs.[73]

Manetti's hedonic calculus reckons that people, on balance, are happy. While locating channels of pleasure in the external and the internal senses, he also puts the senses in a hierarchy but works it out only for taste and touch—perhaps because the flesh of the body, his subject, is their medium. When we quench our thirst and feed our hunger, "enjoyment really is wonderful" in sensations of taste that bring more pleasure than any other tactile experiences, like cooling off or warming up—except one, "the touch specific to the genitals." Except in that case, touch is less pleasurable than taste, where nature's purpose is to nourish individual humans, whereas tactile pleasure in sex preserves the whole species.

Manetti's analysis of nature's purpose in sexual pleasure comports with scholastic doctrine, though he seems more pleased with sex than Aquinas was, for example. Thomas teaches that sight gives the pleasure that works best for knowing things, whereas touch—in eating, drinking, and sex—is best for using them. Taste differs from touch, but flesh is the medium for both, requiring bodily contact in both cases, so that "taste is a kind of touch." The strongest pleasure from touch is sexual. Because touch of that kind propagates the species, it is "the most powerful object of the faculty of desire." Just as the natural desire for food helps the individual survive, so the desire for sex, also natural, helps the species survive. Hence, while the obligation to eat and drink falls on individuals, "the precept of procreation"—fulfilled either by carnal or by spiritual action—obligates the whole human race.[74]

Having given reasons like Thomas's for approving of sex, Manetti next explains how Pope Innocent missed the mark by attack-

ing the body for its slimy, earthy matter, lowest of the elements. On the contrary, housing a mind makes the human body nobler than those of other ensouled creatures, whose bodies are also earthy. Moreover, the aerial or fiery bodies of things above the Moon are neither ensouled nor sentient, hence inferior to human bodies. And Adam's body — still alive and aware after the Fall — could not die at all until sin deposited its wages. Clearly, the earthy matter of this prelapsarian body was no impediment to immortality, mankind's prime endowment. Sperm from the fallen bodies of Adam's progeny is still finer than in other animals because of a richer diet and better blood — biological facts to defeat Innocent's accusation that conception makes humans "vile and rotten" from infancy.[75]

"As for the rest of Innocent's charges about nakedness, weakness and other such disadvantages, I dismiss them," Manetti concludes, closing his defense of the body. Then he salvages the soul by brushing off the pagans who say it is "nothing, that its name is meaningless, that the whole thing is a waste — useless talk." No soul, no mind: evidently — by their own telling — these heathen soul-deniers were mindless, not worth refuting. Epicureans who taught that the soul dies with the body were just as bad, also those who opted for transmigration. Long passages from Aristotle and Cicero reinforce Manetti's thinly argued objections: Cicero's words in the *Tusculans* seem "very much like the truth itself and the Catholic faith of Christians."[76]

With no slurs on the soul by Innocent to reject, Manetti comes back to the "whole human person" and the ancient sages who praised its death — contradicted by Christian wisdom. "Those who talk about death as good," says Lactantius, "know nothing about the truth." In fact, Cato, Socrates, and other wise men did not hate life when they chose death: they hoped for immortal life. But biblical and Christian authorities — Job, Ecclesiastes, and Am-

brose—also seem to preach disdain for life, causing Manetti to proceed carefully.[77]

Finding the teachings of Ecclesiastes "bad and sometimes unsound," Manetti's response is argumentative, using contradictions to weaken the book's authority. But his approach to Job is hermeneutic, seeing contradictions as clues to deeper meaning. Ambrose gets less attention—with a promise to discuss the glorified body later.

Jerome's comments on Ecclesiastes promote "contempt for this world," finding more than *ennui* in the book's famous opening and closing: *vanitas vanitatum*. Told by the Psalmist that "every man alive is emptiness," he concludes that "death is the emptiness of the emptinesses": alas for this unhappy world. Many medieval Christians accepted Jerome's dismal diagnosis, while also—like some Jews—treating the book as problematic, allegorizing its worldlier passages (the only good meal is actually the eucharist, not a hearty dinner) but taking the gloom literally. A few doubted that Ecclesiastes was canonical, as Manetti will note.

However, when Manetti looks for optimism to lighten the preacher's melancholy, he goes against the grain of medieval exegesis. On the other hand, in the passages that he uses to highlight Job's pessimism, Gregory the Great—Job's master interpreter—had found joy: for victory over sin and hope of eternal life. To be sure: it was not this earthly life that made Gregory hopeful; in the "good days and years of glory" promised to Job by Elihu, the only gratification will have been deferred since "by 'good' is meant right conduct and by 'glory' a heavenly reward."[78]

Now that Manetti has dealt with "all the statements by sacred and secular authors previously cited, what remains is . . . Pope Innocent's arguments" on the body/soul composite. His point of attack is ignorance about the first woman's name in the Hebrew Bible: he charges that the pope would "never have slipped into

confusions so great . . . had he not been utterly ignorant of the Hebrew language." This error was basic in two ways: coming near the start of Innocent's book, it discredited everything that follows; and the mistake was about human beginnings.[79]

To illustrate his charge that "we are all born wailing to express our wretched nature," Innocent chose some lines of doggerel,

all of us are born from Eva,
crying either *he* or *ha*.

As Manetti explains, "these interjections from a person in pain express the pain's magnitude. This is why she deserved to be called *he-roine* before her sin and *e-v-a* afterward." Neither Innocent's attack nor Manetti's defense is transparent.

The Bible says that God created the first female from a rib of the first male, who then called her "woman" — *'isshah* in Hebrew — because she came "from a man (*'ish*)." In the Vulgate this etymology became *virago . . . de viro* — a "he-roine" from a "he-man." Later, Adam gave the woman her name, <u>H</u>awwah, which has three letters in Hebrew and starts with a guttural, rendered in the Vulgate by *Hava* or *Heva*, though *Eva* is also common and also has three letters: EVA. If the v in the middle of *Eva* stands for *vel*, meaning "or," the name itself becomes "E OR A," and, if the vowels are aspirated, "HE OR HA." Also, E and A begin the names of Eve and Adam. Perhaps this is why Innocent specifies that HE is the cry of a newborn female, HA of a male, citing the poem that Manetti repeats — while reading the two sounds as Latin interjections, *heu* and *ha*, that express pain. Cries of pain, according to the pope, make a fitting name after the Fall for the woman who had been a heroine before she sinned.

Instead of tangling himself in interjections, Manetti suggests, Innocent could have studied Jerome on Eve's Hebrew name to learn that she was "the mother of all the living." When Jerome says

that "'Eve' is actually transformed into 'life,'" *Eva* is replaced and *vita* is the replacement. Texts of the Vulgate Genesis disagree on how to Latinize <u>Hawwah</u>, and the New Testament settles on *Eva*, though Augustine used *Vita* for *Zoê* in the Septuagint Genesis. So many names for one woman; so much muddle for a pope. Jerome puts *Eva* under E in his list of biblical names, glossing it with *calamitas aut vae vel vita: vae* (woe) is an interjection of anguish or denunciation. Since the Hebrew Bible never uses the woman's name outside of Genesis 2–4, Jerome had few occasions to Latinize it, and since an official text of the Bible took centuries to stabilize, whether he always wrote *Eva* — as Manetti claims — is unknowable.[80]

After this barrage of erudition, Manetti attacks the pope's accusations "about nakedness, about the fruit borne by humans and trees, about the troubles of old age, the shortness of life, the various efforts that people make, their different anxieties and other such topics that I omit."[81]

"Naked he comes out and naked he goes back, starting poor and leaving poor": paraphrasing Job, Innocent reviles the human infant's appearance at birth: "filthy to mention, filthier to hear about, filthiest of all to see." Shameful nakedness, stained by the gore of delivery, displays the "vile unworthiness (*indignitas*) of the human condition." But not for Manetti, who treats nakedness differently: "it was fitting for humans to be born like this," he insists, "for the sake of grace and beauty." There is "immense pleasure" in "seeing . . . fair and shapely people": the naked body is beautiful, not shameful at all. Had it been otherwise, if babies were "born dressed and covered like animals with pelts," the grotesque spectacle would indeed have been "filthy and repulsive." The bloody afterbirth is good, however, because it is physically necessary.[82]

The pope also gets it wrong by preferring the fruits of plants and trees to the body's products — unpleasant ones — giving Manetti the chance to put some revolting papal prose on display:

They produce flowers, foliage and fruit, and from yourself you get nits, lice and tapeworms. They exude oil, wine and gum from themselves, while your discharges are spit, piss and shit. They breathe a smell of sweetness out of themselves, but from yourselves you exhale a detestable stench.

Cutting short the "dirt and defilement," Manetti objects that nature's real fruits in humans — man's essential products — are thinking and acting. But even the wastes oozing through the pope's sentences — "saliva, urine, excrement and hair" — are good in their uses. Saliva cures snakebite; urine helps the eyes; dung and hair are fertilizers: nothing goes to waste, and "the Gospel teaches us that not even a single hair shall perish." Even sewage teaches a lesson about providence.[83]

Since Manetti wrote about *Famous People Who Lived Long*, he could call on his own research to answer another of Innocent's accusations: that life had become meaner than it used to be, when the patriarchs lived much longer. He takes his lead from Josephus, however, who claims that the heroes of old survived so long not just because their conduct was virtuous but also because God's love for them was extraordinary, because their food was better, and because their discoveries in astronomy and geometry took time. But later, as fewer things needed inventing, extra years became unnecessary — permitting an efficiency that Manetti also chalks up to providence.[84]

As for "the troubles of old age," he has already calculated that people feel less pain than pleasure, an advantage that he now extends to "the whole course of a person's life," adding that "there is always enjoyment at every moment. But if this is so, the clear consequence is more pleasure than hardship," and the pope has been caught wrong once again, reproved this time by Aristotle as well as Manetti. The philosopher taught not only that "pleasure is produced for every sense" but also that "without activity no plea-

sure occurs, and pleasure completes every activity." Since Manetti holds that action, like understanding, is essential for humans, it follows that regular pleasure comes with human nature.[85]

Pleasure is neither unmixed nor constant, however, and people are often frustrated in what they try to enjoy. The result—as confirmed by Innocent from Ecclesiastes—is "toil and pain and a spirit afflicted," but Manetti is not distressed. In fact, all the pope's "charges already made, along with all the remaining statements about human disasters that might produce new charges, are easily resolved by the final resurrection of our bodies." Manetti takes Scripture's promise of glorification literally: "All of us shall rise," he declares, "at the full and perfect age of thirty years, . . . not only at Christ's age but also, amazing to say, with the size of his body."[86]

Then he details the happy results of transfiguration, looking beyond what Antonio da Barga and Facio had provided and introducing new material from Augustine and Aquinas. He seems more enthusiastic about eternal torment than Thomas does, though less callous than Facio, who looks forward to "washing his hands in the blood of sinners." Manetti too believes that the saved and the damned will be alert to one another, but he stops short of bloodlust while foreseeing jubilation for the elect when they realize "that the damned will go on being punished forever."[87]

As an ending for Manetti's last book, this long, rambling coda on the damned and the saved is out of proportion and out of place, especially after the tidy tripartitions (body, soul, composite; pagans, Christians, pope) that precede it. By contrast, when Manetti sums up for Alfonso, he takes charge of his argument again, choosing flattery that will give the king a personal stake in his new theory of roles: "your roles of knowing and acting," he assures his patron, are "shared with Almighty God."

If the royal roles really were divine, Manetti's theory of *officia* would have been the perfect capstone for his book. And the adula-

tion was true to Catholic dogma. Aquinas confirms that the just can share some *officia*, like "scattering the proud," with God, even though such roles are primarily divine. "There is nothing worthier (*dignius*) in the role (*officium*) of humans than to become God's co-worker," according to Thomas, though "man's only worth (*dignitas*) lies in brightness"—a mystical illumination that doubles as one of the joys of heaven. Incomplete happiness here and now comes mainly from contemplation but also from "the work of the practical intellect as it directs what humans do and feel (*actiones et passiones*)." With or without such limits on human *officia*, the price of Manetti's theory—of the resemblance to God promised by it—is to be not fully human, and since knowing, for ordinary mortals, is not always contemplative, man's transient happiness is a lesser reward.[88]

Manetti—a pious Christian of the fifteenth century—would have paid this price gladly. But Antonio and Facio, also living piously in the same place at the same time, thought differently about how humans excel, about their *excellentia* and *dignitas*. As for *miseria* and *vilitas*, neither of them complained about the pope's diatribe against humanity: they wanted to complete Innocent's project, not repudiate it. To contradict the pope and disclaim his message was Manetti's aim, however: the vile invective disgusted him.[89]

The heart of his optimist Christian anthropology is a transcendent ideal, immortality: this is what makes imperfect, embodied humans authentically like a perfect, bodiless God. Other facts about humans show that goodness—also a divine ideal—belongs naturally to them and their earthly world, governed by God with providential care. The natural state of humans is original justice, not original sin, which defiles nature but does not liquidate it. Human life on earth is happy, even joyous, made so by pleasures—including sexual pleasure—that are good and part of God's plan. A

sublime piece of God's craftwork is the human body — including the naked body, outside and inside, guts and all — whose image in art is mankind's visible divinity, whether painted on a church wall or carved in antique marble. The art itself — like technology and other vehicles of material culture — manifests human thought in action. Energy, effort, ingenuity, and invention are forces of cultural, intellectual, and material progress.

"Progressive" seems the right word — adjusted for time and place — to use about these attitudes of Manetti's. To call them enlightened — stunningly so in contrast to Innocent's or Facio's or Antonio's — is also fair to his ideas about *dignitas*, which are ideas rooted in antiquity and renewed in the Renaissance, not ideas about the dignity invented in the Enlightenment.

For advice and assistance, I owe thanks to Michael Allen, Stefano Baldassarri, Rebecca Copenhaver, Remy Debes, Jim Hankins, Giuseppe Marcellino, John Monfasani, Ingrid Rowland, and Peter Stacey.

NOTES

1. Luke 22:44; Lugano, "De vita," xxvii–xxxii; Kristeller, "Frater Antonius Bargensis," 531–32. [Full citations of works cited briefly here may be found in the Bibliography.]

2. Pico della Mirandola, *Discorso*, 22 (49–50), 48 (103); see also Bausi's introduction, xv–xviii.

3. Gianfrancesco Pico, in *Commentationes Ioannis Pici Mirandulae in hoc volumine contenta, quibus anteponitur vita per Iohannem Franciscum illustris principis Galeotti Pici filium conscripta* (Bologna: Benedictus Hectoris, 1496), sig. QQii^v. A summary of my views on Pico's speech can be found online in the *Stanford Encyclopedia of Philosophy*: https://plato.stanford.edu/entries/pico-della-mirandola/.

4. Psalm 8:5; Hebrews 2:7–9; *ADE* 13.

5. ADE 28–32, 45.

6. ADE 9–45, where the section on the glorified body begins; my Appendix I omits this, about ten of sixteen pages from the Latin text of Kristeller. Almost all of ADE 9–27 comes from Peter Lombard, Sent. 2.1.3–5, 16.2–4: Kristeller, "Frater Antonius Bargensis," 542, citing Trinkaus, Image and Likeness, 1:212–13, refers to the material from Peter's Distinction 16—but not from Distinction 1. Antonio mentions Cicero in ADE 6, in the preliminaries to Facio; Lactantius appears in ADE 30.

7. ADE 15–16.

8. ADE 27, 30; cf. 9, 15–19.

9. ADE 5; 2 Corinthians 4:10; Rabanus Maurus, Homiliae de festis praecipuis, in MPL 110:36A–B.

10. Peter Comestor, Serm. 14 in MPL 198:1761B–62A; Lugano, "De vita," xxxv–xl.

11. ADE 1–4; Kristeller, "Bartolomeo Facio," 268.

12. ADE 2–6; LDM prol. (93).

13. ADE 28–44.

14. FEP 159.46; Kristeller, "Bartolomeo Facio," 268–70; Foà, "Manetti," and Viti, "Facio," both in DBI.

15. MDE pr. 2; FEP 149; Lotario dei Segni, ed. Maccarrone, ix–xxiii; Lotario di Segni, De miseria, ed. and trans. Lewis, 226–53; Paravicini Bagliani, "Papa Innocenzo IV" in DBI.

16. FEP 149.1–2, 4; 151.11; 156.34; 158.42; 159.45, 47; 164.64; 167.77, 80; LDM prol. (93); Francesco Petrarca, Les Remèdes aux deux fortunes (1354–1366) (Grenoble: Millon, 2002), 2:303; see also Letters of Old Age (Rerum senilium libri), vol. 2: Books X–XVIII, trans. A. Bernardo, S. Levin, and R. Bernardo (New York: Italica Press, 2005), 641 (16.9); Trinkaus, Image and Likeness, 1:173–82.

17. FEP 152.11–54.25; for Cicero see 152.17, for Peter Lombard 155.27.

18. FEP 151.12–52.15, 156.34–58.41; Augustine, Trin. 10.10–12.15; Peter Lombard, Sent. 2.1.6, 16.2–4; Dicta Albini de imagine Dei, in John Marenbon, From the Circle of Alcuin to the School of Auxerre: Logic and Philosophy in

the Early Middle Ages (Cambridge: Cambridge University Press, 2006), 33, 43, 158–61.

19. *FEP* 151.13, 152.15, 153.20, 154.24, 156.33, 158.41, 161.53, 165.70, 167.76.

20. *FEP* 156.33, 159.46, 159.48, 164.64, 165.68–70, 167.77.

21. *FEP* 160.51–61.56, 162.60–63.63.

22. *MDE* pr. 2; 4.43, 58–70; for Manetti's use of Antonio, see 1.13; 2.44; 3.27; 4.58, 61.

23. *FEP* 149.2; Botley, *Latin Translation,* 73, 78, 88, 99–100; Foà, "Manetti."

24. Published in this I Tatti Renaissance Library as *A Translator's Defense,* ed. and trans. Myron McShane and Mark Young (Cambridge, MA: Harvard University Press, 2016).

25. Books I to IV are published in this I Tatti Renaissance Library, *Against the Jews and the Gentiles,* ed. and trans. Stefano U. Baldassarri, Daniela Pagliara, and David Marsh (Cambridge, MA: Harvard University Press, 2017).

26. Botley, *Latin Translation,* 79–80, 93–114; Foà, "Manetti." For Manetti's biographies, see *Biographical Writings,* ed. and trans. Stephano U. Baldassarri and Rolf Bagemihl in this I Tatti Renaissance Library (Cambridge, MA: Harvard University Press, 2003).

27. *LDM.*

28. *MDE* 4.19; *LDM* 1.3 (99).

29. *ADE* 2–4; *FEP* 149.1–2; *MDE* 3.59, 4.45.

30. *MDE* pr. 4–5; *FEP* 148.41; note 19 of this Introduction.

31. *MDE* 1.34, 39, 50–53.

32. *MDE* 1.1.

33. *MDE* 1.3–12.

34. *MDE* 1.13–32.

35. *MDE* 1.5, 29–36; 4.52.

36. *MDE* 1.34–35, 38–39.

37. *MDE* 1.41–42.

38. *MDE* 1.50–51.

39. *MDE* 1.53–54, 4.58–68; *ADE* 45–48; *FEP* 160.48–167.76; note 6 in this Introduction.

40. *MDE* 2.1–3.

41. *MDE* 2.2–12.

42. *MDE* 2.19–23.

43. *MDE* 2.13–16.

44. *MDE* 2.17–19.

45. *MDE* 2.36–44. Augustine, *Trin.* 10.10–12.15.

46. *MDE* 2.37–40; Pliny the Elder, *HN* 19.2–6.

47. *MDE* 2.37.

48. *MDE* 2.45–47.

49. *MDE* 3.11, 20, 30.

50. *MDE* 3.1–2.

51. *MDE* 3.3; Peter of Spain, *Summaries of Logic*, ed. and trans. Brian Copenhaver, Calvin Normore, and Terence Parsons (Oxford: Oxford University Press, 2014), 136–37.

52. *MDE* 3.56.

53. *MDE* 3.58.

54. *MDE* 3.38–39.

55. *MDE* 3.31–32, 38.

56. *MDE* 3.44–50; Aristotle, *Eth. Nic.* 1097b22–98a20; Cicero, *Fin.* 2.40.

57. *MDE* 3.45, 59.

58. *MDE* pr. 4–5; 4.1, 36.

59. *MDE* 4.71; *OLD* s.vv.

60. Kant, *Grundlegung zur Metaphysik der Sitten*, ed. W. Weischedel (Frankfurt am Main: Suhrkamp, 1974), 68–69; *Die Metaphysik der Sitten*, ed. W. Weischedel (Frankfurt am Main: Suhrkamp, 1977), 569–70; for modern conceptions of dignity, see Marcus Düwell et al., eds., *The Cambridge Handbook of Human Dignity* (Cambridge: Cambridge University

Press, 2014); *Dignity: A History*, ed. Remy Debes (Oxford: Oxford University Press, 2017).

61. *MDE* 1.1, 40, 48–49; 2.3, 11, 14, 16, 18, 26, 38; 3.15, 28, 38–39, 42; 4.5, 23, 40, 46–48, 69–70.

62. *MDE* 2.13, 15, 17; 3.6, 7, 35.

63. *MDE* pr. 1; 1.1 (tit.), 25, 34, 43–45, 52–53; 2.8, 16, 18, 20, 23, 30, 46; 3.11, 13, 22, 37–38, 41, 45, 49–50, 56–57, 59; 4.1, 18, 25, 28, 62, 71, 73–74: this list includes *dignus* as well as *dignitas*.

64. Atkins, "Cicero," 481–83; Balsdon, "*Auctoritas*"; Grant, "Cicero"; Pöschl, *Begriff der Würde*; Radin, "Roman Concepts of Equality"; Schofield, "The Fourth Virtue"; Wirszubski, "*Cum dignitate otium*" and idem, *Libertas as a Political Ideal*, 15–17; also Hugo Merguet, *Handlexicon zu Cicero* (Leipzig: Weicher, 1905), s.vv. *dignitas, dignus* (199–200).

65. Genesis 1:26; Ezekial 24:25; Proverbs 14:28, 16:31, 20:29; Ecclesiastes 10:6; Ecclesiasticus 44:3, 45:30; Esther 9:3, 10:2; Baruch 4:3; 1 Maccabees 10:24, 55; 3 Ezra 8:3; Matthew 24:12; Mark 4:39; Luke 2:9; John 11:4; Romans 1:20, 2:4, 3:1, 3:3, 3:16; 2 Corinthians 4:7, 8:14; Ephesians 5:4; Galatians 5:22; 1 Timothy 6:10.

66. *Dicta Albini* in Marenbon, *Circle of Alcuin*, 33, 43, 158–61; Ps.-Anselm, *Liber meditationum et orationum*, in *MPL* 158:709–22A; for even earlier uses of *dignitas* by an authoritative figure, see also *Letters and Sermons of Pope St. Leo I (the Great)*, ed. and trans. P. Boer and C. Feltoe (Lexington: Veritatis Splendor, 2012).

67. *LDM* prol. (93).

68. *MDE* 4.3, 18, 26, 44, 48, 54; Dante, *Inf.* 19.100–101; cf. *ADE* 2–4; *FEP* 149.1–2.

69. *MDE* 4.2–8.

70. *MDE* 4.9–16; Job 10:18–19.

71. *MDE* 4.17; Ambrose, *Bon. mort.* 3, 52–57; cf. Augustine, *De civ. D.* 13.2–6.

72. *MDE* 4.18.

73. *MDE* 4.19–22.

74. *MDE* 4.23–24; Aquinas, *ST* I–II.31.6, 83.4; II–II.152.2, 155.2; *Sent. de an.* 2.14.20, 21.2, 10.

75. *MDE* 4.18, 25–29.

76. *MDE* 4.29–34.

77. *MDE* 4.35–40; Lactantius, *Div. inst.* 3.18.18, 19.1.

78. *MDE* 4.40–42; Jerome, *Comm. Eccl.*, in *MPL* 23:1061–66, commenting on Ecclesiastes 1:2; 3:19–21; 12:5–8; Psalm 39:6; Gregory the Great, *Moral.* 2.83; 4 pr., 48–53; 8.8–12, 63–64; 9.46–48; 12.1; 32.4, 10, 39, 43; 33.26; 35:8–21; 36.57, commenting on Job 1:20; 32–37, esp. 33:14–16; 36:11; 38:2; 41:2; 42:7–10; Ecclesiastes 2:24, 7:2, 11:9–10.

79. *MDE* 4.44, 48.

80. *MDE* 4.18, 44–47: the scriptural texts are Genesis 2:23, 3:20; 2 Corinthians 11:3; 1 Timothy 2:13–14, with comments by Jerome, *Qu. hebr. Gen.* ad loc.; *Nom. hebr.* s.v. *Eva*; Augustine, *Gen. litt.* 11.51; Josephus, *Jewish Antiquities* 1.1.2.36; *LDM* 1.6 (103): after paraphrasing Lotario's description of wailing infants at 4.18, Manetti reproduces it exactly at 4.44.

81. *MDE* 4.49.

82. *MDE* 4.50–51, 64; Job 1:21; *LDM* 1.7 (105).

83. *MDE* 4.52–53; *LDM* 1.8 (105–7).

84. *MDE* 4.54–56; Josephus, *Jewish Antiquities* 1.3.9.104–8; 1.6.5.152; Foà, "Manetti." *De illustribus longaevis* survives in three manuscripts and remains unpublished, though parts can be read in Manetti, *Biographical Writings*, 106–31.

85. *MDE* 4.57; Aristotle, *Eth. Nic.* 1174b26–27, 1175a18–21; *LDM* 1.10 (109).

86. *MDE* 4.58–59; Ephesians 4:11–16; Romans 8:29; *LDM* 1.10 (109).

87. *MDE* 4.59–68; *FEP* 166.74, quoting from Psalm 58:10; Aquinas, *Script. sent.* 4.49.4.5.3; 50.2.4; *ST* III.81.3; *SCG* 4.86–8; [Aquinas], *ST Suppl.* 82–5, 94.1–3.

88. *MDE* 4.73; Aquinas, *Comm. Job* ad 40:6; [Aquinas], *Comm. Matt.* ad 4:19.

89. *ADE* 2–4; *FEP* 149.1–2; cf. *MDE* 4.18, 45, 52–53.

IANNOTII MANETTI
DE DIGNITATE ET
EXCELLENTIA HOMINIS
AD ALFONSUM CLARISSIMUM
ET GLORIOSISSIMUM
ARAGONUM REGEM

GIANNOZZO MANETTI
ON HUMAN WORTH AND
EXCELLENCE
TO THE MOST FAMOUS AND
GLORIOUS ALFONSO
KING OF THE ARAGONESE

PRAEFATIO[1]

1   Vetus quaedam, Serenissime Princeps, eruditorum virorum qui cogitationes suas litteris mandabant consuetudo fuit ut egregia laborum suorum opera ad principes scriberent. Quod eos duabus dumtaxat causis adductos fecisse existimabam: una ut exinde illorum amor ac benevolentia bonis principibus innotesceret; altera ut operibus ipsis quae dignis illorum principum nominibus dedicabantur maior propterea auctoritas proveniret. Ceterum mihi hanc laudabilem doctorum hominum consuetudinem nunc sequi et eorum vestigia imitari vel maxime cupienti duae aliae causae accedebant. Quibus ego inductus et quasi compulsus, me ipsum ulterius continere non poteram quin novum quoddam opus nuper a me compositum cuius titulus est *De dignitate et excellentia hominis* — cum omni reverentia tuo nomini — perscriberem.

    Harum prima erat ut cunctas humani corporis et animi dotes et omnia totius hominis privilegia — tribus prioribus libris antea explicata — in dignissima et admirabili persona tua affatim convenire abundeque concurrere hac nostra praefatione ostenderemus. Quae singillatim inpraesentiarum recenseremus, nisi ad te scribentes adulationis crimen timeremus, praesertim cum id ipsum pluribus scriptorum nostrorum locis diligenter et accurate hactenus fecisse meminerimus. Unum tamen taciti praeterire non possumus: cuncta hoc opere late copioseque tractata totiens certa ac vera videri nobis quotiens in singulares quasdam ac vere admirabiles et paene divinas personae tuae dotes animum mentemque convertimus.

2   Secunda talis occurrebat: cum enim non multo ante Florentini populi nomine legati et oratores Neapoli apud te commoraremur, factum est ut semel opusculum quoddam — praecipuum et

PREFACE

Following a certain ancient custom, my Fairest Prince, learned   1
men who put their thoughts in writing used to address the finest
products of their labors to princes. Only two motives led them to
do this, in my view: first, for these writings to make their love and
friendship known to the good princes; next, for the works themselves to gain greater authority by being dedicated to the worthy
names of those princes. Yet for me, as one most highly desirous of
imitating this laudable custom of learned men and following their
footsteps, two other motives arose. Persuaded by these thoughts
and all but compelled, I could no longer restrain myself from making you a copy of a new work that I have recently put together,
titled — with complete reverence for your name — *On the Worth and
Excellence of Man*.[1]

Of these other motives, the first was this: to declare in this
preface of mine that all man's gifts of body and soul and all the
privileges of the whole human being — those set forth in my first
three books — combine bountifully in your most worthy and admirable person, where they conjoin in abundance. I would list them
one by one right now, especially since I recall having done that very
job with care and attention in various parts of my works, except
that I fear to offend by fawning as I write you. One thing I cannot
pass by in silence, however: all the topics discussed at length and
in detail by this work seem true and sure to me whenever I turn
my mind and soul to the various matchless gifts of your person,
which truly are astonishing and nearly divine.[2]

I had a second such motive: for when I was staying with you   2
in Naples not long ago, representing the Florentine people as
ambassador and spokesman, I happened to read quickly and for
the first time a certain little work — excellent, outstanding, worth

3

egregium et magnis insuper laudibus et memoratu dignum—cursim legeremus, quod a Bartholomeo Fatio, viro eruditissimo simul atque elegantissimo, de eadem materia Nicolao Quinto, Summo Pontifici, scriptum et dedicatum fuerat. Unde cum non multo post forte ad Graecam illam celeberrimam ac famosissimam Turrim semel essemus atque pro humanitate tua prolixum quendam de studiosis atque eruditis hominibus sermonem simul haberemus, modo nescio quo evenit ut in particularem praedicti opusculi mentionem incideremus. Quocirca paulo post—benigne et perhumane quidem—a nobis exegisti ut de eisdem rebus scribere vellemus tibique opus dedicaremus. Nos vero, qui Maiestati Tuae in primis morem gerere et obsequi maxime[2] cupiebamus, nihil nobis gratius fore respondere non dubitavimus quam ut tibi gratificari et famulari possemus. Ideo nos, ut nosti, libenter scripturos et opus tuo nomini dedicaturos hilariter iocundeque promisimus.

3   Unde cum paulo post scribere incoassemus ac prae brevitate temporis incoatum opus perficere et absolvere nequivissemus, rursus postea resumpsimus ac nempe multo prius absolvissemus nisi repentinus Federici Tertii, novelli Imperatoris, in Italiam adventus nos quotidie aliquid describentes parumper retardasset. Nam nostrae rei publicae legati honorandae coronationis eius[3] causa Romam venimus, atque ibi tantum commorati sumus quoad ipse exinde recederet. Ex hac itaque legatione postea in patriam reversi, ultimas demum praedicto operi iam pridem incoato manus imposuimus, atque commemoratis causis adducti tuo nomini dedicavimus, ut—certi pollicitationum nostrarum debitores tibi, ceu vero illorum promissorum creditori—tandem aliquando contracta debita solveremus.

4   Totum autem opus in quatuor libros non temere et fortuito sed singulari quadam et praecipua consideratione divisimus. Nam cum primo singula quaeque quae in corpore humano ac deinde in eius anima et in tota hominis persona aliquatenus apparebant

remembering and deserving much praise besides — that Bartolomeo Facio, an exceedingly learned man and equally refined, had
written on the same subject and dedicated to Nicholas V, the supreme pontiff. Not long after, when I chanced to be at the very
famous and populous Torre del Greco and, in keeping with your
good taste, we had a long talk together about studious and learned
people, I somehow came to mention exactly that work. This was
why you asked a bit later — so kindly and with great refinement
indeed — if I might wish to write about the same issues and dedicate the work to you. Desiring above all to comply with Your
Majesty's desire and to be accommodating, I never really imagined
that any answer would please me more than that I might serve you
and oblige. As you know, I therefore gladly promised to write the
work and dedicate it to your name cheerfully and with pleasure.[3]

And then, shortly after I had begun to write and yet, because   3
time was short, could not complete what I had started and bring it
to an end, I took it up again and surely would have finished much
sooner were it not that the new emperor, Frederick III, arrived
unexpectedly in Italy and slowed me down for a while, since this
gave me something to report every day. For in order to pay respects at his coronation, I went to Rome to represent my government, staying there only until he left. Then, after returning home
from this assignment, I finally put the finishing touches on the
work I have described, long after starting it, and, moved by the
reasons I have given, I dedicated it to your name so that — since
my promises had confirmed my debt to you, just as you were the
creditor of those pledges — I might finally pay a bill already con-
tracted.[4]

Furthermore, I divided the whole work into four books, not   4
casually and haphazardly but after thorough reflection on each
particular. For when I had first gone some way in thinking carefully and attentively about each and every aspect of the human
body and then its soul and the whole human person, it seemed

diligenter et accurate consideraremus, non iniuria visum est nobis — tum pro maiori quadam rerum tractandarum dignitate, tum
etiam pro certiori et planiori omnium cognitione — singularia illa
singulis libris seorsum ac separatim oportunius et convenientius
explicare.

5   Quocirca in primo de egregiis dumtaxat humani corporis dotibus, in secundo de praecipuis quibusdam rationalis animae privilegiis, in tertio de admirabilibus totius hominis muneribus — quanto
a nobis fieri potuit — diligentius et accuratius explicavimus. Quae
omnia cum tribus prioribus libris fecisse videremur, quartum insuper adhibere placuit, in quo ea confutaremus quae a pluribus
idoneis auctoribus de laudatione et bono mortis et de miseria humanae vitae conscripta fuisse intelligebamus — quoniam illa nostris
quodammodo adversari et repugnare non ignoramus.

6   Verum ut haec nostra parva munuscula tibi gratiora viderentur,
non nulla etiam partim in laudem Maiestatis Tuae a nobis antea
descripta, partim nomini tuo dedicata in uno et eodem volumine
coartavimus. Atque ad te summa cum devotione e Florentia usque
Neapolim perferenda curavimus. Humiliter itaque rogamus ac
suppliciter obsecramus ne haec nostra parvula munuscula ullatenus spernas, sed potius propterea gratanter accipias quaesumus,
quoniam a nobis Maiestati Tuae nimirum deditissimis libentissime
simul atque devotissime transmittuntur.

right to me—recognizing the considerable merit of the issues under discussion and wishing to understand them all with greater
purpose and clarity—that it would be more fitting and appropriate to deal with each topic separately in its own book and apart
from the others.

As much as I could, then, I have given a rather careful and at-   5
tentive account limited, in the first book, to the outstanding gifts
of the human body, in the second to certain special privileges of
the rational soul, and in the third to the admirable faculties of the
whole human person. Though plainly I have dealt with all this in
the first three books, I decided to add a fourth as well, in which to
refute what (as I understand it) many capable authors have written
on death as good and praiseworthy and on the misery of human
life—by no means unaware that these writings are in some way
opposed to my own and inconsistent with them.

Actually, to make these little presents of mine seem more pleas-   6
ing to you, I have bound various pieces together in one and the
same volume, one part being what I had written before in praise of
Your Majesty, another what I have dedicated to your name. And
with the greatest devotion, I have arranged for them to be sent
from Florence to you in Naples. Humbly I ask, then, and respectfully pray that you in no way spurn these little presents of mine,
begging you to accept them joyfully instead, because it is Your
Majesty to whom I have dedicated and sent them with truly perfect goodwill and utmost devotion.[5]

LIBER PRIMUS[4]

1 Cum igitur hoc nostrum quodcunque opus ab humano corpore
feliciter incipere debeamus, ipsum vel ex limo terrae et humo unde
hominem appellatum putant — vel potius, si Iosepho vernaculo Iudaeorum historico credimus, ex rubea terra conspersa quae Hebraice *adom*[5] nuncupatur, ex quo *Adam* euphoniae causa paululum
immutatum dictum esse arbitratur, quanquam eo illius linguae
nomine homo significetur — in sacris litteris ab omnipotenti Deo
mirabiliter formatum fuisse legimus. Quod ipse per rationalis animae creationem atque inspirationem divinitus vivificans ad contemplationem sui artificis erexit, ut optime simul atque elegantissime ingeniosus poeta his carminibus signasse visus est:

> pronaque cum spectent animalia cetera terram,
> os homini sublime dedit, caelumque videre
> iussit et erectos ad sidera tollere vultus.

Unde Graeci rectius et expressius *antropon* — quod sursum spec-
tet — quam nos *hominem*[6] ab humo vel quam Hebraei *adam* ab
adama appellasse et cognominasse videntur.

2 De perfecta igitur humanae naturae formatione diligenter et
accurate indagare[7] et investigare cupientes, quid duo excellentis-
sima commemorandorum philosophorum et oratorum ingenia de
hoc ipso senserint parumper videamus, ut quantum praestantes et
excellentes homines — partim puris suis naturalibus constituti,
partim superno lumine illustrati — in eo ipso valuerint, capere et
intelligere possimus. Proinde propria dumtaxat Ciceronis ac Lac-
tantii verba, ceteris omnibus omissis, in hoc loco ponere et in medium afferre curabimus.

BOOK ONE

Since I should begin my book, whatever it amounts to, in a happy 1
way with the human body, I have read in Sacred Scripture that
Almighty God formed it miraculously from the slime and soil of
the earth, the humus from which the name *human* supposedly
came—or else, if I believe Josephus, a native Jewish historian, it
came from the moist red earth called *adom* in Hebrew and after
which, with a very small change for the sake of euphony, they believe that *Adam* was called, though *man* is the meaning of the
name in that tongue. By creating the rational soul and breathing it
into the body, God brought the body to life by divine power and
made it erect to observe its maker, as the gifted poet evidently
pointed out in these verses, quite elegantly and expertly:

> While other animals stoop to see the earth,
> he put man's head up high, directing him
> to look skyward and raise his face erected to the stars.

Hence the Greek *anthropos*—meaning *up-looker*—seems a more
correct and descriptive name and designation, better than our taking *human* from *humus* or the Hebrews taking *Adam* from *adama*.[6]

Though I want to explore human nature's perfect design and 2
examine it with care and attention, let me take a quick look at
thoughts on this topic from the two best minds among notewor-
thy philosophers and orators, so that we can grasp and understand
how much has been achieved in this matter by people of excellence
and distinction—some enabled just by their own natural gifts,
others illuminated by light from on high. Accordingly, I shall take
care to cite here and put into play only the relevant words of Cicero and Lactantius, skipping all the rest.

3   Cicero namque, cum contra Epicurum hominem ab immortali
Deo factum fuisse contenderet, in secundo *De natura deorum* in
hunc modum locutus est.

> Cum tribus rebus animantium vita teneatur, cibo, potione,
> spiritu: ad haec omnia percipienda os est aptissimum quod
> adiunctis naribus spiritu augetur. Dentibus in ore construc-
> tis manditur atque ab his extenuatur et demollitur cibus.
> Eorum adversi acuti morsu dividunt escas. Intimi autem
> conficiunt, qui *genuini* vocantur, quae confectio etiam a lin-
> gua adiuvari videtur.
>
> Linguam autem ad radices eius haerens excipit stomacus,
> quo primum illabuntur ea quae accepta sunt. Hic oris utra-
> que ex parte tosillas attingens palato extremo atque intimo
> terminatur. Atque is agitationibus et motibus linguae cum
> depulsum et quasi detrusum cibum accipiat, depellit: ipsius
> autem partes hae quae sunt infra, in quas id quod devoratur
> descendit, dilatantur, quae autem supra contrahuntur. Sed
> cum *aspera arteria* (sic enim a medicis appellatur) ostium
> habeat adiunctum linguae radicibus paulo supra quam ad
> linguam stomacus annectitur, ea quae ad pulmones usque
> pertineat excipiatque animam eam, quae ducta sit spiritu
> eandemque[8] a pulmonibus respiret et redeat, tegitur quasi
> quodam operculo, quod ob eam causam datum est ne, siquid
> in eam cibi forte incidisset, spiritus impediretur.

4   Sed cum alvi natura subiecta stomaco cibi et potionis sit
receptaculum, pulmones autem et cor extrinsecus spiritum
adducant. In alvo multa sunt mirabiliter effecta, quae constat
fere e nervis. Est autem multiplex et tortuosa arcetque et
continet — sive illud aridum est sive humidum — quod recipit
ut id mutari[9] et concoqui possit. Eaque tum astringitur tum

Now Cicero, arguing against Epicurus that man was made by 3
an immortal God, has put it like this in his second book *On the
Nature of the Gods:*[7]

> For ensouled beings, life is maintained by three things, food,
> drink and breathing: the mouth, nourished with breath from
> the adjoining nostrils, is perfectly suited to take them all in.
> Food is chewed, thinned and softened up by the teeth built
> up in the mouth. The sharp teeth in front bite and divide
> what is eaten. But those at the back, called *jaw-teeth,* are
> grinders, and the tongue also seems to help the grinding.
>
> After the tongue and attached to its roots comes the gul-
> let, where the material taken in starts to slide down. Its edge
> is where the tonsils at the end of the mouth on both sides
> attach to the palate within. And as the tongue's actions and
> motions bring the food in, pushing it down and away, so to
> speak, the gullet pushes the food down farther: where the
> consumed food goes lower down, the gullet's lower parts ex-
> pand, as its upper parts contract. Now the *rough tube* (the
> medical term for the windpipe) has an opening next to the
> roots of the tongue, and a little above this the gullet connects
> to the tongue. The windpipe reaches all the way to the lungs
> and receives the air drawn in by breathing; then it exhales,
> bringing the same air up from the lungs. Covering it is a sort
> of lid, provided to keep the breath free of blockage in case
> any food should fall in.
>
> Set below the gullet, the belly is a natural receptacle for 4
> food and drink, while the lungs and heart bring the breath
> from outside, and the belly, made almost entirely of muscle
> fibers, does many amazing things. It is full of folds and
> turns, to confine and contain what it takes in — dry or wet,
> as the case may be — so that this can be transformed and
> digested. The belly then tightens and loosens to press and

relaxatur atque omne quod accipit cogit et confundit ut facile
et calore—quem multum habet—in terendo cibo et praeterea spiritu omnia cocta[10] atque confecta in reliquum corpus
dividantur. In pulmonibus autem inest raritas quaedam et
assimilis spongiis mollitudo ad hauriendum spiritum aptis-
sima, qui tum se contrahunt aspirantes, tum se spiritu dila-
tant, ut frequenter ducatur cibus animalis quo maxime aluntur animantes.

5   Ex intestinis autem, alvo secretus a reliquo cibo, succus is
quo alimur[11] permanat ad iecur per quasdam a medio intes-
tino usque ad *portas* iecoris (sic enim appellantur) ductas et
directas vias quae pertinent ad iecur eique adhaerent. Atque
inde aliae pertinentes sunt per quas cadit cibus a iecore di-
lapsus. Ab eo cibo cum est secreta bilis eique humores qui e
renibus profunduntur, reliqua se in sanguinem vertunt ad
easdemque portas[12] iecoris confluunt ad quas omnes eius
viae pertinent.

Per quas lapsus cibus in hoc ipso loco in eam venam quae
cava appellatur confunditur, perque eam ad cor—confectus
iam coctusque—perlabitur.[13] A corde autem in totum corpus distribuitur per venas admodum multas in omnes partes
corporis pertinentes. Quemadmodum autem reliquiae cibi
depellantur, tum astringentibus se intestinis tum relaxanti-
bus, haud sane difficile dictu est, sed tamen praetereundum
est ne quid habeat iniucunditatis oratio.[14]

6   Illa potius explicetur incredibilis fabrica naturae, nam
quae spiritu in pulmones anima ducitur, ea calescit—primum ipso ab spiritu, deinde coagitatione[15] pulmonum—ex
eaque pars redditur respirando, pars concipitur cordis parte
quadam quam *ventriculum* cordis appellant. Cui similis alter
adiunctus est in quem sanguis a iecore[16] per venam illam

mix all its contents, quickly distributing through the rest of
the body everything that it has ground up and digested by
breaking up the food, by heat — of which it has plenty — and
also by breathing. Perfectly suited to drawing in the breath,
however, is a certain looseness and spongy flexibility in the
lungs: in exhaling they contract, and then to breathe they
expand, producing a constant supply of the soul's food,
which is the main nourishment of ensouled beings.

Separated by the stomach from the remaining food, the   5
juice that nourishes us flows out of the intestines, led by way
of the midgut toward the liver and straight to its *portals* (that
is their name) through various channels that reach to the
liver and connect with it. And there are others reaching away
from it through which the food goes when discharged from
the liver. After the bile has been separated from this food,
along with those fluids that pour out of the kidneys, the rest
turn into blood and flow together to those same portals of
the kidney where all its blood-channels go.

In this location, the discharged food mixes together into
the vein called *hollow* and — already ground up and digested — flows through it to the heart. From the heart the
food is then distributed through a multitude of veins into all
the connecting parts of the body. As for expelling what is left
of the food as the intestines tighten and then loosen, this is
not at all hard to describe, but to avoid nasty language I
should skip it.

Better to set forth this extraordinary production of na-   6
ture, how the air comes into the lungs by breathing and
grows warm — initially from that very breathing, then by
contact with the lungs. A part of it goes back out by exhaling, while another part is kept in a certain region of the
heart that they call the heart's *little pouch*. Like this is another
adjoining pouch into which the blood flows from the liver

cavam influit, eoque modo ex his partibus et sanguis per venas in omne corpus diffunditur et spiritus per arterias. Utraeque autem crebrae multaeque toto corpore intextae vim quandam incredibilem artificiosi operis divinique testantur.

7   Quid dicam de ossibus? Quae subiecta corpori mirabiles commissuras habent et ad stabilitatem aptas et ad artus finiendos accomodatas et ad motum et ad omnem corporis actionem. Huc adde nervos a quibus artus continentur eorumque implicationem corpore toto pertinentem, qui sicut venae et arteriae a corde tractae et profectae in corpus omne ducuntur.

Ad hanc providentiam naturae tam diligentem tamque solertem adiungi multa possunt e quibus intelligatur[17] quantae res hominibus a diis quamque eximiae tributae sint. Quae primum eos humo excitatos celsos et rectos constituit ut deorum cognitionem caelum intuentes capere possent. Sunt enim ex terra homines non ut incolae atque habitatores sed quasi spectatores supernarum rerum atque caelestium, quarum spectaculum ad nullum aliud genus animantium pertinet.

8   Sensus autem interpretes ac nuntii rerum in capite — tanquam in arce — mirifice ad usus necessarios et facti et collocati sunt. Nam oculi tanquam speculatores altissimum locum obtinent, ex quo plurima conspicientes fungantur suo munere. Et aures cum sonum percipere debeant qui natura in sublime fertur, recte in altis corporum partibus collocate sunt. Itemque nares eo quod omnis odor ad superiora fertur recte sursum sunt, et quod cibi et potionis iudicium magnum earum est non sine causa vicinitatem oris secutae sunt. Iam gustatus, qui sentire eorum quibus vescimur genera

through that hollow vein. In this way, blood spreads from these parts into the whole body through the veins, as breath spreads through the arteries. The interweaving of veins and arteries through the whole body is large and dense, showing extraordinary power in workmanship which is artful and divine.

What to say about the bones? Lying under the body, they 7 join together in amazing ways, adapted for stability and suited to terminate the joints, both in moving and in the body's every action. Here also notice the sinews holding the joints together and their branching through the whole body, reaching into every part of it just like the veins and arteries that go through it everywhere from the heart.

About this foresight of nature, so skillful and so careful, many things can be added that help one understand how much the gods have given to humans and how excellent those gifts are. It was this foresight that first made people tall and straight, raised up from the ground, so that they could look heavenward to get knowledge of the gods. Humans come out of the earth not to dwell and reside there, in fact, but to gaze at the heavens on high, a sight accessible to ensouled beings of no other kind.

Made for the head, moreover, are the senses — messengers 8 and interpreters of things and admirably placed, as if in a citadel, for the required purposes. Like lookouts, for example, are the eyes whose place is the highest, where they observe all around to do their work. The ears are also properly located in the body's upper parts because they are meant to perceive the sound that naturally goes up high. And because every smell rises, the nostrils too are properly elevated: their being in the neighborhood of the mouth makes sense since judging food and drink is a major task for them. The organ of taste, because it must distinguish flavors in what we eat,

deberet, habitat in ea parte oris qua esculentis et poculentis iter natura patefecit. Tactus autem toto corpore aequabiliter fusus est ut omnes ictus omnesque minimos[18] et frigoris et caloris appulsus sentire possimus.

Atque ut in aedificiis architecti avertunt ab oculis naribusque dominorum ea quae profluentia[19] necessario tetri essent aliquid habitura, sic natura res similes procul amandavit a sensibus. Quis vero opifex praeter naturam, qua nihil potest esse callidius, tantam solertiam persequi potuisset in sensibus?

9

Quae[20] primum oculos membranis tenuissimis vestivit et saepsit, quas primum perlucidas fecit ut per eas cerni posset, firmas autem ut continerentur. Sed lubricos oculos fecit et mobiles ut et declinarent siquid noceret et aspectum quo vellent facile converterent. Aciesque ipsa qua cernimus, quae pupilla vocatur, ita parva est ut ea quae nocere possint facile vitet.

Palpebraeque, quae sunt tegmenta oculorum, mollissimae tactu ne laederent[21] aciem, aptissimae factae et ad claudendas pupillas ne quid incideret et ad aperiendas, idque providit ut identidem fieri posset cum maxima celeritate. Munitaeque sunt palpebrae tanquam vallo pilorum, quibus et apertis oculis si quid incideret repelleretur, et somno conniventibus, cum oculis ad cernendum non egeremus, ut tanquam involuti quiescerent. Latent praeterea utiliter et excelsis[22] undique partibus saepiuntur: primum enim superiora superciliis obducta sudorem a capite et fronte defluentem repellunt; genae deinde ab inferiore parte tutantur subiectae leviterque eminentes. Nasus ita locatus est ut quasi murus oculis interiectus esse videatur.

resides in the part of the face that is the natural pathway for eating and drinking. Touch spreads evenly over the whole body, however, so that we can feel every blow and even the least effects of all the cold and heat.

And just as architects design buildings to keep the eyes and noses of owners away from those effluents that would inevitably seem somewhat disgusting, so has nature removed things like this far from our senses. Indeed, who but she could have been so ingenious with the senses, since no builder has more skill than nature?

9

First she clothed and covered the eyes with extremely thin membranes, starting by making them transparent so we can see through them but then firm so that they hold the eyes in place. But the eyes she made slippery and mobile so that they could turn aside anything that might injure them and also shift the gaze quickly as needed. The point of the eye through which we see, called the pupil, is small so that it can readily avoid things that might cause injury.

And the eyelids that cover the eyes, very soft to the touch so as not to damage the point of vision, are perfectly constructed for hiding the pupils, to prevent anything from falling in — and for uncovering them — so arranged that this can be done very quickly and repeatedly. The eyelids are also fortified with a palisade of hairs, as it were, to keep out anything that might fall into the eyes when open, and to let them rest closed and blanketed for sleep, so to speak, when we do not need the eyes to see anything. Besides, it helps that the eyes lie hidden and enclosed all around by raised parts: first, the places above, covered by eyebrows, keep the sweat away as it runs down from the head and brow; next, the cheeks, underneath and slightly raised, give protection below. Evidently the nose has been located to stand between the eyes like a wall.

10   Auditus autem semper patet, eius enim sensu etiam dormientes egemus, a quo cum sonus acceptus est ex somno excitamur. Flexuosum iter habet, ne quid intrare possit si simplex et directum pateret;[23] provisum etiam ut siqua minima bestiola conaretur irrumpere in sordibus aurium tanquam in visco inhaeresceret. Extra autem eminent quae appellantur *aures*, et tegendi causa factae tutandique sensus et ne adiectae[24] voces laberentur atque errarent priusquam sensus ab his pulsus esset. Sed duros et quasi corneos habent introitus multisque cum flexibus quod his naturis relatus amplificatur sonus. Quocirca et in fidibus testudine resonatur aut cornu, et ex tortuosis locis et inclusis referuntur ampliores.

    Similiter nares, quae semper propter necessarias utilitates patent, contractiores habent introitus ne quid in eas quod noceat possit pervadere, humoremque semper habent ad pulverem multaque alia depellenda non inutilem. Gustatus praeclare saeptus est, ore enim continetur et ad usum apte et ad incolumitatis custodiam.

    Omnisque sensus hominum multo antecellit sensibus bestiarum. Primum enim oculi — in his artibus quarum iudicium est oculorum, in pictis, fictis, caelatisque formis, in corporum etiam motione ac gestu — multa cernunt subtilius. Colorum etiam et figurarum tum venustatem atque ordinem et — ut ita dicam — decentiam oculi iudicant, atque etiam alia maiora. Nam et virtutes et vitia cognoscunt: iratum, propitium, laetantem, dolentem, fortem, ignavum, audacem, timidumque cognoscunt.

The way is always clear for hearing, however, because we
need this sense even while sleeping to stir us from sleep
when sound gets in. Since the path is crooked, nothing can
enter that could get through if the way were clear and
straight: also, the arrangement is such that the tiniest little
bug that tries to pass through will get stuck in the ear's dirt
as if it were glue. The parts that stick out are called *ears*,
made for the purpose of covering and protecting the sense
and to prevent sounds that come in from slipping away and
getting lost before they make contact with the sense. But
ears have hard and horn-like entrances with many bends,
and the sound that enters is amplified by such features. This
is also why stringed instruments get resonance from tortoise-
shell or horn, and the sound passed through from the twisted
places inside them is amplified.[8]

The nostrils, which always remain open because their
functions are needed, also have entrances that are more confined so that nothing harmful to them can get through, and
they always contain moisture which is quite helpful for getting rid of dust and much else. Taste is covered up quite effectively by being contained in the mouth, which suits its
operation and guards against injury.

Every sense in humans far surpasses the senses of animals. First of all, our eyes perceive many things in more detail—in those arts that use the eyes to judge, in painted,
molded and carved shapes, and also in the movement and
posture of bodies. The eyes judge the beauty, order and—if
I may—propriety of colors and figures as well, along with
other things that are more important. For they recognize
virtues and vices, sensing when someone is angry or agreeable, happy or sad, brave or cowardly, bold or fearful.

Aurium item est admirabile quoddam artificiosumque iudicium, quo iudicatur—et in vocis et in tibiarum nervorumque cantibus varietas sonorum intervalla distinctio, et vocis genera permulta, canorum fuscum, lene[25] asperum, grave acutum, flexibile durum, quae hominum solum auribus iudicantur. Nariumque item—et gustandi parte et[26] tangendi—magna iudicia sunt: ad quos sensus capiendos et perfruendos plures etiam quam vellem artes repertae sunt. Perspicuum est enim quo compositiones unguentorum, quo ciborum conditiones, quo corporum lenocinia processerint.

11 Ad usum autem orationis incredibile est, nisi diligenter attenderis, quanta opera machinata natura sit. Primum enim a pulmonibus arteria usque ad os intimum pertinet, per quam vox principium a mente ducens percipitur et funditur. Deinde in ore sita lingua est finita dentibus; ea vocem immoderate profusam fingit et terminat, quae sonos vocis distinctos et pressos efficit cum et ad dentes et ad alias partes pellit oris. Itaque plectri similem linguam nostri solent dicere, cordarum dentes, nares cornibus his qui ad nervos resonant in cantibus. Quam vero aptas quamque multarum artium mi-

12 nistras manus natura homini dedit.[27] Digitorum enim contractio facilis[28] facilisque porrectio propter molles commissuras et artus nullo in motu laborat. Itaque ad pingendum, ad fingendum, ad sculpendum, ad nervorum[29] eliciendos sonos ac tibiarum apta manus est admotione digitorum. Atque haec oblectationis, illa necessitatis, cultus dico agrorum extructionesque tectorum.

13 Et reliqua. Atque haec Cicero de corpore humano ieiune et exiliter, ut Lactantio viro eloquentissimo, ut mihi vero homini non diserto videri solet mirabiliter ac divinitus, elocutus est. Nunc de

The ears too have judgment of a kind that is striking and ingenious, judging—both for sung music and for wind and string instruments—how sounds vary by interval and contrast, along with the many types of voice that only human ears can judge: ringing or muffled, smooth or rough, low or high, soft or hard. Judgments made by the nose—and partly by tasting as well as touching—are important: to take in those sensations and enjoy them, more techniques have been invented than I, for one, would like. For it is obvious how far things have gone in blending perfumes, seasoning food and pandering to the body.[9]

Unless you pay close attention, it is impossible to believe   11
how much nature has devised for the purpose of speaking. First, extending from the lungs to inside the mouth is the windpipe through which speech, originating from the mind, is received and uttered. Then the tongue, situated in the mouth, is confined by the teeth. It shapes and limits speech that has poured out without restraint, making the sounds of the voice distinct and compact by pushing against the teeth and other parts of the mouth. This is why our people often say that the tongue is like a lyre's pick, the teeth like strings and the nostrils like these horns that make the strings resonate when playing a song. But nature has also given hu-   12
mans the hands that are so well suited to serve many arts. With their flexible joints, never straining no matter what the movement, the fingers close easily and open easily, which is why the motion of the fingers suits the hand for painting, molding, engraving and for getting sounds from strings and flutes.[10]

And Cicero goes on. For Lactantius, a man of enormous elo-   13
quence, the account that Cicero has given of the human body is thin and scanty, while to me—not a well-spoken person—it seems

ipso Lactantio videamus, quem in libro *De opificio hominis* sic disserentem legisse meminimus.

14   Cum igitur statuisset Deus ex omnibus animalibus solum
hominem facere caelestem, cetera universa terrena, hunc ad
caeli contemplationem rigidum erexit bipedemque constituit — scilicet ut eadem spectaret unde illi origo est. Illa vero
depressit ad terram ut, quia nulla his immortalitatis expecta-
tio erat, toto corpore in humum proiecta ventri pabuloque
servirent. Hominis itaque solius recta ratio et sublimis status
et vultus Deo patri communis ac proximus originem suam
fictoremque testatur.

15   Eius prope divina mens, quia non tantum animantium
quae sunt in terra sed etiam sui corporis est sortita domina-
tum, in summo capite collocata tanquam in arce sublimi
speculatur omnia et contuetur. Hanc eius aulam Deus non[30]
obductam porrectamque formavit ut in mutis animalibus sed
orbi et globo similem quod orbis rotunditas perfectae rationis est ac figurae. Eo igitur mens et ignis ille divinus tanquam caelo tegitur.

16   Cuius cum summum fastigium naturali veste texisset, pri-
orem partem, quae dicitur facies, necessariis membrorum
ministeriis et instruxit pariter et ornavit. Ac primum oculorum orbes concavis foraminibus conclusit — a quo *foratu fron-
tem* nominatam Varro existimavit. Et eos neque minus neque
amplius quam duos esse voluit quod ad speciem nullus est
perfectior numerus quam duorum, sicut et aures duas: quarum duplicitas incredibile est quantam pulchritudinem prae-
ferat, quod cum[31] pars utraque similitudine ornata est tum[32]
ut venientes extrinsecus voces facilius colligantur.

miraculous and divine. Now let me have a look at Lactantius, noting what he writes in his book *On the Workmanship in Man*.[11]

> Since God determined to make man alone, of all the animals, for heaven and all the rest for earth, he stood him up straight and put him on two feet to gaze at the heavens — to look on those same places whence he came. Since the others had no expectation of immortality, he bent them down toward the earth to feed and serve the belly, their whole bodies lying on the ground. Only for man, then, do right reason, an elevated posture and looks shared with God the Father — and very much like him — bear witness to his Maker and origin.[12] 14

> Man's nearly divine mind, because it was assigned the lordship not only of living things that are in the earth but also of its own body, observes and surveys everything from its location at the top of the head, as if in a lofty citadel. God did not give the mind's castle a stretched and extended form as in mute animals but made it spherical like a globe because the roundness of a sphere is perfect in shape and proportion. Like the sky, then, the head covers the mind and the divine fire there.[13] 15

> After covering man's top end with a natural garment, he fitted out the front part, called the face, equally well, furnishing it with the parts needed to serve it. First he enclosed the eyeballs in hollow openings — the *boring* from which the *brow* got its name, so Varro thought. And God wanted two of them, neither more nor less, because no number is more perfect to look at than the twos, so that there are two ears as well. Astonishing how much beauty comes from their being doubled: each side looks better by resembling the other, which also makes it easier to collect sounds coming in from outside.[14] 16

Nam et forma ipsa mirandum in modum ficta: quod earum foramina noluit[33] esse nuda et inobsaepta; quod minus
decorum et minus utile fuisset quoniam simplicium caverna-
rum angustias praetervolare vox posset et spargi,[34] nisi per-
ceptam per cavos sinus et repercussu retentam foramina ipsa
conveherent, illis simillima vasculis quibus impositis solent
angusti oris vasa[35] impleri. Eas igitur aures noluit Deus Artifex mollibus pelliculis informare quae pulchritudinem deme-
rent pendulae ac flaccentes, neque duris atque solidis ossibus, ne ad usum inhabiles essent immobiles ac rigentes. Sed
quod esset eorum medium excogitavit ut eas cartilago mol-
lior alligaret et haberent aptam simul et flexibilem firmita-
tem. In his audiendi tantum officium constitutum est — sicut
in oculis videndi.

Quorum praecipue inexplicabilis est et mira subtilitas
quia eorum orbes — gemmarum similitudinem praeferentes — ab ea parte qua videndum fuit membranis perlucenti-
bus texit ut imagines rerum contrapositarum tanquam in
speculo refulgentes ad sensum intimum penetrarent. Ineffa-
bilis ergo divinae providentiae virtus fecit duos simillimos
orbes eosque ita devinxit ut non in totum converti sed moveri tamen et flecti cum modo possent. Orbes autem ipsos
humoris puri et liquidi plenos esse voluit, in quorum media
parte scintillae luminum conclusae tenerentur. Quas pupillas
nuncupamus, in quibus puris ac subtilibus cernendi sensus
ac ratio continetur. Per eos igitur orbes se ipsam[36] mens intendit ut videat, miraque ratione in unum miscetur et con-
iungitur amborum luminum visus.[37]

17

Now God also fashioned the shape itself in a wonderful way: he did not want the openings to be bare and unclosed; this would be less elegant and less useful because the sound might fly past the holes and scatter if these were straight and narrow, unless the openings themselves—just like those little funnels often used to fill containers with small mouths—would take it in as the hollow folds receive it and counter-pressure holds it back. In making the ears, the divine Crafts-man wanted to form them neither with soft, flabby bits of skin, which would hang down and droop, detracting from their beauty, nor with hard and solid bones, wanting the ears not to be stiff, unmovable and unwieldy for use. Instead he devised something in between, so that a softer cartilage would connect them, making them firm enough but also flexible at the same time. The only function assigned them is hearing—just like seeing for the eyes.[15]

The delicacy of the eyes is particularly astonishing and inexplicable in that God covered the eyeballs—which give the appearance of jewels—with transparent membranes, starting from the part needed for seeing, so that images of things facing them would penetrate to the sense inside as if gleaming in a mirror. Accordingly, the indescribable power of divine providence made the two spheres entirely alike and fastened them down in a way that prevents them from turn-ing all the way around, while still letting them move and re-volve to some extent. But he wanted those same spheres to be filled with a clear, transparent liquid, with their centers holding the bright points of the eyes and keeping them in. These we call pupils, clear and delicate, which contain the sense and faculty of seeing. Through these spheres, then, the mind reaches out to see, and an amazing mechanism mixes the sight of the paired eyes and blends it into one.[16]

17

18   Ut igitur oculi munitiores essent ab iniuria, eos ciliorum tegminibus *occuluit,* unde *oculos* dictos esse Varroni placet. Nam et ipsae *palpebrae* — quibus mobilitas, id est[38] *palpitatio,* vocabulum tribuit — pilis in ordinem stantibus vallatae[39] saeptum oculis decentissimum praebent. Quarum motus assiduus incomprehensibili celeritate concurrens et videndi tenorem non impedit et reficit obtusum. Acies enim — id est membrana illa perlucens quam siccari et obarescere non oportet — nisi humore assiduo tersa pure niteat obsolescit.

    Quid? Ipsa superciliorum fastigia pilis brevibus adornata, nonne quasi aggeribus et munimentum oculis, ne quid superne incidat et speciem simul praestant? Ex quorum confinio nasus exoriens[40] et veluti aequali porrectus iugo utramque aciem et discernit et munit. Inferius quoque genarum non indecens tumor, in similitudinem collium leviter[41] exsurgens, ab omni parte oculos efficit tutiores — provisumque est ab Artifice Summo ut, siquis forte vehementior ictus extiterit, eminentibus repellatur.

19   Nasi vero pars superior usque ad medium solida formata est, inferior autem cartilagine adhaeret mollita ut ad usum digitorum possit esse tractabilis. In hoc autem quamvis simplici membro tria sunt officia constituta: unum ducendi spiritus, alterum capiendi odoris, tertium ut per eius cavernas purgamenta cerebri defluant. Quas ipse Deus tam mirabili quam divina ratione molitus est, ut tamen hiatus nasi oris speciem non deformaret — quod erat plane futurum si simplex foramen pateret. At id veluti pariete per medium ducto

Then, to give the eyes better protection from injury, he 18
laid them under *lids* to cover them—the reason for calling
them that, according to Varro. The *lashes* themselves—to
whose rapid movement or *lashing about* Varro attributes the
term—make a very handsome fence for the eyes, with hairs
standing in a row to defend them. Their constant movement
in unison at unbelievable speed does not obstruct the flow of
vision and makes the gaze steady again. The iris—meaning a
transparent membrane that must not dry out and wither—
becomes useless unless it sparkles when regularly cleaned by
moisture.[17]

What next? Those gabling eyebrows adorned with short
hairs, are they not like ramparts, providing protection for the
eyes, lest something fall in from above, and making them
beautiful as well? The nose, like a ridge rising up from their
common boundary and spreading out equally, both protects
and separates the two eyes. Lower down, the rise of the
cheeks is also not unattractive, swelling gently like hills to
make the eyes safer on all sides—the Great Maker's provi-
sion for places that project to ward off any blow that happens to fall too hard.

From the upper part to the middle, the form of the nose 19
has been made solid, but the lower part is softened by connecting cartilage that makes it possible to use the fingers.
Although this organ is quite simple, it comes with three
functions: one to guide the breath, another to receive smell
and a third so that the waste from the brain flows down
through its openings. God himself has constructed these on
a plan both wonderful and divine so that the nose opens up
but still does not disfigure the appearance of the face—
which clearly would have happened if just a single hole
opened there. But he divided it as if by a wall going through

intersaepsit atque divisit, fecitque ipsa duplicitate pulcherrimum. Ex quo intelligimus quantum dualis numerus, una et simplici compage solidatus, ad rerum valeat perfectionem.

20   Nam cum sit corpus unum, tamen totum ex simplicibus membris constare non poterat, nisi ut essent partes vel dextrae vel sinistrae. Itaque ut pedes duo[42] et item manus non tantum ad utilitatem aliquam usumque vel gradiendi vel faciendi valent sed et[43] habitum decoremque admirabilem conferunt, sic in capite, quod totius divini operis quasi culmen est, et auditus in duas aures[44] et visus in duas acies et odoratus in duas nares a Summo Artifice divisus est, quia cerebrum in quo sentiendi ratio est, quamvis sit unum, tamen in duas partes membrana interveniente discretum est. Sed et cor, quod sapientiae domicilium videtur, licet sit unum, duos tamen intrinsecos sinus habet, quibus fontes vivi sanguinis continentur saepto intercidente divisi ut—sicut in ipso[45] mundo summa rerum vel de simplici duplex vel de duplici simplex et gubernat et continet totum—ita in corpore de duobus universa compacta indissociabilem praetenderent unitatem.

21   Oris quoque species et rictus[46] ex transverso patefactus quam utilis quamque decens sit enarrari non potest, cuius usus in duobus constat officiis, sumendi victus et eloquendi. Lingua intus inclusa, quae vocem motibus suis in verba discernit et est interpres animi nec tamen sola potest per se loquendi munus adimplere, nisi acumen suum palato illiserit, nisi adiuta vel offensione dentium vel compressione labiorum. Dentes tamen plus conferunt ad eloquendum. Nam et *infantes* non ante incipiunt *fari* quam dentes habuerint, et senes amissis dentibus ita balbutiunt ut ad infantiam revoluti denuo esse videantur.

the middle and blocking it off, using this very two-sidedness to make it quite beautiful. From this we understand how the dual number, made whole in one simple structure, contributes so much to nature's perfection.

Besides, even though the body is one, it still could not be made entirely of simple organs without there being right or left parts. Accordingly, just as two feet and hands not only work for a particular use and function, either to walk or to make something, but also join to provide a remarkably beautiful appearance, so likewise in the head, which in a sense is the summit of the whole divine work, the Great Maker has divided hearing into two ears, seeing into two eyes and smelling into two nostrils because, even though there is a single brain where the sensory faculty is located, this is still separated into two parts by a membrane that comes in between. And the heart, apparently where wisdom resides, is also one, yet it too has twin chambers inside that contain sources of living blood divided by a wall in the middle, so that—just as the ultimate power governing things in the universe contains and controls the whole by making one out of two or else two out of one—likewise in the body all its components use twos to present an indivisible unity.[18] 20

The appearance of the mouth and the way it opens from side to side is also indescribably attractive and helpful, and its use includes two functions, eating food and speaking. The tongue enclosed inside, the mind's interpreter that separates sound into words with its movements, still cannot complete the task of speaking by itself alone unless its point strikes the palate, unless it gets help from contacting the teeth or pressing against the lips. Yet the teeth do more for speaking. *Babies* do not start *babbling*, in fact, until they have teeth, and when old people lose their teeth, they babble so much that they seem to return to infancy again.[19] 21

22   Atque ipsos, ne nudi ac restricti magis horrori quam or-
namento essent, *gingivis* mollibus — quae a *gignendis* dentibus
nominantur — ac deinde labrorum[47] tegminibus honestavit.
Quorum durities, sicut in molari lapide, maior est et asperior
quam in ceteris ossibus ut ad conterendos cibos pabulumque
sufficeret. Labra[48] ipsa, quae quasi antea cohaerebant, quam
decenter intercidit! Quorum superius sub ipsa medietate
narium lacuna quadam levi[49] quasi valle signavit, inferius
honestatis gratia foras molliter explicavit.

Nam quod attinet ad saporem capiendum, fallitur quis-
quis hunc sensum palato inesse arbitratur. Lingua est enim
qua sapores sentiuntur — nec tamen tota, nam partes eius
quae sunt ab utroque latere teneriores saporem subtilissimis
sensibus trahunt. Et cum neque ex cibo quicquam neque ex
potione minuatur, tamen inenarrabili modo penetrat ad sensum sapor eadem ratione qua[50] nihil de quacunque materia
odoris decerpit.

23   Cetera quam decora sint vix exprimi potest: deductum
clementer a genis mentum et ita inferius conclusum ut acumen eius extremum signare videatur leviter impressa divisio;
rigidum ac teres collum; scapulae velut mollibus iugis a cer-
vice demissae; valida et substricta nervis ad fortitudinem
bracchia; insignibus toris extantium lacertorum vigens robur;
utilis ac decens flexura cubitorum.

24   Quid dicam de manibus, rationis ac sapientiae ministris?
Quas solertissimus Artifex plano ac modice concavo sinu
fictas ut si[51] quid tenendum sit apte possit insidere, in digitos
terminavit in quibus difficile est expedire utrum ne species

And God adorned these teeth with soft *gums* — named 22
from the teeth that *grow* there — and then shielded them
with lips, lest we bare them uncovered, more horror than
ornament. Their hardness, like a millstone, is greater and
rougher than in other bones, enough to grind food for nourishment. And the lips, how beautifully he divided them, as if
they had been stuck together before! Their upper part under
the middle of the nostrils he marked with a somewhat shal-
low depression, like a valley, and for the sake of adornment
he gave the lower part a gentle outward fold.[20]

As to how we perceive taste, however, anyone who thinks
that this sense is in the palate is mistaken. It is the tongue, in
fact, by which we sense tastes — but not the whole tongue,
for it is the softer parts on either side that take taste in with
extremely delicate sense organs. Although nothing is lost
from the food or drink, nonetheless, in a manner that cannot
be described, their taste gets through in the same way that
prevents anything from being taken away from the content
of smell.

One can scarcely express how handsome the rest is: a chin 23
descending smoothly from the cheeks and closed off below
so that a division lightly impressed appears at the bottom
end to mark it; a neck round and unbending; shoulders like
a smooth collar coming down from the neck; powerful fore-
arms undergirded with muscles for strength; hard, brawny
upper arms bulging with muscle; a functional and attractive
bend at the elbows.

What to say about the hands, these agents of reason and 24
wisdom? The most skilled Maker of all made them with a
flat yet slightly hollow surface so that whatever they might
hold will fit inside them, ended by fingers, and it is hard to
say whether their beauty or their use is the greater. It is hard
to disentangle whether the beauty or the utility of fingers is

an utilitas maior sit. Nam et numerus perfectus ac plenus et
ordo ac gradus decentissimus et articulorum parium cur-
vatura flexibilis et forma unguium rotunda, concavis tegminibus digitorum fastigia comprehendens ac firmans ne
mollitudo carnis in tenendo cederet — magnum praebet ornamentum.

Illud vero ad usum miris modis habile quod unus a ceteris
separatus cum ipsa manu oritur et in diversum maturius
finditur. Qui se velut obvium ceteris praebens omnem te-
nendi faciendique rationem — vel solus vel praecipue — possi-
det, tanquam rector omnium et moderator. Unde igitur *polli-*
cis nomen[52] accepit, quod vi et potestate inter ceteros *polleat*.
Duos quidem articulos extantes habet, non ut alii ternos, sed
unus ad manus carnem nectitur pulchritudinis gratia. Si
enim fuisset tribus[53] articulis et ipse discretus, foeda et inde-
cora species ademisset manibus honestatem.

25   Nam pectoris latitudo sublimis et exposita oculis mirabi-
lem prae se fert habitus sui dignitatem. Cuius haec causa est
quod videtur hominem solum Deus veluti supinum formasse, nam fere nullum animal in tergum iacere potest; mu-
tas autem animantes — quasi *a-frona* — alterno[54] latere iacentes
finxisse et ad terram compressisse. Idcirco illis angustum
pectus, et ab aspectu remotum et ad terram versus abiectum,
homini autem patens et erectum quia plenum rationis a caelo
datae humile aut indecens esse non debuit. Papillae quoque — leviter eminentes et fuscioribus ac parvis orbibus coro-
natae — non nihil addunt venustatis, feminis ad alendos fetus
datae, maribus ad solum decus ne informe pectus et quasi
mutilum videretur.

the greater. For their completely perfect number and order, their very attractive rise and fall, their flexible bending with the same number of joints as well as the round shape of the nails that cover, enclose and strengthen the fingertips so that the soft flesh does not give way when holding things — all this fits them out beautifully.

But this beauty is wonderfully suited for many applications because one digit, separate from the rest, comes from the same hand but extends quite properly in a different direction. This one digit, as if ruling and regulating them all by opposing the rest of them, has in it — either alone or especially — the whole basis of holding and making. From this it gets the name *thumb* because its power and strength *thrive* more than the others. It actually has two joints that are prominent, not three like the rest, but flesh links one joint to the hand for the sake of beauty. For if it were off by itself with three joints, an ugly and disfiguring appearance would deprive the hands of beauty.[21]

Furthermore, a broad and elevated chest exposed to the eyes displays the remarkable grandeur of its situation. The cause of this is that when God shaped man, so it seems, he alone was facing up, since almost no animal can lie on its back; but God fashioned the dumb animals to lie face down on either side — as if *sense-less* or *a-phrona* — and pushed down to the ground. This is why the chest is narrow in these animals, removed from sight and put away near the ground, while man's is broad and prominent, full of heaven-sent reason and not meant to be lowly or unlovely. The breasts — slightly raised and crowned with little orbs a bit darker — also add some beauty: they were given to females for feeding children, to males just for adornment, so that the chest would not seem malformed and a bit maimed.[22]

25

Huic subdita est planities ventris, quam mediam fere umbilicus non indecenti nota signat, ad hoc factus ut per eum
fetus dum est in utero nutriatur. Sequitur necessario ut de
internis quoque visceribus dicere incipiamus, quibus non
pulchritudo, quia sunt abdita, sed utilitas incredibilis attri-
buta est. Quoniam opus fuit ut terrenum hoc corpus succo
aliquo de cibis et potibus aleretur — sicut[55] terra ipsa imbri-
bus ac pruinis — providentissimus Artifex in medio eius receptaculum cibis fecit, quibus concoctis et liquefactis vitales
succos membris omnibus dispartiret.

Sed cum homo constet ex corpore et anima, id quod supra dixi receptaculum soli corpori praestat alimentum, animae vero aliam sedem dedit. Fecit enim quoddam genus
viscerum molle atque rarum quod *pulmonem* vocamus. Eumque non in utri[56] modum finxit ne effunderetur simul spiritus aut inflaret simul. Ideoque plenum viscus effecit sed in-
flabile atque aeris capax, ut paulatim spiritum reciperet dum
vitalis ventus per illam spargitur raritatem et eundem rursus
paulatim redderet dum se ex illo explicat. Ipsa enim vicissi-
tudo spirandi respirandique tractus vitam sustentat in corpore.

Quoniam ergo duo sunt in homine receptacula — unum
aeris quod alit animam, alterum ciborum quod alit corpus —
duas per collum esse fistulas necesse est, cibalem ac spiritalem, quarum superior ab ore ad ventrem ferat, inferior vero a
naribus ad pulmonem, quarum natura et ratio diversa est.
Ille enim qui est ab ore transitus mollis effectus est, et qui
semper clausus cohaereat sibi sicut os ipsum, quoniam potus
et cibus, dimota et patefacta gula, quia corporales sunt, spatium sibi transmeandi faciunt.

26

27

28

Below this comes the flat surface of the belly, its center marked by the umbilicus, a rather handsome way to indicate something made to feed the infant while still in the womb. This obliges me to begin discussing the internal organs as well, provided not with beauty, since they are concealed, but with unbelievable usefulness. Because it had been necessary to nourish this earthly body with juices from food and drink — like rain and frost for the earth — the most provident Maker fashioned a receptacle for food in the middle of the body, to distribute the vital juices to all the body's parts after the food is digested and liquefied.[23]

Since man is made of body and soul, however, the receptacle that I have just described provides nourishment only for the body, and God gave the air a different location. For he made internal organs of a special kind — we call them *lungs* — that are soft and loosely textured. But to keep the breath from being let out just once or taken in just once, he did not fashion the lung like a bag. This is why he made its flesh plump but inflatable to hold air, permitting it to inhale in short breaths as the vital wind diffuses through its loose fabric and then to exhale again in short breaths as the wind escapes from it. In fact, this alternating inflation sustains life in the body as the breathing goes in and out.

Hence, since humans have the two receptacles — one for air to nourish the soul, another for foods to nourish the body — two pipes differing in nature and design must go through the neck for eating and for breathing, the one above leading from the mouth to the stomach, the one below from the nostrils to the lungs. The passage from the mouth has been made soft, and it always fits together when closed, like the mouth itself, because the drink and the food, being physical things, make their own space as they pass through the gullet when it parts and opens up.

26

27

28

Spiritus contra, qui est incorporalis ac tenuis, quia spatium sibi facere non poterat, accepit viam patentem, quae vocatur *gurgulio*. Is constat ex ossibus flexuosis ac mollibus quasi ex anulis in cicutae modum invicem compactis et cohaerentibus, patetque semper hic transitus. Nullam enim requiem meandi potest habere spiritus, quia is qui semper commeat demissa utiliter de cerebro membri portione cui *uva* nomen est velut occursu quodam refrenatur, ne aut teneritudinem domicilii cum impetu veniens,[57] attracta pestilenti aura, corrumpat aut totam nocendi violentiam internis receptaculis perferat.

Ideoque etiam *nares* breviter sunt apertae, quae idcirco sic nominantur quia per eas vel odor vel spiritus *nare* non desinit. Tamen haec fistula spiritalis non tantum ad nares verum ad os quoque interpatet[58] in extremis palati regionibus, ubi se *tolles*[59] faucium spectantes uvam *tollere* incipiunt in tumorem, cuius rei causa et ratio non obscura est. Loquendi enim facultatem non[60] haberemus si sicut iter gulae ad os tantum, ita et gurgulio ad nares tantum pateret. Aperuit igitur viam voci divina solertia ex illa fistula spiritali ut posset lingua ministerio suo fungi et vocis ipsius inoffensum tenorem pulsibus suis[61] in verba concidere.

29   Cibi vero in alvum recepti et cum potus humore permixti, cum iam calore percocti fuerint, eorum succus inenarrabili modo per membra diffusus irrigat universum corpus et vegetat. Intestinorum quoque multiplices spirae ac longitudo in se convoluta et uno tantum substricta vinculo — quam mirificum Dei opus est! Nam ubi maceratos ex se cibos alvus emiserit, paulatim per illos internorum anfractus extruduntur, ut quicquid ipsis inest succi quo corpus alitur membris

But the breath, which is thin and immaterial and could make no space for itself, has taken the way that is open, called the *windpipe*. This consists of soft and flexible bones sticking together and fitting like rings from a stalk of hemlock—a passageway that always opens wide. For the breath can get no rest as it moves through: because it always keeps going, part of an organ—called the *grape*—helps by hanging down from the brain for the breath to meet it and be held back a bit, kept from entering with a rush and dragging infected air with it, which would damage its fragile abode or else transmit all the harmful power to the receptacles inside.[24]

This is also why the *nostrils* open a little and how they get their name because smell and breath never cease *nosing* through them. Yet this tube for breathing opens not only between the nostrils but also to the mouth at the back parts of the palate, where the *tonsils* in the jaws, facing the grape, begin to rise and *tumesce*, and the cause that explains this is not hard to see. For we would not have the faculty of speech if the path of the windpipe opened only to the nostrils, as the gullet opens only to the mouth. This is why divine skill cleared a path for speech out of that breathing channel so that the tongue could do its job by beating on the air and cutting the unobstructed flow of speech into words.[25]

But once the stomach receives the food, thoroughly mixed   29
with moisture from what we drink and then digested by heat, the juice from this spreads in an indescribable manner through the limbs, watering and enlivening the whole body. Also, the many coils of the intestines, folding lengthwise upon themselves and tied together in just one cord—what an amazing work of God this is! For when the stomach ejects the softened food, it is pressed out little by little through those internal bendings, and any juice inside that

omnibus dividatur. Et tamen necubi[62] forte obhaereant ac resistant—quod fieri poterat propter ipsorum voluminum flexiones in se saepe redeuntes, et fieri sine pernicie non poterat—opplevit ea intrinsecus crassiore succo ut purgamenta illa ventris ad exitus suos facilius per lubricum niterentur.

Illa quoque ratio subtillissima est quod vesica—cuius usum volucres non habent—cum sit ab intestinis separata nec ullam habeat fistulam qua ex illis urinam trahat, completur tamen et humore distenditur. Id quomodo fiat non est difficile pervidere. Intestinorum enim partes quae ab alvo cibum potumque suscipiunt patentiores sunt quam ceterae spirae et multo tenuiores. Hae vesicam complectuntur et continent: ad quas partes cum potus et cibus mixti pervenerint, fimum quidem crassius fit et transmeat. Humor autem omnis per illam teneritudinem percolatur, eumque vesica, cuius aeque tenuis subtilisque membrana est, absorbet ac colligit ut foras qua natura exitum patefecit emittat.

30   De utero quoque et conceptione, quoniam de internis loquimur, dici necesse est ne quid praeteriisse videamur. Quae quanquam in operto lateant, sensum tamen atque intelligentiam latere non possunt. Vena in maribus quae semen[63] continet duplex est, paulo interior quam illud humoris obscaeni receptaculum. Sicut enim renes duo sunt, itemque testes ita[64] et venae seminales duae in una tantum compage cohaerentes. Ipsum semen quidam aiunt ex omni corpore ad venam genitalem[65] confluere.

Et reliqua huiusmodi prosecutus, paulo post ita inquit:

Ego ipsorum genitalium membrorum nunc mirificam rationem poteram exponere nisi me pudor ab huiusmodi sermone

nourishes the body divides among all the parts. However, so that nothing gets stuck and stays back anywhere—a disastrous result that could occur because the bends in those rolls often turn back on themselves—God filled them inside with thicker juice so that what is cleaned from the stomach can push its way out more easily through something slippery.

This structure is also quite intricate because the bladder—whose use birds do not have—fills up with fluid and swells even though it is separated from the intestines and has no tube to get urine from them. How this happens is not hard to see. For the parts of the intestines that get food and drink from the stomach are more open than the other coils and much finer. These surround and contain the bladder: when the mixed food and drink get to these parts, the excrement actually becomes thicker and passes through. But all the moisture is strained through its thin fabric, and the bladder, whose membrane is equally thin and delicate, absorbs and collects it in order to expel it outside where nature makes an opening.[26]

Since I am talking about the insides, I must discuss the uterus and conception as well lest I seem to have skipped something. Although these are hidden and covered up, they cannot hide their intelligent design and purpose. The vein in males that contains the semen is double, a little farther in than that other receptacle for foul liquid. For just as there are two kidneys, so also two testicles and veins for seed fit together in just one structure. Some say that the seed itself flows to the genital vein from the whole body.

Lactantius proceeds with other such information, saying this a bit later:

I could have explained the amazing design of those genital parts now except that shame restrained me from such a dis-

30

revocaret. Itaque a nobis indumento verecundiae quae sunt pudenda velentur.

31   Quid reliquae corporis partes? Num carent ratione ac pulchritudine? Conglobata in nates caro — quam sedendi officio apta! Et eadem firmior quam in ceteris membris ne premente corporis mole ossibus cederet. Item femorum deducta et latioribus toris valida longitudo quo facilius onus corporis sustineret, quam paulatim deficientem in angustum genua determinant — quorum decentes nodi flexuram pedibus ad gradiendum sedendumque aptissimam praebent. Item crura non aequali modo ducta ne indecens habitudo deformaret pedes, sed teretibus suris clementer extantibus sensimque tenuatis et firmata sunt et ornata.

32   In *plantis* vero eadem quidem sed tamen longe dispar quam in manibus ratio est. Quae quoniam totius operis fundamenta sunt, mirificus eas Artifex non rotunda specie ne homo stare non posset neve aliis ad standum pedibus indigeret sicut quadrupedes, sed porrectiores longioresque formavit ut stabile corpus efficerent[66] *planitie* sua, unde illis inditum nomen est. Digiti aeque[67] totidem quot in manibus, speciem magis quam usum maiorem praeferentes. Ideo et iuncti et breves gradatim compositi, quorum qui est maximus, quoniam illum sicut in manu[68] discerni a ceteris opus non erat, ita in ordinem redactus est, ut tamen ab aliis magnitudine ac modico intervallo distare videatur. Haec eorum speciosa germanitas non levi adiumento nisum pedum firmat: concitari enim ad cursum non possumus nisi digitis in humum pressis soloque nitentibus impetum saltumque capiamus.

cussion. So let the nature of the private parts be veiled from us under cover of modesty.

What of the body's other parts? Do they lack beauty and design? The mass of flesh rounded in the buttocks — how well suited for the purpose of sitting! And the same flesh is firmer than in other parts so that it will not collapse with the bones when the weight of the body presses on it. Likewise, to bear the body's weight more easily, the thighs are extended in length and strengthened with broader muscles: they gradually get thinner and narrow where the knees end them — this handsome linkage supplying the feet with a bend perfectly suited to walking and sitting. The shins are unequal along their length lest an ungainly appearance disfigure the feet; instead they are fitted out and strengthened with rounded calves that rise gently and gradually thin.

The *soles* are actually the same in design as the hands, and yet quite different. Because the soles are foundations for the whole construction, the wonder-working Maker has not shaped them in a round form: that would make humans unable to stand or, like quadrupeds, in need of other feet for standing. Instead, he gave the feet a longer and more extended shape to stabilize the body with their flat *surface*, from which they get their name. They have the same number of digits as the hands — more for appearance than use. And this is why they are shorter, joined together and arranged by size: since there was no need to separate the largest one from the others, as in the hand, that largest one has stayed in line with the others, though evidently differing in size and standing a bit apart. The handsome sameness of the digits is no small help in making the feet firmer when they push: we cannot start to run, in fact, unless we jump to a fast start with the toes pressing the ground and pushing on the soil.[27]

33   Atque haec omnia Lactantius de corpore humano mirabiliter
profecto ac divinitus explicasse deprehenditur. Et tamen ipse multa
de industria praetermisisse confirmat quae usque adeo dubia et
obscura esse videbantur ut nemo eorum vim rationemque nisi Fa-
bricator ille omnipotentissimus clare et aperte perspicere potuisset.

34   Cum igitur ea superius enarrarimus quae de corpore humano
duo divini homines—et Latinae linguae illustratores—perpetuis
litterarum monumentis mandare non dubitarunt, reliquum est ut
quid de eisdem rebus physici senserint, qui accuratam quandam
humani corporis anatomiam scriptam reliquerunt, vel parumper
videamus. Quoniam vero haec praedicti corporis fabricatio ceteris
animantibus longe dignior atque admirabilior esse videtur, non
absurdum fore putamus si antequam ad membra particularia singillatim descendamus, aliqua memoratu digna de corporis nostri
excellentia cunctorumque aliorum differentia breviter disseramus.

35   Corpus igitur nostrum, si diligenter et accurate proprias eius
conditiones et nonnullas praecipuas qualitates consideraverimus,
cum figura tum generali et universali magisterio tum quoque necessaria quarumdam superfluarum partium carentia, tribus pecu-
liaribus et egregiis dotibus cetera omnia multum admodum excellere ab aliisque differre distareque comperiemus.

36   Figura—ut de singulis pauca quaedam brevissime referamus—
ceterarum omnium nobilissima ita intuentibus apparet ut de ea
nullatenus ambigi dubitarive possit. Nam sic rigida et erecta[69] est
ut cunctis aliis animantibus in terram pronis humique depressis—
quasi solus eorum omnium dominus et rex et imperator in universo terrarum orbe—non immerito dominari ac regnare et imperare videatur.

Cuius quidem erectionis et staturae cum causas quaereremus,
quatuor dumtaxat apud physicos fuisse reperiebamus. Prima erat

All this Lactantius explained about the human body, as we see, 33
in a truly remarkable and inspired account. Yet he himself confirms that he purposely passed over many things which still
seemed so doubtful and so obscure that no one but the mightiest
Artisan of all could perceive, clearly and plainly, their meaning and
design.[28]

Therefore, after recounting what two inspired people—both 34
glories of the Latin language—did not hesitate to say about the
human body for the permanent literary record, it now remains to
take a quick look at what scientists have thought about the same
topics because the writing they have left amounts to an accurate
anatomy. But since the making of the body just described seems
worthier and more wonderful than in other living things, I think it
not unreasonable, before moving on in detail to each particular
part of the body, to give a brief account of certain points worth
remembering about the excellence of our body and how it differs
from all others.

If we have considered the special circumstances of our body 35
carefully and accurately, then, along with some of its outstanding
features, we shall find that it very much surpasses all others in
three special and outstanding endowments, differing and standing
apart from the rest first in form, then in general dominion over
everything, and also in lacking, as it must, certain superfluous
parts.[29]

Its form—to make a few, very brief points about each of these 36
three—has the noblest appearance of all, so that no one seeing it
can in any way doubt or question this. So erect and unbending is
this form that it seems, quite justly, to command, rule and lord it
over all the other living things that face the earth, forced down to
the ground—as the sole lord, king and commander of them all
across the whole world.

Seeking causes of man's erect stature, we have found just four in
the works of the scientists. First was the lightness of matter which,

materiae levitas quae, cum esset spumosa et aerea—praesertim si cum ceteris animantibus compararetur—ab aliis causis adiuta in altum elevabatur. Secunda caloris magnitudo afferebatur: quippe humanum corpus eiusdem quantitatis animalibus ampliorem et intensiorem calorem habere perhibetur et creditur. Tertio loco formae perfectio accedebat: perfectissima enim humanae intelligentiae forma excellentissimam atque rectissimam figuram exigebat. Quarta ratione finis ostendebatur. Nam homo suapte natura ad intelligendum natus et institutus erat.

In quo quidem eius proprio et peculiari officio, nobilitas et excellentia visus et auditus—sensuum, ut ita dixerim, sensatorum ac sagacium—apprime sibi famulantur et serviunt, quod efficere nequaquam potuissent nisi editum aliquem et eminentem locum positionibus suis obtinuissent. Cuius similitudinem in urbium oppidorumque praesidibus et gubernatoribus prospicere et intueri licet, qui in altis magnarum turrium aedificationibus arduisque arcium munitionibus urbanorum custodum habitacula construere et aedificare consueverunt.

37   Circa secundam vero differentiam vel potius excellentiam considerandum est: quod pleraque animalia ad alicuius sive artis sive artificii participationem naturali quodam instinctu[70] inclinata feruntur, quod in araneis et apibus atque hirundinibus et aliis quibusdam solertibus animantibus manifeste deprehenditur. Hoc autem rationale idcirco a natura ita factum itaque institutum esse creditur ut ad cuiuslibet artis, non ad unius solius, perceptionem aptius habiliusque oriretur. Si enim homo ad certam quandam artem, ceu de araneis et apibus dicitur, a natura instructus accessisset, profecto quemadmodum illis animalibus contigisse videmus ceteris paene omnibus exercitiis et professionibus caruisset.

38   At vero ei datae et exhibitae fuerunt manus, ut per huiusmodi—non inanimata sed quasi viva instrumenta et, ut inquit Aristoteles, organorum organa—varia diversarum artium iam perceptarum opera et officia exercere et exsequi posset. Quocirca

44

being foamy and airy—especially compared to other animals—rises high when helped by other causes. The second cause declared was the magnitude of heat: indeed, they assert with confidence that a human's heat is fuller and more intense than an animal's when the body is the same size. In third place came perfection of form: for human intelligence, most perfect in form, needed the tallest figure, towering above all. The end was the fourth reason shown. For by his own nature man was born and ordained to understand.[30]

Assuredly, for this special and distinct purpose of man, superiority and excellence of sight and hearing—those keen and, if I may, perceptive senses—are his chief servants and assistants, as they could never have been unless by their locations they had occupied some lofty and elevated place. Something like this can be seen and observed in the guardians and governors of towns and cities who used to build places to house their urban troops by piling up tall structures for high towers and lofty citadels with castles.[31]

But consider this about the second difference—or excellence, 37 rather: that some natural instinct makes many animals disposed to take up an art or craft, as we plainly see in spiders, bees, swallows and certain other clever beasts. Yet they believe that nature has made this one animal rational and prepared it to grow up better equipped and adapted to grasp any art—not just one. For if nature had arranged for man to take up some particular skill, just like spiders and bees, humans would have been deprived of almost all other practices and professions, exactly as we see it happened with those other animals.[32]

To man, however, hands were presented and given—not lifeless 38 but living instruments and, as Aristotle says, tools of tools—to pursue and practice the various actions and purposes of the different arts, once he saw what they were. Scientists conclude with

multis superfluis et supervacaneis partibus, ut cornibus, rostris, aduncis unguibus, villosis pellibus, pinnis et squamis, caudisque et huiusmodi deformationibus,[71] omnino caruisse existimatur et creditur.

39   Cum itaque de talibus humani corporis vel differentiis vel excellentiis pauca haec retulerimus, restat ut ad particularia eius membra breviter accedamus. Non enim inpraesentiarum id agimus ut cuncta illa referamus quae Aristoteles et Albertus, summi philosophi, in suis illis praeclaris et decantatis animalium voluminibus, nec ea insuper quae Galienus et Avicenna, excellentissimi medicinae artis auctores, in propriis ipsarum anatomiarum codicibus tradiderunt. Hanc humani corporis fabricationem supra quam dici potest admirantibus nobis et solemnem quandam ac divinam diversorum membrorum compactionem singulari admiratione saepenumero considerantibus — de ossibus primo tanquam de necessariis quibusdam futuri aedificii fundamentis; de extrinsecis deinde membris quae sensibus patent; tertio de intrinsecis et occultis — brevius quoad fieri poterit scribere ac referre placuit.

40   Cunctorum ossium quae in toto corpore[72] reperiuntur — ut omissis particularibus ne forte in rebus superfluis nimis curiosi ac superstitiosi fuisse videremur, et universali quadam relatione contenti simus — partim velut quaedam reliquorum membrorum fundamenta putantur quoniam in his, ceu in nonnullis solidis fundamentis, totum corpus constructum et fabricatum esse conspicitur. Qualia sunt dorsi spondyli,[73] haec enim non aliter humani corporis cernuntur quam illud lignum alicuius navis videatur,[74] quod in ea primum collocatur et ponitur.

Partim vero ita existimantur velut si clipeus quidam ad tuitionem et protectionem militis cuiusdam accommodaretur: qualia sunt cranei ossa. Partim insuper velut arma quaedam perhibentur: nam his ipsis quasi armis quibusdam propugnatores offendere ac laedere cupientes longe repelluntur. Cuiusmodi minuta quaedam ossa comperiuntur, quae a medicis *sisamina* nuncupantur. Partim

confidence that this is why man completely lacks many useless and unnecessary parts like horns, beaks, hooked claws, shaggy pelts, feathers and scales, tails and other such disfigurements.[33]

So then, having made these few points about such differences or excellences of the human body, it remains for me to add a little about each of its parts. Actually, my plan here is not to review everything said by those eminent philosophers, Aristotle and Albertus, in their brilliant and charming books on animals, nor everything related by those distinguished authorities on medicine, Galen and Avicenna, in their special works on anatomy. My intention — beyond what I can say in praise of the body, as someone who has often observed with special admiration the grand and godlike conjoining of its different parts — has been to report on this structure and describe it as briefly as possible: first, the bones as foundations needed for the future edifice; next, the external members accessible to the senses; third, the internal and concealed parts.[34]

Of all the bones found in the whole body — leaving some out so that I do not seem too inquisitive or wonder-struck and resting content with a general sort of account — some are thought of as foundations for other parts because the whole body seems to be built and erected upon them, as on physical foundations of various kinds. Like this are the joints of the spine in the back, for in the human body they look no different than the same sort of timber looks in any ship, where it is the first to be set up and put in place.

But partly the bones are regarded as a kind of shield, suited to guard and protect a soldier: like this are the bones of the skull. Partly the bones are also treated as a kind of weaponry: attackers who want to strike and cause injury are driven far away by them, as if they were weapons of some sort. Certain very small bones of this kind are found, called *sesamoid* by physicians. Finally, some

39

40

denique velut columnae et bases ad suspensionem et erectionem aliquorum membrorum institutae videntur. Quale esse dicitur *lambda*[75] os, sic ad similitudinem Graeci illius caracteris nuncupatum.

Quorum omnium quantae et quales sint in corpore nostro utilitates variis necessitatibus conditae, quoniam difficile dictu est et nimis supervacaneum esset si singula quaeque prosequeremur, idcirco de industria praetermisimus, ad extrinseca membra celerrime ac brevissime festinantes.

41 Pedes — ut ab inferioribus incipiamus — homini movendi et ambulandi gratia dati sunt, ideoque ita instructi itaque fabricati esse cernuntur ut, si aliter facti fuissent, officio suo fungi nequaquam potuissent. Mirabilis profecto est eorum forma, admirabilior musculorum contextio, admirabilissima omnium digitorum inter se cum tanto decore distinctio et separatio. Quid de tibiis et cruribus, quid de genibus et coxis dicemus? Nonne haec omnia subtili quodam solertique artificio ita constructa ac sic vicissim compacta esse videmus ut sponte sua moveri et reliquum corpus ferre ac sustentare facile queant?

42 De testiculis rursus ac pudendis — quanta solertia ad generandum instituta et procreata sint explicare difficile foret. Quid insuper de ventre, umbilico, stomacho, thorace ac pectore et intestinis sentiemus? Quid praeterea de scapulis[76] et brachiis, quid de cubitis et manibus, quid de renibus et nuca, quid denique de collo et gutture referemus? Nonne singula quaeque tanto ac tam mirabili opificio constructa et fabricata fuisse conspicimus ut de Deo humani corporis auctore nullatenus ambigere suspicarive debeamus?

43 De quibus singillatim nonnulla memoratu digna scribere et litteris mandare voluissem nisi nimiam orationis prolixitatem timuissem. Quod de industria vitavi, praesertim cum plura doctissimorum et elegantissimorum hominum documenta superius a nobis

look like columns and bases, arranged to hold other parts up and keep them straight: the bone called *lambda*, named for its likeness to the Greek letter, is of this kind.[35]

For all these, because it is hard to say how many uses and what kind have been built into our body to meet various needs, and since chasing each one down would be a waste of time, I have purposely left them out, moving on quickly to a few words about external parts.

The feet — starting from the lower end — were given to man for   41 moving and walking, which is why we see them built and arranged in such a way that they could never have done their job had they been made differently. Their form is truly a wonder, more wonderful the joining together of muscles, most wonderful of all the dividing and separating of all the toes from one another with such elegance. What about the legs and shins, and what to say of the knees and hips? Do we not see that they have all been constructed with a certain intricate and exact artifice, and then put together so that they can easily move on their own, bear the rest of the body's weight and hold it up?[36]

And then the testicles and private parts: the great skill that   42 produced and arranged them for procreation would be hard to explain. Furthermore, what to think about the belly, navel, stomach, chest, breast and intestines? What shall we say about the shoulders and the arms as well, the elbows and hands, the midriff and nape and finally the neck and throat? Do we not see that each was fashioned and assembled by workmanship so great and wondrous that we should have no doubt or hesitation at all about God as maker of the human body?[37]

I had wanted to write down some points worth remembering   43 about each of these and record them except that I feared saying too much. This I purposely avoided, especially after mentioning above the many things written by people of the greatest learning

recitata fuisse meminissem. Ceterum de capite—reliquis extrinsecis una cum pulmone et epate, splene et corde, intestinis et cunctis
aliis interioribus omissis—quoniam id ipsum ceterorum membrorum nobilissimum et praestantissimum esse iure existimatur et
creditur, nonnulla excelsa et digna eius privilegia paulo accuratius
et diligentius recensebimus.

44   Quocirca ante omnia singulares quasdam totius ipsius conditiones et[77] praecipuas deinde partium suarum qualitates parumper
attingemus. Plura de capite nostro etiam atque etiam considerantibus nobis, prae ceteris membris data ei et exhibita privilegia fuisse
constabat. Primo namque ipsum nobiliori et excelsiori loco constitutum et collocatum, digniori deinde et ampliori figura ornatum,
postremo maiori quantitate praeditum extitisse conspiciebamus.
Etenim ut de singulis pauca quaedam brevissime simul atque verissime expediamus, nimirum superiorem ac supremum arcis locum ob sensus homini ad scientiam et intelligentiam famulantes
obtinuisse perhibetur et creditur.

Figurae vero rotundae ac spericae, ita utrinque pressae ut ante
et retro aliqualiter tumidum, dextrorsum vero et sinistrorsum leviter planum cerneretur, ob cerebri magnitudinem ac necessariam
quandam ventriculorum suorum distinctionem fuisse traditur. Talis quippe figura et ceterarum omnium capacissima est, et nisi in
solo puncto—quemadmodum a mathematicis plane et aperte de-
monstratur—tangi nequaquam potest. Proinde ea ipsum figura
praeditum et ornatum apparuisse videmus ut et cerebrum cum
variis ventriculorum suorum distinctionibus caperet simul atque
ab extrinsecis laesionibus tutaretur. Magnitudinis postremo et mo-
lis quantitas, praeter aliqualem illius figurae rotunditatem, ideo
necessaria fuit ut et amplitudinem cerebri et quae ab eo oriebantur
venuste apteque complecterentur.[78]

45   Decem praeterea praecipua et singularia in hoc nobilissimo
atque dignissimo membro a medicis medicinaeque auctoribus

and refinement. Otherwise—having omitted the remaining external members, together with the lungs, liver, spleen, heart, intestines and all the other internal organs—I shall give a somewhat more exact and careful account of the head, and some of its worthy and exalted distinctions, because it is correctly reckoned and thought to be the noblest and most outstanding of the parts remaining.

Accordingly, I shall deal mainly with certain features of the 44 whole head and then touch briefly on special attributes of its parts. As I examined several aspects of it again and again, it remained clear that more distinctions were given to it and shown than for other parts of the body. First, I observed its station and placement, plainly a nobler and higher location, then how it is furnished with a fuller and more becoming shape, and finally the bigger size provided for it. In fact, to make a few very brief but accurate points about each of these, one claim you may trust is that the head got its higher place—that of a citadel on top—because of the senses that serve man for knowing and understanding.[38]

But they say it was circular and spherical in shape, compressed on all sides to look somewhat rounded from front to back, yet basically flat from left to right, because of the brain's size and because some separation was needed between its ventricles. That shape is the most capacious of all, in fact, and also protected from contact except at a single point—as mathematicians have shown clearly and plainly. This is why we see the head appearing with that shape, equipped both to receive the brain and its various separate ventricles and also to protect it against injuries from outside. Finally, besides some roundness in shape, the head needed its considerable size and weight as a handsome and functional enclosure for the bulk of the brain and its outgrowths.[39]

Furthermore, we read that physicians and authorities on medi- 45 cine thought there to be ten special and singular things in this

considerata fuisse legimus. De quorum singulis—ceu de capillis et cute, de carne ac *panniculo* exteriori, de craneo, de duobus panniculis interioribus, de cerebro, de duobus item panniculis inferioribus, de *rete* insuper *mirabili* et de osse *basilari*,[79] sic enim ab illis nuncupantur—quaedam enarrabimus.[80]

Capilli, quanquam ex necessitate materiae generati esse viderentur, quoniam caput est in arce, velut unicum quoddam et solum totius aedificii caminum, quo omnes corporis vapores et fumi rediguntur, ad necessitatem[81] tamen finis—extrinsecarum scilicet[82] laesionum tuitionem ac protectionem—referuntur. Cutis ob duas dumtaxat causas robusta ac grossa extitisse creditur,[83] cum ut capilli in ea tanquam in tenaci quadam radice fortius figerentur, tum etiam quia honestum quoddam et solidum ossis et cerebri velamen erat, quoniam supra craneum nulli musculi extare et apparere cernuntur.

46   De carne in fronte, in temporibus, in mandibulis extrinsecus apparente nihil aliud brevitatis causa dicimus quam si de aliquo pulchro cooperimento ac velamine diceremus. Panniculus ille exterior ob tres praesertim utilitates institutus et factus fuisse scribitur: primo ne craneum a cute et rursus cutis a craneo nullo mediante tangeretur; deinde ut craneum per hunc panniculum sentiendi vigorem perciperet ac sentiret, quo sine expers sensus et, ut ita dixerim, insensatum remansisset; postremo ut mediatore hoc panniculo *dura mater* a craneo suspenderetur. Etenim hic panniculus ex nervis et ligaminibus generatur quae a dura matre per commissuras et poros cerebri extra craneum penetrare videntur.[84]

47   Craneum os magnum cerebrum ipsum extrinsecus[85] penitus circumdans a medicis diffinitur, in cuius concavitate cerebrum, unde nervi ac sensus oriuntur, constitutum et collocatum esse confitentur et dicunt. Hoc autem unum et continuum ob multas ac diver-

noblest and worthiest part of the body. I shall say something about each one — the hair and skin, the flesh and the *garment* outside, the skull, the two garments inside, the brain, also the two garments underneath, the *wonderful net* as well and the *basilar* bone, for these are the names they give them.[40]

Even though hair seems to be produced automatically from a material cause, still — because the head is on a peak and serves as a special chimney, the only one in the whole structure, to collect all the body's vapors and fumes — hair is explained as the necessary effect of a final cause: namely, to protect and defend against external injuries. They believe the skin became thick and strong for just two reasons, so the hair would have a foundation firm enough to root in, and also, since no muscles are seen coming out of the skull on top, this skin would make a solid and rather attractive covering for the bone and brain.[41]

For brevity's sake, I say nothing more about the flesh appearing   46
outside the forehead, the temples and the jaws except to describe it as a handsome covering and wrapping. They write that this external garment was made and applied for three special purposes: first, with nothing else in between, to prevent the skull from touching the skin and the skin from touching the skull; next, to make the skull sensitive, feeling the force of sensation through this garment, without which the skull would have remained devoid of sensation and, so to speak, insensate; finally, for this garment to come in between and lift the *tough shelter* off the skull. In fact, the garment is produced from muscles and connections that seem to penetrate from the tough shelter through the brain's pores and seams to the outside of its casing.[42]

Physicians define the skull as the large bone completely sur-   47
rounding the brain itself from outside, saying and avowing that the brain, from where the nerves and senses originate, sits placed in its hollow. But for many different reasons it could not be made as one

sas causas fieri non potuit. Nam si unum et continuum fuisset, profecto nullatenus laedi offendive valuisset ut[86] laesio et offensio illa in totum non redundasset, ac per hoc ea continuatio sibi multum admodum obfuisset. Deinde ut vapores plerunque ad caput ascendentes per varias iuncturas diversasque compages extra craneum expellerentur, postremo—ut medicamentorum vires ac virtutes—quandocunque incumbente necessitate expediret ad cerebri substantiam penetrarent.

48   Post craneum duo panniculi cooperientes ac velantes idcirco demonstrantur ne eius mollities a duritie et soliditate cranei ullatenus tangeretur. Horum alter craneum ipsum sequitur qui *dura mater* propter soliditatem ac duritiem appellatur. *Pia* deinde *mater* accedit, sic ob mollitiem et humiditatem dicta. Quae mollis idcirco facta fuit ne sua mollitie cerebrum laedere valeret, et venas insuper quasdam contineret a quibus cerebrum aleretur et nutriretur.

Cuius quidem cerebri tres—anteriorem scilicet et intermediam ac posteriorem—principales partes esse contendimus. In quibus profecto—sensus communis (ut vulgaribus[87] physicorum et medicorum verbis utamur), cogitativa,[88] imaginativa, aestimativa atque memorativa facultas—quinque illi sensus interiores, quibus[89] exterioribus praetermissis, admirabiliter profecto ac paene incredibiliter latere et contineri cernuntur. Quorum omnium quanta et quam mirabilis sit nervorum inter se contextio et vicissitudinaria quaedam colligatio difficile dictu est, accommodatissimi namque (ut ita dixerim) loculi quinque illas intrinsecas—per cunctas philosophorum scholas iam dudum celebratas commemoratasque virtutes—tanto ac tam mirabili artificio complectuntur ut hoc singulare ac particulare opificium nisi ab omnipotenti Deo nullatenus fieri potuisse intelligatur.

Qui quidem si optionem naturae nostrae largiretur ab eaque requireret contenta ne esset suis integris nobilitatisque membris—quae ad formationem corporis pertinerent—an quicquam melius

continuous object. For if the bone were one and continuous, surely it could never be damaged or injured without the damage and injury spreading everywhere, and the injury continuing through the bone would do a great deal of damage to the brain. Then, as vapors commonly rise toward the head through various sutures and different joints to be expelled outside the skull, they finally penetrate — like the powers and properties of drugs — to the substance of the brain whenever this serves a pressing need.[43]

They point out two garments under the skull, veiling the brain   48
and shielding it so that the skull's solidity and hardness never contact the brain's soft tissue. The second of these garments comes after the skull itself and is called the *tough shelter* because of its solidity and hardness. Next is the *tender shelter,* so called because it is soft and moist. It was made soft to keep it from injuring the brain and also to contain various veins that feed and nourish the brain.[44]

This brain, I assert, has three main parts — namely, front, middle and back. Skipping the external senses, I find it truly surprising and almost unbelievable that these parts are seen to contain and conceal the five internal senses — the common sense (if I may use terms familiar to scientists and physicians) and the faculties of cogitation, imagination, estimation and memory. For all of them, the amazing and extensive interweaving of nerves with one another as well as a sort of alternating connectivity are hard to describe, for those five little sites (if I may call them that) are perfectly suited to contain the internal faculties — celebrated and long since recorded by all the schools of philosophers — by a skill so great and so amazing that it makes us realize that only God Almighty could ever have produced this special and singular workmanship.[45]

If God bestowed choice on our nature and then asked if this choice would leave our nature content to keep its own ennobled parts — those affecting the structure of the body — or whether it

postularet, quid amplius quaereret porro nescire atque ignorare confitemur. De panniculis inferioribus, de rete atque pasillari osse, reliquis tribus, ne nimii simus, deinceps dicere omittamus.

49   Quae ergo compositio membrorum, quae conformatio lineamentorum, quae figura, quae species quam humana pulchrior aut esse aut excogitari potest? Quod cum illi veteres sapientissimique homines animadverterent, deos in humana esse specie confiteri audebant. Quorum vestigia plerique ex nostris imitati, in quibusdam apostolorum ac martyrum ceterorumque sanctorum basilicis, Deum instar hominis idcirco pingi voluerunt ut ad divinam contemplationem rudibus ignarisque hominibus aliquatenus opitularentur. Quapropter non defuerunt doctissimi ac sapientissimi viri qui, cum praedicta omnia et alia huiusmodi humani corporis machinamenta diligenter et accurate contemplarentur, talem fabricationem instar mundi formatam et factam fuisse arbitrarentur, unde hominem a Graecis *microcosmum*, quasi parvum mundum, appellatum fuisse[90] putaverunt.

50   Nec defuerunt etiam qui famosissimam illam et saluberrimam Noae archam — in qua parvas quasdam humani generis, quod iam paene totum primo et generali diluvio perierat, reliquias incolumes remansisse novimus ex quibus reparati sumus — ad hanc perfectissimam humani corporis fabricam constructam fuisse propterea existimarent quod propria sui ipsius longitudo a vertice usque ad vestigia sexies tantum habet quantum latitudo quae est ab uno ad alterum latus et decies tantum quantum altitudo. Cuius altitudinis mensura in latere a dorso ad ventrem reperitur seu si iacentem hominem supinum seu pronum metiaris. Sexies tantum longus est a capite ad pedes quantum latus est a dextera in sinistram vel a sinistra in dexteram, et decies tantum quantum altus a terra. Proinde commemorata archa trecentorum in longitudine cubitorum, quinquaginta in latitudine et triginta in altitudine facta fuisse scribitur.

would need something else, I confess that I neither know nor understand at all what more might be asked. And then, to avoid going on too much, let me omit describing the lower garments, the net and basilar bone and the other three.[46]

This fitting together of parts, this shaping of features, this fig- 49 ure, this form — can any be more beautiful than the human or so devised? Taking note of this, those ancient and most sagacious people dared avow that gods are human in appearance. Many of our people have followed their path, deciding, in certain grand churches dedicated to apostles, martyrs and other saints, to depict God as a man in order to give ignorant and uninformed people a little help in contemplating the divine. Accordingly, there were plenty of very wise and learned men who, while carefully and exactly observing everything described above and also other machinery of the human body, judged that such a construction had been made like the world in form, reckoning that this was why the Greeks had called man a *microcosm* or *little world*.[47]

There were also some who thought that Noah's most saving 50 and celebrated ark — where we know that certain small remnants of the human race stayed safe so that we could be recovered from them, after mankind was almost wholly destroyed in the first and universal flood — was built on this most perfect plan of the human body because its own length from top to bottom is six times the width from side to side and ten times the depth. This depth is calculated for the side from back to belly when you measure a man lying either face up or down. From head to foot he is six times longer than wide, from right to left or left to right, and ten times the depth from the ground. Hence it is written and recorded that the ark was built three hundred cubits long, fifty wide and thirty deep.[48]

Vir enim suapte natura prudentissimus et multarum quoque rerum experientia in tanta ac tam diuturna sexcentorum[91] annorum vita, nam hac eius aetate generale illud diluvium universum terrarum orbem inundasse legimus. Apprime edoctus et divino insuper quodam spiritu afflatus, cum hoc mirabile ac perfectum hominis opificium ab omnipotenti Deo profluxisse et emanasse intelligeret, tale tanti auctoris supremique magistri exemplum sibi archam fabricaturo—archam, inquam, illam humani generis servatricem quod, ipse maximus eorum temporum propheta, suis flagitiis facinoribusque periturum divinitus acceperat, non immerito ad fabricandum imitandumque proposuit.

51   Et quanquam multa de hoc corpore nostro hactenus dixisse meminerimus, unum tamen de humana facie ceteris forte mirabilius in calce huius primi libri taciti praeterire non possumus. De quo, cum beatus Augustinus satis superque[92] admirari non posset, quodam loco verba haec posuit:

> Quis enim consulta ratione non viderit in hominum innumerabili numerositate et tanta naturae similitudine tam valde mirabiliter sic habere singulos singulas facies ut, nisi inter se similes[93] essent, nequaquam species eorum ab animalibus ceteris discerneretur? Et rursus, nisi inter se dissimiles essent, nempe singuli a ceteris hominibus haudquaquam discernerentur. Quos ergo similes confitemur eosdem dissimiles invenimus, sed multo mirabilior est consideratio dissimilitudinis quoniam similitudinem natura communis iustius exposcere videtur.

> Illud vero ceteris omnibus mirabilius iure existimatur et creditur, quippe singula quaeque humani corporis membra tam subtili

Now Noah was a man of great natural foresight and wide experience of the world who lived very long and went on for six hundred years, for we read that he was that old when the universal flood drowned the whole earth. Superbly informed and also stirred by a sort of divine inspiration, he understood that this miraculous and perfect construct of humanity had come flowing down from its source in Almighty God: hence, when he was about to make himself an ark — meaning the ark that preserved the human race — he was quite right to plan to build it by copying from such a model by so great a worker and supreme master because, being the greatest prophet of those times, he had accepted that he would perish at God's hand because of his own crimes and outrages.[49]

Although by now I have had much to say about this body of ours, there is perhaps still one topic — the human face — more amazing than the rest, that I cannot pass by silently as I end this first book. St. Augustine, since he could not admire it enough or too much, left this passage about it:

> Would anyone thinking rationally not see how very astonishing it is that humans, in numbers beyond counting and with natures so much the same, each have faces of their own such that, unless they were like one another, they could not be told apart from other animals as a species. On the other hand, were they not unlike, there would certainly be no way to tell any one person apart from the rest. The same ones that we acknowledge to be similar we find dissimilar, then, but the dissimilarity is much more surprising to contemplate because it seems more fitting for a common nature to require similarity.

Truly, it is right to reckon this more surprising than anything else and believe it so, for we really see each and every part of the human body formed on so exact a plan and with such great inge-

ratione ac tanta divinae providentiae solertia formata cernuntur ut
tantumdem ad usus necessitatem quantum ad pulchritudinem valere videantur.

52   Si quis igitur — ut hanc primam nostri operis particulam tandem aliquando concludamus — cuncta haec et generalia et particularia humani corporis privilegia praecipuaque munera diligenter
et accurate animadverterit, profecto ipsum ab omnipotenti Deo
idcirco egregie ac mirabiliter fabrefactum non iniuria fuisse cense-
bit ut dignum quoddam simul atque accommodatum rationalis
animae receptaculum formaretur.

53   Unde, cum tales tantasque corporis nostri dignitates et excel-
lentias esse videamus, haudquaquam mirari debemus si antiquorum iustorum funera officiosa pietate curata sunt et exequiae cele-
bratae et sepultura provisa, quemadmodum ex pluribus Veteris et
Novi Testamenti exemplis luce clarius apparet, [94] licet hoc totum
humationis genus idcirco a plerisque philosophis contemneretur,
quoniam nulla defunctorum hominum corpora ullo unquam tempore resurrectura arbitrabantur. Nam et Tobias sepeliendo mortuos Deum promeruisse teste angelo commendatur. Et Dominus
noster die tertio[95] resurrecturus religiosae mulieris bonum opus
praedicat praedicandumque commendat quod unguentum praetio-
sum super membra eius effuderit atque hoc ad eum sepeliendum
fecerit. Et in Evangelio etiam ii laudantur qui corpus eius de cruce
acceptum diligenter atque honorifice tegendum sepeliendumque
curarunt. Et quod mirabilius videri debet: omnes patriarchae et
plerique prophetae dum viverent propriis testamentis curam sepe-
liendorum et humandorum cadaverum suorum domesticis et posteris relinquebant.

54   Quod si animorum nostrorum vascula talia ac tam mirabilia
esse videmus ut de Deo eorum auctore iure dubitare suspicarive
nequeamus, quid de ipso animo peculiari quodam ac praecipuo
omnium rerum thesauro dicemus? An usque adeo hebetes et

nuity from God's providence that those parts are observed to be as good for practical needs as for looks.[50]

Therefore, no one—if now I may finally conclude this first section of my work—who has taken exact and careful note of all these general and particular privileges of the human body and all its special functions, will make a mistake in judging that Almighty God fashioned the body as so splendid a marvel in order to form a worthy and also a fitting vessel for the rational soul.[51]   52

Hence, since we see our body with so many features of such worth and excellence, we should not be at all surprised if funeral rites were held with dutiful piety for the righteous ancients, honoring their remains and providing burial, as is evident—clearer than day—from many examples of the Old and New Testament, even though most philosophers disliked this whole type of burial, thinking that no bodies of the deceased would ever be resurrected at any time. For an angel tells Tobias that he has earned favor from God by burying the dead. And our Lord, who would rise on the third day, tells beforehand about the good deed of a pious woman, whom he commends for anointing his body with precious oil, thereby foretelling his preparation for burial. The Gospel also praises those who carefully took his body from the cross, covered it respectfully and saw to the burial. And this must be seen as more astonishing: while they lived, all the patriarchs and most of the prophets made wills entrusting to their heirs and servants the duty of interring their own bodies and burying them.[52]   53

But if we see these vessels for our souls in this way, as wonders so great that we cannot really doubt or question that God is their maker, what shall we say about the soul itself, that special and extraordinary treasury that holds everything? Will we be so dull and   54

obtusi erimus ut de divino humanarum animarum auctore titube-
mus cum de hominum corporibus — ceteris[96] earum vasculis ac
receptaculis — id ipsum plane et aperte sentiamus? Quod sequenti
libro, quantum parva ingenii nostri facultas efficere conarive poterit, quemadmodum ab initio promisimus, paulo latius et uberius
explicabimus.

obtuse that we hesitate about a divine Maker of human souls while we think this very point is plain and clear about the bodies of humans — those other vessels that really are containers of souls? As I promised from the start, and as much as my modest insight permits me to make the attempt and get it done, in the next book I will go into this a bit more extensively and provide more detail.

LIBER SECUNDUS

1   Vellem nobis, nunc de anima humana breviter conscripturis, tantum ingenii, facultatis et eloquentiae dari, si optata fierent, ut in hac tam obscura et tam abstrusa materia, de qua philosophi varia et inter se diversa ac paene contraria scripsisse comperiuntur, nonnulla praecipua et singularia in medium afferre possemus. Sed quoniam tantam in rebus ipsis difficultatem inesse latereque conspicimus, ut Cicero — Romanae eloquentiae princeps, cum de anima dissereret ac quid foret in praeclaro illo *Tusculanarum disputationum* dialogo diligenter et accurate perscrutaretur — magnam quandam de eius origine, loco et qualitate dissensionem fuisse describat. Et Lactantius quoque — vir doctissimus atque elegantissimus, cum de eisdem conditionibus in commemorato *De opificio hominis* opusculo investigaret — in hunc modum scribens dixisse deprehenditur: quid autem sit anima nondum inter philosophos convenit nec fortasse unquam[1] conveniet. Idcirco omnibus, quemadmodum dicitur, animi et corporis viribus aliqua fortasse non indigna Maiestatis Tuae lectione referre et explicare conabimur.

2   Proinde ad perfectam et veram eius definitionem quoad fieri poterat anhelantes, veterem Aristotelis morem in rebus seriis ac gravibus prosequi imitarique decrevimus: qui in omnibus fere libris suis ea antea recitabat quae a prioribus philosophis de illis rebus dicebantur — de quibus ipse disserere et disputare contendebat — eorumque postea opiniones singillatim confutabat. Atque haec omnia ideo faciebat ut quid ipse sentiret, quando cum ceteris compararetur, facilius et clarius appareret. Nos igitur certa quaedam et solita[2] tanti viri vestigia in recitandis dumtaxat opinionibus antiquorum breviter imitabimur.

BOOK TWO

Now that I am about to write a little about the human soul, a   1
subject so hard and obscure that I find philosophers changing, differing and all but contradicting themselves about it, I would
wish — were my hopes fulfilled — to be given enough insight, information and eloquence to bring some singularly important points
before the public. But look: I have seen the difficulty that these
very problems contain and conceal, so much that Cicero — the
prince of Roman eloquence, discussing the soul in that brilliant
dialogue, his *Tusculan Disputations*, where he carefully and correctly
investigates what it might be — described some considerable dis-
agreement about its origin, place and quality. I also find Lactantius — another very learned and refined investigator of the same
topic in his book *On the Workmanship in Man*, previously cited —
writing this: that among philosophers no agreement exists, and
perhaps none ever will exist, about what the soul is. And so, with
all my powers of mind (so to speak) and body, I shall strive to report and explain a few things perhaps not unfit for Your Majesty
to read.[1]

Yearning for a definition of the soul as complete and correct as   2
could be made, I accordingly decided to imitate Aristotle by following the ancient custom that he used for serious and weighty
subjects. In nearly all his books, he would first list what earlier
philosophers had said about the topics at hand — topics that he
himself was trying to examine and dispute — and later he would
refute the views of those thinkers one after another. He did all this
so that his own position, compared with the rest, would seem
simpler and clearer. Hence, in that my task is to give a short account of what the ancients thought, in listing them I shall follow
the sure and familiar tracks left by that great man.

Non enim ita arrogantes itaque impudentes neque sumus neque videri volumus ut in tot et tantis occultarum rerum difficultatibus nostram sententiam explicaremus. Sed postquam ea ipsa recitarimus, recitataque leviter confutarimus, quae philosophos suis puris naturalibus constitutos conscripsisse percipimus,[3] ad nostros theologos, quibus haec et cetera huiusmodi naturae mysteria divinitus revelata fuisse constabat, tanquam in unum[4] humanae salutis portum magna iactati tempestate confugiemus.

3   Cum autem nonnullos doctissimos simul atque elegantissimos viros — praecipue Ciceronem ac Lactantium — *animum* ab *anima* ita inter se differre voluisse intelligamus ut altero *vivere* altero vero *sentire et sapere* significaretur, quoniam satis superque satis esse arbitramur ut magnis tam arduarum rerum difficultatibus opprimamur, de nomine minime laborandum fore censemus. Unde quanquam utroque — ut suis locis aptius et accommodatius fieri posse videbitur — pro eodem uteremur, animam tamen quam animum propterea crebrius frequentare maluimus, quoniam Catholicos doctores nostros, sive ex Hebraea sive ex Graeca sacras scripturas in Latinam linguam convertentes sive aliter quomodolibet explanantes, eo verbo semper usos fuisse comperimus. Quorum nos veneranda ac sacrosancta vestigia tantummodo observare et imitari constituimus, licet gentiles philosophi plerumque animum raro vero animam posuerint.

4   Thales Milesius, ut ab antiquioribus ordiamur, quem in numero illorum septem celebratorum sapientum Romulo regnante extitisse ac primum in philosophia claruisse manifestum est, quanquam de anima particularem quandam mentionem nequaquam fecisse memoraretur.[5] Cum tamen aquam omnium rerum principium fuisse existimaret atque exinde cuncta mundi elementa ipsumque mundum et quaecunque in eo gignerentur oriri et nasci opinaretur, animam ab aqua sicut cetera originem trahere eius opinio iure censenda est.

I am not, to be sure, so shameless and overbearing—nor do I wish to seem so—that I would argue for a conclusion of my own about the many serious problems involved in these puzzling matters. But after listing the views that I see philosophers have written down based on purely natural reasons, and after giving a swift refutation of what I have listed, I will take shelter with our theologians—the lone harbor that saves mankind from the great storm swirling around—since plainly it was to them that God revealed these and other mysteries of this kind.

Because problems this hard make troubles bad enough—or more than enough—to overwhelm me, I propose not to worry much about the terminology, though I realize that some quite learned and eloquent men—Cicero and Lactantius especially—have thought that a *mind* differs from a *soul* so that one means *living* and the other *perceiving and knowing*. Hence, while using both words to mean the same thing—as each will seem a better fit and more appropriate for a particular context—I have still preferred to write *soul* more often than *mind* because I find that our Catholic teachers have always used that word, either to translate Sacred Scripture from Hebrew or Greek into Latin or to comment on it in some way. My plan is just to observe and follow their revered and most holy footsteps, even though pagan philosophers have mostly written *mind* and rarely *soul*.[2]

To start with older thinkers: Thales of Miletus is obviously well known as one of those seven sages renowned when Romulus was king, and as the first famous philosopher: the point is not that he ever made any special remark about the soul. Still, since he thought that water is the basis of all things and that all the world's elements, the world itself and whatever comes to be in the world originate and emerge from water, we may fairly conclude that in his view the soul, like other things, gets its start from water.

Anaximander, eius auditor, non ex aqua ut magister sed ex suis principiis infinitis omnia produci et progredi asserebat. Cui Anaximenes succedens infinitis illis praeceptoris sui principiis aerem adhibuisse perhibetur. Anaxagoras, eius discipulus — praeter generalem quandam de initiis rerum ex similibus inter se particulis opinionem — de anima disserens, rem se ipsam moventem esse et dixit et sensit. Diogenes, alter Anaximenis auditor, eam quemadmodum cetera ad aera unum omnium principium retulisse scribitur.

5   Leucippus et Democritus — athomorum, hoc est levium et individuorum corpusculorum, auctores et principes, ex quibus omnia confici volebant — animam nihilominus calorem et ignem quendam esse arbitrabantur. Heraclitus, cognomento *scotinos* quoniam de natura rerum ita obscure scripsisse videbatur ut illius temporis philosophi perplexas eius sententias vix sudantes intelligere potuissent, eam ipsam vaporem subtilissimum censebat. Empedocles, qui de rebus naturalibus Graecis carminibus scripsisse laudatur, quemadmodum apud nos Lucretium latine fecisse novimus — si Ciceroni credimus — animam esse dicit cordi suffusum sanguinem.

Si vero potius Aristoteli adhaeremus, ex elementis eam fecit,[6] Hippias sophista aquam, Critias autem illam sanguinem definivit. Archelaus, Anaxagorae auditor, sive ex similibus sive ex dissimilibus inter se particulis omnia quecunque essent et mentem et animum constare arbitratus est. Zenoni Stoico animus ignis videtur, quem Aristoxenus, musicus idemque philosophus, harmoniam ut in cantu et fidibus, Pythagoras vero ac Xenocrates, Platonis auditor, numerum se ipsum moventem putaverunt.

6   Socrates, Archelai discipulus, omissis naturalium rerum difficultatibus, quoniam eas Academicorum more nullatenus sciri cognoscive posse autumabat, ac propterea de anima quid esset nihil perscrutatus, sese ad moralis philosophiae studia converterat. Eam

Anaximander, his student, claimed that all things are produced and proceed not from water, as his teacher thought, but from infinite principles of his own devising. Anaximenes, his successor, claims to have used air for those infinite principles of his teacher. Anaxagoras, his disciple—going beyond a common view that things originate from particles resembling one another—discussed the soul, believing and stating that it is a self-moving thing. People describe Diogenes, another student of Anaximenes, as having traced the soul, like everything else, to air as the single origin of them all.[3]

Leucippus and Democritus—leading authorities and inventors 5 of atoms, those tiny undivided particles from which they supposed all things are made—still reckoned the soul to be heat and fire of some sort. Heraclitus took it to be a very thin vapor: his nickname was *dark* because he seemed to write so obscurely about nature that the philosophers of his time sweated over his tangled statements yet could barely understand them. Empedocles, famed for writing about nature in Greek verse, just as we know Lucretius did in Latin, says that the soul is the blood that fills the heart—if we believe Cicero.

Yet if we stick with Aristotle instead, Empedocles made it out of elements, while Hippias the Sophist defined it as water but Critias as blood. Archelaus, a student of Anaxagoras, reckoned that all things, including both mind and soul, consist of particles, either like or unlike one another. For Zeno the Stoic mind seems to be fire. But Aristoxenus, a musician and a philosopher, thought of it as an attunement, as in singing or playing instruments, while for Pythagoras and Xenocrates, Plato's student, it was self-moving number.[4]

Socrates, a follower of Archelaus, turned to the study of moral 6 philosophy, skipping problems about nature because, in the Academic manner, he thought there was just no way to know or understand them, so he never investigated what the soul might be.

tamen immortalem et perpetuam esse describit, quemadmodum
et Alcmaeon nescio quis et Pherecides Syrus antea tradiderant.
Hunc Socratem Plato, celeberrimus eius discipulus, postea secutus. Quamvis omnium philosophorum disertissimus haberetur, de
anima tamen obscura quaedam ac metaforis tropisque refercta
pluribus librorum suorum locis ita locutus est, ut vix intelligi
potuerit, ac pleraque in eum librum congessit cui titulus est *De
immortalitate animorum.*

Ex quibus eam potius suis quibusdam persuasionibus immortalem fore quam quid propriis descriptionibus esset haurire et augu-
rari valeamus. Quod Cicero eo loco maxime sensisse videtur ubi
verba haec posuit: quid tibi ergo opera nostra opus est? Num eloquentia Platonem superare possumus? Evolve diligenter eius eum
librum qui est de animo, amplius quod desideres nihil erit. Et
paulo post ita subdit: feci mehercule et quidem saepius. Sed nescio
quomodo evenit, dum lego assentior. Cum posui librum et mecum
ipse de immortalitate animorum coepi[7] cogitare, assensio illa omnis elabitur.

Ex pluribus tamen eius dictis deprehendi et elici potest eum
idem sensisse quod Pythagoram et Xenocratem vel de substantia,
quemadmodum ab Alberto philosopho traditur, vel de numero se
7   ipsum movente paulo superius intellexisse diximus. Nec defuerunt
etiam qui eam ipsam cor esse opinarentur, ex quo plerique homines excordes, vecordes, concordesque dicebantur.

Aristoteles insuper, cum haec omnia quae ab antiquioribus de
anima ferebantur frivola et paene inania esse animadverteret,
quoniam cunctae fere eorum opiniones ad res corporeas referri
videbantur—praeter elementa quibus haec corpora constare non
dubitabat—praetermissis duabus aliis eius definitionibus, quintam
naturam esse voluit unde humana anima conficeretur. Quam

Yet he still describes the soul as immortal and eternal, just as a certain Alcmaeon, like Pherecydes of Syros, had passed this view on before him. Plato, the most famous student of Socrates, followed him later. Although people consider Plato the cleverest philosopher of all, in many passages of his books he still makes rather obscure statements about the soul, stuffed with metaphors and figures of speech that are barely intelligible, and most of them are brought together in the book titled *On the Immortality of Souls*.[5]

From those remarks by Plato, we may be able to draw out and divine that the soul will be immortal — more from various opinions of his than from anything based on genuine analysis. Cicero seems to have realized this, especially in that passage where he asks this: Why do you need my help, then? Can I do better at eloquence than Plato? Go carefully through this book of his on the soul, and you'll need nothing more. A little farther on he puts it this way: I've done this, by God, and quite often! But as I read, I don't know how it happens, I end up agreeing. When I've put the book down and started to think to myself about the immortality of souls, all that agreement slips away.[6]

Yet from several of Plato's statements one can detect and infer that he felt the same as Pythagoras and Xenocrates, whether about the soul's substance — just as the philosopher Albert reports — or in what he meant by the self-moving number mentioned just above. Some have even thought that the soul is actually the heart, 7 which is why many people have been called stupid, foolish or agreeable — at heart.[7]

Since Aristotle considered everything said by older thinkers about the soul to be unimportant and basically worthless, in that nearly all such opinions — over and above statements about elements constituting bodies, which he did not question — were seen to refer to material objects, he thought (if we omit two other definitions of his) that there is an additional fifth nature from which

Graeco, et tunc novo sed nunc iam dudum per omnes philosophorum scholas celebrato, nomine *entelechiam*[8] appellavit, non quasi continuatam, ut ait Cicero, motionem et perennem sed potius spiritalem quandam humani corporis perfectionem — licet ipse pluribus verbis inter definiendum uteretur, quemadmodum Avicenna et Averois exponere et explanare videntur.

Varro denique, etsi divinarum et humanarum rerum peritissimus putaretur, quid tamen esset anima definire volens, eam aerem quendam ore conceptum, in pulmone defervefactum, in corpore temperatum, et in totum[9] corpus diffusum esse terminavit. Seneca vero substantiam incorpoream rationis participem credebat.

8   Contra quos omnes — Aristotele, cum ob dignam tanti philosophi venerationem tum ob subtilem quandam ac veracem eius, licet non perfectam et ex omni parte absolutam, determinationem, semper excepto — dicendum breviter existimamus. Nam quemadmodum nos, de Deo rebusque caelestibus ac divinis animadvertentes, magis quid *non sit* quam quid *sit* unum quodque dicere et excogitare possumus, ita de anima humana considerantes, eadem propemodum credere et existimare debemus, praesertim cum in omnibus obscuris rebus multo facilius falsa convinci quam vera inveniri posse videamus.

9   Ad levem vero illam praedictarum opinionum confutationem quam nos facturos esse praediximus, ea plurimum conferre ac satisfacere putavimus: quae Ciceronem partim in *Tusculanis disputationibus* conscripsisse, partim etiam in *Consolatione* sua posuisse meminimus. Cuius verba, quoniam nobis summopere placuerunt et ad nostrum pro positum apprime valere videbantur, in hoc loco ponere et hic scribere curavimus. Sic enim ait:

Animorum in terris nulla origo est, nam nihil est in animis mixtum ac concretum aut quod ex terra natum ac fictum

the soul is made In Greek he called this nature *entelecheia*, a new name at the time that by now has long been famous in all the schools of philosophy; this is not like a sustained and everlasting motion, as Cicero describes it, but a sort of spiritual perfecting of the human body — though Aristotle actually uses many words while defining it, as we see Avicenna and Averroes revealing and explaining.[8]

Despite Varro's reputation for great expertise on theological and human subjects, when he wanted to define what the soul is, he finally determined that it is a kind of air taken in by the mouth, heated up in the lungs, tempered in the body and then diffused through the whole body. But Seneca believed that the soul is a nonbodily substance that shares in reason.[9]

My own judgment is that brief statements are required against 8 all these thinkers — Aristotle always excepted, both because so great a philosopher deserves respect and also because his account is acute and truthful, though not complete on every point or finished. For just as I am better able to think and say what something *is not* than what it *is* when I turn to God, divinity or heavenly matters, so also should my judgments and beliefs be basically the same in dealing with the human soul, especially since I observe that in all obscure questions defeating false claims is much easier than finding the truth.[10]

For the swift refutation that I promised of the views previously 9 stated, I have concluded that the helpful and sufficient findings are these: some that Cicero described in his *Tusculan Disputations*, as I recall, with others that he proposed in his *Consolation*. I have taken the trouble to copy his words here because I agree with them entirely and because they look like the best support for my position. This is what he says:

> there is no origin of souls on earth, for in souls there is nothing mixed or compounded or appearing to be born and

esse videatur, nihil humidum quidem aut flabile aut igneum;
his enim in[10] naturis nihil inest[11] quod vim memoriae, mentis, cogitationis habeat, quod[12] et praeterita teneat et futura
praevideat et complecti possit praesentia — quae sola divina
sunt. Nec invenimus unde ad hominem venire possint nisi a
deo,

et reliqua.[13]

10   Aristoteles quippe, vir sapientissimus, intelligentiam, volunta-
tem, memoriam — naturalia quaedam et communia humanarum
animarum munera — nisi meditantibus[14] illis quorum propria dona
esse videantur[15] nullatenus provenire posse excogitavit. Itaque omnia elementa — licet sola terra ab anima iuxta veteres philosophorum traditiones, eo ipso recitante, separaretur — et non modo elementa sed cuncta quaeque corporea a spiritali eius natura merito
distinxisse et segregasse laudatur. Hanc egregiam supradictarum
paene omnium opinionum confutationem Cicero ab Aristotele
magistro — sic enim eum quodam loco appellare non dubitavit —
ex secundo *De anima* sumpsisse et accepisse creditur.

   In quo quidem libro, cum ille verae philosophiae princeps animae essentiam — sic enim interpretari placuit quod Graeci οὐ-
σίαν[16] dicunt, quamvis eo verbo Latini veteres minime uteren-
tur — paulo accuratius perscrutaretur quam ceteros philosophos
antea fecisse constaret, eam corpoream esse non posse plane et
aperte[17] vidit et sensit. Itaque cuncta corpora sua cogitatione
transcendens atque optimum quiddam perfectumque non iniuria
oportere esse[18] existimans, ipsam in genere substantiae ponere et
collocare constituit, nec *materiam* quam philosophi *substantiae* ap-
pellatione censebant sed *formam,* et non cuiuslibet corporis sed talis utique quale *humanum* corpus dicimus formam esse declaravit et
voluit. Quo facto, cum de eius potentiis postea dissereret atque

shaped from the earth, nothing even moist or airy or fiery:
nothing in these natures has the power to remember, understand and reason, nothing to hold on to the past, foresee the
future and grasp the present — faculties that are only divine.
Nor, except from God, do we find whence they could come
to man,

and so on.[11]

Aristotle, a person of great wisdom, reasoned that there is no   10
way to get intelligence, will and memory — functions that are natural and shared by human souls — except from the mental activity
of those whose own special gifts they are. This is why he famously
and correctly separated *all* the elements — and any bodily thing
whatever, not just elements — and divided them from the soul's
spiritual nature, even though earth on its own had been excluded
from soul by the ancient philosophical tradition, according to Aristotle's own account of it. The claim is that Cicero accepted this
remarkable refutation of nearly all past views that he took from
the second book *On the Soul* by Aristotle, his teacher — and he did
not mind calling him that in a certain passage.[12]

In that book, as we all know, when this prince of true philosophy went farther than other philosophers and looked a bit closer
at the soul's essence — this being the usual translation of the Greek
ousia, even though ancient Latin writers never used the word — he
certainly saw plainly and clearly understood that this essence could
not be bodily. Thinking beyond all bodies, then, and judging
rightly that the soul must be something excellent and perfect, he
decided to classify it by putting it in the genus of substance,
believing and declaring that this is *form* and not the *matter* that
philosophers usually assessed with the word *substance* — and not
the form of just any body but of the type we call a *human* body.
With that done, when Aristotle later discussed the soul's powers,

intellectivam tanquam perpetuam a reliquis corruptibilibus separa-
ret, prioribus definitionum[19] particulis ita adhibuisse et adiecisse
videtur—ut animam humani corporis rationalem atque immortalem et incorruptibilem formam plane et aperte diffiniret.

11   Si autem circumscriptos naturalis philosophi, qualem se ipsum
esse profitebatur, limites transgredi et transcendere voluisset (vide
quid homini tribuam!) ab omnipotenti Deo ex nihilo mirabiliter,
ut arbitror, creatam fuisse adiecisset. Quod si fecisset, nimirum
cunctis naturae legibus et omnibus quoque naturalium philosophorum decretis ac dogmatibus repugnasset, quibus ex nihilo aliquid fieri posse negabatur—ac propterea animam humani corporis
immortalem et incorruptibilem formam, rationis et intelligentiae
capacem, ex nihilo a Deo creatam verissime ac perfectissime diffi-
nisset.

Huiusmodi enim vera vel definitio, vel potius descriptio, ex
sacris Catholicorum doctorum sententiis elici posse existimatur
et creditur, quanquam talia suapte natura abstrusa et obscura in
tenebris latere videantur, quo humanae mentis acies invalida penetrare non potest, nisi iam superno lumine illustraretur, quemadmodum optimis illis ac sanctissimis viris contigisse novimus,
quorum sententias inpraesentiarum haurire et explanare contendimus.

12   Nam ex uno homine quem primum a Deo secundum sacras
scripturas conditum fuisse legimus, et ideo Graece expressius *protoplastus* appellatur—contra falsas philosophorum de aeternitate
mundi sententias—genus humanum in hunc mundum[20] sumpsit
exordium. Moyses enim, omni sapientia Aegyptiorum eruditus ac
primus et maximus eorum prophetarum qui prophetias suas litteris mandabant, cum sese a sensibus revocare cuperet, in vastas
Aethiopiae solitudines peragrare non dubitavit, ubi, cunctis saecu-
laribus negotiis praetermissis ac neglectis, ad altissimarum dumtaxat et divinarum rerum meditationem animum mentemque

separating the intellective from all the other destructible powers because it is everlasting, he seems to have added this point, attaching it to previous clauses of his definitions — in order to define the soul of a human body, plainly and clearly, as rational, immortal and indestructible.[13]

But if Aristotle (see what I attribute to this man!) had wanted 11
to cross boundaries and pass beyond the constraints on a natural philosopher, such as he professed to be, I believe he might have added that God created the soul miraculously from nothing. Had he done so, however — thus giving a perfectly correct and complete definition of the soul as the human body's immortal and indestructible form, capable of reason and intelligence and created by God from nothing — this surely would have overturned all the laws of nature and also all the decrees and dogmas of the natural philosophers, which forbid something to come from nothing.[14]

In fact, one trusts and reckons that a correct definition of this sort, or perhaps a description, can be had from the sacred statements of Catholic teachers, even though such things seem obscure by nature, hidden in shadows where the human mind's feeble vision cannot penetrate unless already illuminated by light from above, which happened, as we know, to those most holy and virtuous men whose views I have tried to draw out and explain in this present writing.

Now contrary to false claims made by philosophers about the 12
world's eternity, the human race got its start in this world, as we read in sacred Scripture, from the one human first created by God — hence called *prôtoplastos* more graphically in Greek. For when Moses, instructed in all the wisdom of Egypt and the first and greatest prophet to put his prophecies in writing, longed to withdraw himself from the senses, he did not hesitate to wander through the vast deserts of Ethiopia where, leaving all worldly cares aside and unattended, he turned his mind and intellect to meditate only on the highest matters of divinity. I believe —

convertit. In quo quidem ita omnipotenti Deo placuisse creditur, ut eum non per aenigmata aut per somnia obscurasque visiones instar ceterorum prophetarum sed facie ad faciem videre et intueri ac plura et stupenda miracula facere meruerit, quemadmodum sacrae litterae plane et aperte asserere testificarique videntur.

13   Talis igitur Moyses per hunc modum, divino spiritu afflatu nec humanae sapientiae nec saecularis philosophiae professor sed potius idoneus quidam divinorum operum testis et assertor, *Pentatheucum* suum sic incipere ausus est: In principio creavit Deus caelum et terram—ac reliqua usque ad integram et absolutam cunctorum brutorum productionem. Deinceps prosecutus, tandem inquit: faciamus[21] hominem ad imaginem et similitudinem nostram—quae quidem verba, secundum certam quandam et unicam omnium theologorum explanationem, non ad corpus sed ad animam tantummodo referuntur. Nam quid est Deus qui ita dixit? Caro an spiritus? Non caro utique sed spiritus, cui similis caro esse non potest quia ipse incorporeus et invisibilis est, caro autem et comprehenditur et videtur.

14   De qua quidem re, etsi multa immo paene infinita esse videantur quae de ea subtiliter quaeri et investigari soleant, animam tamen non a parentibus et *ex traduce* (ut theologico verbo utamur) instar corporum processisse, quemadmodum quidam haeretici et in primis Apollonius nescio quis falso opinabantur, sed a Deo ex nihilo factam in lucem prodisse ita existimamus et credimus, ut de eo ipso ullatenus dubitare et ambigere nequeamus. Cui quidem sententiae—vero enim omnia consonant—cuncti fere sacrarum litterarum explanatores Catholicique doctores adhaerere et assentiri perhibentur.

    Unde eius quasi materiem quam nullam fuisse manifestum est nequaquam quaerere et investigare debemus. Non enim tale quiddam esse scimus sicut terram humani corporis materiam extitisse diximus[22] e cuius limo vel humefacto pulvere fingeretur.

because I see the testimony of sacred Scripture plainly and clearly saying so — that this pleased the Almighty so much that Moses earned the privilege of doing many astonishing miracles and also looking on God and seeing him face to face, not through dark sights or dreams or obscure visions like other prophets.[15]

This Moses, a person so inspired by the spirit of God, and no 13 professor of human wisdom or worldly philosophy but a capable witness and advocate of God's works, dared to begin his *Pentateuch* in this way: In the beginning God created heaven and earth — next proceeding to all the beasts and their distinct production. Going on from there, he finally writes this: let us make man in our own image and likeness — words that actually refer only to the soul and not the body, according to a unique explanation and a sound account given by all the theologians. For what is the God who said this? Flesh or spirit? Not flesh, certainly, but spirit, to which flesh cannot be likened since spirit is unbodily and invisible, whereas we see the flesh and grasp it.[16]

I see people often making careful inquiries into many or even 14 countless problems arising from this point. My belief and judgment, nonetheless, allowing no doubt or hesitation at all, is that the soul came into this world made by God from nothing and did not emerge as bodies do, *off the branch* (using the theological term) from parent stock, though certain heretics, especially one Apollonius, had that false view. People say that nearly all Catholic teachers and interpreters of sacred scripture affirm this claim and adhere to it — for with the truth everything harmonizes.

Hence, we must by no means inquire about the soul by looking for its material where plainly there is none. For we know it was not the sort of thing I have described as the human body's matter — the earth from whose mud or wet dust a body might be

15 Ex quo Iudaeorum et Arrianorum stultam opinionem falsam esse convincitur qui verba illa *faciamus* et *nostram* Dei ad angelos fuisse putant. Non enim sive imaginem ad formam sive similitudinem ad naturam referant, ut sunt variae de hac re theologorum nostrorum sententiae.

Ceteris praedictorum verborum explanationibus praetermissis, quae paene innumerabiles afferuntur, parum attendisse ac considerasse videntur quonammodo iure fieri potuerit ut creationis operatio — quae ad solum Creatorem pertineret qui usque adeo omnipotens est ut ex nihilo cuncta facere ac creare valuerit — angelis tribueretur communicareturque, quos creaturas esse constabat. Quod si fuisset, utique creaturae simul atque creatores plane et aperte apparuissent. Si vero quam illud absurdum et quam impossibile esset aliquatenus excogitassent, profecto nunquam in tantum ac tam evidentem errorem incidissent. Neque etiam *eandem* imaginem ac similitudinem Dei et angelorum esse non potuisse animadverterunt. At si creationis operatio cum angelis communis extitisset, nunquid imago et similitudo Deo et angelis communis esse potuisset? Tantum enim abest ut angeli in potestate ac maiestate Deo pares esse videantur ut ipsos ab eius natura maxime ac longissime abesse sentiamus.

16 At vero propheta ille supremus non temere sed potius mirabiliter sentiens ac supra humanum modum sese inter contemplandum attollens, ut quandam divinarum personarum distinctionem latentem et occultam paucis verbis, quoad fieri poterat, planius et apertius explicaret, in creatione animae pluraliter loqui et enuntiare non dubitavit. Quod et antea fecerat, quando *in principia creavit Deus Eloyn* Hebraice dixerat, non temere et fortuito plurali numero[23] usus, cum in ceteris cunctarum rerum et animalium productionibus semper *Deum* singulariter dixisse meminisset. Quod ad praecipuam quandam et egregiam animarum excellentiam vel

fashioned. This proves false the stupid idea of the Jews and Arians 15 who suppose that God's words *let us make* and *our* applied to angels. They do not connect an image with form or a likeness with nature, as do various statements on this point by our theologians.[17]

Leaving aside other interpretations, nearly beyond counting, given to the words just quoted, these people evidently paid little heed or mind to just how the creative act — belonging only to a Creator so exceedingly powerful that he had the ability to make and create everything from nothing — could rightly be assigned to angels, whom we all know to be creatures, and transferred to them. Sure enough: had this been so, creatures would have seemed the same as creators, plain and simple. But if those people had given a little thought to something so absurd and impossible, surely they would never have fallen into so great and obvious an error. They did not even notice that the *same* image and likeness could not have belonged to God and angels. Really, if the act of creating had been shared with the angels, could an image and likeness actually have been shared by God and angels? So far are angels from seeming to be God's peers in power and majesty that we understand them to be totally distant from his nature — as far removed as possible.[18]

That supreme prophet, by contrast, was miraculously percep- 16 tive and not thoughtless, rising within himself to superhuman contemplation. Hence, in describing the soul's creation, he did not hesitate to speak expressly in the plural, so that a few words could display, as clearly and plainly as possible, the special distinction among the divine persons that is hidden and mysterious. Before he did this, having said *Elohim* in Hebrew for *in the beginning God created*, his use of the plural number was not thoughtless or by chance, since he always remembered to say *God* in the singular for the making of all the other things and animals. This actually has to do with souls, we realize, pertaining most of all to a special and

maxime pertinere et spectare cognoscitur, ut omnes divinae personae ad solam earum creationem expresse fuisse videantur.

Nec his adhuc contentus, postquam Deus creavit homines, *benedixit* — inquit — illis eosque omnium rerum productarum dominos universique terrarum orbis reges imperatoresque constituit. Et ut maiorem ipsarum animarum praestantiam dignitatemque monstraret, tandem in hunc modum secure intrepideque adiecit: formavit Dominus Deus hominem de limo terrae et inspiravit in faciem eius spiraculum vitae, et reliqua. *Dominus*, inquit, *Deus*: hoc est illud ineffabile nomen quod Graece *tetragrammaton* appellatur ac propria ipsius[24] essentia significatur.

Sic enim hoc loco quam substantiam dicere maluimus. Et usque adeo ab Hebraeis observatur et colitur ut quemadmodum sacris caracteribus venerandis eorum codicibus expressum et scriptum sit — nisi summis dumtaxat sacerdotibus quotannis semel et in sancto[25] sanctorum pronuntiari — explicarique non liceat. Quod attendentes Manichaei — perversi et acuti haeretici — verba illa ita interpretabantur ut animas de substantia Dei factas esse affirmarent. In qua quidem opinione Euripides poeta una cum quibusdam philosophis fuisse traditur.

17 Verumenimvero quid nos de theologis nostris dicemus, quandoquidem — secundum poetas et philosophos — humanas animas e caelis in terras descendisse intelligimus, quod Virgilius his versibus ostendit:

Igneus est ollis vigor et caelestis origo
seminibus quantum non noxia corpora tardant
terrenique hebetant artus moribundaque membra.

Id ipsum a Lucretio poeta praedictum fuisse constat, ita canente:

denique caelesti sumus omnes semine oriundi,
omnibus ille idem pater est.

distinguished excellence that they have, so that all the divine persons are distinctly seen to attend only their creation.[19]

Still not content with these words, Moses writes that after God created humans he *blessed* them, making them masters of all he had produced, kings and emperors of the whole earthly globe. Fearless and unshaken, and wishing to demonstrate the greater eminence and value of souls themselves, Moses finally added this along the same lines: the Lord God formed a human from the mud of the earth and breathed the breath of life into his face, and so on. *Lord*, he says, and then *God*: the latter is the unsayable word called *tetragrammaton* in Greek that signifies God's own essence.[20]

Actually, I would rather put it that way in this passage than talk about God's substance. So much do the Hebrews cherish and honor this name that they may not reveal it by pronouncing it as shown in their scrolls and written in the revered sacred letters — except for the chief priests once a year and in their Holy of Holies. When the Manichees noticed this — those perverse and passionate heretics — they interpreted the words to claim that souls were made from God's substance. Incidentally, Euripides the poet is said to have had this view, along with certain philosophers.[21]

Then what to say about our theologians, seeing that we understand — from poets and philosophers — that human souls have come down to earth from the heavens, as Vergil shows in these lines:

17

Fiery the power of their sky-sourced seeds
until slowed by hurtful bodies, dulled
by deathward limbs and earthbound joints.

The poet Lucretius had plainly said the same thing, singing that

we are all sprouts of the sky-seed,
the same father for us all.

Et Hermes quoque ille (ob excellentiam suam) cognomento Tri-
megistus — quod Graece Mercurium Ter Maximum significat —
hominem et a Deo et ad Dei similitudinem factum esse non
ignoravit, quando humanam formam *theoeidem*,[26] hoc est deo similem, appellare et nuncupare non formidavit. Hunc Platonem
postea secutum eodem Graeco verbo usum fuisse legimus. Cicero
etiam pluribus locis hominibus nihil mente melius, nihil praestantius, nihil denique divinius ab omnipotenti Deo dari potuisse testatur.

18   Sed ut alia multa omittamus quae a plerisque Catholicae ecclesiae doctoribus circa huiusmodi geneseos auctoritatem addu-
cuntur, his beati Augustini verbis ad veram quandam et brevem
commemoratarum divinarum sententiarum explanationem contenti erimus. Qui quidem, cum per totum septimum et octavum
librum *Super genesim ad litteram* de animarum dignitate plura copiosissime quaesivisset atque elegantissime disputasset, longis tandem
disputationibus defessus, in calce eius[27] codicis de anima, quam
Deus homini in faciem eius sufflans inspirasse dicitur, nihil se nisi
hoc solum confirmare testatur: quod sic *ex Deo* erat ut substantia
Dei non esset, et sic incorporea ut non esset corpus sed spiritus,
non de substantia Dei genitus nec de substantia Dei procedens sed
factus a Deo, nec ita factus ut in eius naturam natura ulla corporis
vel irrationalis[28] animae verteretur — unde ex his ac ceteris huiusmodi *de nihilo* factam ac creatam esse concluditur.

19   Fecit igitur Deus hominem ad imaginem et similitudinem
suam. Talem quippe illi animam creavit qua — ratione et immortalitate, intelligentia ac memoria et voluntate praedita — ceteris
omnibus animalibus praestaret ac dominaretur. Hanc nostram —
immo potius Catholicam et, ut ita dixerim, theologicam — ipsius
animae definitionem veram ac perfectam idcirco esse contendimus
quoniam ipsam cum ex ante dictis Moysaicorum verborum explanationibus, tum etiam ex pluribus aliis sanctorum virorum et

Nor did this escape the Hermes called (because of his nobility) Trismegistus — meaning Mercury Thrice-Greatest in Greek — that man was created by God and made in God's likeness, in that he did not fear calling the human form by the name *theoeidês* or god-like. I read that Plato followed Hermes later, using the same Greek word. Cicero also testifies in many places that Almighty God could have given man nothing better than mind, nothing excelling it, even nothing more divine.[22]

However, while omitting much else cited by many teachers of 18 the Catholic Church to confirm a genesis of this sort, I will be content with what St. Augustine writes to give a correct and rather brief explanation of the divine statements already mentioned. In fact, after presenting a most elegant discussion and a very rich inquiry into many aspects of the value of souls, throughout the whole seventh and eighth books of his *Literal Commentary on Genesis*, Augustine finally tired of lengthy debates. And then — talking at the end of his text about God's having breathed a soul into man by blowing into his face — he says that he has just one thing to confirm: that the soul came *out of God* in such a way that it was not God's substance, hence nonbodily and so not body but spirit, neither begotten from God's substance nor proceeding from God's substance but made by God, yet not so made that any nature of a body or unreasoning soul would turn into God's nature; Augustine concludes from this and other such points that the soul was made and created *from nothing*.[23]

So God made man in his image and likeness. And yes, God 19 created a soul for man to surpass and master all other animals, equipping it with reason and immortality, with intelligence and memory and will. This definition of the soul — not just mine but Catholic and, if I may, theological — I claim to be correct and complete because, while keeping it short, I have compiled a summary both from explanations of the words of Moses already discussed

maxime Ambrosii et Gregorii, Damasceni ac Remigii descriptionibus hinc inde conflantes breviter compilavimus.

20 Cum itaque eam substantiam et formam incorpoream et a Deo ex nihilo creatam ex his quae diximus antea probaverimus, reliquum est ut nonnulla de ipsius immor talitate in medium adducamus. Quo facto, de tribus suis naturalibus potentiis superius commemoratis pauca quaedam brevissime referemus. Ad certam igitur quandam et indubitatam animarum immortalitatem graviter secundum dignitatem rei procedere et progredi cupientes, primo hoc ipsum nonnullis rationibus et argumentis ac persuasionibus ostendemus, quibusdam deinde poetarum ac philosophorum auctoritatibus confirmabimus, adamantinis denique sacrarum scripturarum testimoniis comprobabimus. Rationibus igitur niti et insistere volentes, pauca e multis in hunc modum tanquam aliis probabiliora delegimus.

21 Ceterae animantes tribus dumtaxat elementis quasi ponderosis ac terrestribus utuntur, solus vero homo ignem, utpote leve et sublime ac caeleste elementum sine quo vivere non posset, in quotidianum vitae suae usum assumit. Quod ideo non exiguum, ut ait quidam, immortalitatis argumentum videri debet: quoniam Deum, qui singula quaeque bruta ignis utilitate privavit, hominibus vero tantummodo largitus est, nihil temere ac frustra facere operarive intelligimus, praesertim cum ad generales quasdam aliquorum, nedum ad cunctas omnium, animalium species intendere ac prospicere videatur. Sed cum cetera animalia mortalia efficeret, hominem autem solum immortalem generaret, per huiusmodi elementorum discretionem quae ad viventium usum utilitatemque creaverat, ea ut re vera inter se discreverat ita, per hunc diversarum naturarum modum ab invicem discreta, ab illis intelligi voluit qui, subtili ingenio praediti, paulo altius a terrenis cogitationibus elevarentur.

and also from many other accounts given by saintly men, especially Ambrose and Gregory, Damascene and Remigius.[24]

And so, having proved from the foregoing statements that the 20 soul is a substance, an incorporeal form and created by God out of nothing, it remains to bring up some things about its immortality. After that, I will make a few very brief points about its three natural powers as mentioned above. Wishing to move forward and proceed with gravity worthy of the topic — that souls have an immortality which is certain and beyond doubt — I will first demonstrate this with various opinions, reasons and arguments, then confirm it with certain views of poets and philosophers, and finally prove it with rigorous testimonies of sacred Scripture. Wanting to rely on reasons, then, and take my stand, I have chosen a few that are more convincing from the many like them.

Other living things use only the three elements that are heavy 21 and earthy, while man alone also takes fire to use in his daily life because it is the light, exalted and celestial element without which he cannot live. Someone said that this should be seen as no small evidence of immortality: that we understand God as acting not at all in vain nor working without purpose by depriving every beast of the advantage of fire to bestow it only on humans, especially since he evidently looks out for certain general types of animals — only some — without attending to each and every one. But when God made the rest of the animals mortal (man alone he created immortal), when he also distinguished in this way among elements created for the use and advantage of living things, he actually made creatures distinct for this purpose: that once they were distinguished from one another by means of their different natures, he wanted them known apart from the others that he equipped with a finer temperament and raised a bit higher, away from earthly designs.[25]

22   Si omnes etiam viventes homines longe post mortem prospicere ac futuris saeculis magnis cum laboribus nec minoribus sumptibus, naturali quodam desiderio allecti et instigati, quantum possunt semper prodesse conantur—partim crebris procerarum arborum consitionibus, partim diuturnis magnorum aedificiorum constructionibus, partim continuis filiorum procreationibus, partim denique (ne cuncta in hoc loco complectamur) perpetuis liberalium artium et ingenuarum scientiarum conscriptionibus ut sunt varia diversorum hominum ingenia quae omnia Cicero in *Tusculanis* suis multo latius et uberius prosecutus est—quemadmodum luce clarius constare et apparere dignoscimus, profecto eorum animam immortalem fore iure dubitare et ambigere non possumus, praesertim cum huiusmodi desiderium cunctis hominibus vel potius toti humano generi ab ipsa natura, rerum omnium parente, inditum fuisse videamus: quoniam aliter sequeretur ut innatae eorum animalium quae Deus prae ceteris nobilitata condidisset cupiditates appetitionesque evanescerent.

Eosdem quoque homines natura duce felicitatem appetere videmus quam nullatenus nisi per animae dumtaxat immortalitatem adipisci et assequi possent. Nam si omnino extingueretur,[29] quonam modo felices esse viderentur intelligere excogitareque nequimus, praesertim cum in hac vita mortali ob singularem quandam eius varietatem nullatenus beati esse valeamus. Itaque similiter vana et stulta naturae cupiditas et appetitio resultaret. Omnes insuper naturali et innata voluntate immortales fore exoptamus et cupimus, sed huiusmodi nostra voluntas, quam philosophi appetitum cum ratione definierunt, omnino falli decipive non potest. Quod si eveniret, in idem utique inanis cupiditatis naturalis absurdum laberemur. Quae quidem quoniam impossibilia sunt ac naturae ipsi plane et aperte repugnare cernuntur, profecto animas una cum corporibus interire falsum esse convicitur.

23   Quod si fieri potuisset ut animae simul cum corporibus interirent, porro Deum iniustum fuisse manifeste concluderetur. Nam

If all humans still living, stirred and drawn by a kind of natural 22
desire, can, with great labor and at no less cost, care so much for
ages to come long after they have died that they try to make their
help go on — sometimes by planting tall trees close together, sometimes by building great structures to last, sometimes by continuing
to bear children and finally (not to include everything in this passage) sometimes by writing books to endure in the liberal arts and
noble sciences, according to all the various inclinations of different
people that Cicero has described much more fully and extensively
in his *Tusculans* — then, seeing all this clearly and plainer than day,
surely we cannot rightly doubt or disbelieve that the soul will be
immortal, especially since we see such a longing planted by Nature
herself, the parent of all, in all people, in the whole human race:
otherwise, the result would be that the inborn desires and appe-
tites of these animals that God created nobler than others would
come to nothing.[26]

We also see the same humans guided by Nature in their appetite for a happiness which they could never pursue or attain except
through the soul's immortality. Now if this were completely eliminated, I cannot understand or imagine how people might appear
happy, especially since we cannot find bliss in this mortal life,
given its remarkable inconstancy. Nature's desire and appetite
would then turn out to be useless and foolish. Moreover, we all
desire and long to be immortal by a natural and inborn will, but
this will of ours, defined by philosophers as appetite plus reason,
cannot be duped and deceived entirely. Were that to happen, we
would fall into the same absurdity — a natural desire utterly without hope. In fact, because these things are plainly impossible and
perceived as clearly repugnant to Nature herself, the obvious ver-
dict is that it is false to say that souls perish with bodies.[27]

But if it could be that souls perish along with bodies, another 23
obvious conclusion would be that God has been unjust. For in an

magna quaedam perditis hominibus suorum malorum facinorum praemia — vel divitias vel honores ac potentatus et regna — indignissime simul atque iniquissime largiretur. Viris vero probis atque optimis — qui cuncta haec quae nos bona appellare solemus frivola et inania contempserunt, atque inediam, parsimoniam, verbera, eculeos et singula quaeque corporum tormenta sponte sua susceperunt ut caelestem illam ac beatam et immarcescibilem vitam nanciscerentur — non modo dignam laborum suorum mercedem non praeberet, sed pro operibus iustis glorioseque gestis cunctas huius humanae vitae miserias, cruciatus et neces tribueret. Quo quid absurdius dici excogitarive possit nequaquam intelligere valemus.

24 Unde Dicaearchus et Democritus, Epicurus ac Panaetius et quicunque alii animas una cum corporibus interire putaverunt proculdubio aberrasse deprehenduntur. Quod quidem plurimis tam poetarum quam philosophorum et sanctorum virorum auctoritatibus deinceps clarius apparebit.

Atque ut a poematibus fabularumque figmentis tanquam a leviusculis testimoniis breviter recedamus, omnes poetas Graecos pariter ac Latinos Inferos et Infernum pro malorum punitionibus, Elysios vero Campos et Beatorum Insulas pro bonorum hominum praemiis posuisse manifestum est, quod Virgilius his versibus expressit:

Hic locus est partes ubi se via findit in ambas:
dextera quae Ditis magni sub moenia tendit,
hac iter Elisium nobis; at laeva malorum
exercet poenas et ad impia Tartara mittit.

Id ipsum et *Carmina sibyllina* tunc vel maxime confirmare videntur cum ultimum de vivis ac mortuis Dei iudicium futurum vaticinantur.

25 Ad philosophos severiores veritatis magistros et professores accedamus. Quorum primus — ut ait Cicero — Pherecides Syrus

absolutely unbecoming and shameless way, he would have bestowed various great prizes — wealth, honor, power, kingdoms — on wicked people for their evil deeds. But to the upright and excellent — those who have disdained all those goods that we usually call trifling and worthless, people who have freely submitted to starvation, frugality, scourging, the rack and all such bodily tortures in order to attain the blessed and heavenly life that never fades — not only would God have offered no reward befitting their labors, but, in return for their righteous works and glorious deeds, he would have doled out all the misery, agony and slaughter of this human life. In no way can I understand how anything more absurd could be said or imagined.[28]

Hence, we find beyond any doubt that those people were mistaken — Dicaearchus and Democritus, Epicurus and Panaetius, as well as any others who thought that souls perish along with bodies. This will be even clearer from many declarations to come of poets, philosophers and holy men.[29] 24

And to move on quickly from the insubstantial witness of poetry and mythical fiction, all the Greek poets as well as the Latin have plainly set up an Underworld and a Hell to punish the wicked, but to reward the good an Elysian Fields and Blessed Isles, as depicted by Vergil in these lines:

This place is where the way divides in two parts:
the right road, our Elysian path, goes by
the walls of mighty Dis; the left leads down
to Tartarus, pain and torment for the wicked.

Then the *Sibylline Verses* give great support to the very same idea when they prophesy about God's future judgment of the living and the dead.[30]

Let me move on to philosophers, stricter teachers and professors of truth. The first of them — as Cicero reports — was 25

animos hominum sempiternos esse dixit. Cuius opinionem Pythagoras, eius discipulus, non modo comprobavit sed causam etiam cur ita esset adiunxit. Qui enim ante Pherecidem extiterant philosophi, quoniam intelligere non poterant quonam modo anima sine corpore vivere valeret, utrunque simul interire putaverunt. Itaque simplici praedicti praeceptoris sui de aeternitate animorum sententiae perpetuam quandam in varia et diversa corpora revolutionem adinvenisse dicitur qua mediante perpetuo servarentur. Sed hic et ceteri superiores viderint qualem incorpoream formam in ipso corpore intelligant. Ciceroni enim nostro naturam animi intuenti, non immerito multo difficilior cogitatio multoque obscurior occurrebat, qualis animus esset in corpore tanquam alienae domui, quam qualis remaneret postquam exierit et in liberum caelum tanquam in domum suam emigraverit.

Alcmaeon — secundum Aristotelis sententiam idoneus immortalitatis animorum assertor — accedit: sic enim ipsum quodam loco

26 existimasse refert. Plato quanquam ut Pythagoreos cognosceret in eam Italiae partem venisse memoretur quae quondam Magna Graecia dicebatur, ubi Pythagoras primo et qui eum sequebantur postea celebres scholarum suarum sedes constituerant, non solum de aeternitate animorum idem sensisse quod Pythagoram sed plures etiam rationes cur ita esset attulisse existimetur. Ipsum tamen a Socrate eius magistro idcirco illud accepisse credimus quoniam Socratem in extremo mortis articulo constitutum de eorum immortalitate divinitus disseruisse ac disputasse comperimus. Atque ab eodem praeceptore Xenophontem quoque — cognomento Socraticum, Platonis condiscipulum — illam ipsam opinionem exhausisse putamus, quando Cyrum maiorem, clarissimum Persarum regem, celebrato illo *Paediae* suae volumine (quod nos *De infantia Cyri* Latine interpretari solemus) de aeternitate animorum disserentem inducit.

Pherecydes of Syros, who said that human souls are everlasting. Pythagoras, his student, not only approved this belief but also added the reason why it is true. The philosophers who had lived before Pherecydes thought that body and soul perish together because they could not understand how one could live without the other. Then, to complement the straightforward statement by his teacher — the one I have mentioned — about souls being eternal, they say that Pythagoras devised a kind of cycling into various different bodies as a means of preserving them perpetually. But let him and the rest of the ancients figure out what a bodiless form in a body would be like. When our Cicero considered the soul's nature, he encountered no idea more obscure and difficult, and no wonder: what sort of mind would exist in a body, as in a stranger's house, and then still exist after exiting and leaving for the open sky — as for its own house?[31]

Alcmaeon agrees — a capable supporter of the immortality of souls, according to a statement by Aristotle: for somewhere he expressed the same thought, as Aristotle reports. The records 26 show Plato coming to the part of Italy once called Great Greece to meet Pythagoreans, in the place where Pythagoras first, and then his followers, set up centers for their schools that were well-attended. And they say he not only felt the same as Pythagoras about the immortality of souls but also gave several reasons why this is so. Yet I believe Plato learned this from his teacher, Socrates, for this reason: I see that Socrates, inspired in the final moment of death, chose to discuss and debate the immortality of souls. And I think that Xenophon — called a Socratic and a fellow student with Plato — also got that belief from the same teacher, since in his famous book on *Paideia* (which in Latin we usually call the *Childhood of Cyrus*) he introduces the elder Cyrus, the noblest Persian king, talking about the eternity of souls.[32]

Aristoteles — magister omnium — idem plane et aperte asserere et confirmare non dubitavit, quem Porphirius in eandem sententiam secutus est, sed et quosdam antiquiores et celeberrimos viros hoc idem sensisse constat. Nam et commemoratus Hermes ex duabus diversis naturis hominem conflatum arbitrabatur, quarum alteram mortalem, alteram vero immortalem esse existimabat. At Polites quidam Apollinem Milesium consuluisse dicitur utrum post mortem anima vel dissolveretur vel remaneret, atque eam post separationem a corpore perpetuo remanere atque in aeternum vivere ex Oraculi responsis intellexit. Cicero denique et Seneca pluribus librorum suorum locis, per multa argumenta perque varias persuasiones huiusmodi, animorum immortalitatem probare et attestari conantur.

27   Ceterum si his omnibus sapientibus viris magnisque philosophis credimus qui hanc animorum aeternitatem verbis dumtaxat et scriptis suis confirmaverunt, quid de illis sentiemus qui ea de causa mortem sibi ipsis consciverunt ut, vinculis corporis soluti, liberius vivere valerent? Quales Cleantem, Chrisippum, Zenonem, Empedoclem, qui sese in ardentis Aethnae specum intempesta nocte deiecisse scribitur; quales insuper Catonem Romanum et Theombrotum[30] Ambrachiotam fuisse legimus. Quos, lecto Platonis libro qui est de aeternitate animorum, se ipsos interemisse comperimus. Nonne tales et tantos viros animorum aeternitatem recepisse existimabimus, quandoquidem eos ad voluntariam mortem sponte sua accessisse non dubitamus?

28   Cum itaque nonnullis rationibus pluribusque poetarum ac philosophorum allegationibus de animorum immortalitate aliqua memoratu digna breviter recitarimus, reliquum est ut ad sanctorum auctoritates et ad divina oracula parumper accedamus, et, quanquam cuncta quae in utroque, Veteri scilicet ac Novo Testamento, scripta sunt hanc animorum immortalitatem praesupponere

Aristotle—everybody's teacher—had no doubts about asserting the same thing clearly and plainly affirming it, with Porphyry following him in the same opinion, though obviously there were also some older and very distinguished men who felt the same. In fact, the Hermes previously mentioned thought that the human is an amalgam of two different natures, reckoning the one to be mortal, the other immortal. But a certain Polites is said to have asked the Milesian Apollo whether the soul remains after death or is destroyed, and from the Oracle's responses he understood that, after separating from the body, it remains forever and lives on into eternity. Finally, with many arguments and various reasons of this kind, Cicero and Seneca try in several passages of their books to prove the immortality of souls and confirm it.[33]

Besides, if we believe all the wise men and great philosophers 27 who have confirmed this eternity of souls just with words and in their writings, what shall we think of those who killed themselves because of it so that they could live a freer life when released from the body's chains? Such were Cleanthes, Chrysippus, Zeno and Empedocles, described as having thrown himself into flaming Aetna's crater in the dead of night. Such also, I read, were Cato the Roman and Theombrotus of Ambracia: I find that they did themselves in after reading Plato's book on the eternity of souls. Shall we not reckon that men of such character and greatness accepted the eternity of souls, seeing that we have no doubt that they went willingly to deaths of their own choosing?[34]

And now, since I have given a brief listing of a few memorable 28 points about the immortality of souls, along with some theories from poets and several proofs from philosophers, it remains for me to spend a little time with the records of the saints and the sacred oracles. Even though we see that everything written in both Testaments, Old and New, presupposes this immortality of souls, from many texts I shall still cite a few summarily as clearer and

videantur, pauca tamen e multis clariora et expressiora brevitatis simul atque illustrandae veritatis causa breviter referemus.

29   Et ut a vetustioribus ordiamur, Moyses in commemorata Geneseos auctoritate animam immortalem fore plane et aperte declaravit. Per hoc enim solum propior ac Deo similior quam per quaecunque alia facile videri et apparere potest. Nam cognitione, sapientia, potestate ac ceteris omnibus longe dissimilis est cum sola immortalitate Deo consimilis appareat. Atque in eodem libro id ipsum manifestius expressisse videtur quando Enoch — illum septimum ab Adam *protoplasto*[31] — sexagesimo quinto aetatis anno non obiisse sed cum Deo ambulasse et in caelum ascendisse testatur. Quod et Heliae in libris Regum contigisse legimus, ut curru igneo vivus ab ignitis equis in caelum veheretur. Quo in loco Helisaeum prophetam, memorati Heliae discipulum, puerulum quendam, viduae Sunamitis filium, paulo ante defunctum e tenebris in lucero revocasse novimus.

    In sacro quoque et admirabili illo patientissimi viri dialogo — quem librum a praedicto Moyse Hebraei compositum fuisse opinantur — cum de certa quadam et expressa defunctorum hominum resurrectione determinetur, profecto animam immortalem esse non dubitatur. David etiam pluribus Psalmorum suorum locis his et huiusmodi verbis usus: qui sperant in te, Domine, in aeternum exultabunt, manifestam animarum perpetuitatem ostendere et demonstrare dignoscitur. Isaias quando de Deo loquens, praecipitabit — inquit — mortem in sempiternum et mortui tui vivent, quid aliud quam animorum aeternitatem per haec et huiusmodi verba sensisse videtur? Si enim interirent, quomodo in sempiternum mors praecipitaretur? Et quonam modo mortuos corpore aliter quam per animarum perpetuitatem vivere posse putandum est?

30   Cum deinde apud Hieremiam Infernum et inferos crebro scriptum fuisse cognovimus, non de cadaveribus quae in hoc saeculo ante oculos nostros quotidie humari et sepeliri videmus, sed de

more distinct, both by reason of their brevity and because they shed light on the truth.

To begin with the more ancient witnesses, Moses declared 29 plainly and openly in the aforementioned passage of Genesis that the soul is immortal. For only through this, more than anything else, can the soul be seen as closer to God and appear somewhat like him. In knowledge, wisdom, power and all other ways it is actually much different; the soul is very like God only by being immortal. In the same book Moses seems to express the same thing more explicitly when he testifies that Enoch—seventh in line from Adam *prôtoplastos*—did not die in the sixty-fifth year of life but walked with God and ascended to heaven. I read in the Books of Kings that this also happened to Elias, who was carried up to heaven alive in a fiery chariot by flaming horses. And in this place I learn that the prophet Elisha, a follower of that Elias, called back from death to life a little boy, the son of a Shunamite widow, shortly after he passed away.[35]

Also, since the sure and certain resurrection of the dead is discussed explicitly in the sacred and astonishing conversation of the most patient man of all—a book that the Hebrews think was composed by the aforesaid Moses—there is surely no doubt that the soul is immortal. In several passages of his Psalms, David also used these and similar words: those who hope in you, Lord, shall exult eternally—taken to show and demonstrate that souls are plainly perpetual. When Isaiah says, talking about God, that he will hurl death down eternally and that your dead shall live, what else do we take him to have meant by these and other such words but that souls are eternal? For if they perished, how would death be hurled down forever? And how do we suppose the dead can live in the body unless souls go on forever?[36]

Then, when I have noticed Jeremiah writing in quick succession 30 about Hell and those in Hell, I understand that what he really means is souls—not the corpses that we see being covered with

animabus iure intelligimus. Et rursus quando Ezechielem viventium terram saepenumero repetentem et iustum vita victurum et non moriturum dicentem audivimus,[32] quid aliud nisi humanas animas non morituras merito interpretamur? Daniel—a Dario Medorum rege omnibus regni sui provinciis ob admirabilem illam ac divinam diversorum somniorum interpretationem digne praefectus—nunquam in lacum leonum crudelibus feris laniandum se[33] mitti passus esset, sed potius saevo et impio illius gentis Satrapum edicto paruisset, nisi animam immortalem esse credidisset.

31   Quid vero haec celebrata Oseae prophetae verba, in forma Dei ita dicentis: de manu mortis liberabo eos; de morte redimam eos; ero mors tua, o mors; ero mors tua, Inferne, et reliqua, nisi animarum aeternitatem sonant ac plane aperteque significant? Convertimini ad me, per Ioelem dicit Dominus, in ieiuniis, in fletibus et planctibus et reliquis huiusmodi humanorum corporum cruciatibus. Cur inquit convertimini? Ut scilicet, per aspera illa tormentorum genera ad quae nos exhortatur et invitat celerius anima sui corporis compage separata, omnino pereat? Quin immo potius ut in aeternum vivat.

32   Amos Dominum super altare stantem et sic loquentem se vidisse dicit: Fugientes non salvabuntur. Nam si descenderint in Infernum, exinde manus mea educet, et si ascenderint usque ad Caelum, inde pariter eos extraham, et cetera huiusmodi. Ex quibus quidem verbis animas defunctorum nequaquam cum corporibus interire declarat, quoniam ex omnibus locis extrahendas esse testatur. Hic non verbis solum sed rebus quoque et corporali morte, tanquam verus omnipotentis Dei athleta, id ipsum approbasse traditur.

Nam primum ab Amasia sacerdote multis plagis afflictus, ab Ozia deinde, eius filio, Iudaeorum Rege, vecte quadam per tempora transfixus, innocens perire quam divinae legis transgressor

earth and buried every day in our world. And since I have also heard Ezekiel constantly talking about the land of the living, repeating that the just shall have a life to live and shall not die, what is the right interpretation except that human souls will not die? Daniel—deservedly made governor of all the provinces of his realm by Darius, king of the Medes, because he interpreted various dreams with amazing, godlike skill—would never have allowed himself to be sent to the lions' den, to be mangled by wild beasts, had he not believed the soul to be immortal; instead, as Satrap of that people, he would have complied with the cruel and ungodly edict.[37]

But what about the prophet Hosea's famous words, in the form 31 of a speech by God: I will free them from death's hand; from death will I redeem them; death—I will be the death of you; Hell—I will be your death, and so on? This can only be about the eternity of souls—the meaning plain and clear. Return to me, says the Lord through Joel, in fasting, weeping, wailing and other such torments for human bodies. Why does he say to return? Is it so that the soul, separated more speedily from the body's embrace by the harsh tortures to which he invites and urges us, might perish altogether? Of course not: the point is to live eternally.[38]

Amos says that he saw the Lord standing above an altar and 32 saying this: You shall not flee and be saved. For if you go down to Hell, my hand will bring you out, and if you go up to Heaven, from there too I will take you out, and so on. With these words he declares that the souls of the dead by no means perish with their bodies, testifying that they are to be taken out from everywhere. They say he made good on this not just with words but with deeds and the death of his body, like a true athlete of God Almighty.

First he was beaten with many blows by the priest Amaziah, then pierced through the temples with a kind of rod by the priest's son, Uzziah, king of the Jews, preferring to die innocent rather

vivere maluit — quemadmodum Isaiam saevis impii regis Manasses temporibus antea fecisse legimus, quando serra aequanimiter secari se[34] passus est. Quod nullo unquam tempore adducti essent ut facerent si animam ullatenus mortalem credidissent, praesertim cum utranque violentam et crudelem mortem faciliter fugere et evitare possent.

33   Abdiam insuper et Ionam, Michaeam, Naum, Abachucum, Sophoniam, Aggeum, Zachariam, Malachiam — ut uno verborum contextu brevitatis gratia reliquos fere omnes prophetas complectamur — certam quandam et indubitatam humanarum animarum immortalitatem codicibus suis declarasse et conscripsisse scimus. Partim namque beatos homines, partim ad Deum conversos, partim prophetas per multa saecula antea mortuos, iustosque et sanctos viros pariter defunctos, in aeternum vivere, partim denique dominum Heliam, ante quam veniat dies magnus et horribilis, missurum plane et aperte testantur. Quae quidem omnia, si anima interiret, nullatenus fieri poterant. Quid autem de Machabaeis fratribus dicemus, quoniam[35] inclita et gloriosa gesta — et dura et aspera sub Anthioco, Armeniorum rege, inflicta pro sacris legibus tormenta — aliam nempe quam istam qua vivimus vitam fore declarant?

34   Ceterum multis et aliis et huiusmodi Veteris Instrumenti, quae paene infinita sunt, praetermissis, deinceps ad Testamentum Novum summatim ac brevissime accedamus.[36] Mathaeus, Marcus, Lucas, Iohannes in omnibus Evangeliis suis nihil aliud legentibus et audientibus — et toti ferme humano generi — quam aeternitatem animarum significare et manifestare contendunt. Nam et regna caelorum et plures beatitudinum species et inferorum poenae et iniuriarum patientiae et crebra ieiunia et mutuae inimicorum dilectiones et asperae propriorum corporum castigationes et plures defunctorum hominum suscitationes et novissimae mortuorum omnium, quibus resurrectiones et alia similia quorum [omnium]

than live and break the divine law—just as Isaiah had done before, so I read, in the savage times of the godless king Manasseh, when he calmly submitted to being cut up with a saw. Never would they have been led to do this had they believed the soul to be in any way mortal, especially since both prophets could easily have fled, avoiding deaths that were violent and cruel.[39]

In addition, I know that Obadiah, Jonah, Micah, Nahum, Habakkuk, Zephaniah, Haggai, Zechariah and Malachi—to cover almost all the other prophets with one fabric of words, for the sake of brevity—wrote about the immortality of human souls in their books, showing this to be something certain and beyond doubt. In some passages they testify, plainly and clearly, that the blessed live for eternity, while elsewhere they mention either those who return to God or prophets already dead for centuries or the righteous and the saints who were also deceased, and finally some say that the Lord—before that great and terrible day arrives—will send Elias. But there would be no way for any of this to happen if the soul were to perish. Then what to say about the Maccabee brothers, since their noble and glorious deeds—those hard and bitter sufferings on behalf of the sacred laws inflicted under Antiochus, king of Armenia—surely mean that there will be a life other than this one for us to live?[40]

For the rest, leaving out many other such texts of the Old Testament, which are nearly countless, let me come next to the New Testament, but for a very brief summary. In all their Gospels, what Matthew, Mark, Luke and John strive to make evident and obvious to all who hear and read them—to the whole human race, essentially—is nothing else but the eternity of souls. For all the copious contents of the Gospels—statements about kingdoms in Heaven, beatitude of various kinds, the pains of Hell, the suffering of wrongs, frequent fasting, enemies loving one another, harsh punishment for one's own body, the many deceased who are raised and then finally all the dead risen—resurrections and other

33

34

Evangelia referctissima sunt, nequaquam animas interire sed in aeternum potius vivere plane et aperte significant. Actus Apostolorum atque Pauli, Petri, Iohannis, et Iudae Epistolae, ne solis eorum allegationibus contenti simus (quid enim verbis opus est ubi manifesta et certa rerum testimonia cernuntur?), nonne propriis martyriis — quae plerique ipsorum sponte sua subierunt cum fugere et evitare facile possent — et pluribus etiam mortuorum hominum suscitationibus animas remanere post mortem ostenderunt?

35 Innumerabiles infinitorum paene martyrum catervas omittamus, qui certatim undecim illis famosis diversorum impiorum imperatorum adversus Christianos persecutionibus ad aspera et diversa martyria concurrebant atque exinde ad aeterna caelorum regna aspirabant. Missos insuper faciamus Iohannem Chrisostomum, Gregorium Nazanzenum, Magnum Basilium, Cirillum, Origenem reliquosque externos, Hilarium, Cyprianum, Lactantium, Ambrosium, Hieronymum, Augustinum, Gregorium pontificem, et ceteros Catholicae Ecclesiae doctores, Graecos pariter ac Latinos, quandoquidem omnes ipsi in cunctis operibus suis, quae paene infinita reliquerunt, nihil aliud agere operarive contenderunt nisi ut optima ac vera et solida utriusque Testamenti fundamenta quodammodo obscura et involuta explanarentur atque, quoad fieri poterat, paulo clarius explicarentur.

36 Cum itaque pluribus rationibus multisque tam profanis quam sacris praestantissimorum virorum auctoritatibus animam immortalem esse antea probaverimus, nunc de tribus eius naturalibus potentiis — quemadmodum nos facturos esse promiseramus — deinceps pauca dicemus, ac primo de ipsa hominis intelligentia brevissime agemus, cuius quidem quantae et quam excellentes vires sint pleraque magna et ingentia vel facinora vel machinamenta admirabiliter inventa et intellecta declarant.

37 Nam ut a levioribus incipiamus, quanto et quam mirabili ingenio praeditum Iasonem, Argonautarum principem, fuisse

like events of which the Gospels are stuffed full—plainly and clearly indicate that souls by no means perish but live eternally instead. As for the Acts of the Apostles and the Letters of Paul, Peter, John and Jude, let me not rest just with what they claim (what need for words where we see sure and certain evidence of deeds?), for by their own martyrdoms—to which they often willingly submitted when they could easily flee and escape—and also by frequently raising the dead, did they not show that souls remain after death?[41]

Let me skip the countless throngs of martyrs, nearly beyond   35
number, who banded together, eager for harsh and varied martyrdoms in those famous persecutions—eleven of them—by a variety of godless emperors, attacking Christians who wished to go from there to the eternal realms of Heaven. Let me also set aside John Chrysostom, Gregory of Nazianzus, Basil the Great, Cyril, Origen and the rest of the foreigners, Hilary, Cyprian, Lactantius, Ambrose, Jerome, Augustine, Pope Gregory and the other Doctors of the Catholic Church, both Greek and Latin, seeing that, in all the nearly countless works left by them, what they all tried to accomplish was simply to make plain and effective what was somehow obscure and tangled in both Testaments, explaining the basics—the best, true and solid foundations—and laying this out a little more clearly, as best they could.[42]

Now, since I have already proved that the soul is immortal, us-   36
ing many arguments and many citations, both sacred and profane, from the most eminent men, I shall next say a little—doing just as I promised—about the soul's three natural powers, dealing first and very briefly with human intelligence, which is shown to have abilities of large scope and excellence by the great deeds and remarkable devices that people have thought up and invented so admirably.

To start with less weighty evidence, I reckon that Jason's en-   37
dowment of genius was huge and astounding, since this chief of

existimamus, quando primum illud navigium construxit quo
Argonautae, eius collegae, vecti horrisonum mare ingredi atque
horribiles saevi pelagi fluctus secure et intrepide—incredibile
dictu—transire ausi sunt! Id cuique ita mirabile videri poterat ut
unumquemque videntem in sui admirationem compulisset—ceu
ille apud Accium poetam pastor qui navem nunquam antea vidis-
set, ut procul divinum et novum illud vehiculum ex alto conspexit
perterritus et admirabundus, hoc modo loquebatur:

> tanta moles labitur
> fremebunda ex alto ingenti sonitu et strepitu;
> prae se undas evolvit,

et reliqua. Huiusmodi navigandi artificium—paulatim per multa
temporum momenta usque ad hanc nostram aetatem—ita excre-
visse videmus ut in miraculum usque processerit. Nam non modo
Britannicum et glacialem Occeanum, ut inquit poeta, quotidie
navigare consueverunt, sed etiam in intimam paene Mauritaniam
ultra terminos antea navigabiles nuper penetrare contenderunt, ubi
plures cultas et habitatas insulas penitus ante hac incognitas reper-
tas fuisse audivimus.

38   Quanta quoque industria ingentes illas ac celeberrimas Aegypti
pyramides atque illam etiam quae Romae cernitur altissimam turrim in pyramidalem formam redactam factas fuisse arbitramur!
Quanta insuper arte Philo Atheniensibus armamentarium, illud a
Graecis scriptoribus tantopere laudatum opus, ut scribitur, im-
pensa et elegantia visendum, construxisse creditur! Quanta praeterea solertia arcam illam ob priscam generalis diluvii tempestatem
a Noe—humani generis vel conservatore vel consolatore potius,
quod nomen eius ex Hebraea in Latinam linguam interpretatum
significare videtur—fabrefactam fuisse putamus. Et, ne de vetustis
et admirabilibus aedificiis, quae paene innumerabilia fuerunt,
inpraesentiarum plura dicamus, et ad nova et recentiora paulisper

the Argonauts was the first to build the ship in which his companions dared to go out to sea, sail toward the horizon and—astonishing to say—cross the dreadful surges of the savage deep fearlessly and undaunted! So amazing was this spectacle to anyone
seeing it that everyone was forced to wonder at it—like that
shepherd in the poem by Accius who had never seen a ship before.
Spying this strange and godlike vessel at some distance from the
sea, completely terrified and thoroughly astonished, he spoke as
follows:

> so huge a mass glides
> groaning on the deep, with a great roar
> and rumble, rolling the waves before it,

and so on. I see that this technology of sailing has grown so
much—bit by bit through many ages up to our own day—that
progress has been miraculous. For they have not only become used
to daily trips on the British and icy Ocean, as the poet calls it, but
recently they have also tried to penetrate almost into deepest
Moor Land, beyond the former limits of navigation, where—so
I've heard—many islands, inhabited and cultivated but completely
unknown up to now, have been discovered.[43]

I also observe the enormous energy it took to build those huge 38
and celebrated pyramids in Egypt, as well as the very tall tower
seen in Rome that was made in the shape of a pyramid. What
great skill went into the arsenal that they believe Philo built in
Athens, so much praised by Greek writers as a work that must be
seen for its elegance and expense. I think that Noah—mankind's
defender or comforter, rather, which apparently is the meaning of
his name translated from Hebrew into Latin—also had such ingenuity when he constructed the ark in response to the original calamity caused by the universal flood. And, to say no more at present about antiquity's marvelous buildings, which were nearly
numberless, let me spend a moment on new and more recent

accedamus: quanto mentis acumine Philippus, cognomento Bru-
nelleschius, architectorum omnium nostri temporis facile princeps, magnum—vel potius maximum—Florentinae Aedis forni-
cem illum admirabilem nullis lignorum ferrorumve armamentis,
incredibile dictu, fabricatus est!

39   Nec minori vel maiori potius industria egregios pictores praeci-
puosque sculptores quaedam solemnia pinxisse et exculpsisse novimus. Quippe Zeusim, Apellem, Euphranorem tanto et tam subtili
artificio picturas suas effinxisse legimus, ut unus pictam Helenam
artificiosis liniamentis talem expressisse laudetur qualem Leda eius
mater caelesti partu edidisse videbatur. Alter equam canemque
tales depinxerat ut equi canesve transeuntes, viva quasi imagine
capti allectique, interdum hinnire ac latrare cogerentur quoniam ea
animalia vera esse existimabant quae in pariete picta in propatulo
cernebantur. Alius tanta arte recentes uvas una cum racemis ef-
fingebat ut volantes aves falsa specie deceptas parietem pictum
cum rostris pulsandum pascendi gratia compelleret. Quid de Iotto
nostro, optimo suorum temporum pictore, dicemus? Quem Romae, quem Neapoli, quem Venetiis, quem Florentiae, quem denique pluribus aliis celebratis urbibus multa ita egregie depinxisse
constat ut cum antiquis illis maximis eius artis magistris non
iniuria conferri et computari[37] posse videatur.

40   De Praxitele, Phidia, et Policleto, optimis et excellentissimis
statuariis, idem sentimus quod de commemoratis pictoribus paulo
ante sensisse diximus. Quorum primus Venerem in quodam Cni-
diorum[38] templo marmore ita venuste expressit ut vix a libidinosis
transeuntium complexibus[39] tuta et pudica servaretur. Ab alio
tamen nescio quo Syracusis vacca quaedam aenea conflata prae-
tereuntem taurum ad eius amorem et concubitum excitavit.
Duorum quoque aliorum pleraque maxima et admirabilia adhuc
Romae signa visuntur. Quid de Laurentio, peregregio nostri

structures: how sharp was the mind of Filippo, called Brunelleschi, in our own day surely the prince of all architects, who constructed an amazingly large vault — no, the largest one of all — for
Florence's Temple with no wooden or iron armature, as stunning
as that is to say!⁴⁴

I note that the best painters and leading sculptors had no less   39
energy (or even more) when they carved and painted certain public works. Indeed, Zeuxis, Apelles and Euphranor painted pictures
with such skill and delicacy — so I read — that one of them gets
praise for representing Helen with lines so refined that Leda, her
mother, might have given birth to her in Heaven. Another depicted a mare and a bitch so that horses and dogs passing by, at-
tracted and captivated as if the image were alive, sometimes felt a
need to whinny and bark because they thought they were seeing
real animals when they were painted on a public wall. Another
depicted fresh grapes so artfully on their stalks that birds flying by
were tricked by the false sight and felt compelled to peck the
painted wall with their beaks in order to eat. What to say about
our Giotto, the best painter of his time? He made many paintings
of such excellence in Rome, Naples, Venice, Florence and many
other famous cities that it seems right to add him in with those
ancient and supreme masters of this art and compare them.⁴⁵

About Praxiteles, Phidias and Polyclitus, the best and most   40
outstanding sculptors of all, my feeling is the same as what I said
about the painters just mentioned. The first of them represented
Venus so beautifully in marble for a certain temple of Cnidos that
it was hard to keep her safe and undefiled by the lustful embraces
of bypassers. In Syracuse, however, some other artist cast a cow in
bronze that aroused a bull that was passing by to love her and
mount her. To this day, many remains of the greatest and most
amazing works by the other two are seen in Rome. What to report
about Lorenzo, the most eminent sculptor of our time, whose

temporis statuario, referemus, cuius quidem excellentes admirabilesque virtutes in nobilitatis praesertim et celebratis sacrae Aedis nostrae ianuis in propatulo visuntur ?

41 Sed ut ad altiora et liberaliora ingenuarum artium monumenta ascendamus, quid de poetis Homero, Esiodo, Euripide, Pacuvio, Virgilio, Plauto, Horatio et Seneca ceterisque Graecis pariter ac Latinis commemorabimus? Quos poemata et figmenta sua tanta ingenii acie finxisse constat ut non sine aliquo caelestis mentis instinctu ea perfecisse et absolvisse videantur.

42 Nobilitatos historicos et oratores ac iurisconsultos, Tuchididem dicimus et Polibium, Herodotum ac Diodorum, Livium et Sallustium, Curtium ac Iustinum, Demosthenem et Aeschinem, Ciceronem et Hortensium, Scaevolam et Paulum, et reliquos huiusmodi praestantissimos viros omittamus: quos praecipuam elegantiam et magnam multarum rerum peritiam non sine singulari ingenio acquisivisse manifestum est. Philosophos insuper missos faciamus, Pythagoram, Platonem, Aristotelem, Theophrastum, Varronem, Ciceronem, Senecam et Plinium, quos in philosophia ita claruisse manifestum est ut de cunctis naturalibus rebus mirabiliter perscrutarentur subtilesque et acutas cogitationes suas Graecis et Latinis litteris commendarent. Iam de medicis medicinaeque auctoribus pariter sileamus. Quod quidem artificium accurata et diligens hominum solertia ad utilitatem suam mirum in modum excogitavit ut aegrotis et infirmis corporibus suis adinventionibus et oportunis pharmaciis[40] salubriter mederentur.

43 Astrologi insuper, motus conversionesque siderum ortus obitusque signorum et planetarum magna cum attentione suspicientes, in tantam eorum cognitionem pervenerunt ut varias Solis Lunaeque eclipses defectionesque multo ante praedicerent, et futuras frumentorum, olei, vini ubertates inopiasque praenoscerent. Quales multos et in primis Thalem Milesium, qui ob magnam quandam olei emptionem, cuius penuriam per astrologiam

outstanding and amazing talents are on public display, especially on the doors of our sacred Temple that he ennobled and glorified?[46]

But as I move up to the higher and nobler monuments of the 41 liberal arts, what shall I record about the poets — Homer, Hesiod, Euripides, Pacuvius, Vergil, Plautus, Horace, Seneca and the rest of the Greek and Latin authors? Everyone agrees that they composed their poetry and fiction with such great vision and talent that it must have been some prompting from a celestial mind by which they seem to have perfected these works and finished them.

Let me omit the eminent historians, orators and jurists whom I 42 say to be Thucydides and Polybius, Herodotus and Diodorus, Livy and Sallust, Curtius and Justinus, Demosthenes and Aeschines, Cicero and Hortensius, Scaevola and Paulus as well as other such outstanding figures: plainly, it took singular genius for them to acquire their special elegance and great expertise on many subjects. Let me also skip the philosophers whose brilliance in that field plainly enabled them to make amazing investigations of all kinds into nature and put their subtle and precise thoughts into Greek and Latin prose: Pythagoras, Plato, Aristotle, Theophrastus, Varro, Cicero, Seneca and Pliny. I shall also say nothing now about physicians and writers on medicine. Their careful and exact ingenuity devised this technology that they used, with astonishing effect, to provide healthy treatments for ailing and infirm bodies with suitable drugs and by means of their own discoveries.[47]

The astrologers too: by gazing up with great attention at the 43 motions and turnings of the stars and the risings and settings of the signs and planets, they came to know them so well that they predicted various eclipses of the Sun and disappearances of the Moon long in advance, foretelling abundance or scarcity of grain, oil and wine for the future. Many made such predictions, they say, especially Thales of Miletus: because of a large purchase of oil, having foreseen a lack of it by astrology, this poor man was made

futuram esse praeviderat, ex paupere dives effectus est. Et Archi-
medem Syracusanum extitisse tradunt, quem diversos Lunae, Solis
ac quinque errantium stellarum motus in sphaera nescio qua ab eo
mirabiliter fabrefacta ita illigasse dicitur ut omnes eorum dissimil-
limos motus, mirabile dictu, una regeret conversio. De quo Lactantius vehementer admiratus in secunda *Divinarum institutionum*
libro verba haec ponit:

> An Archimedes Siculus concavo aere similitudinem mundi
> ac figuram potuit machinari in quo ita Solem Lunamque
> composuit ut inaequales motus et caelestibus similes con-
> versionibus singulis quasi diebus efficerent,[41] non modo
> accessus Solis ac recessus vel incrementa diminutionesque
> Lunae verum etiam stellarum vel errantium vel vagantium
> dispares cursus orbis ille dum vertitur exhiberet?

44   Postremo quanta et quam magna theologorum nostrorum ingenia fuerint facile arbitrari et cogitare poterimus, si multiplices
libros eorum[42] accuratissime legere et intelligere voluerimus in quibus praecipua quaedam de mundi creatione, de angelorum pro-
ductione, de providentia Dei, de divinarum personarum distinc-
tione et de incarnatione Verbi ac ceteris huiusmodi vel maxime
continentur. Quae quidem omnia mysteria, etsi prophetis ab initio
divinitus revelata fuisse existimemus. A quibus postea ad supradic-
torum theologorum notitiam provenisse noscuntur.

Tanto tamen artificio ac tam acri et tam subtili ingenio illa prophetarum firma et solida fundamenta confirmasse et corroborasse
videntur, ut obscura illa et occulta et invisibilia atque incompre-
hensibilia propria mentis acie comprehendisse et vidisse compe-
riantur. Unde qui haec et cetera huiusmodi conspexisse putantur,
hi profecto docuisse perhibentur similem animum suum eius esse

wealthy. As for Archimedes, they say he lived in Syracuse and attached a moving Sun, Moon and five planets inside some sort of
marvelous sphere, constructed by him so that turning just the one
part of it, marvelous to relate, would regulate all their completely
different motions. Describing this with amazement in the second
book of his *Elements of Divinity*, Lactantius uses the following
words:

> Could Archimedes the Sicilian construct a likeness out of
> hollow bronze to resemble the world, putting a Sun and a
> Moon in it to produce motions that were unequal and
> aligned with each revolution of the heavens, almost to the
> day, so that when the sphere turns, it shows not only the
> Sun's comings and goings and the Moon's waxings and wan-
> ings but also the dissimilar courses of the stars and planets
> as they move?[48]

Finally, I could easily consider the many insights of our theolo-   44
gians, and judge how important they are, were I to read their
many books with great care and understand the particular teachings in them, especially on the creation of the world, the making
of angels, the providence of God, the distinction among the divine
persons, the incarnation of the Word and other such topics. These
are all mysteries, in fact, though I reckon that God revealed them
to prophets from the beginning. From the prophets — as we recognize — they came to be known by the aforementioned theologians.

Yet with their great skill, both sharp and subtle, the theologians
have evidently confirmed those prophetic fundamentals, corrobo-
rating them as firm and solid, and so we realize that they have
seen and understood, with their own keen intelligence, those
points that are obscure, hidden, unseen and incomprehensible.
Hence, the claim is that theologians, who are thought to have examined these and other such matters, have certainly taught that

qui ea sive in caelo sive in terra sive in mari totove mundo fabricatus esset.

45   Sed ne plura de humana intelligentia dicamus, quid de memoria, altera naturae dote, referemus? Cuius quidem quanta et quam
mirabilis potestas sit summatim dicere nedum explicare difficile vel
impossibile foret. Non quaerimus quanta memoria Simonides,
quanta Theodectes, quanta Cyneas (Pyrrhi ad Senatum legatus),
quanta Charmadas,[43] quanta Speusippus, quanta Metrodorus,
quanta Themistocles, quanta Cyrus, quanta Mitridates (duo
potentissimi reges), quanta Lucullus, quanta Hortensius, quanta
Seneca, quos ceteros praestantes et eruditos viros in hoc ipso memorandi officio excelluisse legimus. De communi hominum memoria loquimur et eorum maxime qui, in[44] quibusdam maioribus
studiis liberalibusque artibus versati, ingenuam magnarum rerum
contemplationi operam navaverunt, quorum quanta mens fuerit
existimare propterea difficile ac paene impossibile esse censemus,
quoniam infinita et quasi innumerabilia rerum et verborum vestigia meminerunt.

46   Cuius quidem etsi tanta vis est ut eam breviter pro dignitate
sua explicare nequeamus, artificium tamen quoddam sive a Simo-
nide poeta Chio sive ab aliquo alio praestantissimo viro repertum
fuisse accepimus quod maximum naturali memoriae lumen affer-
ret. In hoc tam admirabili omnium rerum thesauro inter cetera
duplex vis, una rerum, altera verborum, ita latere perhibetur et
creditur ut, quanquam per eam potentiam simul et res et verba
percipiamus, quosdam tamen una plus quam altera valuisse et vi-
guisse intelligamus, ceu de Lucullo et Hortensio apud Ciceronem
legisse meminimus. Haec enim ipsius in *Academicis* verba sunt:

> Habuit enim Lucullus divinam quandam memoriam rerum,
> verborum maiorem Hortensius, sed quo plus in negotiis

their own minds are like God's who fashioned what is in the heavens, on earth, in the sea or in the whole world.[49]

To say no more about human intelligence, what to report about   45
memory, another gift of nature? This would be difficult or impossible to describe summarily, much less explain how great and how amazing its power is. I am not asking how Simonides, how Theodectes, how Cyneas (legate to the Senate from Pyrrhus), how Charmadas, Speusippus, Metrodorus, Themistocles, Cyrus and Mithridates (either of those mighty kings), how Lucullus, Hortensius and Seneca — I am not asking how far they surpassed, according to what I've read, those other men who were expert and outstanding in this function of memory. I'm talking about ordinary human memory, especially in people devoted to studying the higher and liberal arts and applying themselves seriously to the work of thinking about larger issues. The reason why I reckon it difficult, nearly impossible, to judge how much intelligence they might have is that they remember countless traces, almost beyond number, of things and words.[50]

Even though the power of memory is so great that I cannot give   46
a short account in keeping with its value, I have heard that the poet Simonides of Chios or some other eminent person discovered a technique that would greatly illuminate natural memory. Among the other capacities of this quite marvelous and comprehensive treasury, people believe and assert that a two-part faculty — one for facts, one for words — lies concealed, so that, even though it has the power to grasp facts and words simultaneously, I understand that some have developed more strength and capability for one than for the other, as I recall having read in Cicero about Lucullus and Hortensius. These are his words from the *Academics*, in fact:

Lucullus had a quite divine memory for facts, Hortensius was better at words, but the first type of memory is superior

gerendis res quam verba prosunt, hoc erat memoria illa praestantior. Quam fuisse in Themistocle, quem facile Graeciae principem ponimus, singularem ferunt. Qui quidem etiam pollicenti cuidam se artem ei memoriae, quae tum primum proferebatur, traditurum respondisse dicitur oblivisci se malle discere, credo quod haerebant in memoria quaecunque audierat et viderat. Tali ingenio praeditus, Lucullus adiunxerat etiam illam quam Themistocles spreverat disciplinam; itaque, ut litteris consignamus quae monumentis mandare volumus, sic ille in animo res insculptas habebat,

et reliqua.

47   Duabus supradictis singularibus et praecipuis dotibus, quarum una singula quaeque intelligere, altera vero cuncta quae intellecta essent meminisse valeremus, sive Deum sive naturam liberum voluntatis imperium non immerito adhibuisse cognoscimus, ut per huiusmodi potestatem mala scilicet evitare et effugere, bona vero appetere et eligere possemus. Quod theologi liberum voluntatis arbitrium appellaverunt—de quo quidem quale et ante et post primi hominis transgressionem fuisset, qualeque in posteris remansisset—plura a sacris doctoribus eleganter tractata inpraesentiarum recitaremus, si idoneum in calce huius libri disserendi lo-
48   cum fore putaremus. Sed cum iam pridem de animae definitione et de eius immortalitate ac de tribus suis naturalibus potentiis, quo a nobis brevius et diligentius fieri potuerit, hucusque disseruerimus, multo melius fore existimavimus[45] ut de toto iam homine, adiutore et fautore Deo, dicere et tractare incipiamus—quandoquidem de duabus principalibus partibus ex quibus ipse componitur satis pro facultate nostra disseruisse meminimus.

because facts are more helpful than words for getting things done. They say that this memory was matchless in Themistocles, whom I rank as by far the best of the Greeks. When someone promised to teach him the art of memory, which was first being offered at that time, they say his answer was that he would sooner learn to forget—because everything he had heard or seen stuck in his memory, I believe. Gifted with such talent, Lucullus also added the instruction that Themistocles spurned, so that the facts that we record in letters when we want them to be documented he had engraved in his mind.[51]

To the two special and remarkable gifts just described, one enabling us to understand each and every thing, the other to recall all the things understood, I recognize that God or nature has added the will's free control—and rightly so, since plainly we could avoid and escape evil through such a power while choosing and seeking good. The theologians have called this the will's free authority. If I thought a discussion of this power helpful at the end of this book, here and now I would cite several choice treatments of it by the sacred doctors—what it was like before and after man's first offense and how it remained for later generations. But since by now I have already said as much as I can to give a brief and careful account of the soul's definition, its immortality and its three natural powers, I have thought it much better here, with God's help and support, to begin describing man as a whole—noting that I have given the best treatment I can of the two main parts of which man is composed. 47 48

LIBER TERTIUS

1   Quoniam corpus et animam duo sola esse intelligebamus ex quibus homo constabat, ac quaedam propria et peculiaria corporis,
quaedam vero animi singularia et admirabilia, nonnulla etiam
utrique coniuncto communia videbamus, idcirco, cum plura de
egregiis quibusdam humani corporis muneribus primo atque de
praecipuis quoque rationalis animae dotibus et privilegiis secundo
libro hactenus tractasse meminerimus, deinceps hoc[1] tertio pauca
de toto homine dum erit in hac vita mortali disseremus, quem ab
omnipotenti Deo mirabiliter constitutum fuisse iure dubitare et
ambigere non possumus, quandoquidem partes illas ex quibus
hominem ipsum construi ac componi intelligimus divinitus factas
creatasque antea probaverimus.

2   At vero siquis rudis et ignarus rerum de hoc ipso forte suspica-
retur, tunc profecto omnis eius suspicio scrupulusque cessaret cum
has duas — corpoream scilicet et spiritalem, tam diversas ac tam
distantes naturas inter seque contrarias — simul et in unum ita
admirabiliter ac vere divinitus convenisse vel parumper consideraverit. Quod aliter quam ab omnipotenti Deo nullatenus fieri
potuisse certissime scimus, praesertim cum ea sibi ipsis maxime
adversantia ac repugnantia videamus. Verum quanquam id ipsum
ex his quae in praecedentibus libris late copioseque explicavimus
ita certum et manifestum sit ut nulla ratione nullave auctoritate ad
probandum et confirmandum indigere videatur, quia tamen res
magna et ardua est — ubi omnis nostra disputatio fundatur et
unde quoque reliquus orationis nostrae cursus emanabit et pro-
fluet — paulo altius ab origine repetemus.

BOOK THREE

Since I have learned that body and soul are the only two things 1
that make up a human being, and that some extraordinary items
belong to the body while others are remarkable and unique to the
soul, and since I have also seen that some are shared by body and
soul combined, therefore, since up to this point I have made various claims, in a first book, about certain outstanding endowments
of the human body and, in a second, about the special gifts and
privileges of the rational soul as well, next, in this third book, I
shall discuss a few issues about the human being as a whole during
its existence in this mortal life—a being whose composition is a
miracle of God Almighty, which we have no right to doubt or
dispute, seeing that those parts which I have learned to be the
constituents and components of the human I have already proved
to be creations and products of divine power.[1]

Should some crude and uninformed person waver on this very 2
point, all his problems and worries would surely cease if he took
even a minute to consider how these two natures—the bodily and
the spiritual, so different from one another, so far apart and so
contrary—have joined together as one in a truly divine and marvelous manner. We know with complete certainty that this could
never have been done except by Almighty God, especially when we
see these two natures in all-out clashes and conflicts. However,
even though detailed and extensive explanations in the previous
two books have made this point so manifestly certain that it needs
no confirming by argument or authority, still, because the question
is serious and difficult—forming the basis for my whole presentation and providing the source from which the rest of my account
arises and flows—I shall revisit the problem from the beginning in
a bit more depth.[2]

3   Ac primo quid sit homo breviter ostendemus. Omnis enim quae de aliqua re suscipitur institutio — iuxta veterem illam famosamque sententiam — debet a definitione proficisci ut intelligatur quid sit id de quo disputetur. Hominem animal sociale et civile, rationis et intelligentiae capax, ab errantibus, luscis et caecutientibus philosophis definitum esse novimus. Nos igitur — quibus occultum et abstrusum veritatis lumen ex divinis sacrarum scripturarum oraculis illustratum evidenter apparuit — hanc ipsam (qualiscunque est gentilium et ethnicorum hominum) descriptionem etiam atque etiam considerantes non usquequaque perfectam esse comperimus.

Nam cum eos mentem suam fragili quidem et tenebroso propriorum corporum domicilio illigatam nec ullo nisi naturali dumtaxat lumine sustentatam possedisse, atque propterea reconditam quandam magnarum rerum obscuritatem humanis disputationibus penitus et omnino assequi non potuisse intelligeremus, supernaturali et divino splendore fulciti et adiuti, in hunc certe modum corrigere et sic emendare audebimus: ut homo sit animal cum reliquis adiectionibus supradictis, partim mortale, dum est in hac vita saeculari, partim vero immortale, ubi a mortuis resurrexerit. Sed postquam nonnullam de certis antiquorum philosophorum erroribus quasi fortuitam mentionem fecimus, hanc partem, quantum ad praesens propositum spectare et pertinere censebimus, parumper prosequamur.[2]

4   Multi mundum fortuito, ut Leucippus, Democritus, Dicaearchus et Epicurus factum, multi vero ut Peripatetici semper fuisse opinantur; Stoici autem mundum ab omnipotenti Deo formatum et constitutum esse dicunt. Qui fortuito factum contendunt nulla Dei providentia regi gubernarive confirmant. Peripatetici, quamvis semper fuisse existimaverint, divina tamen providentia — una cum Stoicis — administrari gubernarive senserunt. Sed, ne forte aliqua

First, let me briefly show what a human is. To begin any in- 3
struction about anything—according to that ancient and famous
statement—one must start with a definition in order to understand what it is that is being discussed. We know that the human
has been defined as a social and civic animal, capable of reason and
understanding, by philosophers who wander about with one eye
shut and find it hard to see. We therefore—to whom the reserved
and hidden light of truth has been plainly revealed and clarified by
the divine oracles of sacred Scripture—after repeatedly examining
this description (whatever its standing may be among heathens
and pagan people), we find it not altogether complete.[3]

In fact, with help and support from God's supernatural illumination, I have come to see that the thinking of these philosophers
was actually tied to the frail and gloomy habitation of their own
bodies and sustained only by the natural light. Hence, since their
human deliberations could not get them a thorough and complete
grasp of the special secret that these great problems conceal, I shall
venture some corrections and improvements—on this point, to be
sure: that man is the animal with the extra features described
above, being partly mortal, while existing in this temporal life, but
partly immortal, when he rises from the dead. Having noted—
where they happened to come up—particular mistakes made by
ancient philosophers, let me pursue this point for a moment, to
the extent that I judge it pertinent to the present subject.

Many, like Leucippus, Democritus, Dicaearchus and Epicurus, 4
think that the world was produced by chance, while many Peripatetics think it has always existed, but the Stoics say that the world
was formed and put in place by an all-powerful God. Those who
maintain that it was produced by chance assert that no divine
providence rules and governs it. The Peripatetics, while supposing
that the world has always existed, still thought—along with the
Stoics—that divine providence rules and governs it. And yet, even

praedictorum philosophorum haeresis (vel, ut planius et expressius loquamur, secta) ab humanis erroribus aliena esset, Stoici—nimirum ceteris omnibus graviores—de hac ipsa materia ita confuse disseruisse comperiuntur ut Deum quem mundi fabricatorem arbitrabantur operi suo immiscuisse videantur, unde illud Virgilianum natum esse creditur:

> totamque infusa per artus
> mens agitat molem et magno se corpore miscet.

Itaque—Academicis tanquam de omnibus ambigentibus quoniam nihil sciri posse existimabant penitus praetermissis—et Epicureos divinam providentiam omnino tollentes et Peripateticos mundi creationem abnegantes et Stoicos Deum operi suo immiscentes aberrasse constat.

5   Ceterum nos—quanquam homunculi et ignari simus, praesertim si cum tantis ac tam magnis philosophis comparemur—per sacras tamen scripturas caelitus edocti et divino quodam splendore illuminati, contra falsam gentilium ethnicorumque virorum sapientiam dicere ac disserere praesumentes, mundum ab omnipotenti Deo ex nihilo creatum ac gratia hominis constitutum asserere et confirmare non dubitamus. Credere namque ipsum frustra et incassum tanta ac tam miranda opera constituisse absurdum quiddam et longe a veritate alienum esse quis inficias ibit? Nec quoque propter mundum mundus ipse factus est, nullo enim harum rerum usu indigere videtur, cum omnino sensu careat. Nec etiam dici potest Deum propter se ipsum mundum fabricasse cum sine ipso esse potuisset et posset, quemadmodum ante creationem plane et aperte fuisse cognovimus.

Relinquitur ergo animantium causa mundum esse constructum, cum rebus ipsis ex quibus constat animantes ipsas—uti videamus, quatenus per praedictum earum rerum usum sese conservare ac per hunc modum degere et vivere valeant. Si ceteras igitur

though no group (or sect, to put it more plainly and directly) of the philosophers just mentioned may be strangers to human error, the Stoics—certainly more serious than all the rest—are regarded as so confused on this point that evidently they mixed God up with his work, while still taking him to be the maker of the world, which is thought to be the source of Vergil's remark:

> spread through every joint,
> mind activates the mass, mingling with that great body.

Plainly they were mistaken, then: Epicureans by completely eliminating divine providence, Peripatetics by denying the creation of the world and Stoics by mixing God in with his work—though I leave the Academics out entirely as doubting everything because they thought that nothing can be known.[4]

But I—ignorant little person though I am, especially compared   5 with philosophers of such great stature—still presume to dispute with pagan men and speak against the false wisdom of heathens because heaven has instructed me with sacred Scripture and enlightened me with a kind of divine light, leaving me with no doubt about asserting that Almighty God created the world from nothing or affirming that he put it in place for mankind's sake. For who will deny that it would be absurd and a far cry from the truth to believe that God made so many wonderful things without reason or use? Moreover, it was not because of the world that the world itself was made: in fact, what we see is a world not needing to enjoy the things in it since it is utterly insentient. Nor can it be said that God constructed the world for his own sake since he can and could exist without it, just as we know he did before the creation—clearly and plainly.[5]

The alternative, then, is a world constructed because of what lives in it and providing the makings of such beings—as we may see, in that they can keep themselves in existence by using such things, which enable them to live and carry on. If it is clear that

animantes hominis tantummodo causa factas esse appareret, mundum utique hominis dumtaxat gratia a Deo factum et constitutum fuisse concluderetur, quoniam ipsum propter animantes factum et eas propter hominem factas dicimus. At hoc ipsum ex eo certum esse declaratur quod omnia quaecunque facta sunt soli homini deservire ac mirum in modum famulari — meridiana, ut dicitur, luce clarius — conspicimus. Quo quidem probato vereque concesso, hominem — cuius gratia mundum creatum confitemur — utique a Deo factum fuisse manifestum est.

6   Unde frivolae et vanae de formatione hominis cunctorum poetarum opiniones extiterunt. Poetae namque hominem a Prometheo, Iapeti filio, de luto factum esse finxerunt. Sed fieri non potuit ut homo verum et vivum hominem faceret, cum posset eadem ratione generari qua ipse Prometheus ex Iapeto natus erat. Qui quidem, si fuit homo, generare hominem potuit, facere vero non potuit. Verum quia poetas non omnino mentiri solere sed figuris et aenigmatibus sententias suas involvere et obscurare vulgo existimatur et creditur, Lactantius et Augustinus, huiusmodi vulgi opinionem apprime secuti, eos in hac ipsa fictione non usque quaque fuisse mentitos putaverunt, sed primum omnium Prometheum de molli ac pingui luto simulachrum hominis formasse ab eoque primitus natam esse artem statuas et simulachra fingendi tradiderunt, siquidem Iovis eum temporibus fuisse scribunt, quibus primum templa construi et novi deorum cultus esse coeperunt.

7   Proinde formatio hominis proprium quoddam solius Dei opus est: nam ipse rerum omnium machinator, cum cuncta antea creasset, postremo fecit et formavit hominem. Quod Cicero, quamvis expers caelestium litterarum, plane tamen et aperte sensisse

the other living things have been made only on account of humans, the obvious conclusion is that God made the world and set it up only for mankind's sake, the reason being that the world was made for living beings and they were made because of man, showing the following to be a certainty: we see—clearer than the light of noon, as they say—that whatever exists has been made just to serve humans and supply their needs wonderfully well. Once this has been accepted and recognized, it is surely obvious that man—for whose sake we grant that the world was created—was made by God.[6]

Hence, the views of all the poets about the forming of man 6 have been conspicuously silly and worthless. The fact is that poets have fabricated the story that Prometheus, the son of Iapetus, made a man from mud. But a human could not possibly have made a real, living human, though a man could be begotten in the same way that Prometheus was born of Iapetus. If Iapetus was a man, he could certainly beget a man, but he could not really make one. People ordinarily think that poets are not habitual and complete liars, however, usually believing that they wrap their views in riddles and hide them under metaphors. This is why Lactantius and Augustine, who were much taken with the ordinary view, thought that the poets were not lying about everything when they made this story up. What poets reported was that Prometheus first shaped a human likeness from soft, thick mud, and that the art of fashioning statues and likenesses started with him: they write that Prometheus lived in the time of Jupiter, in fact, when worshipping the gods was new and people first started to build temples.[7]

Accordingly, the work of forming a man is something that be- 7 longs only to God: having already created everything else, this architect of all things made man last of all and gave him form. Although Cicero was without the heavenly writings, we still see—plainly and clearly—that he had this view, noting that he has used

videtur, quandoquidem in primo *De legibus* libro verba haec apposita fuisse cernuntur: animal hoc providum, sagax, multiplex, acutum, plenum rationis et consilii, quem vocamus hominem, praeclara quadam conditione generatum a summo Deo solum extitisse cognovimus. Est enim ex tot animantium generibus ac naturis particeps rationis et cogitationis, cum cetera sint omnia expertia.

Quod veteres — et novi, ut ita dixerim — theologi multo clarius et evidentius aperuerunt. Nam Deum, consumato et perfecto mundo, animalia varii generis ex dissimilibus formis, magna et minora, ut fierent imperasse prodiderunt. Unde facta sunt bina, idest diversi sexus singula, ex quorum variis fetibus et aer et terra et maria complerentur. Deditque eis omnibus generatim Deus alimenta de terra ut usui esse hominibus[3] possent — alia nimirum ad cibos, alia vero ad vestimentum. Quae autem magnarum erant virium idcirco praebuit ut in excolenda terra *iuvarent*, unde sunt dicta *iumenta*.

Item, rebus omnibus mirabili descriptione compositis, regnum sibi aeternum parare constituit et innumerabiles paene animas procreare voluit, quibus immortalitatem largitus est. Tum fecit ipse sibi simulachrum sensibile atque intelligens — hoc est ad imaginis sui ipsius formam, qua nihil poterat esse perfectius. Hominem figuravit ex limo terrae, unde *homo* nuncupatus est, quod sit fictus ex *humo*.

Atque hoc ipsum cuncta prophetarum, evangelistarum et apostolorum oracula et singula quaeque Catholicorum doctorum eloquia plane et aperte declarant. Quae, ne nimii simus, perpetuo silentio praeterire quam prolixo sermone explicare maluimus, praesertim cum talia sint ut de eis nullatenus ambigere et dubitare valeamus.

these words in the first book *On the Laws*: we have recognized this prudent animal that we call human — careful, shrewd, clear-sighted, full of reason and counsel — to be the only one produced by the greatest God in a special state of nobility. Out of all the types and kinds of living things, this is actually the one that shares in reason and thought, while all others lack them.[8]

Theologians in antiquity — and today, in my opinion — have shown this much more clearly and plainly. For they have noted that God, once he had done with the world and made it complete, commanded that there should be animals of various kinds with different forms, large and smaller. He made these two-by-two, each of a different sex, to fill the air, the land and the seas with their young of various types. And from the earth he gave them all nourishment suited to their kinds so that they could be of use to humans — some for food, obviously, but others for clothing. But those that had great strength he provided for the purpose of *helping* to cultivate the land, which is why they are called *hauling* beasts.[9]

Also, after everything was put in place and wonderfully ordered, God determined to set up an eternal kingdom for himself and wished to go on creating souls almost beyond number, endowing them with immortality. Then he made himself a likeness that was sentient and intelligent — a form in his own image, in other words, than which nothing could have been more perfect. He fashioned a man from the mud of the earth, which is why he was named *human* from the *humus*.[10]

This is the declaration — plain and clear — of all the oracles of prophets, evangelists and apostles, of each and every utterance by Catholic teachers. Lest I go on too long, I prefer to keep my silence unbroken and pass their statements over rather than comment on them extensively, especially since they are such that we can have no doubt about them or any hesitation.

8   Quod si veteres illi sapientes viri, Graeci ac[4] Latini, picturam
sculpturamve aliquam propterea apprime laudare et commendare
solebant, quod Zeusim, quod Appellem, quod Euphranorem,
quod Fabium, peregregios pictores, vel quod Phidiam, quod Prax-
itelem, quod Policletum, quod Parrhasium optimos illorum temporum sculptores habuisse arbitrarentur, quid nos in hac ipsa hominis fabricatione certa quadam omnipotentis Dei figura facere
debemus—qui de Deo vero et solo humani generis auctore non
immerito gloriamur? Et si enim illi summi earum artium magistri
fuisse viderentur, homines tamen erant, qui facile labi et aberrare
poterant. Quod de hoc nostro opificio iure suspicari et titubare
non possumus, cum id a Deo optimo maximo, eius conditore,
profluxisse et emanasse sentiamus, qui falli decipere non potest.

9   At dicet fortasse quispiam statuam picturamve aliquam apud
veteres non tam ob id laudari et commendari consuevisse quod
optimos statuarios pictoresque opifices habuerint[5] sed potius quod
egregie decenterque formata et pulchris quoque liniamentis distincta videbatur. Quod si nos ita antiquitus contigisse conce-
deremus—ut debita membrorum conformatio ad pulchritudinem
cuiuscunque operis maxime valeret, quanquam summa eorum
magistrorum excellentia ad magnitudinem laudum plurimum con-
ferebat—quid nos de hac hominis fabricatione respondebimus?
Nonne—cum ex his quae corporibus extrinsecus apparent, tum ex
illis etiam quae in intimo et pretioso humanarum animarum thesauro inclusa perhibentur—pulcherrime et admirabiliter ac divinitus factam fuisse asseremus? Sed ne forte maxima ac nimia huma-
nitatis nostrae gloria allecti ac protracti longius a proposito evagari
videamur, ad id parumper redeamus unde digressi sumus.

10   Cum igitur hominem ab omnipotenti Deo factum esse antea
probaverimus, reliquum est ut qualem ipsum magister ille supremus fecerit primum paulo latius ostendamus. Quod deinde et
quale ei ita mirabiliter constituto officium exercitiumque dederit
breviter enarrabimus. Postremo cur eum talem constituerit

But if those ancient wise men, Greek as well as Latin, used to 8
give special praise and honor to painting and sculpture, concluding
that Zeuxis, Apelles, Euphranor and Fabius should be seen as
painters of great excellence or deeming Phidias, Praxiteles, Polycle-
tus and Parrhasius to be the best sculptors of their day, what
should we decide about the making of man with a figure that is
God Almighty's in some sure sense — we who rightly exult in the
true God and sole author of the human race? Although those
masters were indeed seen as supreme in their crafts, they were still
human, quick to err and go astray. About the workmanship that
made us we cannot rightly suppose this and waver since we realize
that the best and supreme God, who cannot go wrong or be deceived, is its source, origin and framer.[11]

Yet someone might say that the ancients used to praise a statue 9
or honor a picture not so much because they regarded the craftsmen as the best sculptors or painters but rather because the art
seemed beautifully and fitly shaped and was also adorned with
lovely lines. But if I grant this situation in ancient times — that the
beauty of any work at all would be most enhanced by a becoming
arrangement of parts, even though it was the supreme excellence
of their masters that most often produced great praise — how shall
I respond about this making of a human? Shall I not assert — both
from how bodies look on the outside and also from what we ascribe to the inside, within the rich inner treasury of human
souls — that this was done, most beautifully and wonderfully, by
divine power? But let me not seem to stray from my topic, drawn
on and distracted by loud and excessive boasting about our own
humanity: I shall go back for a moment to where I left off.

And so, since I have already confirmed that man was made by 10
Almighty God, what remains is to show in a little more detail
what sort of being that supreme master made. Then I shall briefly
explain what role and what kind of employment God gave to this
human who was so wonderfully put together. Finally I shall say

deinceps referemus. Quibus pro facultate nostra ieiune exiliterque tractatis, nonnullas praeterea nobilitatas et egregias humanae naturae conditiones adhibere et adiungere conabimur.

11   Primum itaque Deus hoc—tam dignum ac tam praestans— eius opificium tanti fecisse et existimasse videtur ut hominem formosissimum, ingeniosissimum, sapientissimum, opulentissimum ac denique potentissimum efficeret. Eius namque forma ita sublimis et excellens est (quemadmodum in primo libro uberrime ac latissime explicavimus) ut plerique tam profani quam sacri scriptores deos immortales nulla alia praeter quam humana figura velut ceteris omnibus longe sublimiore atque excellentiore in templis delubrisque pingi et effingi voluerint—quorum formam vel humanam vel potius nostram divinam fore oportere censebant, ceu Cicero in primo *De natura deorum* plane et aperte declarat, cuius verba haec sunt: auxerunt haec eadem poetae, pictores, opifices; erat autem non facile agentis aliquid et molientis deos in aliarum formarum imitatione servare.

Quippe huiusmodi vana vel picta vel sculpta deorum *simulachra* a *similitudine* nomen acceperunt, sed solum et verum Dei simulachrum homo est: in quo quidem quibuscunque eruditis simul atque piis consideratoribus divina quaedam similitudo apparere et relucere dignoscitur. Quae enim compositio membrorum, quae conformatio liniamentorum, quae figura, quae species—ut de extrinsecis et apparentibus dicamus—quam humana potest esse pulchrior? Nam si mundus ipse ita decorus et pulcher est ut pulchrior esse excogitarive non possit, siquidem ab ornatu et munditie nomen accepit, quam pulchrum et quam formosum illud existimare debemus cuius gratia mundi pulchritudinem factam fuisse novimus?

12   At vero terras, maria, caelos astris stellisque distinctos, diversas solarium et lunarium luminum varietates, eorumque omnium ortus et occasus atque in omni aeternitate ratos immutabilesque

why God put him together in that way—and so on. After covering these topics in my thin and scanty way, I shall try to bring in some especially renowned features of human nature and add them on.[12]

First then, God evidently prized this work of his—so worthy 11 and so extraordinary—finding it so important it that he made humankind the most handsome, clever, judicious, noble and finally the most capable of all. For the human figure towers so high (as my first book showed abundantly and in detail) that many writers, both sacred and secular, would have it that the immortal gods were painted in temples and portrayed in shrines only as human just because that form stands so much taller and higher—a form, this human form or rather our own, that had to be divine, they thought, as Cicero explains fully and clearly in his first book *On the Nature of the Gods*, using these words: poets, painters and artisans have developed the same practices; it hadn't been easy to preserve the actions or undertakings of gods while representing them in other forms.[13]

False *semblances* of the gods, whether painted or carved, actually got that name from *resemblance*, though the human is God's sole and true semblance: in it we perceive a kind of divine resemblance showing itself and shining forth, according to those who have reflected on this with reverence as well as learning. What framing of limbs, what symmetry of lines, what shape, what looks—meaning the external and visible—can be more beautiful than the human? For if the universe itself is so lovely and beautiful that nothing more beautiful can be imagined, seeing that it gets its name from universal splendor and elegance, then how fair and beautiful must we judge the one for whose sake we know the beauty of the universe to have been produced?[14]

But with the aim of surveying lands and seas and the heavens 12 marked with stars and luminaries, of observing the solar and lunar lights in their variety, putting all the risings and settings before our

cursus ante oculos nostros considerandi et contemplandi causa parumper constituamus,[6] ut qualis et quantus sit huiusmodi totus mundi ornatus paulo clarius et evidentius elucescat.

Ideo varia supradictarum rerum ornamenta paulisper consideremus. Fontium gelidas perennitates, liquores perlucidos amnium, riparum vestitus viridissimos — diversis coloribus atque dissimilibus, ut ita dixerim, inter se viriditatibus distinctos — speluncarum concavas profunditates, saxorum asperitates, impendentium montium altitudines immensitatesque camporum circumspiciamus: quae vero et quam varia genera bestiarum, vel cicurum vel ferarum, qui volucrum lapsus atque cantus, qui pastus, quae vita silvestrium. Quid denique de humano genere dicemus? Qui quasi cultores terrae constituti, non patiuntur eam nec immanitate beluarum efferari nec stirpium asperitate vastari; quorumque operibus agri, insulae, litoraque collucent distincta terris et urbibus.

Quae quidem omnia si ut animis sic oculis uno aspectu videre et conspicere possemus, quale et quam mirabile spectaculum nobis ita videntibus et conspicientibus appareret, nec verbis abunde explicare nec mente satis excogitare valeremus!

13   Etenim si priscis temporibus illi praestantissimi viri se aliquid dignum assecutos fuisse putabant qui ostium Ponti viderant et eas angustias per quas penetraverat Argos, prima illa et celebrata navis, aut ii qui Occeani freta illa conspexerant, ubi rapax unda Europam Libiamque dividens ab invicem dirimebat, quod et quale spectaculum fore censeremus si totam terram — situm, formam, circumscriptionem, pulchritudinem — simul contueri liceret? At vero, quoniam omnia in unum simul collecta corporeo visu conspicere videreque nequimus, saltem singula quaeque maiora et digniora paulo uberius designemus atque aliquanto latius amplificemus, ut per hanc amplificationem nostram — haec ipsa tam pulchra et tam decora ac tam admirabilia quandoquidem conspicari non

eyes, the changeless circuits fixed for all eternity, surely I may take a moment to describe these things, so that the whole beauty of such a universe might be a bit plainer in nature and clearer in extent.[15]

So for a minute let me review the glories of what I have named. All around I see ageless icy springs, rivers of clear water, their banks clothed in brightest green — different shades of green, if I may call them that, distinct and varicolored — deep and hollow caverns, craggy rocks, peaks tall and overhanging, fields without measure, with animals wild and tame in their many different kinds, birds soaring and singing, pasture and thriving woodland. Then what to say of humankind? Put here to till the land, humans will not let the earth be ravaged by wild animals or remain a wilderness of barren stalks; dividing every field, island and shore into districts and cities, they make them all resplendent with their labors.[16]

If we could take all this in and see it with ours eyes at a single glance, as the mind can do, what a great and astonishing vision would be ours to gaze at and observe, though we would not have words enough to describe it or thoughts to conceive such a thing![17]

Indeed, if those eminent men of ancient times thought they had achieved something worthwhile by looking on the Black Sea's entry and those narrows penetrated by the Argos, that first and celebrated ship, or by sighting the straits that lead to Ocean, where the furious waters divide to separate Europe from Africa, then what a spectacular scene might we think lay before us if the whole earth — place, form, outline and beauty — could be taken in all at once? But in fact, since we cannot gather it all together to see with the eyes of our bodies and observe, we can at least mark certain items out as a bit more important or worthier and give them a little more attention, so that then — even though we cannot really have a view of all this that is so fine, so lovely and so amazing — we

13

possumus — saltem multo melius comminisci et contemplari valeamus.

14   Quanta itaque est Maris Occeani pulchritudo quamque incredibilis magnitudo, quo universus terrarum orbis ambiri et circuiri videtur; quantus deinde huius nostri Mediterranei decor et ornatus quod ab illo, velut a fonte et a capite profluens, plerasque provincias regionesque mirabiliter abluit: quae deinde species, quae magnitudo, quae moles, quae varietas universi, quae amoenitates orarum ac litorum, quot genera quanque disparia, partim submersarum, partim fluitantium et innantium beluarum!

15   Quanta quoque sunt caelorum ornamenta! Sol enim, qui nobis ita parvus apparet ut humanum caput vel paululum excedere videatur, magnitudine tamen sua multis partibus tota Terra circa quam continuo quodam ac perpetuo motu volvitur maior est. Isque oriens et occidens diem noctemque conficit, et modo accedens ac modo recedens binas in singulos annos reversiones ab extremo contrarias facit, quarum intervallo tum quasi tristitia quadam contrahit Terram, tum vicissim laetificat ut cum caelo hilarata videatur. Luna — cuius magnitudo Terra ipsa minor est — his quibus Sol spatiis vagatur. Reliquae stellae, quas *vagas* et *errantes* Graeco verbo *planetas* dicimus, circa Terram feruntur; eodemque motu oriuntur et occidunt — quorum motus tum incitantur, tum retardantur, saepe etiam insistunt. Sequitur stellarum inerrantium maxima multitudo: quarum distinctio profecto talis et tanta est ut eo spectaculo nihil pulchrius, nihil ornatius, nihil denique admirabilius fieri reperirive[7] excogitari poterat.

16   Quod quidem omnipotens Deus non solum idcirco fecisse videtur ut maius et evidentius ipsius universi ornamentum appareret sed etiam ne, Solis lumine ad occasum decedente, obscura et caeca nox taetris atque horrentibus tenebris nimium ingravesceret noceretque viventibus hominique obesset — cuius gratia cuncta

can still get a much better idea of it by directing our attention in this way.[18]

How great is the beauty of the Ocean Sea, then, and how un- 14 believable its extent, seen to enclose and encircle the whole globe of the Earth; next how great the splendor and grace of this Mediterranean of ours that flows from that Ocean, its source and origin, to wash many tracts and territories with its wonders: so what a sight it all is—in size, in bulk, in variety, in delights of coast and shore, with so many types, no two alike, of beasts swimming in it, some afloat and some below![19]

How great likewise are heaven's beauties. Though the Sun may 15 look so small to us that it seems not much bigger than a person's head, its actual size is larger by many increments than the whole Earth around which it revolves with a motion that always keeps going. Rising and setting, the Sun makes day and night, sometimes approaching, sometimes withdrawing, making two opposed turns every year from the opposite end, and in the interval between these turns it constricts the Earth as if to sadden it, then reversing to make it happy, so it seems, and cheered to be in heaven's company. The Moon—smaller in size than the Earth— goes back and forth in those spaces where the Sun is. The rest of the stars, which we call *planets* from the Greek word for *roaming* or *wandering*, go around the Earth; they rise and set with the same motion—moving sometimes at full speed, sometimes slowing, sometimes stopping. Next comes the greatest possible multitude of fixed stars: so much do they stand out that no sight can have been made, found, or imagined to be fairer, lovelier or more amazing.[20]

Almighty God seems to have done this not only to make the 16 beauty of the universe greater and more visible but also, as the Sun's light vanishes in the west, to lighten the nighttime burden of foul and fearful darkness, dense and dreary, lest living things be injured and mankind hindered—for whose sake he knew how to

quaeque viventia instituisse et ordinasse noverat. Proinde ipsas noctis tenebras ob tantam ac tam incredibilem parvarum stellarum numerositatem multis minutisque luminibus temperavit.

17   Quae quidem quasi omnia Cicero in primo *Tusculanarum disputationum* his verbis comprehendere et complecti videtur:

> Primum videmus speciem candoremque caeli, deinde conversionis celeritatem tantam quantam cogitare non possumus, tum vicissitudines dierum ac noctium, commutationesque temporum quadripartitas ad maturitatem frugum et ad temperationem corporum aptas, eorumque omnium[8] moderatorem et ducem Solem, Lunamque accretione et diminutione luminis quasi fastorum notantem et significantem dies; tum in eodem orbe in duodecim partes distributo quinque stellas ferri eosdem cursus constantissime servantes disparibus inter se motibus, nocturnamque caeli formam undique sideribus ornatam; tum globum Terrae eminentem e mari, fixum in medio mundi universi loco, duabus oris distantibus habitabilem et cultum — quarum altera, quam nos incolimus,
>
> > sub axe posita ad stellas septem, unde horrifer
> > aquilonis stridor gelidas molitur nives,
>
> altera australis ignota nobis, quam Graeci vocant[9] *antitona*, ceteras partes incultas quod aut frigore rigeant aut urantur calore. Hic autem ubi habitamus non intermittit suo tempore
>
> > caelum nitescere, arbores frondescere,
> > vites laetifice pampinis pubescere,
> > ramos bacharum ubertate incurvescere,
> > segetes largiri fruges, florere omnia,
> > fontes scatere, herbis prata convestirier;

put every living thing in its place and order. To this end, he tempered the dark night with many tiny lights from an astonishingly great multitude of little stars.

Cicero seems to have understood almost all of this, covering it   17
in the first book of his *Tusculan Disputations* and using these words:

> First we see heaven's beauty and brightness, then a turning so fast we cannot comprehend it, next days alternating with nights, fourfold changes of season suited to ripen crops and keep bodies well tempered, all of them commanded and governed by the Sun, while the Moon's light waxes and wanes as if she were keeping track of the days and marking a calendar; then five stars distributed through the twelve regions of the same sphere, keeping their orbits with complete regularity as each one moves differently than the others, and the sky's beauty at night, attired everywhere with stars; next the ball of the Earth pushing up from the sea, fixed at the center point of the whole universe, habitable and cultivated in two regions far apart — one of them, where we live,
>
> > sits under seven polar stars, where horrid
> > noisy northern winds push at frozen snow,
>
> while the other region in the south, unknown to us, the Greeks call *antichthona* — and other parts are not cultivated because they are either frozen stiff or else blazing hot. Here where we live, however, the seasons never fail with
>
> > a sky that glitters, trees in bud and leaf,
> > joyous tendrils worn by springtime vines,
> > branches bending down with ripened berries,
> > fields all lush with fruit and all in flower,
> > brooks that babble, meadows clothed in green;

tum multitudinem pecudum, partim ad vescendum, partim
ad cultus agrorum, partim ad vehendum, partim ad corpora
vestienda; hominemque ipsum — quasi contemplatorem caeli
ac deorum eorumque cultorem, atque hominis utilitati agros
omnes et maria parentia.

18   Si ergo mundi huius ornatus (ne forte in rebus tam claris tamque evidentibus longiores simus), talis ac tantus esse perhibetur et
creditur, qua forma, qua pulchritudine, quo decore hominem praeditum existimare debemus, cuius solius causa mundum ipsum
pulcherrimum et ornatissimum factum esse non dubitamus? Non
mirum igitur si veteres novique ingeniosarum artium inventores —
quoniam naturam divinam omnibus rebus tum[10] inanimatis tum
animatis[11] excellere ac praestare arbitrabantur, nec ullam figuram
humana forma pulchriorem existimabant — ut dii instar hominum
effingerentur pingerenturve consensisse videbantur.

19   At quam pulchra et quam decora sit haec hominis species ex eo
maxime[12] intueri licet quod nemo est quin emori malit quam converti in aliquam figuram bestiae, quamvis, si fieri posset, sibi hominis mentem reservaret — ceu de Apuleio quodam Madaurensi fertur, quem in asellum reservata sibi humana mente conversum
fabulantur. Sed postquam ad pristinum veri hominis statum mirabiliter redierat, de omnibus quae ea[13] tempestate evenerant librum
quendam composuit, quem *De asino aureo* appellavit.

Ac profecto talis — hoc est pulcherrima et decentissima — huius
divini potius quam humani animalis forma, quemadmodum re
vera fuit, ita esse fierique debebat, ut idoneum quoddam et oportunum divinae potius quam humanae mentis domicilium non iniuria fore potuisset, ceu in primo huius operis libro multo latius et
uberius explicavimus.

20   Sed haec hactenus de forma. Quid vero de subtili et acuto eius
tam pulchri et tam formosi hominis ingenio dicemus? Quod

also cattle in plenty, some to eat, some to till the fields, some to carry, some to clothe our bodies; and man himself—to survey heaven and its gods, as it were, and worship them, and all the fields and waters spread out for man to use.[21]

So then, if such we take the beauty of this world to be (though   18 I mean not to go on too long about things so clear and obvious), and if we say it is this great, then what form, what grace, what beauty must we think has been bestowed on man, who is the only reason, beyond all doubt, for making the world so very fair and beautiful? No wonder, then, if we see that ancient and modern innovators in the fine arts—believing that in all things, both ensouled and soulless, a divine nature stands out and excels, and thinking no form more beautiful than the human—agreed that the gods should be painted and portrayed in the likeness of humans.[22]

However, to see how very fair and seemly man's appearance is,   19 the most important fact is that anyone would prefer death to being changed into some beastly shape, even though, if this could be done, the person would still have a human mind—as they say about Apuleius, a native of Madaurus who was turned into an ass while keeping his human mind, so the story goes. But after he returned by some miracle to his original state as a real human, he wrote a book about everything that happened during that time and called it *The Golden Ass*.[23]

Such a form—the most beautiful and becoming of all—should have been, and should have been made to be, the form of this animal that is more divine than human, as in fact it was, so that by rights it could be a suitable and fit habitation for a mind more divine than human, as I explained at much greater length and in more detail in the first book of this work.

Up to now the form has been my subject. But what to say   20 about the sharp and subtle intellect of this human, so very fair and

equidem tantum et tale est ut cuncta quaeque—post primam illam novam ac rudem mundi creationem—ex singulari quodam et praecipuo humanae mentis acumine a nobis adinventa ac confecta et absoluta fuisse videantur. Nostra namque—hoc est humana—sunt, quoniam ab hominibus quae[14] effecta cernuntur: omnes domos,[15] omnia oppida, omnes urbes, omnia denique orbis terrarum aedificia. Quae nimirum tanta et talia sunt ut potius angelorum quam hominum opera ob magnam quandam eorum excellentiam iure censeri debeant.

Nostrae sunt picturae, nostre sculpturae; nostrae sunt artes, nostrae scientie, nostrae—vel volentibus vel invitis Academicis, qui nihil omnino a nobis nescientia, ut ita dixerim, dumtaxat excepta sciri posse arbitrabantur—sapientiae; nostrae sunt denique, ne de singulis longius disseramus cum prope infinita sint, omnes adinventiones.

Nostra omnia diversarum linguarum ac variarum litterarum genera, de quarum necessariis usibus quanto magis magisque cogitamus, tanto vehementius admirari et obstupescere cogimur. Nam cum primi illi homines ac vetusti eorum successores sine mutuis quibusdam et vicissitudinariis favoribus per se solos nequaquam vivere posse animadverterent, subtile quoddam et acutum loquendi artificium adinvenerunt ut per linguam, intercedentibus verbis, abstrusa quaeque[16] intimae mentis sensa cunctis audientibus innotescerent. Cum deinde, tractu ut fit temporis, genus humanum mirum in modum multiplicaretur ac diversas orbis regiones provinciasque incoleret, necessarium fuit ut elementorum caracteres invenirentur, quibus absentes amicos de cogitationibus nostris certiores reddere valeremus. Unde tam varia linguarum genera et tam diversae litterarum figurae emanasse et profluxisse cernuntur.

Nostra sunt denique[17] omnia machinamenta quae admirabilis et paene incredibilis humani—vel divini potius—ingenii acies et

handsome? This mind is so great and remarkable that all later discoveries and inventions — after the first creation of a world fresh and wild — have evidently been products of ourselves, coming from that special, singular shrewdness of human thinking. Ours indeed are those inventions — they are human — because it is those that are seen as made by humans: all the houses, all the towns, all the cities, including all the structures on earth. Truly, because of their immense excellence, these are so great and remarkable that they might well be judged the works of angels rather than men.

Ours are the paintings, ours the sculptures; ours are the crafts, ours the sciences and ours the knowledge — whether the Academics like it or not, who reckoned that nothing at all can be known by us, excepting only what I might call our "unknowing"; they are all our discoveries in the end, not to describe each and every one at length since they are almost without end.[24]

Ours are all the kinds of different languages and various alphabets, and the more we realize how indispensable it is to have the use of them, the more forcefully are we compelled to be amazed and marvel at them. For when those first humans and their ancient descendants saw that there was no way to live by themselves and not deal with one another in mutually beneficial relations, they devised a method of speaking, elegant and accurate, using the tongue, with words as intermediaries, to make known to all who heard them whatever ideas were hidden deep in their minds. Then, in the course of time, as the human race multiplied to an amazing extent and settled the globe's different regions and territories, it was necessary to invent marks for letters, enabling us to give absent friends better assurance of our thoughts. This is why we see that so many different forms of writing have developed and spread with so many different kinds of language.[25]

Ours, in sum, are all the devices that the human — or better, divine — intellect, with its nearly incredible power and astonishing

acrimonia singulari quadam ac praecipua solertia moliri fabrica-
21 rique constituit. Haec quidem et cetera huiusmodi tot ac talia
undique conspiciuntur, ut mundus et cuncta eius ornamenta, ab
omnipotenti Deo ad usus hominum primo inventa institutaque et
ab ipsis postea hominibus gratanter accepta, multo pulchriora
multoque ornatiora ac longe politiora effecta fuisse videantur.
Unde factum est ut primi quarumcunque artium inventores pro
diis a priscis gentibus colerentur. De quibus quidem credibilior, ut
in septimo *De civitate dei* inquit Augustinus, redditur ratio cum
perhibentur homines fuisse et unicuique eorum ab his qui illos
adulando deos esse voluerunt ex eorum ingenio, moribus, actibus,
casibus sacra et solemnia constituebantur.

22   Quid insuper de humana sapientia referemus, cum ipsa ordi-
nandi operatio ad dignum quoddam et unicum solius sapientis
officium spectare pertinereque[18] existimetur? Illum enim sapientem esse iure dubitare et ambigere non possumus cuius proprium
officium sapere dicimus, quod in nullo alio magis consistere videtur quam ut ordine suo inter agendum utatur. Sed ut paulo apertius disseramus, sapientis proprium officium esse creditur ut
omnia quaecunque facta sunt singulari sua[19] sapientia instituat,
ordinet et gubernet. Atqui haec quae in mundo cernuntur pleraque ab hominibus ordinata et instituta fuisse nemo inficias ibit.
Homines enim—velut omnium domini terraeque cultores—variis
eam diversisque operibus suis mirum in modum coluerunt atque
agros et insulas litoraque terris et urbibus distinxerunt. Quae si ut
animis ita oculis videre atque conspicere valeremus, nemo cuncta
uno aspectu intuens (quemadmodum supra diximus) ullo unquam
tempore admirari atque obstupescere desisteret.

23   Ceterum—non ut oratorum solum sed etiam ut dialecticorum
more argumentandi et declarandi causa quandoque argumenta
stringamus—sapientia ipsa de qua inpraesentiarum disserimus in
solum hominem cadit, licet calliditas et astutia in mutis quoque

sharpness, has labored with special and singular skill to put in place. These and other such discoveries are so many and so im- 21 pressive, as we observe, that the world with all its beauties, originally devised by Almighty God and set up for human use and then happily accepted by those very humans, seems to have been fitted out much better and made far more cultivated. This is why the ancient pagans came to worship the first inventors of various arts as gods. It certainly gives a more credible account of those gods—says Augustine in the seventh book of the *City of God*—to claim that they were human and that rites and ceremonies suited to each god's nature, character, activity and circumstances were established by those who flattered them by treating them as divine.[26]

Besides, why report on human wisdom when we reckon that 22 the very activity of ordering belongs only to what is in some sense, the uniquely worthy office of the sage, and relates to it alone? We cannot rightly doubt or question that it is the sage whose proper role is to be wise, as we say, and plainly this belongs nowhere more than with his making use of an order of his own while acting. To put this a bit more clearly, however, people think the wise man's proper role is to prepare, organize and regulate by his own singular wisdom each and every thing created. But no one will deny that humans have prepared and organized most of what we see in the world. Humans, in fact—as masters of all and tillers of the earth—have tended the land admirably with their various labors by dividing fields, islands and plains into districts and cities. If we could look at these things and see them with our eyes as in our minds, no one could ever take them all in at once (as I said before) without being astonished and dumbstruck.[27]

Besides—not to restrict myself to orators in making my case 23 and clarifying it but sometimes to use the dialectical style as well in touching on various topics—the wisdom under discussion here belongs only to humans, even though cunning and craft are also

animalibus reperiatur, vel cum aliis insidiantur et devorandi gratia
dolo capiunt vel cum insidias ceterorum vario quodam lusionis
genere deludunt.

Est enim sapientia, ut inquit Aristoteles, scientia et intellectus
pretiosissimorum natura; vel — ut Lactantio placet — intelligentia
vel ad bonum rectumque faciendum vel abstinentia dictorum fac-
torumque improborum; vel, ut aliquanto clarius explicemus, profecto nihil aliud sapientia[20] est quam certa quaedam unius ac veri
Dei notitia. Omnis enim hominis sapientia in hoc uno et solo
consistere et residere videtur, ut Deum prae ceteris cognoscat et
colat.

24   Praeterea alia intellectivarum ac moralium virtutum opera ad
quem alterum quam ad sapientem hominem spectare et pertinere
videantur nequaquam intelligimus. Qui, cum cerneret duplicem
illum — irascibilem scilicet et concupiscibilem — appetitum nobis
cum brutis esse communem, ad cohibendum effrenatos rebellesque
huiusmodi appetitus impetus praedictas intellectus morisque virtutes adinvenisse ac reperisse perhibetur, quibus veluti frenis quibusdam varias ac multiplices et obscaenas voluptates compesceret,
quarum humanum dumtaxat quam illum ceterarum animantium
appetitum fertiliorem et abundantiorem esse voluit.

Nam ceterae animantes praeter unam libidinis voluptatem quae
ad generandum pertinet nullam sentiunt. Utuntur ergo sensibus
ad naturae suae necessitatem: vident ut appetant ea quibus opus
est ad vitam tuendam, audiunt invicem seque dignoscunt ut possint congregare, quae utilia sunt ad victum aut ex odore inveniunt
aut ex sapore percipiunt, inutilia respuunt ac recusant, edendi et
bibendi officium ventris plenitudine metiuntur.

25   At, ne plura de humana sapientia dicamus, quid de hominum
divitiis atque opibus referemus? Nostrae sunt terrae, nostri sunt
agri, nostri sunt campi,[21] nostri montes, nostri colles, nostrae
valles, nostrae vites, nostrae oleae, nostrae piri, nostrae mali, nos-

found in dumb animals, whether they trap other beasts and use trickery to catch and eat them, or they play a different game, toying in various ways with the traps set by the rest.[28]

In fact, wisdom is the knowledge and understanding of things that are the most valuable by nature, as Aristotle says; or else — according to Lactantius — wisdom is the intelligence needed to do what is right and good, or it is refraining from bad speech and actions; or, to put it a bit more clearly, wisdom is actually nothing but a sure and certain acquaintance with the true God. For it is evident that all human wisdom consists and rests only in this: knowing God and honoring him before all others.[29]

Furthermore, I know nothing at all of any acts of intellectual 24 and moral virtue that should be seen as belonging or relating to anyone but a wise man. They say that some such sage, noticing that we share with animals a twofold appetite — namely, tendencies to anger and desire — discovered the aforesaid virtues of mind and morals and developed them to restrain the unbridled and insurgent impulses of such an appetite, using virtues like reins to pull back on various pleasures, manifold and indecent, and considering the human appetite at least as fertile as that of other animals in producing them abundantly.

Now the other animals feel nothing that extends beyond the single pleasure of desire that goes with reproducing. They use their senses for natural needs, then — seeing in order to seek what's necessary to preserve life, hearing and recognizing each other in order to join together, smelling to find things good to eat or tasting to tell them apart, then spitting the bad things out and rejecting them, regulating by a full belly their role of eating and drinking.[30]

And then, to say no more about human wisdom, what about 25 mankind's riches and resources? Ours is the land, ours are the fields and plains, ours the mountains, hills and valleys, ours the vines, olives, pears, apples, figs, peaches, cherries, plums, walnuts,

trae ficus, nostrae persici, nostrae cerasi, nostrae pruni, nostrae nuces, nostrae avellanae, nostrae aranci, nostrae mespilae, nostrae sorbi, nostrae castaneae, nostrae quercus, nostrae ilices, nostrae fraxini, nostrae platani, nostrae abietes, nostrae cupressi, nostrae pini, nostrae denique — ne de pluribus singillatim dicamus — omnes cum domesticae tum silvestres arbores. Postremo nostri cunctarum herbarum fructus, quarum[22] genera tot et tanta esse perhibentur ut paene infinita videantur.

26   Nostri equi, nostri muli, nostri asini, nostri boves, nostri tauri, nostri cameli, nostri canes, nostra iumenta, nostra pecora, nostra omnia armenta, nostri sues, nostrae oves, nostrae caprae, nostri agni, nostri haedi, nostri arietes, nostrae cunctae quaeque greges. Et, ne de cicuribus dumtaxat disseruisse videamur, nostri praeterea sunt lepores, nostri capreoli, nostri apri, nostri cervi, nostrae vulpes, nostri lupi, nostrae natrices et cetera reptilia, nostre cunctae quaeque fere et omnia silvestria, nostri homines. Nostra flumina, nostra fluenta, nostri fluvii, nostri torrentes, nostri lacus, nostra stagna, nostri fontes, nostri rivuli, nostra maria, nostri omnes pisces quorum species innumerabiles praedicantur. Nostra pariter reliqua duo elementa, aer et aether, siquidem nostre aves.

Quarum diversitates tot et tantae esse perhibentur ut providentia divina (quam Graeci πρόνοιαν[23] nuncupant) Epicurea fuisse videatur, cum tam varia ac tam voluptuosa, partim[24] animatarum, partim inanimatarum, rerum genera hominibus ipsis parare et administrare voluerit — quoniam multiplices et varias diversorum animalium species in terris, in aquis, in aere ad usum hominis effectas affatim collocavit abundeque constituit. Quod in aethere similiter fecisset, si eius elementi natura omnium consumptrix fieri permisisset.

27   Quid plura? Nostri sunt caeli, nostra astra, nostra sidera, nostrae stellae, nostri planetae et — quod mirabilius videri potest — nostri sunt angeli qui, ut inquit Apostolus, administratorii spiritus in usum hominum creati fuisse creduntur. Quod Dionysius

hazelnuts, oranges, medlars, serviceberries and chestnuts, ours the oaks, the holly, the ash, plane, fir, cypress, pine and—not to list more one by one—all the trees, both wild and cultivated. Finally, ours are the fruits of all the plants, whose kinds are said to be so many that they seem nearly endless.

Ours are the horses, mules and donkeys, ours the cows, bulls 26 and camels, ours the dogs, draft animals and cattle in all their herds, ours the pigs, sheep, she-goats, lambs, kids, rams and flocks of every kind. Then, moving beyond tame animals, ours too are the hares, ours the wild goats and wild boars, ours the deer, foxes and wolves, ours the snakes and other reptiles—all are ours, basically every animal in the woods and also the human animal. The brooks and streams are ours, the rivers, torrents, lakes, swamps, springs and rills, ours the seas and all the fish whose species are said to be uncountable. Ours also are the other two elements, the air and upper sky, seeing that the birds are ours.

These things are so vastly diverse, people say, that divine providence (called *pronoia* by the Greeks) might seem to have been Epicurean when it chose to supply humans and help them with so many different types of things, living and not living, that give so much pleasure—the fact being that on land, in water and in the air it was providence that located an abundance of animals of many different kinds made for man's use, supplying them in plenty. And the same would have happened in the upper sky, had the nature of its element—which is to destroy everything—allowed it.[31]

Can there be more? Ours are the heavens, ours the stars, lumi- 27 naries, planets and constellations and—as amazing as this may seem—ours are the angels, believed to have been created as ministering spirits for the welfare of humans, as the Apostle says.

Areopagita, peregregius eius discipulus, in praeclaris illis de angelica et ecclesiastica hierarchia voluminibus interpretari et explanare
cupiens, inter cetera angelorum officia id praecipuum et peculiare
esse confirmavit et voluit—ut homines angelicis inspirationibus
illuminarent, illuminatosque purgarent purgatosque perficerent,
nec solum praedictis huiusmodi illuminandi, purgandi ac perfi-
ciendi ministeriis sed pluribus quoque aliis famulatibus humano
generi inservire et obsequi comperiuntur.

28   Quod multa et quidem celebrata Veteris ac Novi Testamenti
exempla plane et aperte declarant. Nam et Abrahae ad ilicem
Mambre, ut scribitur, sedenti tres angelos, ut filium sibi ex Sara
iam nonagenaria nasciturum significarent, apparuisse legimus.
Quem Isaac propterea cognominavit—quoniam Sara, quasi id impossibile foret, quod muliebria multo ante fieri desierant, risisse
dicitur—huiusmodi enim nomen ex Hebraea in Latinam linguam
conversum *risus* interpretatur. Et unum alterum postea, cum Iacob,
ut admirabilem quandam sui ipsius virtutem comprobaret, con-
flixisse novimus, ex quo Israelis cognomen accepit, quoniam angelo in mutuo congressu angelicoque duello viriliter restitisset.

Ac Raphaelem insuper Tobiae filio, cum a patre eiusdem nomi-
nis exigendi decem talentorum argenti gratia, quae ipse Gabello
cuidam amico suo mutuo dederat, e Galilea unde oriundus erat
usque in Mediam provinciam mitteretur, peregrini ac longinqui
itineris ducem et comitem extitisse accepimus. Daniel praeterea
cum in lacum leonum iussu Darii Medorum Principis a feris la-
niandus mitteretur, atque tres quoque viri eius socii in maximum
quendam ardentis fornacis rogum ex praecepto Nabucdonosor,
Regis Babilonis, ligatis manibus et pedibus proiicerentur, omnes
angelicis obsequiis a crudelibus feris a flammaque illaesos et ab
igne demum liberatos fuisse scimus.

Dionysius the Areopagite, the Apostle's most distinguished disciple, wants to explain and interpret this in those outstanding works on hierarchy, ecclesiastical and angelic, where he taught and proved that among the various roles of angels this one is special and comes first—to enlighten humans with angelic inspiration, to cleanse the enlightened and perfect the cleansed, which shows that angels serve and submit to the human race not only in those ministries of enlightening, cleansing and perfecting but also in finding many other ways to help.[32]

Many examples from the Old and New Testaments, some really   28
quite famous, show this plainly and clearly. Where Scripture says that three angels appeared to Abraham when he was sitting at the oak of Mamre, we read that they announced a son to be born to him from Sara, who by that time was ninety years old. So he named this child Isaac—for Sara is described as laughing, as if this would be impossible since her woman's cycles had long since ceased—because that name, taken from Hebrew into Latin, translates as *laughter*. Later a human battled an angel, as we know: to show that he had amazing strength of his own, Jacob took the name Israel because he had held his own bravely when he and an angel fought in single combat.[33]

I have also learned that Raphael became a companion and guide to the boy Tobias on the long journey that he made to foreign lands: the boy's father (of the same name) sent his son out from Galilee all the way to the territory of the Medes because ten talents of silver, loaned by the father to a friend named Gabellus, had to be collected. And when Darius, prince of the Medes, had Daniel put in the lions' den to be torn by wild beasts, and when Nebuchadnezzar, king of Babylon, ordered three men who were Daniel's companions to be bound hand and foot and thrown into the fiery furnace, blazing at its hottest, we know that angels took care of them all, so that the cruel beasts and flames did them no harm, and in the end they were freed from the fire.[34]

29   Sed quid nos plura vel Veteris vel Novi Testamenti exempla
conquirimus cum omnia sacrarum scripturarum loca angelicis ministeriis referctissima videamus, siquidem Gabrielem Mariae Vir-
gini salutiferam Christi conceptionem, et beatis quoque pastoribus
non unum angelum sed potius angelorum agmen (nam multos
fuisse constat) eius nativitatem nuntiasse, et Ioseph patri de pueri
nati in Aegyptum delatione et non multo[25] exinde reversione angelos retulisse meminimus—et sexcenta alia huiusmodi ex evangelica
lectione provenisse cognovimus? In *Vitis* denique sanctorum patrum angelos plures defunctorum hominum animas in caelum
portasse et obsequia in funeribus frequenter exhibuisse non dubitamus. Quae, ne nimii simus, praetermittere quam recitare maluimus, praesertim cum talia sint ut neminem vel mediocriter quidem doctum latere debeant.

30   Ex quibus omnibus superius a nobis enarratis et satis superque
satis confirmatis, hominem opulentissimum ac potentissimum esse
plane et aperte[26] concluditur, quandoquidem cunctis quae creata
sunt sua voluntate uti propriaque potestate dominari et imperare
potest. Haec omnia cum veteres Romani humano generi divinitus
a natura data esse cognoscerent atque ipsi Iovi[27] utpote ceterorum
deorum (quemadmodum ipsi opinabantur) principalissimo accepta referrent, idcirco Optimum Maximum appellabant.

31   Praeterea solertissimi Artificis Providentia homini ipsi, quem
tam formosum, tam ingeniosum, tam sapientem, tam opulentum
et ad extremum tam praepotentem—ac tantum principem et ubique imperantem—constituerat, voluptatem praebuit paene infinitam, quam ex omnibus creatarum rerum generibus delibaret et
caperet, sed in vitium cadentem quia praeposuit ei virtutem quae
cum voluptate semper tanquam cum domestico hoste pugnaret.
Nam singulis sensibus—visus, auditus, odoratus, gustus, et tactus—certiores ac vehementiores et plures ab hominibus quam a
ceteris animalibus voluptates et delectationes capiuntur.

But why hunt for more examples from the Old Testament or 29
the New since I see that all the texts of sacred Scripture are full of
ministering angels? I note that Gabriel declared Christ's saving
conception to the Virgin Mary, that not one angel but a troop of
them (for clearly there were many) announced his birth to the
blessed shepherds, and that angels spoke to Joseph, the father,
about taking the newborn child into Egypt and not long afterward
about his return—these and hundreds of other such examples
that come from Gospel reading. And then by the *Lives* of the
sainted fathers I am assured that angels carried souls of the deceased to heaven and often paid their respects at funerals. Wishing
not to go on too long, I have preferred to move on without telling
these stories, especially since they are the kind that no one with
even a little education would miss.[35]

My conclusion—from everything I have said above and have 30
confirmed more than sufficiently—is clear and obvious: that humankind is immensely powerful and well endowed, seeing that
humans can use all created things as they will, also commanding
them by their own might and having dominion. The ancient Romans recognized that nature gave all these to the human race as
gifts from heaven and traced what was received to Jupiter himself
as (so they thought) supreme chief over the other gods, and for
this reason they called him Best and Greatest.[36]

To the human whom Providence had made so handsome, cle- 31
ver, wise and well endowed, so utterly powerful—a mighty prince
ruling everywhere—to him that skilled Craftsman also granted
nearly limitless pleasure, picking and choosing it from creatures of
every type, though the human would also fall into vice because the
virtue that God planned for man always clashes with a pleasure,
like an enemy in one's home. Through each of the senses—sight,
hearing, smell, taste and touch—the pleasures and delights enjoyed by humans are certainly stronger, surer and more abundant
than those had by other animals.[37]

32   Quod in venereis paulo manifestius apparet, ceu Lactantius in sexto[28] *Institutionum* adversus gentes his verbis innuere videtur:

> Cum excogitaret Deus duorum sexuum rationem, attribuit his ut sese invicem appeterent et coniunctione gauderent. Itaque ardentissimam cupiditatem cunctorum animantium corporibus admiscuit, ut in hos affectus avidissime ruerent eaque ratione propagari et multiplicari genera possent. Quae cupiditas et appetentia in homine vehementior et acrior quam in ceteris animalibus invenitur, vel quia hominum multitudinem voluit esse maiorem vel quia virtutem soli homini dedit ut esset laus et gloria in cohercendis voluptatibus et abstinentia sui,

et reliqua.

33   Quibusdam deinde sanctis hominibus data fuit caelitus potestas ut plura miracula facerent pluresque[29] defunctos ab ipsa morte ad veram et certam vitam—mirabile dictu—suscitarent: ceu de Moyse, Iosue, Helia, Helisaeo, Daniele pluribusque aliis Veteris Testamenti prophetis, ac etiam de Petro, Paulo, Iohanne reliquisque apostolis, Stefano, Laurentio, Gervasio ac Prothasio multisque aliis martyribus ab idoneis auctoribus scriptum legisse meminimus. Omnibus insuper sacerdotibus concessum est ut non modo—per baptismum quibusdam suis formalibus verbis—peccatum originale quo omnes homines infecti oriuntur sed cetera quoque humana delicta, facinora ac flagitia per indulgentiam et veniam dimittere delereque valerent, ac praeterea sacratissimum Christi corpus conficere et consecrare vel maxime possent. Episcopos aliosque Romanae ecclesiae praelatos et summos pontifices omittamus, quibus certa quaedam ac mirabilia damnandorum et salvandorum hominum privilegia ab omnipotenti Deo indulta et exhibita fuisse legimus.

For sexual pleasures this is a bit more obvious, as Lactantius 32
seems to suggest in the sixth book of his *Elements* against the pagans, saying this:

By devising a plan for two sexes, God gave them the feature
of wanting one another and finding joy in their intimacy. He
therefore blended the most intense desire into the bodies of
all living things, making them very eager to rush into those
feelings, and in this way their offspring could be propagated
and multiplied. One finds that such desire and longing are
stronger and sharper in humans than in other animals, either because God wanted their number to be greater or because to them alone he gave the virtue that would bring
praise and glory for limiting their pleasures and controlling
themselves,

and so on.[38]

Next, heaven gave certain holy people the power to work many 33
miracles and—astonishing to say—to waken many of the departed even from death back to true and certain life: I remember
having read exactly this in the writings of reliable authorities about
Moses, Elijah, Elisha, Daniel and several other Old Testament
prophets, as well as Peter, Paul, John and the rest of the apostles,
also Stephen, Lawrence, Gervase, Protasius and a multitude of
other martyrs. Furthermore, all priests have been divinely granted
the power not only to remit—through the form of words used
when they baptize—the original sin that infects all people from
birth but also to wipe away other human offenses, wrongs and
outrages by indulgence and forgiveness, beyond which priests have
the ultimate power to prepare and consecrate Christ's most sacred
body. Let me omit what I have read about bishops and other prelates or supreme pontiffs of the Roman Church, to whom Almighty God has granted and allowed certain specific and miraculous privileges to save people and condemn them.[39]

34   Haec omnia superius a nobis commemorata poetae, philosophi ac theologi et ceteri omnes scriptores, Graeci pariter et Latini ac Hebraei quoque, pluribus librorum suorum locis plane et aperte asserere et confirmare videntur. Ovidius namque, ut sola eius auctoritate ex poetis contenti simus, ubi Deum mundum formasse atque partes illius[30] ab invicem separasse contendit—etsi nos divinitus creatum fuisse non dubitemus—demum in productionem hominis carmina haec posuit:

> Sanctius his animal mentisque capacius altae
> deerat adhuc et quod dominari in cetera posset:
> natus est homo.

Plato in *Timaeo* Deum fabricatorem mundi constituit, quem ad utilitatem tantummodo hominum ab eo creatum et formatum esse voluit.

35   Moyses—prophetarum et omnium veterum theologorum, pace aliorum dixerim, princeps et caput—postquam ab omnipotenti Deo cuncta quaeque, homine dumtaxat excepto, vel facta vel creata fuisse dixit: faciamus, inquit, hominem ad imaginem et similitudinem nostram, ut praesit piscibus maris et volatilibus caeli et bestiis terrae universaeque creaturae omnibusque reptilibus quae moventur in terra. Quem quidem, uti praedixerat, tanquam unicum cunctorum antea factorum dominum possessoremque postea creavit et benedixit et ait: crescite et multiplicamini et replete terram et subiicite eam et dominamini piscibus maris et volatilibus caeli et universis animantibus quae moventur super terram.

36   Paulus Apostolus, vas electionis et magister gentium ac novorum theologorum doctor veterumque explanator, omnia quaecunque facta sunt nostra esse confirmat. Nam ad Corinthios scribens ita inquit: Omnia enim nostra sunt, sive Paulus sive Apollo sive Cephas, sive mundus sive vita sive mors, sive praesentia sive futura; omnia enim nostra sunt, vos autem Christi, Christus vero

Poets, philosophers, theologians and all other writers, Greek as 34
well as Latin and also Hebrew, are seen to declare and confirm,
plainly and clearly, in many passages of their books all these points
that I have already made. To content myself with Ovid's single
authority among the poets, right after having asserted that God
shaped the world and separated its parts from one another—
whereas I have no doubt that the world was God's creation—he
immediately put the producing of man into these verses:

Still lacking was a better animal, one more fit
to think high thoughts and capable of ruling others:
so the human race came forth.

In the *Timaeus* Plato established that God constructed the world,
thinking it to be a creation formed by him only for human use.[40]

After each and every thing had been made or created by God 35
Almighty, said Moses—whom I would call the prince and chief of
prophets and of all ancient theologians, whatever others may
think—all that remained was mankind. Let us make man in our
image and likeness, God said, so that he might rule the fish of the
sea, the flying things of the sky, the beasts of the earth and every
creature, with all the reptiles that move on the land. Accordingly,
as he had already announced, God then created this human and
blessed him as the only lord and possessor of all that had been
made previously, saying this: increase and multiply, fill the earth,
make it subject to you and rule the fish of the sea, the flying things
of the sky with all the living things that move upon the land.[41]

The Apostle Paul, chosen vessel, teacher of the Gentiles, master 36
of modern theologians and interpreter of the ancients, confirms
that whatever has been made is all ours. For when he writes to the
Corinthians, he says this: Everything is ours, in fact, whether it is
Paul or Apollo or Cephas, the world or life or death, the present
or future; all things indeed are ours, but you are of Christ and
Christ is of God. In their very great desire to interpret these

Dei. Quae quidem verba Catholici explanatores nostri, recte interpretari et declarare maxime cupientes, tanti fecisse videntur ut in
hunc modum ab invicem distinxerint:[31] quippe infima, aequalia et
superiora hinc inde distinguentes, infima ad utendum, aequalia ad
convivendum, superiora ad fruendum, pulcherrime atque optime
interpretantur.

37   David denique, hanc maximam ac praestantissimam ipsius hominis dignitatem supra quam dici potest admirans, in octavo illo
celebratissimo et vulgatissimo Psalmo, quasi Deum percontaretur
et paulo post sibi ipsi sic interroganti responderet, carmina haec
ponit:

> Quid est homo quod memor es eius? Aut filius hominis
>   quoniam visitas eum?
> Minuisti eum paulo minus ab angelis, gloria et honore
>   coronasti eum:
> et constituisti eum super opera manuum tuarum. Omnia
>   subiecisti sub pedibus eius:
> oves et boves universas, insuper et pecora campi,
> volucres caeli et pisces maris qui perambulant semitas maris.

Quorum quidem verborum commemoratus Apostolus dum ad
Hebraeos scriberet, meminisse legitur, quando in eo, inquit, quod
omnia ei subiecit, nihil praetermiserit quod humanae potestati
largiri voluerit: cum paulo superius ad maximam quandam humani generis dignitatem universum terrarum orbem non angelis,
quos in admirabili quadam excellentia constituerat, sed hominibus
dumtaxat subiecisse ac tribuisse testatur.[32] Atque haec omnia quae
praedicta sunt, dum in hac vita mortali peregrinatur,[33] a Domino
quasi invitus repugnansque consequitur.

38   Perpetuam praeterea felicitatem sempiternamque post corpoream mortem beatitudinem ei, ut diximus, tot tantisque muneribus mirabiliter constituto et ornato, ferre ac promittere et largiri
insuper, modo non repugnaret, concupivit et voluit, atque ut sibi

words and explain them correctly, our Catholic exegetes have plainly made much of the following distinctions: telling the lower apart from the equal apart from the higher, such that the lower is to be used, the equal shared and the higher enjoyed, according to their excellent and very elegant interpretation.[42]

And then David, stunned beyond speech by this human's eminent and enormous worth, puts these verses into his eighth Psalm, so very famous and so well known, as if he were quizzing God and then answering his own questions just a moment later:

37

> What is man that you attend to him? Or the son of man that you look after him?
> You have made him little lower than angels, crowning him with glory and honor;
> you have set him over your handiwork. You have put it all under his feet:
> all the oxen and cattle, and the flocks of the field besides, birds in the sky, fish in the sea who go by the sea paths.

We read the Apostle attending to these words as he wrote to the Hebrews, since when God made all things subject to man, as Paul writes, he left nothing out because he wanted to be generous with human power: just before this, Paul notes, God assigned the whole earth and made it subject not to the angels — whom he had put in a wonderfully eminent condition — but only to man, in order to give the human race a special and supreme rank. And so from the Lord, though man resists him while on pilgrimage in this mortal life, he gets everything previously described — but against his own will.[43]

Moreover, to this human whom he had appointed so wonderfully and equipped with so many great gifts, God wanted to offer unending happiness, choosing in his bounty to provide eternal bliss after the body's death, if only man would not resist, having

38

recte admonenti crederet multifariam et apprime exhortatus est. Ante omnia namque duobus primis hominibus, quos in maiori quadam dignitate—ceu *iustitia originali,* ut theologico verbo utamur—praeditos quam ceteros omnes, post detestandam illam eorum transgressionem in peccato originali conceptos constituerat, praeter illa naturalia intelligendi, memorandi ac volendi dona, expressam quandam veri boni cognitionem ipsorum mentibus impresserat. Et ne sua mandata transgrederentur, non modo propriis suasionibus admonuit, sed terribiles quoque metus mortisque terrores adiecit ut eos a malis facinoribus vehementius deterreret.

39   At vero nec suasionibus nec minis neque terroribus profecisse videtur. Nam dum ipsi diabolicis laqueis irretiti labuntur in praeceps, nimirum sese genusque humanum ab illis propagandum perpetuo damnaverunt. Posteri autem, qui post plura saecula primis illis parentibus successerunt, deterioribus peccandi conditionibus depravati, suis malis facinoribus scelestisque flagitiis sese ita inquinaverunt ut Deum ad generalem quandam humani generis punitionem provocarent. Ex quo universum terrarum orbem ab illo generali et admirabili diluvio inundatum fuisse constat, ubi cuncta viventia (piscibus dumtaxat reptilibusque exceptis) aquis submersa nisi ea sola interierunt quae in arca illa famosissima a Noe—iusto[34] consolatore, quemadmodum eius nomen ex Hebraea in Latinam linguam conversum, ceu in secundo huius operis libro dixisse meminimus, significare videtur—divinitus fabrefacta incolumia remanserunt, ex quibus cuncta quaeque diversorum animalium genera novam quandam originem traxisse non dubitamus.

40   Abrahae deinde temporibus eadem monita per vicissitudinarios angelos eo usque subsecuta sunt quoad Deus Moysi divinam legem per duas illas celeberrimas decantatasque tabulas largiretur. In qua quidem lege quibuscunque praevaricatoribus suis plura maledictionum et execrationum genera imprecatus est, servatoribus vero omnes benedictionum et indulgentiarum species promittere atque offerre decrevit et voluit.

been urged to put his trust first in the one whose instructions are just and so many. Above all, after God equipped the first two humans with a special worth greater than he gave to any other creatures — a sort of *original justice* (if I may use the theological term) — and after he had arranged for those who would be conceived in original sin after the detestable lapse of that pair, he actually impressed on their minds a clear knowledge of the true good, beyond the natural gifts of understanding, memory and will. And to keep them from breaking his commandments, he not only counseled them with those special warnings, he also added fear and terror of death to deter them from evil deeds in a stronger way.[44]

We see that neither advice nor threats nor terror succeeded, 39 however. Falling headlong into the Devil's traps and snares, the two humans truly damned themselves forever, along with the race that they were to propagate. And the generations who followed the first parents in later ages were corrupted by worse states of sin, befouling themselves with deeds so evil and shame so abominable that they provoked God to a universal punishment for humankind. We all know the result: when the whole earthly globe was flooded by that general and astonishing deluge, all living things (except fish and reptiles) sank in the waters and perished, save only those that remained safe in that most celebrated ark which Noah built by divine command — Noah, the just consoler, which is the meaning of his Hebrew name translated into Latin, as noted in the second book of this work; and from those animals, no doubt, all the different species got a new start, as it were.[45]

Then, through angels traveling back and forth in the days of 40 Abraham, the same warnings followed until God granted the divine law to Moses on those two most famous and much described tablets. In that law, God assuredly called down many kinds of curses and maledictions on whoever violated it, while choosing to promise every sort of blessing and also decreeing that he would offer a kind of forbearance to those who kept the law.[46]

41   Cum aliquot deinde annorum milia intercessissent, divina illa et antiqua praecepta vilescere coeperunt. Unde, ne totum genus humanum suis iniquis operationibus merito damnaretur—appropinquante temporis plenitudine, quemadmodum ait Apostolus—misit Deus Filium suum humani generis redemptorem, ut eadem veteris legis praecepta renovaret, renovataque multo clarius et apertius explicaret. Atque temporales illas contemptorum et spretorum mandatorum punitiones per diversas detestationes in perpetuas Tartari poenas, et versa vice priscam lactis mellisque dulcedinem in dignissima quaedam virtutum praemia—hoc est in aeternum caelorum regnum—converteret. Per tot igitur modos—praeter naturales quasdam et gratuitas humani generis conditiones—ipsum in tot tantisque dignitatibus constitutum felix ac beatum, dummodo vellet, ut diximus, efficere concupivit et voluit.

42   Quod ut facilius ordinare et assequi ac parare posset, singulis hominibus singulos angelos ab initio nativitatis attribuit, ut eos, quasi paedagogi forent, a malis facinoribus scelestisque flagitiis custodirent. In quo quidem Deus toti generi humano ita fecisse itaque indulsisse videtur, quemadmodum diligentes patres pueris et adultis filiis facere et indulgere consueverunt: quibus in puerili et adulta aetate constitutis non solum litterarum et primorum elementorum magistros sed morum etiam doctores quasi continuos quosdam comites custodesque largiri et assignare solent, quos Graeco verbo *paedagogos*, hoc est, ut Latine interpretemur, quasi *puerorum ductores*, appellarunt.

43   Hanc de singulis angelis perpetuis singulorum hominum custodibus non modo Catholicam sententiam ex accurata quadam sacrarum scripturarum lectione sed ex quibusdam etiam gentilibus et ethnicis auctoribus certam et veram esse non dubitamus. Nam et priscae historiae sanctorum virorum auctoritatibus praetermissis, Pyrrhi Epyrotarum Regis bello Curium, Fabritium,

After some thousands of years went by, God's ancient rules 41
began to weaken. So that the whole human race would not be
damned by its own wicked deeds, and justly so — as the fullness of
time drew near, in the Apostle's words — God then sent his Son to
redeem mankind by renewing those same rules of the old law and
by setting forth the renewed precepts much more clearly and
openly. For those who scorned and spurned the commandments,
God also used various curses to convert temporal penalties into
Hell's eternal punishments and, conversely, he transformed the
old-time sweetness of milk and honey into virtue's most valuable
rewards — meaning the eternal kingdom of heaven. In so many
ways, then — ways exceeding mankind's natural and spontaneous
dispositions — God wanted to make the race happy and chose to
bless it by equipping it with so many eminent features of such
value, provided that man was willing, as I have said.[47]

So that people could more easily adjust and follow and prepare, 42
God assigned each person a special angel from the moment of
birth in order to guard them from wicked deeds and shameful
acts, as if angels were taking them to school. In doing so, God
seems to have done a kindness for the whole human race, just as
good parents have customarily been kind to their younger and
their grown children: whether these children are young or grown,
parents usually treat them kindly by providing not only teachers
for the alphabet and elementary lessons but also instructors in
good behavior: these are the attendants and constant companions
whom the Greeks call *pedagogues* — or *child-guides* if we put it into
Latin.[48]

I have no doubt that this Catholic belief about each person hav- 43
ing a particular angel as a perpetual guardian is true and certain
not only from a correct reading of sacred Scripture but also from
various gentile and pagan authorities. For even if I omit examples
from the saints, ancient stories give evidence of many noble and
outstanding men — Curius, Fabricius and Coruncanius during the

Coruncanium;[35] primo Punico Calatinum, Duellium, Metellum, Lutatium; secundo Maximum, Marcellum, Africanum; post hos Paulum, Graccum, Catonem, Scipionem, Laelium multosque praeterea Graecos et Latinos praestantissimos et excellentissimos viros extitisse testantur—quorum neminem nisi iuvante Deo, ut ait Cicero, hoc est favente angelo suasore et impulsore, talem fuisse credendum est.

Poetae quoque eorum poemata fingentes hoc idem suis carminibus fabulantur. Quae enim alia ratio poetas, maxime Homerum, impulit ut principibus heroum, Ulixi, Diomedi, Agamennoni, Achilli certos deos quasi divinos ministros, quos nos iam pridem paulo evidentius angelos nuncupare et appellare consuevimus, discriminum et periculorum adiutores comitesque adiungerent?[36] Philosophi insuper id ipsum asserere et confirmare videntur quando Socrates, oraculo Apollinis sapientissimus ceterorum omnium iudicatus, daemonem quendam sibi in custodiam datum cuius consilio in rebus seriis ac gravibus uteretur coram omnibus praedicabat, ceu ex pluribus Platonis libris et dialogis atque ex celebrato illo praedicti Apulei Madaurensis opusculo, cuius titulus est *De deo Socratis*, plane et aperte deprehendimus.

44 Cum igitur Deus hominem ipsum talem esse constituerit qualem supra brevius, quoad fieri potuit, verbis designare ac figuris depingere valuimus, atque illum pulchritudine, ingenio, sapientia, divitiis et opibus, potestatibus[37] insuper et imperiis pluribusque aliis admirabilibus privilegiis vel maxime ornaverit, quod deinde et quale ei caelesti et divino animali atque ita mirabiliter constituto officium exhibuerit parumper consideremus.

45 Postquam ergo Deus in constitutione mundi cuncta prius effecerat, postremo hominem creavit. Hunc Hebraice *Adam* appellamus, quod nomen primaevo illi nostro parenti propterea non immerito attributum fuisse accepimus quoniam verus et dignus

War with Pyrrhus, king of Epirus; Calatinus, Duellius, Metellus and Lutatius in the First Punic War; Maximus, Marcellus and Africanus in the Second; after them Paulus, Gracchus, Cato, Scipio, Laelius and many more besides, both Greek and Latin — none of whom would have been what they were, people believe, without help from a god, as Cicero says, meaning a protecting angel to advise and urge them on.[49]

Poets who devise fictions about such people tell the same tales in their verses. What other reason moved them, Homer especially, to connect various gods with their chief heroes? They linked them with Ulysses, Diomedes, Agamemnon and Achilles as companions in danger and helpers at risky moments, treating them like the divine attendants that for a long time we Christians have usually called *angels*, using clearer language. We also see philosophers making the same claim and confirming it: Socrates, judged the wisest of all by Apollo's oracle, stated in public that he had been given a special daemon as a guardian from whom he took advice on serious and weighty issues, as I have learned quite clearly from several books and dialogues by Plato and from that well-known essay *On the God of Socrates* by Apuleius of Madaura, whom I have already mentioned.[50]

Therefore, since God created man as I have been able to de-   44
scribe him in words, up to now, and sketch him briefly in language, as much as I could, and since he equipped man with the
maximum of beauty, wit, wisdom, riches and resources, as well as
several other astonishing prerogatives of power and authority, let
me next take a little time to examine what role he has conferred —
and what its nature was — on this heavenly and divine animal
whose constitution was such a miracle![51]

God created man last of all, having first made all the other   45
things that constitute the world. In Hebrew we call this man
Adam, which name I have taken to be given correctly to this primal
parent of ours because God made him, and in a godlike way, as *the*

homo a Deo divinitus factus erat. Unde vetus illius sacri idiomatis consuetudo *Adam* primum ad certam quandam aliorum hominum differentiam nuncupat et appellat—cuius gratia omnia paulo ante constituerat atque praecepit ut illis omnibus antea creatis domi naretur atque ad utilitatem quamadmodum vellet suam uteretur.

Proinde, ut magna et recta et admirabilis est vis et ratio et potestas hominis—propter quem mundum ipsum et omnia quae in mundo sunt creata fuisse—ostendimus, sic pariter rectum et simplex atque unicum officium suum tale esse existimamus et credimus, ut mundum eius causa factum, ac praesertim cuncta quae in hoc universo terrarum orbe constituta videmus, gubernare et administrare cognoscat et valeat, quod nequaquam nisi cum agendo tum intelligendo penitus perficere et omnino adimplere poterit.

46 Itaque non iniuria agere et intelligere proprium ipsius solius hominis officium fore dicemus. Atque ita proprium eius esse existimamus et credimus, ut intelligere et agere quam ridere—quod antiqui et nostri temporis philosophi (ut suis verbis declarandi et explicandi gratia utamur) *proprie proprium* appellare consueverunt—magis humanae naturae conveniat. Nam cum utrunque omnibus hominibus pariter competere minime ambigamus, homines tamen sine risu officium suum recte et probe administrare et exercere posse atque homines remanere cognovimus, quod absque intellectu nequaquam efficere et adimplere valerent. Hominesque esse desinerent, quorum solum officium intelligere sentimus et dicimus.

47 Et si hoc intelligendi et agendi munus, quod homini ab omnipotenti Deo tributum videmus et scimus, aliis utpote angelis et Creatori, et non ridendi exercitium, convenire videatur, in hoc certe homo melioris qualitatis et conditionis habetur et creditur, ut in proprio eius officio una cum angelicis spiritibus et cum ipso Deo communicaverit, quoniam aliter—hoc est sine operatione et

human, true and fitting. This is why that sacred language, in its ancient usage, calls the first man *Adam*, giving him that name to indicate a definite difference from all other humans — the one for whose sake God had just recently created everything, directing him to rule all that had been created already and use it for his own benefit as he might wish.[52]

Accordingly, as I have shown that man's power is great, his reason upright and his strength amazing — this man for whom the world itself and everything in the world has been created — so I conclude and believe that his role is equally upright, honest and singular: he has the ability to manage and the knowledge to govern the world that was made on his account, in particular each thing that we see existing on this earthly globe, and he could by no means achieve all this unless he could do it all by acting and understanding.

Therefore I will say — and rightly — that to act and to understand is the proper role of man alone. So properly is this role his, as I believe and conclude, that acting and understanding suit human nature more than laughing — though philosophers in ancient times and in our own day (if I may use their own words to explain and clarify) have customarily said that laughing is *properly proper*. Though I have no doubt that both belong equally to all people, I have ascertained that mankind can play its role correctly, manage suitably and still remain human without laughing, whereas without understanding they could not succeed or get anything done at all. And they would cease to be humans, whose only role is understanding — so I believe and declare.[53]

And if this function of understanding and acting, which I see and know to be assigned to mankind by Almighty God, seems suited to such others as angels and the Creator, while the use of laughter does not, because of this people confidently view the human state and condition as of a better kind, sharing its proper role with angelic spirits and God himself, because otherwise — without

46

47

intellectione—mundo eius causa facto ipsum nequaquam uti posse intelligimus. Nullum quoque aliud animal praeter hominem solum per suam naturam operationis et intellectionis particeps fieri potuisse novimus.

Quod Ciceronem in secundo *De finibus bonorum et malorum*, dum contra Epicureos disputaret, his verbis et in hunc modum declarare et explicare comperimus. Sic enim inquit: hi non viderunt, ut ad currendum equum, ad arandum bovem, ad indagandum canem, sic hominem ad duas res, ut ait Aristoteles, ad intelligendum et ad agendum esse natum—quasi quendam mortalem deum. Et Philosophus quoque ipse, cum in primo *Ethicorum* de proprio quodam hominis opere et officio investigaret, absurdum fore putavit ut fabri et sutoris ac cunctorum aliorum opificum et omnium insuper humanorum membrorum, ut oculi, manus et pedis et ceterorum, proprium aliquod opus et officium esset, homini vero nullum singulare peculiareque exercitium, utpote otioso et ad nihil agendum nato, tribueretur. Atque eam quam Cicero eleganter terminavit sententiam ita diffinivit, ut homo scilicet ad agendum et ad intelligendum tanquam quidam mortalis deus nasceretur.

48   Quod si recte decenterque faceret, quemadmodum fieri oporteret, profecto Deum per ea quae facta sunt visibilia cognosceret, eumque cognitum adamaret, veneraretur et observaret. Id enim proprium solius hominis officium esse creditur, in eoque solo summa rerum et omnis beatae vitae ratio consistit, quandoquidem propterea facti et constituti ab eo sumus—ut non caelum videremus et Solem, quod Anaxagoras putavit, sed ut artificem Solis et caeli Deum pura et integra mente coleremus. Deus namque voluit ut caelum spectaremus non utique frustra: quippe aves et ex mutis paene omnia caelum videre et suspicere possunt. Sed nobis proprie datum est rigidis ac stantibus intueri ut religionem ibi quaeramus et Deum, cuius illa sedes est, quoniam oculis non possumus,

activity and understanding, in other words — my understanding is that man could make no use at all of a world made for his sake. I also know of no animal, except the human alone, that by its own nature could have been made to share in activity and understanding.[54]

When Cicero argues against the Epicureans in his second book *On Ends of Goods and Evils*, I find him explaining and clarifying this point as follows: These people have not seen, he writes, that just as a horse is meant to run, an ox to plow and a dog to hunt, so man — like a mortal god of some sort — was born to do two things, as Aristotle says, to understand and to act. While looking for man's proper work and role in the first book of his *Ethics*, the Philosopher himself also thought it would be absurd if the smith, the cobbler, all other craftsmen and also every human organ, including eyes, hands, feet and so on, had some proper work and role assigned to them, yet there was no special function peculiar to man, as if he were born for no purpose, with nothing to do. Thus Aristotle explained the thought that Cicero brought to so graceful a close, meaning that it was action and understanding for which man was born as a kind of mortal god.[55]

But if man were to do what is right and proper, as things 48 should be done, he would certainly recognize God through the visible creation, and then he would observe, revere and come to love what he recognized. We believe this to be the proper role of man alone, and in this alone lies the ultimate reason for existence and the whole of the blessed life, since this is why God made and created us — not to see the sky and Sun, as Anaxagoras supposed, but, with a mind pure and spotless, to worship God as the maker of sky and Sun. Surely it was not for nothing that God wanted us to gaze at the sky: plainly, birds and almost all dumb animals can look up and see it. But as we stand firm, our proper endowment is to observe the sky and look there for religion, using the mind to contemplate God, whose throne is there, because we cannot do

animo contemplemur. Naturam enim hominis Deus hanc esse voluit, ut duarum rerum cupidus et appetens esset, religionis et sapientiae, quoniam in his duobus inseparabiliter connexis officium
hominis et veritas omnis inclusa est.

49   Itaque omnipotens Dominus ei in tanta ac tam sublimi dignitate constituto suapte natura indidit ut se ipsum conservandi sui
causa diligeret. Ceteris vero, per certa quaedam et expressa scriptae
legis mandata, iniunxit quatenus omnes proximos—hoc est omnes
homines—amarent, honorarent et observarent. Atque ut hoc dili-
gendi sui officium libentius atque constantius exequerentur, adim-
plerent ac perficerent, singulis quibusque huius divini opificii
dilectoribus et conservatoribus sese pro digna quadam mutuae di-
lectionis mercede aeternum caelorum regnum daturum plane et
aperte pollicitus est. Ceteris autem illius sui operis osoribus, et
tanti aedificii quomodocunque destructoribus et dedecoratoribus,
perpetuas inferorum poenas se ipsum exhibiturum plurimis hor-
rendis et terribilibus comminationibus et nonnullis etiam execran-
dis detestationibus pro conveniente pessimi facinoris sui praemio
claro quodam et aperto sermone significavit.

50   Cum ergo hoc[38] Deus homini—mirum in modum ut diximus
constituto—dignum quoddam agendi et intelligendi atque ad-
ministrandi et imperandi, gubernandi ac dominandi officium tri-
buerit, deinceps cur eum fecerit in calce huius tertii libri paucis
explicabimus.

51   Est autem verisimile—quin immo et decens et verum—cum
ratio corporis recta sit, quod est temporale, ipsum vero animum,
qui sit aeternus, rectiorem esse debere, cum figura et status nihil
aliud significent nisi mentem hominis eo spectare oportere quo
vultum et animum tam rectum esse convenire quam corpus, ut id
cui dominari debet imitetur et superet. Etenim satis homini esse
videbitur si Deum et eius divina opera intelligat, cuius quidem

this with our eyes. For God wished this to be man's nature — to be desirous and eager for two inseparably connected things, religion and wisdom, because they include man's role and the whole truth about him.[56]

In the very nature of the human whom he had placed so high, at so lofty a rank, the Lord Almighty planted love of the self for the sake of self-preservation. Through certain explicit commandments of the written law, he charged the rest of mankind to respect, honor and love all their neighbors — meaning all humans. So that people would more willingly and steadily perform, fulfill and complete this role of loving their own, God clearly and plainly promised to give heaven's eternal kingdom to each and every lover and defender of this divine craftwork, as the sort of reward befitting their mutual affection. But to others who hated this work of his, to those who would revile and somehow tear down so magnificent a structure, he made it known that he would deliver Hell's eternal penalties as a reward befitting the worst wickedness, stating this in clear and certain terms, with many horrid and terrifying threats and awful curses besides.[57]

Accordingly, since God assigned to man — produced in the wonderful way that I have described — this special, worthy role of acting and understanding, of managing, ruling and exercising power, I shall next take a few words at the end of this third book to explain why God made him.[58]

Since the structure of the body, which exists in time, is upright, it is reasonable — even fitting and correct — that the mind should be even more upright since it is eternal: exactly what the body's figure and bearing indicate is that a man's face ought to go the same way as his thoughts, because looking up suits the body as much as the mind, which should imitate and emulate what it must master. Moreover, for man it will plainly suffice to understand God and God's works: in fact, the height and heart of his under-

intelligentiae vis et summa haec est ut suspiciat[39] communem parentem generis humani et rerum mirabilium fabricatorem.

Quod quidem Lactantius in libro *De ira dei* maxime asserere et confirmare videtur, cuius verba haec sunt:

> Sicut mundum propter hominem machinatus est Deus, ita ipsum propter se tanquam divini templi antistitem, spectatorem operum rerumque caelestium. Solus est enim qui, sentiens capaxque rationis, intelligere possit Deum, qui opera eius admirari, virtutem potestatemque perspicere. Idcirco enim consilio, mente, prudentia instructus est. Ideo solus praeter ceteras animantes rectus corpore ac statu factus est, ut ad contemplationem parentis sui excitatus esse videatur. Ideo sermonem solus accepit ac linguam cogitationis interpretem — ut enarrare maiestatem Domini sui posset.
>
> Postremo idcirco cuncta ei subiecta sunt, ut factori atque artifici Deo esset ipse subiectus. Si ergo Deus hominem suum voluit esse cultorem ideoque illi tantum honoris attribuit ut rerum omnium dominaretur, utique iustissimum est ipsum et Deum — videlicet eum qui tanta praestiterit — amare et hominem etiam, qui sit nobiscum divini iuris societate coniunctus. Nec enim fas est cultorem Dei a Dei cultore violari.

52   Unde intelligitur religionis atque iustitiae causa esse hominem figuratum. Cuius rei testis est Marcus Tullius in libris *De legibus* ita dicens: omnium quae in doctorum hominum disputatione versantur, nihil est profecto praestabilius quam plane intelligere nos ad iustitiam esse natos. Quod si est verissimum, Deus vult ergo omnes homines esse ius-

standing is that he can look up at the common Parent of the human race to admire this Maker of wonders.[59]

In fact, we see that Lactantius makes this point best and confirms it in his book *On the Wrath of God*, in the following words:

Just as God constructed the world for the sake of man, so for his own purposes he made man the chief priest of God's temple, as it were, the observer of God's works and of things heavenly. Man alone, sentient and capable of reason, can understand God, wonder at his works and perceive his might and power. For this purpose humans have been furnished with judgment, intellect and prudence. This is why they alone, unlike other living things, have been made upright in body and stature — raised up, it would seem, in order to have their parent in sight. This is why they alone have been given language and a tongue to explain their thinking — so that they can describe their Lord's greatness.[60]

Finally, all things have been made subject to them, as they themselves are subjects of the God who made and produced them. Hence, if God wanted humans to worship him and then gave them honor great enough to make them lords over all things, then surely it is with complete justice that men love God — the one who offered them such great gifts — and humans as well, who are joined with us in the fellowship of divine justice. For a worshipper of God to be injured by a worshipper of God is not right.

We understand, then, that man was fashioned in the 52 cause of religion and justice. Marcus Tullius testifies to this fact in his books *On the Laws*, where he says this: of all the things discussed when learned people debate, surely none is better established than the clear understanding that we were born for justice. If this is completely correct, then God

tos — id est Deum et homines caros habere, Deum scilicet honorare tanquam patrem, hominem diligere velut fratrem. In his enim duobus tota hominis iustitia consistit. Qui ergo aut Deum non agnoscit aut homini nocet iniuste, et contra naturam suam vivit et hoc modo corrumpit institutum legemque divinam.

Et in septimo *Divinarum institutionum* ita inquit:

Eorum omnium summa haec est ut Deum colat. Is enim colit qui haec intelligit; is artificem rerum omnium, is vere patrem suum debita veneratione prosequitur, qui virtutem maiestatis eius de suorum operum inventione, inceptione, perfectione metitur.

53 Ceterum Augustinus rectius quam Lactantius sensisse et gravius ac verius considerasse videtur. Quippe Deum, ob immensam eius bonitatem, non sua utilitate — scriptum est enim, quoniam bonorum nostrorum non eget — sed potius hominis causa hominem fecisse putat. Nam inquit quia bonus est Deus, sumus, et reliqua.

54 Omittamus Platonicos, qui homines factos esse senserunt ut hunc terrarum orbem incolerent. Missos faciamus pariter[40] Stoicos, qui homines ad usum hominum natos fuisse dixerunt. Peripateticos denique ac reliquos ceterarum sectarum philosophos tanquam nocturnos quosdam obscurae et abstrusae veritatis indagatores praetermittamus, et ad Catholicos doctores nostros tanquam in unicum ac tranquillum et securum verae et expressae salutis portum magna iactati tempestate confugientes redeamus.

55 Fecit igitur Deus hominem ut per quandam admirabilium operum suorum intelligentiam certamque cognitionem eorum opificem recognosceret et coleret. Quod *Divinarum sententiarum* magister his

wants all people to be just—to hold God and humans dear, in other words, honoring God like a father and loving men like brothers. In these two lies the whole of human justice. Whoever does not recognize God, then, or harms a human unjustly, lives contrary to his own nature and thereby also spoils God's law and design.[61]

And in the seventh book of the *Elements of Divinity*, Lactantius has this to say:

> The sum of all this is to worship God. For this is what a worshipper of God understands: that he truly honors the Maker of all things, his own Father, with due reverence, judging the power of his greatness from the devising, the undertaking and the completing of his works.[62]

In other ways, Augustine appears to give the better account, 53 having thought about this more accurately and understanding it in more depth. He thinks, as you know, that God made man out of his immense goodness because of man, not for his own benefit: as it is written, he needs not our goods. Augustine also says that because God is good, we exist, and so on.[63]

Let me omit the Platonists, who thought that humans were 54 made in order to inhabit the earth. I shall also leave out the Stoics, who said that people were born to benefit people. Next, while tossed about by this great storm—as I pass by the Peripatetics and the rest of the philosophers from other sects, who are like people hunting at night for a dark and hidden truth—let me turn back for shelter to our Catholic teachers as the only safe and quiet harbor of salvation, distinct and authentic. God made man to wor- 55 ship and recognize him, then—through some understanding of God's own wondrous works and through sure knowledge of Him who made them—as the Maker of those things. The master of

verbis plane et aperte approbare et confirmare videtur, sic enim inquit: fecit Deus hominem ut cum cognosceret, et cognoscendo amaret, et amando possideret, et possidendo denique frueretur.

Itaque dum est in hac vita mortali, mundum ei ipsi habitaculum dedit, ut enim domus unius hominis habitaculum est et ut urbs unius populi, sic mundus pariter domicilium totius generis humani existimatur et creditur. Et postquam defunctus est, pio et iusto homini—hoc est, illi qui legitime vixerit—sempiternam caelorum sedem constituit. Proinde et homo vivens mundi incola fit et pie moriens caeli possessor efficitur, ac per hunc modum, et in hac praesenti et in futura vita, semper et omni quidem tempore felix beatusque habetur.

56   Ex hac igitur tanta ac tam sublimi hominis dignitate et excellentia—velut ab ipsa radice—invidia, superbia, indignatio, dominandi libido et ambitio atque ceterae huiusmodi animi perturbationes non iniuria oriuntur et profluunt. Nam qui sese ita dignum factum fuisse considerat ut cunctis rebus creatis praeesse ac dominari videatur, profecto non modo ab aliis superari non patietur, quod est invidiae, sed potius ceteros excellere vel maxime concupiscet, quod superbiae et ambitionis proprium vitium existimatur et creditur. At si forte contigerit ut aliquando spernatur, negligatur et contemnatur, usque adeo indignatur ut contemptores suos non secus quam capitales et acerrimos hostes ac proprios quosdam excellentiarum suarum violatores et detractores enixe usque ad necem persequatur. Quod ego etiam atque etiam considerans atque hominem noviter describere et diffinire volens, ipsum animal indignabundum mea quidem sententia non iniuria explicavi.

57   Quapropter, ut partes huius tertii libri variae hinc inde dispersas tandem aliquando epilogi gratia in unum concludamus: si

Theological Sentences plainly approves this and confirms it clearly when he uses these words: God made man to know him, and by knowing to love, by loving to possess and then by possessing to enjoy.[64]

While people are living this mortal life, then, God has given them the world to dwell in. For as a house is one person's dwelling and a people's dwelling is a city, so likewise we believe and conclude that the world is the abode of the whole human race. And after death, for the just and pious person — one who has lived by the law — God has established a permanent residence in heaven. Accordingly, as a living person becomes an occupant of the world, one who dies piously is also made an owner of heaven, and in this way, both in the present life and in the future, the human is always counted happy and blessed — for all time, in fact.[65]

In these circumstances, from this human rank and excellence 56
that is so great and so lofty, come envy, pride, indignation, ambition, lust for domination and other such disorders of the soul — emerging as from their very root and not uncaused. For surely those who realize that they have been given such status that they visibly dominate and command all of creation will not only *not* put up with being surpassed by others, which belongs to envy, but rather will feel the greatest urge to outdo the rest, which we regard as a vice belonging to pride and ambition. But should it happen sometimes that people are scorned, slighted and despised, they become so angry that they pursue their detractors zealously and to the death, as if those who pick out someone's particular virtues to dishonor and disparage were the deadliest and fiercest enemies. Thinking about this again and again and wishing to give a novel description and definition of the human, I have shown — correctly, in my view — that this is an animal given to anger.[66]

Accordingly, to bring together the various parts of this third 57
book, scattered here and there, consider this my last word, final

Deus mundum et cuncta quae in eo sunt hominis gratia fabricatus
est, si humanum quoque genus omnibus rebus dominari et
imperare voluit, si ipsum insuper decore, ingenio, sapientia, opibus
et divitiis, regnis praeterea et potestatibus[41] ornavit, si pluribus
denique et admirabilibus cum generalibus tum singularibus et
praecipuis privilegiis insignivit, profecto decere et convenire videbatur ne is — quem in tanto et tam excellenti dignitatis gradu col-
locaverat et cuius occasione cuncta quaeque machinatus erat — in
perpetuum damnaretur. Idcirco, quanquam protoplastus[42] ille noster divina mandata transgrederetur ac per hoc ipse et omnes eius
posteri aeternam damnationis poenam mererentur, ut ex inde redi-
merentur, Filium suum humanam, quando aliter fieri non poterat,
carnem suscipere atque ignominiosam execrandi patibuli mortem
subire constituit.

58   Ceterum si primi nostri parentes nequaquam peccassent, Christus nihilominus e caelis in terras descendisset — non ut humanum
genus redimeret, quod quidem a peccati labe et a reatu immune
extitisset nisi commemorati patres nostri divina mandata temere
nimis et insulse admodum contempsissent. Sed utique in mundum venisset, ut hominem per hanc humilem humanae carnis
susceptionem mirabiliter et incredibiliter honoraret glorificaret-
que — quemadmodum plurimi doctissimi simul atque sanctissimi
viri, pluribus rationibus adducti et singulari religione ac praecipua
devotione praediti, pie admodum crediderunt.

59   Nihil enim aliud quicquam ei naturae — quam tam pulchram,
tam ingeniosam et tam sapientem, ac tam opulentam, tam dignam
et tam potentem, postremo tam felicem et tam beatam constituerat — ad totam et undique absolutam perfectionem suam deesse
putabatur nisi ut ea per admixtionem cum ipsa divinitate non
solum coniuncta in illa Christi persona cum divina sed etiam ut

and alone: if God fashioned the world and everything in it for the sake of man, if he also wanted the human race to rule all things as their commander, if besides he furnished humans with beauty, brilliance, wisdom, riches and resources, as well as kingdoms and dominions, and if he then distinguished mankind with many wonderful and perpetual privileges, both universal and individual, it would certainly seem fitting and proper—for one whom God had placed at so estimable a level and so high a rank and for whose benefit he had devised each and every thing—that mankind should not be damned forever. Hence, even though that *prôtoplastos* of ours broke the divine commandments, thereby earning the eternal penalty of damnation for himself and all his descendants, God arranged for his own human Son to take on flesh and suffer a disgraceful death on the cursed gibbet, doing so to save men from this punishment, since it could not have been done in any other way.[67]

Moreover, had our first parents not sinned at all, Christ would 58 still have come down to earth from the heavens—not to redeem the human race, which then, had our storied ancestors not been so excessively rash and foolish as to disregard God's commandments, would have been unblemished by guilt and the stain of sin. Christ would have come into the world in any case, to give humanity the inconceivable glory and astonishing honor of lowering himself to take on this human flesh—following the quite pious belief of many learned and likewise holy men, who have had many reasons to offer, besides their gifts of special devotion and singular reverence.[68]

From the total perfection, absolute in every respect, of that na- 59 ture—made to be so beautiful, intelligent and wise, so wealthy, worthy and mighty, and finally so happy and so blessed—nothing else at all was thought to be lacking except to make it not only conjoint with divinity itself, by blending with the divine in Christ's

cum divina natura una et sola efficeretur, ac per hunc modum unica facta fuisse videretur. Quod neque angelis neque ulli aliae creaturae nisi homini dumtaxat ad admirabilem quandam humanae naturae dignitatem et ad incredibilem quoque eius ipsius excellentiam datum, concessum et attributum esse novimus.

person, but also the one and only nature to join with a divine nature, and in this way it was evidently made unique. We realize that this has been given, granted and permitted neither to angels nor to any other creature but man, in keeping with the astonishing value of human nature and mankind's unbelievable excellence.[69]

LIBER QUARTUS

1   Hactenus cuncta quae ad singularem quandam et praecipuam dignitatem et excellentiam hominis vel maxime spectare et pertinere
videbantur — quantum parvula ingenii nostri facultas permittere
operarive poterat — tribus praecedentibus libris sparsim ac diffuse
claro quodam et aperto sermone congessimus. Itaque oportunum
quoddam et accommodatum venisse et occurrisse tempus non
iniuria existimavimus ut ultimas huic operi manus imponeremus.

  Quod profecto iam fecissemus nisi nostra interesse putaremus
ut ea refelleremus quae a pluribus priscis novellisque auctoribus
vel de laudatione et bono mortis vel de miseria humanae vitae
scripta fuisse intelligebamus, quoniam ea illis a nobis antea tractatis aliquatenus repugnare animadvertebamus. Sed in hac nostra
praedictarum veluti frivolarum ac falsarum opinionum confutatione, ordine quodam uti constituimus ut res ipsa gravius severius-
que tractetur. Primo namque ad ea quae de fragilitate humani
corporis, ad illa deinde quae de ignobilitate animae, postremo ad
ea quae de tota hominis persona obiciebantur — quantum rerum
tractandarum natura ac materiae de qua agitur conditiones et qualitates permittere et pati videbantur — breviter respondebimus.

2   A corpore igitur incipientes, multos graves et doctos viros fuisse
dicimus qui humanum corpus — suapte natura nudum et inerme —
ita fragile, ita imbecillum, ita caducum esse putabant, ut frigora,
aestus, labores, famem et sitim et ceteras huiusmodi corporeas
molestias, sine aperta quadam et manifesta laesione, pati et tolle-
rare non posset. At si forte quieti otiove se dederit, in ipso rursus
situ ac tabo[1] liquescere, labescere ac marcescere asseverabant.

  Ea insuper quibus vel maxime oblectabatur — et sine quibus
vivere non poterat — plerunque sibi molesta ac mortifera fore

BOOK FOUR

Up to this point, throughout the three preceding books — as far as   1
my small powers of mind have allowed me — I have brought together everything I found relevant to that special worth and singular excellence of man, everything important that bears on it, stating this clearly and openly and dealing with it in detail. Now, since
the moment is opportune, I have determined that the right time
has come to put the last touches to this effort.

I would certainly have done this already except that I thought it
my job to rebut what several ancient and modern authors had
written, as I gathered, either on death as praiseworthy and something good or else on the misery of human life, my reason being
that I noticed their claims clashing somewhat with my previous
findings. To rebut the aforesaid views as worthless and false, I have
chosen a certain sequence in order to deal with this issue in a more
rigorous and sober way. First, then — as much as I am permitted
by the nature of the points to be treated, considering the features
and structure of the material in question — I shall respond briefly
to the complaints these people have made about the frailty of the
human body, then about the inferiority of the soul and finally
about the whole human person.[1]

To start with the body, I affirm that many eminent and learned   2
men have thought the human body — naked and defenseless in its
natural state — so frail, so feeble and such a ruin that it cannot,
without some obvious and manifest injury, bear cold, heat, toil,
hunger, thirst and endure other such physical vexations. And
should the body give itself up to rest and leisure, they maintained
that it would languish, weaken and waste away again in that very
dissipation and decay.

They said besides that what most delighted the body — and
without which it could not live — would generally be harmful to it

aiebant. Nam ingentem et repentinum sonitum, nimiam intuitionem, taetrum odorem, amarum saporem et asperam contactionem magnam quandam earum partium lassitudinem inducere credebant. Vigilia praeterea et somnus, cibus et potus—ut ipsi arbitrabantur—quandoque laetifera efficiebantur. Aquarum denique novitatibus vinorumque mutationibus, ventorum flatibus—et tenuissimis causis atque leviusculis offensionibus—morbidum sua semper natura dignoscebatur, quoniam ipsum ex infimis fluidisque contextum atque constructum fuisse constabat, quemadmodum per plura manifesta experimenta et evidentia quoque exempla plane et aperte deprehendimus.

3   Et Aristoteles etiam et Seneca, Cicero et Plinius multique alii Graeci et Latini sacri et profani scriptores—ne de omnibus particularem quandam mentionem faciamus—pluribus librorum suorum locis hoc idem asserere et confirmare conantur. Nam et Aristoteles in ethicorum libris quodam loco verba haec ponit: Videre et audire, ut naturales testantur sermones, laboriosa sunt. Et Cicero in *Tusculanis quaestionibus* ita inquit: cumque natura corpora nobis infirma dedisset hisque et intolerabiles dolores et morbos insanabiles adiecisset, animos quoque dedit et corporum doloribus congruentes et separatim suis molestiis et angoribus implicatos.

Quantis enim morborum generibus corpora nostra a capite usque ad pedes pullulare et redundare videantur difficile dictu foret. Unde primo suapte natura imbecilla existentia et postea per aliquam aegritudinis speciem debiliora effecta, ad celerem interitum labuntur et currunt: quin immo, ut expressius dixerim, ad quotidianam quandam et repentinam ruinam instar avium volitare et corruere comperiuntur. Proinde humanam vitam brevem et quodammodo momentaneam fieri manifestum est. Et Seneca pluribus scriptorum suorum locis, et maxime in *Consolatione ad Helbiam matrem*, hanc nostri corporis imbecillitatem multum admodum lamentatur. Plinius in suo *Naturalis historiae* volumine inter cetera

and destructive. For they believed that a large and unexpected sound, too much of a dazzling sight, a repulsive smell, a bitter taste or a rough touch would severely weaken the affected parts. Waking and sleeping, eating and drinking would sometimes become deadly — so they felt. Finally, from new wines, changes of water and breezes blowing — trifling mishaps of the least little kind — they diagnosed the body as always sickly by its nature: everyone knew that its parts were tiny and its structure soft, as I have seen from much experience and evidence as well as many plain examples.[2]

Both Aristotle and Seneca too, also Cicero and Pliny, as well as   3 many other Greek and Latin writers, both sacred and secular — not to list each and every one of them — try to make the same point and prove it in various parts of their books. In one passage from his books on ethics, Aristotle uses these words: seeing and hearing trouble us, as shown by scientific discussions. And in the *Tusculan Questions* this is what Cicero says: after giving us feeble bodies and then adding unbearable pains as well as incurable diseases, nature has also supplied bodies with minds to suit their woes, besides wrapping minds up in their own separate griefs and anguish.[3]

It would actually be hard to say how many kinds of disease seem to flourish in our bodies and run over them from head to foot. Naturally feeble to begin with and then weakened by illness of some sort, they quickly slip and fall toward death: to put it more plainly, in fact, we find our bodies in daily life fluttering like birds and suddenly tumbling into catastrophe. Plainly, then, human life is meant to be short — momentary, in a sense. In many passages of his writings, especially the *Consolation to His Mother Helvia*, Seneca also greatly laments this weakness of our bodies. Pliny, while adding a strong complaint about this debility of the

de hac humani corporis debilitate apprime conquestus, propterea naturam potius novercam quam matrem nobis extitisse scribit.

Iob insuper domum istam nostram et hoc habitaculum tuguriumque terrestre—idest ex terra madefacta—et ex luto et limo compactum et constitutum[2] fuisse tradit. Quod Innocentius Tertius Summus Pontifex in eo libro cuius titulus est *De miseria humanae vitae* augere et amplificare volens, de vilitate utriusque materiae, et illius ex qua Adae corpus et alterius etiam ex qua ceterorum hominum corpora confecta fuisse scimus, multa et dicit et sentit. Siquidem primi hominis corpus de limo terrae divinitus factum esse confirmans, planetas et stellas ex igne, flatus et ventos ex aere, pisces et volucres ex aqua, hominem et iumenta de terra ab omnipotenti Deo fabricata fuisse probat, cetera vero aliorum hominum corpora ex humanis seminibus ac spermatibus concepta et postea nata in lucem prodiisse asseverat. Ex quibus tanto viliorem et ignobiliorem primi hominis materiam quam aliorum quorumcunque animatorum extitisse concludit, quanto terrestre elementum ceteris omnibus vilius et ignobilius reperitur.

Et reliqua quoque hominum corpora eandem cum mutis animalibus nascendi conditionem sortita esse refert, nisi forte postquam concepta sunt embriones dumtaxat (hoc est imperfecti solorum hominum fetus) in materno utero ex sanguine menstruo educarentur et nutrirentur. Quod ipse quodam praedicti operis sui loco plane innuisse et aperte sensisse videtur, quandoquidem hoc solum post suam conceptionem hominum et non aliorum animalium corporibus obiecisse legimus. At his ipsis plura alia huiusmodi, dedecoris et vituperationis et ignominiae plena atque referta, subiungit quae, ne longiores simus, brevitatis causa praetermittimus.

Haec igitur sunt quae a plerisque idoneis auctoribus de imbecillitate—vel potius de fragilitate—humani corporis disputari et in medium adduci consueverunt. Nunc vero ad ea quae de ignobilitate animae disseri ac tractari solent parumper accedamus.

human body to other points in his work on *Natural History*, writes
that nature has been more a stepmother to us than a mother.[4]

This house of ours, says Job, this little hut or shed made of
earth — moist earth, that is — was built with mud and stuck together with slime. This is a point that Innocent III, the supreme   4
pontiff, wants to extend and amplify in his book titled *On the Misery of Human Life*: he has strong views and much to say about the
worthlessness of both kinds of matter, both that from which Adam's body was produced, as we know, and also the different matter
for the bodies of other humans. Affirming that the first man's body
was made by divine action from the slime of the earth, he declares
that Almighty God fashioned the planets and stars from fire, the
breezes and winds from air, the fish and birds from water, man and
beasts from earth, but he states that the bodies of other humans
were conceived from human seed and sperm, coming forth later to
be born. From this he concludes that the matter of the first man
was lower and worth less than that of any other ensouled beings,
in that earth is lower and worth less than all the other elements.[5]

And he reports that the rest of the human bodies shared their
situation at birth with the dumb animals, except perhaps that after
conception it was just their embryos (meaning the immature
young of humans only) that were sustained and nourished on
menstrual blood in the mother's womb. In one passage of the work
just mentioned, this plainly appears to have been his view and
clearly what he suggested, since we see him making this charge
against the bodies of men after their conception, not against other
animals. To these he adds many more such accusations, full of
disgrace and dishonor and loaded with blame, but to avoid going
on too long, I am skipping them to keep things short.[6]

So then, concerning the human body's frailty — or fragility, if
you like — these points are what the leading authors have typically
brought up for deliberation. Now let me move on for a moment to   5
their usual discussions when the topic is the soul's worthlessness.

In secundo huius operis libro, ubi varias de conditionibus et qualitatibus animae diversorum auctorum opiniones recitavimus, inter cetera philosophos quosdam fuisse diximus qui humanam animam aliquid corporeum esse opinabantur, ut Thales, Anaximander, Anaximenes, Anaxagoras, Diogenes, Leucippus, Democritus, Heraclitus, Empedocles, Hippias, Archelaus, Zeno, Aristoxenus, Varro et si qui alii fuerunt. Nec defuerunt etiam qui eam nihil omnino esse voluerunt, ut Dicaearchus: qui propterea quod animam nihil esse imaginabatur id nomen irritum et inane frustraque *animantes* et *animalia* appellari asseverabat. Plerique insuper astiterunt qui, et si ipsam quicquam corporeum abnegarent, de potentia tamen materiae et *ex traduce*, ut theologico verbo iterum utamur, *educi* censebant.

6   Atque hi omnes animos humanos una cum suis corporibus interire existimabant — nec solum hi qui animos aliquid corporeum esse foreque credebant, sed etiam quidam alii qui eos spiritus arbitrabantur mori simul cum propriis corporibus putabant: quales Epicureos extitisse novimus et quicunque eos secuti sunt. Animos enim non aliter suis quibusdam perturbationibus vexari quam corpora ac pluribus morborum generibus implicari aiebant.

Nam quemadmodum in humanis corporibus multas aegritudinum species — emigraneam, optalmiam, polipum, lienteriam, cyragras, podagras, lateris dolores, strangurias, tormina,[3] febres et cetera huiusmodi — inter assistendum quandoque acriter vexare et ad extremum in manifestum quendam et certum interitum ducere videbant; ita pariter in animis varia diversarum perturbationum genera assistere arguebant, a quibus ipsi plerunque in contrarias partes distrahebantur ac per hunc modum interibant.

Quales sub aegritudine aemulationem, obtrectationem, misericordiam, angorem, luctum, maerorem, aerumnam, dolorem,

In the second book of this work, where I listed various authoritative opinions about the soul's features and dispositions, one of my points was that some philosophers believed the human soul to be something bodily—like Thales, Anaximander, Anaximenes, Anaxagoras, Diogenes, Leucippus, Democritus, Heraclitus, Empedocles, Hippias, Archelaus, Zeno, Aristoxenus, Varro and various others. There were even some, like Dicaearchus, who thought the soul to be nothing at all: since there was nothing he pictured as a soul, he maintained that its name is empty and meaningless and that calling things *ensouled* and *animate* is nonsense. This discussion involved several people who, even while denying that the soul was anything bodily, judged—if I may use theological language again—that it came *off the branch* and was *educed* from the potency of matter.[7]

All these people also thought that human souls perish with 6 their bodies—not only those who believed that souls are and shall be something bodily, but also certain others who took them to be spirits and imagined they would die simultaneously with their own bodies: we know that Epicureans were of that sort as well as those who followed them. For they said that souls are no different than bodies in being troubled by certain special disorders that tangled them up in many kinds of illness.[8]

They observed many types of sickness in human bodies—migraine, inflamed eyes, polyps, diarrhea, gouty hands and limbs, pains in the side, difficulty urinating, gas pains, fever and other such things—illnesses whose presence sometimes gave people enormous trouble before bringing them in the end to a manifest and certain death; likewise they declared that various kinds of disturbance of a different sort were equally present in souls, often pulling them apart in different directions and thereby killing them.

Under grief they listed jealousy, scorn, pity, anguish, mourning, sorrow, distress, suffering, lamenting, anxiety, vexation, torment

lamentationem, sollicitudinem, molestiam, afflictionem, desperationem constituebant. Sub metu vero pigritiam, pudorem, terrorem, timorem, pavorem, exanimationem, conturbationem, formidinem reponebant. Sub laetitia autem malivolentiam, delectationem, iactationem collocabant. At sub cupiditate excandescentiam, iram, odium, inimicitiam, discordiam, indigentiam, desiderium et reliqua ordinabant. Quae quidem omnia et cetera huiusmodi perturbationum genera Cicero quodam scriptorum suorum loco egregie eleganterque complexus est.

7   Qui vero animos hominum immortales fore autumabant omnes variis perturbationibus dum in corporibus viverent commoveri et conquassari arbitrabantur. Quando vero duarum illarum ab invicem et inter se diversarum naturarum coniunctio per separationem dissolvebatur, partim animos in diversa viventium brutorum corpora, ut ea tempestate casus ferebat, ingredi iudicabant, atque sic eo usque vivere putabant quoad marcescente primo illo corporeo instrumento in aliud quoddam intrare cogerentur. Ac per hunc modum ob varia ac paene infinita brutorum corpora—secundum hanc opinionem—perpetua et aeterna animorum vita servabatur.

Cuius quidem opinionis Pythagoras Samius auctor fuisse perhibetur, qui a Pherecide Syro, eius magistro—primo ex naturalibus immortalitatis repertore—animam immortalem esse accipiens, atque hoc quonam modo sine corporibus evenire fierive posset intelligere non valens, huiusmodi circularem, ut ita dixerim, revolutionem excogitavit atque adinvenit. Proinde homines ex constitutionibus suis brutorum animalium carnibus vesci prohibebat—ne forte defunctorum amicorum et domesticorum animae per humanas eorum corporum commestiones ex inde expellerentur atque alio transmigrare cogerentur. Partim vero eas per centum annos, ut inquit poeta,

    centum errant annos

and despair. Under fear they put sluggishness, shame, dread, panic, alarm, terror, confusion and fright. Under joy they located malice, gloating and boasting. And under passion they classified temper, anger, hatred, hostility, dissension, need, desire and the rest. In one passage of his works, with his great and distinctive elegance, Cicero covered all such types of disturbance and others.[9]

Some who claimed that human souls will be immortal, however, held that they would all be shaken and agitated by various disturbances as long as they lived in bodies. But when these two conjoined natures, so unlike one another, were parted and their union dissolved, they reckoned that some souls entered into various bodies of living animals, as a moment's chance might take them there, surviving until the original bodily material withered away, forcing them to occupy another. Hence, since the bodies of beasts were so different and so many, souls — by this account — would be kept alive perpetually and eternally.[10]

The first actually to state this view, they say, was Pythagoras of Samos. From his teacher, Pherecydes of Syros — the first of the scientists to discover immortality — he learned that the soul is immortal. And since he could not understand how this might possibly happen or come about without bodies, he came upon this turning in a cycle, so to speak, and worked the idea out. Next, because of how humans come to be, he forbade them to eat the flesh of dumb animals — to prevent the souls of friends and family from being driven out and forced to migrate elsewhere because someone had made a meal out of their bodies for humans to eat. They said that another part of these souls fluttered about,

wandering for a hundred years

et reliqua, hoc est per multa temporum curricula — sive per aerem istum crassum et caliginosum sive per purum aethera vagas et errabundas volitare aiebant, donec vel ad Tartara laberentur vel ad caelum,[4] secundum diversas ante actae vitae conditiones, evolarent.

8   Quapropter sive mortales sive immortales essent animae, iuxta commemoratas praedictorum philosophorum de ipsarum qualitatibus et conditionibus sententias, eas tales esse non iniuria concludi videbatur ut sive in corporibus assistentes suis naturalibus perturbationibus vexarentur sive post mortem una cum illis evanescerent. At si remanerent, certe vel in alienis corporibus habitarent vel per aera vel per aethera volitarent vel apud inferos morarentur. Itaque quocunque modo fiebat ut ubicunque existerent, apprime torquerentur. Atque haec sunt quae de indignitate humanae animae in praesentiarum retulisse sufficiat.

9   Deinceps ad ea breviter procedamus[5] quae de tota hominis persona atque de humana vita a nonnullis idoneis auctoribus ignominiae, vituperationis et detestationis causa referebantur. Si igitur dicet quispiam duo illa ex quibus hominem compositum ac confectum esse constat talia sunt qualia supra ostendisse et demonstrasse videmur, quis iure ambigere dubitareve poterit quin illud quod ex eorum compositione resultat componentium naturam redoleat, sapiat atque retineat?

Proinde hominem fragilem, caducum et ignobilem, et multis ac paene infinitis morborum et perturbationum generibus subiectum et implicatum, singulis quibusque eius naturam et conditiones paulo diligentius et accuratius considerantibus plane et aperte ap-
10   parebit. Quocirca plerique veteres doctissimi simul atque sapientissimi viri, haec et cetera huiusmodi corporis et animae incommoda atque humanae vite mala secum ipsi animadvertentes et saepenumero reputantes et recognoscentes, pluribus librorum suo-

and so on, in the poet's words, meaning through many cycles of seasons — whether they described them as roaming through air that was thick with mist or straying through the pure aether, until they either slipped down into Tartarus or else flew up to Heaven, depending on the different states of their past lives.[11]

Hence, given the statements by the aforesaid philosophers un- 8 der review here, dealing with the dispositions of souls and their features, it would not seem wrong — whether souls were mortal or immortal — to conclude that the state they are in is either to be plagued by their own natural disturbances while living in the body or else to vanish after death along with their bodies. If they survive, however, this is certain: either they live in the bodies of others or flit about through the air or aether or else linger in the underworld. Whatever happens, then, wherever they end up, there is immense torment. And this is enough to review here about the worthlessness of the human soul.

So let me move on to a brief account of reports on human life 9 and the whole human person made by certain distinguished authorities for the purpose of disgracing, denouncing and cursing them. On these points, if someone says — thinking of the two parts from which the human composite is known to be made — that they are as I have already shown and proved them to be, then could anyone really hesitate or have any doubt that the resulting composite would retain the nature of the components, keeping the same smell and savor?

For those who think a bit more carefully and accurately about man's nature and the human condition, it will be as clear as day from this that people are frail, fallen and miserable, gripped by many types of sickness and subject to nearly numberless disturbances. This is why we see that many ancient sages — people of the 10 greatest wisdom and learning — when they gave thought to these and other such disadvantages of body and soul, often reflecting and recognizing them as evils in human life, have greatly lamented

rum locis de talibus hominum qualitatibus apprime conquesti ac lamentati fuisse comperiuntur.

Nam et Egesias quidam Cirenaicus philosophus de plurimis humanae vitae incommodis priscis quondam temporibus sic copiose et eleganter disputabat ut is a Ptolomaeo, Aegyptiorum rege, prohibitus esse dicatur illa in scholis dicere quoniam multi his auditis mortem sibi ipsi consciscerent. Unde, cum viva, ut aiunt, voce regia prohibitione impeditus disserere ac disputare non posset, demum sese continere nequivit quin ea litteris mandaret de quibus loqui vetabatur. Ac per hunc modum egregium dialogum composuit ubi quidam inducebatur qui a vita per inediam discedens ab amicis revocabatur, quibus ille respondens varia humanae vitae enumerabat incommoda.

11   Crantor quoque in *Consolatione* nescio qua hoc idem plane et aperte confirmabat, ubi inter cetera—ut refert Cicero—Terrineum[6] quendam Helisium mortem filii graviter maerentem facit. Proinde cum in psicomantium ad Apollinis oraculum accessisset, sciscitaturus quaenam extitisset tantae calamitatis causa, ei sic interroganti in tabellis tres huiuscemodi versiculos datos fuisse scribit:

> Ignaris homines in vita mentibus errant:
> Euthineus potitur Fatorum munere leto;
> sic fuit utilius finiri ipsique tibique.

Alchidamus insuper—rhetor antiquus et, ut ait Cicero, in primis nobilis—laudationem mortis scripsisse perhibetur, quae ex enumeratione humanorum malorum maxime consistere et constare videbatur. Marcus Tullius praeterea in praeclaro illo et celebrato *Consolationis* volumine hanc humanarum calamitatum materiam aureo eloquentiae suae flumine elegantissime simul atque copiosissime prosecutus, vitam hominum usque adeo luxit et

these facts about mankind and complained about them in many passages of their books.

Now in times long gone a person named Hegesias, a philosopher from Cyrene, also discussed the many disadvantages of human life with such style and richness that they say Ptolemy, the king of Egypt, forbade him to lecture about these things in his classes because many who heard him talk did themselves in. Hence, though the royal ban meant that Hegesias could not debate these issues by talking out loud about them, as they say, he was finally unable to restrain himself from putting on paper what he was forbidden to utter. So he wrote a remarkable dialogue that introduces a character called back by his friends from exiting life by starvation, and he answers them by listing various disadvantages of human life.[12]

In some unknown *Consolation*, Crantor also gives clear and full   11 evidence of this — as Cicero reports — where he describes a certain Elysius of Terina as weighed down with grief for his dead son. When Elysius went into the séance room to ask Apollo's oracle what the cause of such a calamity might be, Crantor writes that he was given tablets with three verses like these in reply to his question:

> Humans wander through life with minds knowing nothing:
> In death Euthynous gets a prize from the Fates;
> for him to end it was better — and you too.

They also say that Alcidamas — an ancient rhetorician and very renowned, so Cicero claims — wrote a panegyric on death, and evidently it consisted mainly of a list of human evils. In his brilliant and celebrated work on *Consolation*, in a golden flood of his own eloquence, Cicero too developed this material on human calamities very elegantly and in abundance. He wept for man's life

lamentatus est ut qui ea legerent nihil aliud, ut ait quidam, cupe-
rent quam has res seculares nostrasque relinquere.

12   Plinius denique quodam *Naturalis historiae* loco nihil homine
miserius ac superbius esse testatur. Ceteras quippe animantes solam sine ullis animi angoribus victus curam habere confirmat
et probat, hominem autem praeter illa quae sibi cum brutis
communia sunt multis ac paene infinitis animi perturbationibus
quotidie vexari ac torqueri asseverat.

13   Hinc Herodoti historia quaedam de Cleobe et Biton,[7] duobus
cuiusdam Argivae[8] sacerdotis filiis, predicabatur. Nam cum illa ad
solemne et statutum sacrificium curru de more in urbem veheretur, nescio quo factum est ut iumenta morarentur. Unde filii qui
aderant veste posita adiuvandi gratia corpora perunxerunt; ad iu-
gum accesserunt, ac per hunc modum sacerdos advecta in fanum.
Cum currus ductus esset a filiis, precata a dea dicitur ut illis prae-
mium daret pro pietate, quod maximum homini dari posset a deo.
Post epulatos cum matre adolescentes somno se dedisse, inventos
mane esse mortuos.

Hinc Trophoneus[9] et Agamedes commemorabantur, qui simili
precatione usi dicebantur. Nam cum Apollini Delphis templum
exaedificavissent, venerantes deum petierunt mercedem non par-
vam quidem operis ac laboris sui — nihil certi sed quod esset optimum homini — quibus Apollo id daturum ostendit. Unde cum
post diem tertium mortui reperirentur, mortem optimum quiddam esse iudicatum per eum deum fuisse confirmabant, cui reliqui
dii concessissent ut praeter ceteros divinaret.

Hinc poetarum de Sileno fabella ferebatur, qui ipsum a Mida
Rege captum fabulabantur. Nec prius ab eo dimissum et relaxa-
tum extitisse asseverabant quam regem docuisset non nasci homini

and mourned so much that those who read his words would want
nothing more (as one person said) than to leave this worldly business of ours behind.[13]

And then Pliny, in a passage of his *Natural History*, testifies that   12
nothing is haughtier than man or more wretched. He gives evidence to show that the rest of the animals care only about eating,
without mental anguish. On the other hand, he maintains that
humans — beyond what they have in common with beasts — are
shaken and tormented every day by many disturbances of mind
that almost never end.[14]

Item: Herodotus told a story about Cleobis and Biton, two   13
sons of a certain priestess from Argos. When she was riding in her
chariot in the usual way to a scheduled rite of sacrifice, something
made her horses hold back. Then her sons, who were nearby, removed their clothes so they could smear their bodies with oil to
help: they went and took the yoke, and this was how she was
conducted to the temple. Since her sons had pulled the chariot,
they say she prayed to the goddess to give them a reward for their
dutiful deed and to make it the greatest that a human could get
from a god. After dining with their mother, the boys went to sleep
and were found dead in the morning.[15]

Item: Trophonius and Agamades, they say, were also remembered for using a similar prayer. For after they had built a temple
for Apollo at Delphi, they asked the god while worshipping to
recompense their deed and their toil, and in no small way to be
sure — nothing they could describe, but what would be best for a
human — and Apollo gave them a sign that a gift would come.
Three days later they were found dead, confirming that death was
what this god judged best, the one to whom the rest of the gods
conceded primacy in divination.[16]

Item: the poets used to tell a fable about Silenus, who in the
myth was captured by King Midas. He got the king to untie and
release him, they said, as soon as he explained that not being born

longe optimum esse, proxime autem quam primum mori. Atque hoc ei muneris pro sua missione et relaxatione dedisse scribitur. Qua quidem sententia et Euripides et multi alii poetae in[10] confabulationibus suis usi fuisse perhibentur.

Hinc proveniebant nonnullae pertinaces et obstinatae quarumdam Asiaticarum gentium opiniones, quae familiares et convicinos lugendi causa invitare et domum convocare consueverant ubi esset aliquis in lucem editus, quod humanae vitae varia reputabant mala. Atqui labores morte finisset graves, hunc omnes amicos laude et laetitia exequi.

14   Hinc Theombrotus Ambrachiota, etsi ei nihil accidisset adversi, satius tamen mori quam vivere iudicavit; proinde e muro sese in mare obeundi causa proiecit. Hinc Socrates, cum e vinculis et e carceribus educi facile posset, interire quam vivere maluit. Hinc Cato Uticensis mortem sibi ipse conscivit, atque sic e vita abiisse fertur ut Caii Caesaris victoriam certam quandam moriendi sui causam nactum se esse gauderet. Hinc denique innumerabiles alii, gentiles et ethnici, sapientissimi simul atque fortissimi viri extiterunt qui, his dumtaxat causis adducti, et sese vita privarunt et proprias suas suorumque domesticorum mortes aequo et hilari animo tollerarunt.

15   Sed quid opus est plura profanorum hominum exempla proferre cum Salomonem[11] in libro *Ecclesiastes* hoc idem plane et aperte sentire videamus?[12] Nam in principio a vanitate incipiens et per totum postea procedens: me, quodam loco inquit, taedet vitae meae cum videam universa mala quae sub Sole fiunt. Et paulo post ita scribit:

Unus interitus est hominis et iumentorum et aequa utriusque conditio: sic moritur homo, sicut et illa moriuntur. Similiter spirant omnia, et nihil habet homo amplius iumento. Cuncta subiacent vanitati, et omnia pergunt ad unum locum; de terra facta sunt, et in terram pariter revertuntur. Quis

is the best thing by far for a human and that dying as soon as possible comes next. The story goes that Silenus gave this lesson in payment for being untied and set free. Euripides and many other poets are said to have used this saying in the stories they told.[17]

Item: various fixed and obstinate beliefs arose among certain Asiatic peoples. When someone was born, their custom was to invite family and neighbors and bring them home to mourn, reflecting on life's various evils. But when a person put his heavy burdens down and died, they all followed him to the grave with praise and joy.[18]

Item: Theombrotus of Ambracia, even if nothing bad happened   14 to him, thought it better to die than to live: so to end it all he threw himself from a wall into the sea. Item: Socrates could easily have been released from his chains and prison but chose dying rather than living. Item: when Cato of Utica committed suicide, they say that in making his exit from life he was happy to have lighted on Caesar's certain victory as a reason for dying. Item the last: countless others, pagan sages and heathen heroes, removed themselves from life simply because such reasons persuaded them, also accepting their own deaths and those of family members with a calm and cheerful attitude.[19]

But why offer more examples of ungodly people when we see in   15 the book of Ecclesiastes that Solomon feels the same, clearly and plainly? Starting at the beginning with emptiness and proceeding through the whole work, in one place he says: I am weary of my life when I see that everything happening under the Sun is evil. Shortly after this he writes:

> Death is one for man and beast, and both are in the same state: as the human dies, so do animals. All draw the same breath, and a man gets no more than a beast. All are subject to emptiness, and all move on to a single place; from earth they were made, and into the earth they return just alike.

novit si spiritus filiorum Adam ascendat sursum, et si spiritus iumentorum descendat deorsum?

Et inferius sic ait: laudavi magis mortuos quam viventes, et feliciorem utroque iudicavi qui nondum natus est, nec vidit mala quae
sub Sole fiunt.[13] Et alibi: melior est[14] dies mortis die nativitatis. Et
multa his similia complectitur.

16   Cum Iob quoque, in sacro illo et celebrato eius dialogo, inter
cetera verba haec ponit:[15] homo natus de muliere, brevi vivens
tempore, repletus multis miseriis, qui quasi flos egreditur et conte-
ritur et fugit velut umbra et nunquam in eodem statu permanet.
Et alibi ita inquit: militia est vita hominis super terram, et sicut
dies mercennarii dies eius. Et paulo post sic scribit: hesterni sumus, et ignoramus quoniam sicut umbra dies nostri sunt super
terram. Et infra ait: dies mei velociores fuerunt cursore, fugerunt
et non viderunt bonum, et transierunt quasi naves poma por-
tantes, sicut aquila volans ad escam. Et paulo inferius dicit: quare
de vulva eduxisti me? Qui utinam consumptus essem ne oculus
me videret; fuissem quasi non essem, de utero translatus ad tumu-
lum. Et sexcenta huiusmodi per totum paene librum hinc inde
dispersit, quae omnia singillatim connumerare nimis longum esset.

17   Cum Ambrosius insuper, Mediolanensis Episcopus, vir sanctis-
simus atque doctissimus, seorsum de bono mortis tractare ac singulare quoddam opus separatim scribere non dubitaverit. In quo
quidem opere et multa humanae vitae mala enumerat et ad princi-
palem conclusionem quam intendit praedictas et alias quasdam
ecclesiasticas auctoritates commemorat. Et ad confutationem quo-
rumdam quae prius circa vituperationem mortis sibi ipsi antea
obiecerat, tria eius genera distinxit atque obiecta illa dissolvit, ac
demum id in calce libri quod a principio proposuerat probare et
confirmare conatur.

Who knows whether the spirit of the sons of Adam ascends above and the spirit of beasts goes down below?

He says this farther on: the dead I have praised more than the living, and the one not yet born I have judged happier than both — the one who has not seen what evils happen under the Sun. Elsewhere he says: the day of death is better than the day of birth. And Solomon adds many more comments like these.[20]

Job likewise, in that sacred and celebrated conversation of his, makes this remark among others: man born of woman, living a little while, filled full of misery, comes forth like a flower and wastes away, as fleeting as a shadow and never staying the same. Elsewhere he puts it this way: a person's life upon earth is warfare, and his days are like the days of a hired soldier. A little farther on he writes: we were born yesterday, not knowing that our days on earth are like shadows. After that: my days go faster than a runner, rushing away and seeing no good, passing by like ships carrying fruit, like an eagle flying to its food. And next: why did you bring me out of your belly? Would that I had been eaten up and no eye would see me, as if I had never existed, carried from a womb to a tomb. From there on Job scattered hundreds more statements like this through almost the whole book, but it would take too long to list them all one by one.[21] 16

Ambrose also, bishop of Milan, a very holy and learned man, had no hesitations about dealing separately with death as a good and writing about it in a special work devoted to that subject. In this work, in fact, he lists many evils of human life, also mentioning the religious authorities just named along with others to support the main conclusion that he intends. And to refute certain denunciations of death that he had first set up for himself as objections, he divided them into three kinds and solved the problems, trying at the end of his book to confirm and finally demonstrate what he had proposed at the start.[22] 17

18   Postremo, cum commemoratus Innocentius particularem quendam librum composuerit quem, ut supra diximus, *De miseria humane vite* nuncupavit, ubi a prima nativitatis origine incipiens et
usque ad ultimum finem tendens multa congessit. E quibus nos
illa dumtaxat elegimus quae ceteris memoratu digniora et ad nostrum refellendi et confutandi propositum aptiora fore putabamus.

Postquam enim ipse de putrida quadam et vili embrionis conceptione disseruit, omnes, inquit—tunc cum nascimur, quando
nondum per aetatem infecti et depravati esse possumus—ut certam quandam et veram naturae miseriam exprimeremus, vel mares
vel feminae, querulis et lamentabilibus vocibus lugemus et eiu-
lamus. Cunctos namque—masculos in *ha*, feminas vero in *he*—
cum oriuntur flere ac plorare testatur. Et ad maiorem et eviden-
tiorem huius suae sententiae confirmationem vulgarem illum et
decantatum versum allegans commemorat quo sic enuntiatur:

dicentes *he* vel *ha*
quotquot nascuntur ab Eva.

Et id nomen ita interpretatur: *e-v-a* nihil aliud est quam *heu* et *ha*.
Quorum utrunque dolentis interiectionem esse confirmat, et demum ante peccatum *viraginem* et postea *Evam* appellari meruisse
subiungit.

His igitur et huiusmodi velut solidis quibusdam et optimis—ut
sibi videbatur—futuri aedificii sui fundamentis qualitercunque
iactis,[16] per nuditatem, per pediculos, per sputum,[17] per urinas,
per stercora, per brevitatem temporis, per senectutem, per varios
mortalium labores doloresque, per diversa hominum studia, per
vicinitatem mortis, per multiplicia tormentorum genera, ac per
plura huiusmodi humani corporis incommoda late copioseque
procedit.

19   Quae quidem si nos divina favente gratia quemadmodum cupimus pro modulo nostro confutarimus, oportune finem dicendi faciemus, ubi prius nosmet ipsos et quoscunque huius nostri operis

And finally Innocent — I have mentioned him before — wrote a   18
book dedicated to this topic: as I said, the title he chose is *On the Misery of Human Life*. Starting with the first instant of birth and continuing to the final moment, he crams a lot in. From all this I have chosen only what is more memorable than the rest, thinking it would better suit my task of confuting and refuting.[23]

After describing the conceiving of an embryo as vile and rotten, he says that all of us, male and female alike — from the moment of birth, when we cannot yet have been spoiled and depraved by age — wail and howl with noises of pain and complaint to express our nature's real true misery. For he maintains that all infants start out crying and weeping — males with *ha*, females with *he*. And to give stronger and plainer proof of this claim of his, he quotes the popular verse that people sing, where it says

all of us are born from Eva,
crying either *he* or *ha*.

This is how he interprets her name: *e-v-a* is just *oh!* plus *ah!* Innocent asserts that both are interjections of someone in pain, then adding that *he-roine* was what she deserved to be called before her sin and *e-v-a* afterward.[24]

Treating these points and others like them as quite good and solid — so he imagined — he set them out however it suited him to lay the foundations for what he meant to construct. Then he goes on endlessly with a variety of remarks about many disadvantages of the human body: the nakedness, the lice, the spit, piss, shit, fleeting time, old age, the different pains that mortals suffer as they toil, the various things that people try to do, the nearness of death and many types of torment.[25]

If I am favored by God's grace to refute these claims as I wish,   19
in my own small way, it will be time to finish my discussion, having given us and anyone who reads my work this careful and exact

lectores in calce libri diligenter et accurate admonuerimus: quatenus delectabiles et optimas humanae naturae conditiones — de quibus in tribus praecedentibus libris satis large satisque copiose disputavimus — ab omnipotenti Deo recognoscant, ut per bona opera in hoc saeculo semper laeti et alacres vivere et in futuro postea divina Trinitate a qua praedicta omnia nobis provenerunt perpetuo

20 frui valeamus. Nos igitur cuncta superius commemorata refellere et confutare vel maxime cupientes, eodem ordine ad confutandum procedemus quo inter obiiciendum usi sumus.

Unde a corpore incipientes, ad imbecillitatem et ceteras eius incommoditates sic et in hunc modum respondere non dubitamus. Catholici doctores nostri humanum corpus, quod ab omnipotenti Deo ex limo terrae factum fuisse supra diximus, tale extitisse testantur, ut partim mortale esset, si protoplastus[18] ille peccasset, quemadmodum eum fecisse scimus, partim vero, si non peccasset, immortale efficeretur. Primus enim homo mortale et quodammodo immortale corpus habuisse perhibetur. Unde quaeri solet an utrunque ex conditione ipsius corporis habuerit an potius immortalitas ex gratiae beneficio ac privilegio provenerit.

Proinde in primo eius statu ita factum fuisse dicunt ut, si voluisset, utique non mori potuisset. In secundo vero statu, postquam delinquens transgressus est, a primaeva illa conditione sua ipsum usque adeo degenerasse et defecisse tradunt ut certam quandam et indubitatam moriendi legem contraheret. At in tertio gloriosae resurrectionis statu tale tantumque per gratiam effectum iri dicunt ut mori non poterit, quemadmodum in fine huius nostri operis — adiutore Deo — paulo latius et uberius ostendemus.

Itaque omnem corporis imbecillitatem et quascunque aegritudines et cetera quaeque eius incommoda a nobis antea commemorata non ex natura sua sed potius ex peccati labe contraxit. Unde quicquid mali in praesentiarum habere ac possidere existimatur —

advice when I end this book: that inasmuch as the superb and
delightful features of human nature—those I have discussed so
extensively and in such detail in the three preceding books—are
recognized as coming from Almighty God, then may we have the
strength, through good works, always to live with joy and cheer in
this world, and then later, in the next, to enjoy for eternity the
divine Trinity from which all the aforesaid goods have come to us.
Therefore, since my greatest desire is to expose and refute all the
teachings that I have mentioned above, my rebuttal will go in the
same order used to present them.²⁶

    Starting with the body, then, concerning its weakness and other
disadvantages, I have no doubt how to respond—as follows.
About the human body, which I have already described as made
by Almighty God from the mud of the earth, our Catholic teachers testify that its condition was to be partly mortal, if the primal
man sinned—as we know he did—but if he were not to sin, to be
made partly immortal. In fact, they said that the first man had a
mortal body that was, in some sense, also immortal. The usual
question, then, asks if Adam got both from the state of the body
itself or if immortality came as a privilege with the aid of grace.

    In his original state, then, they say he was made so that, had he
wished, he could have never died at all. But in his later state, after
failing and transgressing, they maintain that he fell so far from his
primeval condition and was so degenerate that he brought a cove-
nant of death—sure and certain—into effect. But in a third state
of glorious resurrection they say that grace will make him so great
that he will be unable to die, as I shall show—with God's help—
in a bit more depth and detail at the end of my book.

    So it was not from his nature but rather from falling into sin
that Adam got every weakness of his body, all its afflictions and
any remaining disadvantages that I have already mentioned. Hence
whatever evil one thinks—and rightly believes—the body to have

et creditur merito — non eius naturae sed primae potius transgressioni, quemadmodum supra diximus, attribuendum est. Itaque omnes profanorum et sacrorum scriptorum conquestiones et lamentationes de laudatione et de bono mortis et de reliquis incommoditatibus suis deficere cessareque deberent quandoquidem tale non ab ipso Deo neque ab eius natura sed a peccato prodiisse et provenisse novimus.

21   Ceterum fortasse dicet quispiam: quanquam ita esse concederetur, consequens tamen non videretur quin quaecunque hominum corpora — sive ex natura sive potius ex peccato, ceu tu probare et asserere conaris — hanc fragilitatis et aegritudinis ac mortis et reliquarum denique incommoditatum necessitatem acceperint acceptamque retulerint. Quin immo talem et tantam molestiarum[19] necessitatem reportarunt ut — quaecunque sit et undecunque provenerit — iam a principio creationis naturalis effecta fuisse videatur, quando eam moriendi et ceterarum malarum conditionum legem cunctis humanis corporibus a principio nativitatis suae et omni quidem tempore imminere et impendere non dubitamus.

22   Haec omnia et cetera huiusmodi etsi nos vera esse fateamur, pluribus tamen — nisi nimis queruli nimisque ingrati ac pertinaces et delicati essemus — voluptatum quam molestiarum generibus potiri in hac nostra communi et pervulgata vita dicere et asseverare auderemus. Nulla est enim, mirabile dictu, hominis operatio, si diligenter et accurate eius naturam adverterimus,[20] ex qua ipse saltem non mediocriter oblectetur. Quippe singulis exterioribus videndi, audiendi, olfaciendi, gustandi, et tangendi sensibus tantas semper et tam vehementes voluptates capit ut quaedam interdum superfluae ac nimiae et supervacaneae fieri videantur. Quantis namque homo voluptatibus capiatur — partim ex certa quadam et expressa pulchrorum corporum visione; partim ex sonorum et simphoniarum et rerum insuper magnarum variarumque auditione; partim ex florum et similium odorum olfatione; partim ex diversa dulcium epularum suaviumque vinorum degustatione;

and keep at present, this must be assigned not to its nature but rather to the first transgression, as previously stated. Therefore, all the complaining and wailing by writers, profane and sacred, in praise of death as something good and about the body's other disadvantages should cease and desist since we know that no such thing has come from God or has been produced by its nature but has resulted from sin.[27]

On the other hand, suppose someone says this: granting what 21 you claim, the consequence is just that whatever human bodies are — and whether nature is the cause or it is sin, as you maintain and try to prove — they have, in fact, acquired this destiny of frailty, affliction, death and other disadvantages, and they have passed on what they received. Look: their destiny of woes is such and so vast — whatever it may be like, no matter its source — that the product seems to have been natural from the beginning of creation. No one doubts that this law of death, with other evil dispositions, threatens all human bodies from the time of birth and hangs over them at every moment.

Even though I admit that all these statements and others like 22 them are true, I would venture to say and declare — wishing not to be too picky, not too fussy, headstrong or hard to please — that more kinds of pleasure than distress rule this ordinary, everyday life of ours. Strange to say, there is no human activity, if we attend carefully and correctly to its nature, that we do not enjoy at least a little. Indeed, we always take such great and intense pleasure from each of the external senses of sight, hearing, smell, taste and touch that sometimes they seem to grow superfluous, redundant and excessive. How many pleasures there are to charm a person would be hard — no, impossible — to say: some from the clear and distinct sight of beautiful bodies; some from hearing tunes, harmonies and other sounds in great variety; some from the scent of

partim denique ex mollissimarum substantiarum attrectatione—
difficile dictu, quin immo impossibile foret.

23   Quid de reliquis interioribus sensibus dicemus? Quantas enim
oblectationes in constituendis sensibilium rerum discretionibus et
differentiis afferre secum sensus ille perhibetur, qui communis a
philosophis appellatur. Quantum quoque nos delectat[21] varia diversarum substantiarum et accidentium imaginatio. Quantum aes-
timatio, quantum memoratio, quantum denique intellectio, cum ea
quae iam aliquo particulari sensu deprehendimus imaginari, com-
ponere, aestimare, meminisse et intelligere constituimus verbis
satis declarare et explicare non possumus!

24   Quocirca si homines quas[22] fert vita communis pluribus inter
vivendum voluptatibus et delectationibus potirentur quam molestiis et angoribus cruciarentur, potius gaudere et consolari quam
conqueri et lamentari deberent, praesertim cum natura plura frigo-
rum, aestuum, laborum, dolorum, morborumque remedia quasi
certa quaedam illarum aegritudinum antidota, non aspera, non
molesta, non amara, ut plerunque in pharmaciis contingere et evenire consuevit, sed potius mollia, grata et dulcia, et voluptuosa
abunde affatimque subministraverit. Quemadmodum enim cum
comedimus et bibimus in depulsione famis et sitis mirabiliter
oblectamur, ita cum concalescimus, cum refrigeramur, cum quies-
cimus pariter laetamur.

Sed quoniam illa a[23] gustu percipiuntur, ceteris omnibus tangi-
bilibus quodammodo delectabiliora videntur quae communi—et
non particulari ipsorum genitalium—tactu apprehenduntur. Quod
a natura—solertissima et callidissima, atque profecto unica rerum
magistra—non temere et fortuito sed certis rationibus et evidentibus causis factum fuisse philosophi tradidere ut longe maiores in
coitu quam in commestionibus ac potationibus voluptates cape-
rentur, quoniam specierum conservationem principalius quam individuorum intendebat, quorum alterum per commixtionem maris

flowers and similar smells; some from the different tastes of sweet dishes and fine wines; and some from touching things that are very soft.

What about the other senses inside? The sense that philoso-   23
phers call "common" — how many pleasures they say it brings along when it sets up distinctions and differences among things that can be sensed. How much we delight in our changing imagination of unlike objects and their features. Although we lack the words to show and explain what happens as we go about imagining, aggregating, appraising, remembering and understanding the things that we have already perceived with some particular sense, what pleasure comes from our faculties of appraisal, memory and understanding![28]

Hence, if most people — rather than being racked by anguish   24
and distress — are more taken with the joys and pleasures that many get from ordinary life, they should be encouraged and happy, not sad and complaining, especially since nature has supplied many remedies for cold, heat, toil, pain and disease, reliable antidotes in some way for those afflictions: they are not sour, nasty and bitter, like the products one usually finds in pharmacies, but mild, pleasant and sweet, a profuse sufficiency of pleasures. Just as the enjoyment really is wonderful when we eat and drink to rid ourselves of hunger and thirst, we take equal joy in warming up, cooling off and resting.[29]

Because the former are sensations of taste, they seem somehow more pleasurable than all the other tactile feelings had by the general sense of touch — but not by the touch specific to the genitals. Philosophers have said that nature — so very skilled and shrewd, and really the sole mistress of things — was not acting casually or by chance but had definite reasons with clear motives when she saw to it that far greater pleasures would be felt in sex than in eating and drinking. Her purpose was to preserve the species more

et feminae, alterum vero per assumptionem alimenti in restaurationem, ut ita dixerim, deperditi conservabatur.

25   Itaque cunctae de fragilitate, de algoribus, de aestibus, de laboribus, de fame et siti, de taetris odoribus et de huiusmodi saporibus, intuitionibus, attrectationibus, lassitudinibus, vigiliis et somniis,[24] cibis et potibus et ceteris similibus humanarum incommoditatum argumentis opiniones ac sententiae, singulis quibusque naturam rerum paulo diligentius animadvertentibus et aliquantulo accuratius considerantibus frivolae et vanae atque inanes esse videbuntur. Nam praeallegatae Aristotelis, Ciceronis, Senecae, Pliniique auctoritates per ea quae antea dicta sunt merito refelluntur et confutantur.

Quippe videre et audire tunc vere laboriosa et molesta sunt cum supervacua et nimia efficiuntur. At cum modice ac mediocriter his et huiusmodi sensibus utimur, non modo neque fatiscimus neque laboramus sed potius refocillamur, gestimus, et gaudemus. Etsi natura corpora nobis infirma, ut ait Cicero, et imbecilla et fragilia largita est (quod negare et inficiari non possumus), iam plurima huius infirmitatis, inbecillitatis et fragilitatis nostrae remedia, ut supra diximus, affatim abundeque subministravit. Etsi hoc nostrum domicilium ex terra madefacta et humo, ut inquit vir patientissimus — hoc est ex infimis fluidisque — contextum esse videmus, nimirum ob admirabilem quandam et delicatam huiuscemodi corporis complexionem, qualis tanto et tam digno ac tam praestanti humanae animae receptaculo competere et convenire putabatur, aliter fieri non poterat.

26   Quapropter, cum rationibus et allegatis antiquorum virorum auctoritatibus abunde, ut credimus, hactenus satisfecisse videamur, reliquum est ut ad Innocentii Summi Pontificis rationes paucis respondeamus, ad quod nos ita parati itaque armati accedimus, ut aptas quasdam et accommodatas responsiones nobis non defuturas existimemus.

than individuals, the one by sex between male and female, the other by taking nourishment in order to restore (if I may) what had been lost.[30]

Therefore, considering each and every one of the opinions and statements about frailty, anguish, heat and toil, about hunger and thirst, about foul odors and then on to tasting, seeing and touching, along with weariness, waking and dreaming, also food and drink and other such items of human disadvantage, any who pay a bit more attention and treat the nature of the facts with a little more care will see that these views are silly, groundless and without merit. What has just been said exposes the claims previously adduced from Aristotle, Cicero, Seneca and Pliny, which deserve to be refuted.[31]

Granted: seeing and hearing can be truly irksome and difficult when done too much and needlessly. But when we use these and other senses in a measured and moderate way, it is not just that we do not wear ourselves out with toil: we revive, we exult and we are happy. Though nature has provided us with feeble bodies, as Cicero states, and they are weak and frail (we cannot deny this or object), surely she has supplied many remedies — a profuse sufficiency, as I said — for our feeble, frail and weak condition. And if we see, according to that most patient of men, that this little house of ours has been built of soil and wet earth — from small, soft parts, in other words — truly it could not have been done differently because the amazing delicacy of this body's constitution was the type thought suitable and seemly for a receptacle so great, so worthy and so superior: a dwelling for the human soul.[32]

Hence, since I have said quite enough — I believe — about the arguments of the ancients and the claims made to support them, what remains is to provide a few answers to the arguments of Innocent, the supreme pontiff, to which I now proceed, armed and equipped, I would judge, so that I will not be caught short for fit and proper replies.

25

26

Si enim primi hominis corpus ex limo terrae, ceterorum vero tam animatorum quam inanimatorum corpora ex aliis elementis facta fuerunt, quae quidem suapte natura quam terra nobiliora et generosiora cernuntur — ut ille et dicit et sentit, et nos facile concedimus — profecto hoc quodcunque terrestre hominis opificium tanto praestabilius et excellentius cunctis aliis videri debuit quanto ceteris et ventis et planetis et stellis nobilius erat. Quae, licet ex aere et ex igne facta essent, insensibilia tamen et inanimata esse constabat.

27   Et piscibus quoque et avibus quae ex ipso aere et iumentis quae ex terra pariter secum animata prodierunt[25] admirabilius apparebat, nam hoc animal rationale, providum, et sagax multo propterea nobilius corpus quam iumenta et pecora habebat, cum quibus in propria materia convenire videbatur, quoniam ad agendum et ad loquendum[26] et ad intelligendum quibus illa carebant longe aptius et accommodatius erat. Ventis vero et stellis, rebus penitus et omnino insensatis, piscibus quoque et volucribus, animantibus utrisque, pariter excellentius putari poterat.

Nam etsi cum nullis praedictarum rerum in propria materia conveniret, insensatis tamen illis ex eisdem rationibus et causis quas de iumentis et pecoribus diximus praestantius concludebatur.

28   Et aquatilibus praeterea et aereis animantibus similiter excellentius credebatur quoniam tale suapte natura factum fuerat, ut nisi peccasset, mori et interire non posset, quemadmodum supra dixisse et ostendisse meminimus — quod nullis aliis corporibus conveniebat. Unde terrestre elementum tanto ceteris admirabilius et praestantius videri debet quanto illis suapte natura ignobilius et ineptius existens in corpore dumtaxat humano altius sublimatum et dignius exaltatum fuisse novimus. Atque haec ad primi hominis corpus breviter dixisse sufficiat.

29   Ad alia vero ceterorum hominum communia corpora[27] et ad alia quae de conceptione eorum et de embrionum educatione

If the first man's body came from the slime of the earth, in fact, while the bodies of other living and lifeless things were made of different elements identified as higher and nobler than earth by their nature—which is the pope's stated view and which I readily concede—then surely whatever earth there was in mankind's making should have been seen as more excellent and preferred to all the others by as much as humanity was nobler than the rest—all the winds and planets and stars. Although those things were made of air and fire, everyone knows they have no senses and no soul.[33]

In appearance humans were also more admirable than the fish 27 and birds that came from air and the beasts that came from earth, ensouled like themselves: this reasoning animal, being shrewd and farsighted, had a body much nobler than horses and cattle, with whom he evidently shares his own type of matter since his body was far more fit and suitable for the acting, speaking and understanding that those creatures lack. This made it possible to judge the body more exalted than winds and stars, which are absolutely insensate in every way, as well as fish and flying things, both of them alive—surpassing them all just the same.[34]

Now even though the body matches none of these in its own type of matter, it was still found superior to those that are insensate, and for the same reasons I gave about horses and cattle. Likewise, the body was also thought more excellent than watery 28 and airy animals because it had by its very nature been made unable, in the absence of sin, to perish and die, as I recall saying and showing previously—something befitting no other bodies. For this reason, the earthy element should be seen as more admirable and outstanding than the rest, and to this extent, as we know: that something more or less wasted and worthless while existing only in the human body was lifted up and raised to greater value. And let this suffice for a brief account of the first man's body.[35]

Now I wish to deal briefly with the other ordinary bodies of 29 the rest of humankind, replying to charges against how they

obiiciebantur brevissime respondere cupientes, quod ad[28] haec duo
pertinere et spectare videbatur, eandem vel potius meliorem cum
ceteris perfectis animalibus conditionem eo sortita fuisse respondemus, quod corpora[29] nostra ex melioribus et delicatioribus
seminibus quam brutorum omnium oriuntur.

Et sic orta ex potioribus et purioribus, ut ita dixerim, sanguini-
bus nutriuntur et educantur quoniam sicut sperma ex superfluo
alimenti, ita pariter sanguinem ex ipsa eiusdem alimenti substantia
generari certa quaedam et celebrata philosophorum omnium sententia est.[30] Quanto igitur cibus cuiuscunque animalis delicatior et
generosior est, tanto sperma ex superfluitatibus illius generatum
melius et prestantius efficietur. Eodemque modo de sanguine sentiendum est, qui quidem in homine tanto praestantior quam in
ceteris animantibus esse debet quanto cibus humanus ceteris quorumcunque animantium alimentis nobilior existimatur et creditur.

Ceteras obiectiones suas de nuditate et de imbecillitate et de
aliis huiusmodi incommoditatibus missas facimus, quoniam supra
in certa quadam plurium communium obiectionum confutatione
30 satis pro facultate nostra diluisse videmur. Nunc ad confutanda ea
quae de ignobilitate animae dicebantur paucis accedamus.

Dicaearchum et siqui alii fuerunt qui ipsam nihil esse totumque
eius nomen irritum et inane frustraque animantes et animalia appellari contenderent penitus omittamus quoniam ea de humana
mente excogitaverunt ut prorsus amentes et omnino inanimati ac
prorsus insensati propterea fuisse videantur quoniam sese ipsam
habere non cernerent. Hos proxime sequuntur Thales, Anaximander, Anaximenes, Anaxagoras, Diogenes, Leucippus, Democritus,
Heraclitus, Empedocles, Hippias, Archelaus, Zeno, Aristoxenus,
Varro et quicunque aliquid corporeum vel ex traduce et de potentia materiae educi et exinde simul cum corporibus interire existi-
maverunt.

31 His hebetibus — et, ut ita dixerim, corpulentis et pinguibus —
philosophis ea respondemus quae in secundo huius operis libro

conceive and breed embryos. My response seems related to these two issues and is pertinent: that our bodies share the same condition with other complete animals — or better, since ours emerge from seeds better and finer than what any beast has.[36]

After this origin, our bodies are bred and fed, I would say, from stronger and purer blood, because — according to a reliable and celebrated view held by all philosophers — just as sperm is produced from excess food, so blood comes in the same way from the substance of the same nourishment. The finer and richer the diet of any animal, the better and stronger the sperm produced by its residue. We should think the same of sperm as of blood, which in humans must excel what other animals have, inasmuch as our diet is more refined — so people believe — than what other animals feed on.[37]

As for the rest of Innocent's charges about nakedness, weakness and other such disadvantages, I dismiss them because I have plainly done enough, as best I could, to remove them when I refuted various general objections previously. Now let me move on to a few rebuttals of statements about the soul's inferiority.[38] 30

I shall simply skip Dicaearchus and any others who insist that the soul is nothing, that the term is meaningless, that the whole thing is a waste, that talk about animals being animate is useless. My reason is that people who have invented such a thing about the human spirit would seem to be completely mindless, utterly soulless and thoroughly insensate, precisely because they don't comprehend that they themselves have one. Right behind them come Thales, Anaximander, Anaximenes, Anaxagoras, Diogenes, Leucippus, Democritus, Heraclitus, Empedocles, Hippias, Archelaus, Zeno, Aristoxenus, Varro and anyone who reckoned that something bodily or off the branch is educed from the potency of matter and then perishes together with the body.[39]

To these thickheaded philosophers — gross and corpulent too, one might say — I reply with words that I recall putting in the 31

posuisse meminimus, ubi inter cetera haec Ciceronis nostri verba
allegavimus, quae ipsi veritati et Catholicae Christianorum fidei
vel maxime consonabant:

> Animorum[31] nulla in terris origo est, nam nihil est in animis
> mixtum ac concretum aut quod ex terra natum ac fictum
> esse videatur, nihil humidum quidem aut flabile aut igneum;
> his naturis nihil est quod vim memoriae, mentis, cogitationis
> habeat, quod et[32] praeterita teneat et futura praevideat et
> complecti possit praesentia — quae sola divina sunt. Nec in-
> venimus unde ad hominem venire possint nisi a Deo. Singu-
> laris est igitur quaedam natura atque vis animi seiuncta ab
> his usitatis notisque naturis. Ita quicquid est illud quod
> sentit, quod sapit, quod vivit, quod viget caeleste et divinum
> ob eamque rem aeternum sit necesse est.

32   Et Aristoteles quoque, philosophorum princeps et caput, cuncta
mixta et simplicia corpora sua cogitatione transcendit atque quintam quandam naturam esse voluit e qua mens emanaret. Cogitare
enim et providere et cetera huiusmodi a nullo praedictorum corporum provenire posse putabat — quemadmodum Cicero, de eo
loquens, quodam loco ita scribit:

> Aristoteles longe omnibus (Platonem semper excipio) praest-
> ans et ingenio et diligentia, cum quatuor nota illa genera
> principiorum esset complexus e quibus omnia orirentur,
> quintam quandam naturam censet esse e qua sit mens. Cogi-
> tare enim et providere et discere et docere et invenire aliquid
> et tam multa alia meminisse, amare, odisse, cupere, timere,
> angi, laetari, haec et similia eorum in horum quatuor ge-
> nerum inesse nullo putat. Quintum genus adhibet, vacans
> nomine, et sic ipsum animum *entelechiam*[33] appellat novo no-
> mine, quasi continuatam quandam motionem et perennem.

second book of this work, where, among other remarks, I cited these from our own Cicero, which actually sound very much like the truth itself and the Catholic faith of Christians:

> On earth there is no origin of souls, for in souls there is nothing mixed or compounded or appearing to be born and shaped from the earth, nothing even moist or airy or fiery: nothing in these natures has the power to remember, understand and reason, nothing to hold on to the past, foresee the future and grasp the present — faculties that are only divine. Nor, except from God, can we find whence they come to man. The soul, then, has some singular nature and power apart from the natures commonly noticed. Whatever it is that feels, understands, lives and flourishes is necessarily heavenly and divine, and that fact makes it eternal.[40]

Aristotle too, the prince and chief of philosophers, reached beyond all mixed and simple bodies in his own thinking and supposed there to be a kind of fifth nature from which mind flows. He thought that cognition, foresight and other such abilities could come from none of those bodies — as indicated by a passage where Cicero says this about him: 32

> Aristotle, who far surpasses all others (Plato always excepted) for talent and application and has grasped the four familiar types of principle from which everything arises, judges there to be some fifth nature that is the source of mind. For any thinking, foreseeing, learning, teaching and discovering, also remembering so many different things to love, hate, desire, fear, suffer, enjoy and so on, cannot — he believes — be found in any of those four types. He adds a fifth that lacks a name, then calling the soul itself by a new name, *entelechy*, as if it were a movement that keeps going perpetually.[41]

33   Ad Epicureos et ad ceteros huiusmodi mortales (et, ut ita dixerim, plebeios et minutos) philosophos parumper veniamus qui
animos una cum corporibus interire putaverunt, eosque ad illa re-
mittamus quae in praedicto huius operis libro affatim et abunde
retulisse meminimus, ne forte, si hic apponeremus, eadem pluribus
locis repetere et replicare obiurgaremur, ubi nos diversas rationes,
multas magnorum philosophorum auctoritates, plurima sanctissimorum virorum oracula, et pleraque celebrata profanorum et
sacrorum scriptorum exempla congessimus.

34   Illis vero qui immortales animos ita esse putaverunt ut in aliena
corpora, quando e propriis recedebant, ingredi cogerentur, quoniam qualis esset animus sine corpore intelligere non poterant,
ideoque formam aliquam figuramque quaerebant ac revolutionem
illam inanem, insulsam, et insanam excogitaverunt; illud Cic-
eronianum in eodem loco a nobis allegatum brevitatis causa repe-
tamus,[34] qui quodam *Tusculanarum* suarum libro ita inquit:

> Sed plurimi contra nituntur animosque quasi capite damna-
> tos morte mulctant. Neque aliud est quicquam cur incredibi-
> lis animorum videatur aeternitas, nisi quod nequeunt qualis
> animus sit *vacans corpore* intelligere et cogitatione comprehen-
> dere, quasi vero intelligant qualis sit *in ipso corpore*, quae
> conformatio, quae magnitudo, qui locus. Ut si iam possent in
> homine uno cerni omnia quae nunc tecta sunt, casurusne in
> conspectum animus an tanta sit eius tenuitas ut fugiat aciem?
>
> Haec reputent isti qui negant animum sine corpore se in-
> telligere posse, videant quem in ipso corpore intelligant.
> Mihi quidem naturam animi intuenti multo difficilior cogita-
> tio occurrit multoque obscurior, qualis animus sit in corpore,
> tanquam alienae domui, quam cum exierit et in liberum cae-
> lum, tanquam domum suam venerit. Nisi enim quod nun-
> quam vidimus id quale sit intelligere non possumus, certe et

Let me come for a moment to the Epicureans and other such 33
philosophers of mortality (vulgar and petty too, may I say) who
thought that souls perish along with bodies: for them I refer to my
full and thorough remarks in the previous book of this work.
Were I to put them in here, I might be scolded for repeating and
duplicating the same things from several earlier passages where I
packed different arguments and many statements by eminent philosophers in with sayings by the most saintly authors as well as
famous examples from writers sacred and profane.[42]

Next consider those who thought that immortality compels 34
souls to enter the bodies of others when they leave their own — the
soul being such that they could not conceive of it without a body.
So in their search for a form or figure, they thought up that cycle
of theirs which is useless, absurd and crazy. To keep things short,
let me repeat for them the same part of Cicero that I just cited,
where he says this in one part of his *Tusculans*:

> Many push against this, however, as if condemning souls to
> death. They find eternity inconceivable for souls only be-
> cause they cannot understand or comprehend in their think-
> ing what a soul would be like *without a body*, as if they ac-
> tually get what it is like *in the body* by shape, size and place. If
> they could actually see everything that now hides inside a
> single person, would the result be a sighting of the soul, or
> would its extreme fineness cause it to evade observation?
>
> Those who deny that a soul is intelligible without a body
> should reflect on this, to let them see what it is in the body
> that they understand. When I consider the soul's nature, I
> find the thinking much harder and far more obscure for a
> soul residing in the body, as if this were someone else's
> house, than for a soul departed into the open sky, as if going
> to its own home. For unless we cannot understand what
> something is like that we have never seen, we surely can

Deum ipsum et divinum animum corpore liberatum cogitatione complecti possumus.

35   Ad illa deinceps veniamus quae adversus totam hominis personam proponebantur. Itaque primo ad auctoritates et postea ad rationes descendemus—quippe ad auctoritates Egesiae, Crantoris,
Alchidami, Ciceronis, Plinii, Herodoti, Euripidis, Theombroti,[35]
Socratis, Catonis: quorum aliqui nonnullas mortis laudationes
conscripserunt; aliqui vero sese propterea interemerunt quod per
mortem multiplicibus humanae vitae incommodis et calamitatibus
36   privarentur. Primo priscas cunctorum gentilium scriptorum opiniones tunc vel maxime floccipendendas fore respondemus cum a
Catholica et ab ortodoxa sententia ullatenus discrepare videantur.

At cuncta a Deo creata valde bona, ut sacra scriptura testatur,
nemo vel sanae mentis ullo unquam tempore dubitavit. Quod
si sic est, profecto hominem, cuius gratia omnia valde bona et
optima facta fuisse constat, non solum optimum quiddam sed
etiam—ut ita dixerim—plusquam optimum esse iure dubitare et
ambigere non possumus. Humana igitur vita qua homo vivere dicitur generaliter misera esse fierive non potest. Aliter sequeretur ut
id quod optimum esse constaret in continua quadam et perpetua
miseria viveret. Quod quoniam falsum esse manifestum est, nimirum praeallegatas vel poetarum vel oratorum vel philosophorum—
qui de miseria humanae vitae disseruisse atque scripsisse perhibentur—auctoritates falsas ac frivolas et inanes extitisse apparet.

37   Quod quidem rationibus superius probatum famoso quoque
beati Augustini testimonio confirmatur, qui duodecimo *De civitate
dei* libro verba haec posuit:

Sicut melior est natura sentiens, etiam cum dolet, quam la-
pis, qui dolere nullo modo potest, ita rationalis natura praestantior, etiam misera, quam illa quae rationis vel sensus est
expers et ideo in eam non cadit miseria. Quod cum ita sit,

comprehend in our thinking both God himself and a godlike soul freed from the body.[43]

Next let me come back to the statements made against the whole human person. For this purpose I shall proceed first to the experts and then on to their arguments — the experts being Hegesias, Crantor, Alcidamas, Cicero, Pliny, Herodotus, Euripides, Theombrotus, Socrates and Cato: some wrote various things in praise of death; others did themselves in because death would relieve them of the many disadvantages and calamities of human life. At the outset I state that the ancient beliefs of all the pagan writers will count for absolutely nothing when they seem to diverge in any way from Catholic and orthodox teaching.[44]

But no really sane person has ever doubted, at any time, that God created everything to be very good, as sacred Scripture testifies. If this is so, surely we cannot rightly doubt or stick at the claim that mankind, for whose sake we know that everything was made good and excellent, is not only something that is the very best but also — to put it this way — better than the very best. The human life that man is said to live, then, cannot be or become totally miserable. Otherwise it would follow that something known to be the best of all would live in some kind of constant, perpetual misery. Since this is obviously false, the views previously cited from poets, orators and philosophers — those put forward as having written about the misery of human life and discussed it — are certainly false, silly and useless.[45]

What my previous arguments confirmed is also famously corroborated by St Augustine, in his words from the twelfth book *On the City of God*:

> Just as a sentient nature is better, even when in pain, than a stone that has no way to feel pain, so a rational nature, even when miserable, surpasses one that lacks reason and sense so that misery cannot fall upon it. This nature, given the facts,

35

36

37

huic nature, quae in tanta excellentia creata est ut, licet sit
ipsa mutabilis, inhaerendo tamen incommutabili bono, idest
summo Bono, beatitudinem consequatur nec expleat indigentiam suam nisi utique beata sit: eique explendae non
sufficiat nisi Deus, profecto non illi adhaerere vitium est.

38   Id ipsum Lactantius pluribus *Institutionum* suarum locis verum
et certum quiddam esse testatur quando, Ciceronis et aliorum qui
de bono mortis nonnulla litterarum monumentis tradiderunt
opiniones refellens, sic inquit:

> Cicero in principio *Consolationis* suae dixit luendorum sce-
> lerum causa nasci homines. Iteravit id ipsum postea quasi
> obiurgans eum qui vitam non esse plenam malis putet. Recte
> ergo profatus est errore ac miserabili veritatis ignoratione se
> teneri.

Et non multo post ita subiungit:

> At illi qui de bono mortis disputant, quia nihil veri sciunt,
> sic argumentantur: si nihil est post mortem, non est malum
> mors, aufert enim sensum mali; si autem supersunt animae,
> etiam bonum est quia immortalitas sequitur.

Quam quidem opinionem illa sua admirabili eloquentia penitus
diluit et omnino refellit ac prorsus redarguit et ad extremum falsam esse convincit.

39   Ad celebrata illa Socratis, Theombroti, Catonis exempla, eos
nullis humanarum calamitatum rationibus sed potius spe immortalitatis ad contemptum vitae tantummodo adductos fuisse dicimus. Quod nisi ita esset, ipsi utique de magnitudine animi non
fuissent a variis scriptoribus tantopere laudati quoniam laboriosa
effugere non fortis et magnanimi sed potius, ut inquit Aristoteles,

was created in such an outstanding state that, even though mutable, it attains bliss by sticking fast to the immutable good that is the greatest Good, and unless bliss is assured, it does not fulfill its own need: for such fulfillment only God is enough, and sticking with him is obviously no vice.[46]

In several passages of his *Elements*, Lactantius testifies that the 38 same point is something true and certain when he rejects the views of Cicero and others who wrote various literary works on death as a good. As Lactantius writes:

Cicero said at the start of his *Consolation* that humans are born because their crimes need to be purged. Later he returned to this thought as if to rebuke the person who thinks that life is not full of evils. Hence he was right to declare that he was hindered by uncertainty and by deplorable ignorance of the truth.

A little further on, Lactantius adds this:

But those who talk about death as good, since they know nothing about the truth, make the following argument: if there is nothing after death, death is no evil since it takes away the sensing of evil; if souls survive, however, death is also good because immortality follows.

With that astonishing eloquence of his, Lactantius completely eliminates this view, exposing it thoroughly, totally refuting it and in the end proving it false.[47]

As for the vaunted examples of Socrates, Theombrotus and 39 Cato, I say that no reasoning about human calamities persuaded them: it was only the hope of immortality that led them to hold life so cheap. Were this not so, surely so many writers would not have praised them so much for greatness of soul, since a person who runs away from trouble is not brave and greathearted but, as

mollis et enervati hominis est. Pythagoras quoque vetat iniussu imperatoris, idest Dei, de praesidio et de statione vitae decedere.

Id ipsum etiam verum esse deprehenditur et ex ea Socratis oratione qua Plato facit eum usum apud iudices iam morte mulctatum. Magna me, inquit,

> spes tenet, iudices, bene mihi evenire quod mittar ad mortem. Necesse est enim sit alterum de duobus, ut aut sensus omnes omnino mors auferat; aut in alium quendam locum ex his locis morte migretur,

et reliqua. Et ex Theombrotica Platonici libri de immortalitate animae lectione qui non alia de causa sese interemit quam quia Platoni de aeternitate animorum in commemorato libro scribenti credidit, quem quidem beatus Augustinus in primo *De civitate dei* antequam se ipsum interficeret legisse testatur.

De Catone, praeclarissimo et animosissimo viro, idem sentiendum est: aliter plus ceteris interemptoribus sui aberrasset si sola evitandi mala quae sibi ex victoria Caesaris proventura suspicabatur causa sesemet ipsum interemisset, nec de magnanimitate etiam a profanis scriptoribus tantis ac tam magnis in caelum laudibus extolleretur. Quod idem Augustinus in eodem *De civitate dei* libro eo loco maxime sentire et innuere videtur, ubi sic inquit: Cato Uticensis se ipsum occidit, sive turpe esse iudicaverit sub victore Caesare vivere sive potius eius gloriae ne sibi ab eo parceretur inviderit—ut ipse Caesar dixisse fertur. Plutarchus insuper ipsum eundem Platonis librum priusquam sibi manus iniiceret in vita sua legisse testatur.

40   Ad sacras illas Salomonis, Iob et Ambrosii auctoritates varie respondendum fore censemus.

Aristotle says, weak and unmanly instead. Pythagoras also forbids deserting the post where we are stationed in life—without orders from the commander, meaning God.[48]

One also grasps the truth of this from the speech that Plato reports by Socrates to his judges after they condemned him to death. A great hope, he tells the judges,

> possesses me: of things turning out well for me because I am sent to die. Things must go one of two ways: either death completely eliminates all sensations; or else we travel in death to some other place apart from these places,

and so on. The only reason—and none other—why Theombrotus killed himself was that he believed what Plato had written about the eternity of spirits in the book on the immortality of souls that I have mentioned before, the one that Saint Augustine, in the first book of the *City of God*, says Theombrotus read before doing away with himself.[49]

About Cato, that most noble and spirited man, the correct view is the same: he would have been less true to himself than other suicides if the reason for killing himself were just to escape the troubles that he believed would follow from Caesar's victory, and then even pagan writers would not have praised him to the skies so often for greatness of spirit. This certainly seems to be what Augustine feels and suggests in a passage from the same book of the *City of God*, where he says this: Cato of Utica slew himself, whether he thought it disgraceful to live under a victorious Caesar or else begrudged Caesar the glory that would come from sparing him—as Caesar himself remarked, so they say. Plutarch also reports that Cato read the same book by Plato before ending his life by his own hand.[50]

To those revered statements by Solomon, Job and Ambrose, I 40 believe I must give different answers.[51]

Nam Salomon in praedicto *Ecclesiastes* libro ita locutus est ut ad omnes totius mundi homines propalam, quasi publicus praeco et manifestissimus contionator loqueretur, quod ipsum et *coeleth* Hebraeum et *ecclesiastes* Graecum nomen plane et aperte significat. Proinde secundum diversas hominum condiciones ita varie et sentit et dicit, ut pluribus locis sibi ipsi manifeste adversari ac maxime repugnare videatur—ceu illi sententiae, cum de uno et de eodem hominis et iumentorum interitu superius allegatum, fuit illud maxime contradicit quod in calce libri postea subiungit, ubi de homine loquens inter cetera ita dicit:

> Ibit in domum[36] aeternitatis suae, et circuibunt in platea plangentes antequam rumpatur funis argenteus et recurrat vitta[37] aurea et conteratur idria super fontem et confringatur rota super cisternam et revertatur pulvis in terram suam unde erat et spiritus redeat ad Deum, qui dedit illum.

Et duobus quoque aliis, videlicet uni quando dicit: Laudavi magis mortuos quam viventes, et feliciorem eum iudicavi qui nondum natus est neque vidit mala quae sub Sole sunt; et illi insuper alteri quando ait: melior est dies mortis die nativitatis. Et cetera huiusmodi, plura apprime repugnant ac praesertim haec alia duo manifestissime contradicunt: unum quando inquit: melior est canis vivus leone mortuo; et alterum quando ita ait: vade ergo et comede in laetitia panem tuum et bibe cum gaudio vinum tuum quia placent Deo opera tua.

41 Quapropter cum ex hac tam diversarum et inter se tam dissidentium sententiarum varietate et dissonantia ac contrarietate, tum etiam ex mala et interdum non sana eius libri doctrina, inter priscos illos primitivae ecclesiae Iudaeorum doctores ac magistros—qui paulo post mortem Christi Redemptoris nostri sacrum Hebraicorum librorum ordinem instituerunt quo nunc

In the aforesaid book of Ecclesiastes, Solomon was actually making a public statement to all the world's people, talking like a town crier and a preacher speaking very bluntly, which is the clear and obvious meaning of the word *qoheleth* in Hebrew and *ecclesiastes* in Greek. Accordingly, his statements and meanings vary as people differ in their situations, so that in many places he obviously goes against himself — visibly with complete contradictions. Take the statement cited before about one and the same death for man and beast. This totally contradicts what he adds later at the end of the book, where he makes this and other remarks about mankind:

> He shall go into the house of his eternity, mourners surrounding him in the street, before the silver cord breaks, the golden band pulls back, the jar crumbles upon the fountain, the wheel on the cistern wears away, the dust goes back to the earth from which it came and the spirit returns to God, who gave it.[52]

Take two other passages. In one he says this: The dead I have praised more than the living, and the one not yet born I have judged happier than both — the one who has not seen what evils there are under the Sun. The other says that the day of death is better than the day of birth. Look also at others of this kind, several quite incompatible, especially these two which are obvious contradictions: better a living dog than a dead lion, says one; and the other says to go eat your bread in happiness and drink your wine with joy because your deeds are pleasing to God.[53]

Hence, because these statements are so different and disagree so much, with all their variations, confusions and contradictions, and also because the book's doctrine is bad and sometimes unsound, the ancient teachers and masters of the Jews in their primitive church — those who shortly after the death of Christ, our Redeemer, established and consecrated the order still used now for

41

utuntur et rabi Hebraice vocantur — diu disputatum et dubitatum fuit utrum praedictus liber in firmo et solido quodam sacrarum scripturarum canone una cum ceteris propheticis codicibus coordinaretur vel potius anathemate damnatus igni combureretur. Et nisi in calce libri verba haec apposita legissent — Deum time et mandata eius observa, hoc est enim omnis homo — et reliqua huiusmodi, proculdubio codex iste, iam dudum secundum praedictorum magistrorum sententiam ignibus combustus, nusquam appareret.

42   Ad tot ac tam varias patientissimi viri auctoritates ac sententias, eum librum a Moyse, sacrosanctae legis latore, in dialogo de providentia divina compositum fuisse respondemus, ubi varias et diversas interloquentium sententias esse necessarium est. Unde, cum omnes illas praeallegatas auctoritates vel proprio ipsius ore vel trium amicorum consolatorum suorum verbis enuntiatas extitisse comperiamus, eas pro falsis ac fallacibus propterea habendas dicere et asserere non dubitamus: quoniam ab Eliu, sapientissimo et optimo viro, et ipse Iob et omnes tres amici in cunctis commemoratis sententiis plane et aperte redarguti, et postea ab omnipotenti Deo ita increpiti et castigati fuisse videntur ut omnes praedictas sententias in alias veras et certas commutaverint commutatasque converterint.

43   Ad Ambrosium et ad ceteros huiusmodi doctores siqui alii fuerunt qui cogitationes suas de bono mortis litteris mandaverunt[38] respondentes, illos propter beatam et felicem bonarum animarum a corporibus separatarum futuram vitam et propter admirabilem et paene incredibilem post novissimam resurrectionem humanorum corporum glorificationem, de qua in fine libri paulo latius et uberius disseremus, ita scripsisse dicimus — quemadmodum ex propriis eorum scriptis plane et aperte deprehenditur.

44   Cum ergo cunctas profanorum et sacrorum scriptorum auctoritates superius allegatas pro facultate nostra diluisse[39] videamur,

the Hebrew books by the teachers called rabbis in that language —
for those reasons they also long doubted and debated whether to
group the book along with other prophetic texts in a complete and
stable canon of sacred Scripture or instead condemn it by anath-
ema to the fire for burning. Had they not read these words placed
at the end of the book and others like them — fear God and keep
his commandments, for this is the whole of humanity — this text,
beyond any doubt, would never have appeared, long since burned
up by order of those teachers.[54]

To the many different statements and declarations by Job, that   42
long-suffering man, my response is that Moses, delivering the sacred law, wrote this book as a conversation about divine providence, where the speakers must make statements that vary and
differ. Hence, though I find that all the statements previously cited
come either from Job's own mouth or from words of his three
sympathetic friends, I have no qualms about stating and maintain-
ing that they should be treated as false and deceptive for this reason: that in the statements mentioned, Job himself and three
friends are plainly and fully contradicted by Elihu, an excellent
man and very wise, and we see Almighty God scolding and chas-
tising them later, so that they might exchange all the cited declarations for others that are true and certain in order to reverse the
ones that are exchanged.[55]

Responding to Ambrose and any other teachers like him who   43
wrote down their thoughts about death as something good, I say
that they made these claims — as one sees, plainly and clearly, from
their own writings — in order to support the blessed and happy life
to come for good souls parted from their bodies, as well as the
astonishing glorification, almost beyond belief, of human bodies
after the final resurrection: at the end of this book, I shall discuss
this glorification a bit more extensively and in detail.[56]

So then, since I seem to have eliminated — to the best of   44
my ability — all the statements by sacred and secular authors

reliquum est ut deinceps ad rationes Innocentii Pontificis parumper accedamus.

Primum nanque et principale Innocentii nostri fundamentum
super quo totum eius miserabile aedificium — ex quo *De miseria*
appellare placuit — firmasse ac stabilisse perhibetur de quorun-
cunque nascentium hominum nativitate esse constat. Quod quasi
in principio commemorati operis sui merito collocavit, ubi de humanis calamitatibus disserens verba haec posuit. Omnes nascimur
eiulantes ut naturae miseriam exprimamus. Masculus enim recen-
ter natus dicit *ha*, femina dicit *he*,

> dicentes *he* vel *ha*,
> quotquot nascuntur ab Eva.

Quid est igitur Eva nisi *heu ha?* Utrunque interiectio dolentis dolo-
ris exprimit magnitudinem. Hinc enim ante peccatum *vir-ago*, post
peccatum *e-v-a* meruit appellari — et reliqua huiusmodi postea
prosequitur.

45   Unde sese optima futuri aedificii fundamenta iactasse putat:
quae profecto talia sunt ut — nisi me debita Summi Pontificis reverentia, quemadmodum ait poeta noster, contineret — levia quaedam et puerilia et a pontificia et apostolica[40] gravitate longe aliena
esse contenderem. Sed honestis quibusdam dumtaxat dictorum
suorum confutationibus ob maximam quandam Defunctae Sancti-
tatis Suae venerationem contenti acquiescemus, ubi nostrae confutandi et refellendi professioni vel mediocriter satisfecisse videbi-
mur. Quale igitur et quantum sit hoc suum tam firmum ac tam
solidum et tam adamantinum (ut ita dixerim) fundamentum ante
omnia pauliser considerandum est, ut eo diligenter accurateque
considerato, qualia et quanta fore debeant reliqua vere debilibus et
harenosis potius et fragilibus quam glareosis et adamantinis fundamentis apposita, facilius animadvertere atque evidentius intelligere valeamus.

previously cited, what remains is to take a moment and approach Pope Innocent's arguments.[57]

Now plainly the first and principal foundation laid by our Innocent to stabilize his whole wretched construction and firm it up—the reason why he chose the title *On Wretchedness*—is the birthing of anyone born to be human. He correctly placed this topic almost at the start of this work, where he discusses human calamities in the following terms. We are all born wailing to express our wretched nature. For a newborn male says *ha*, a female says *he*, so

all of us are born from Eva,
crying either *he* or *ha*.

What is *Eva*, then? Just *oh! ah!* Both these interjections from a person in pain express the pain's magnitude. This is why she deserved to be called *he-roine* before her sin and *e-v-a* afterward—followed by other points of this sort.[58]

With this Innocent thinks he has put down fine foundations for what he will build: truly, what they are—were I not restrained, as our own poet says, by the reverence due to a supreme pontiff—would make me contend that they are trifling, childish and quite remote from pontifical and apostolic seriousness. Restrained, then, by maximal respect for His Deceased Holiness, I shall rest content with some few honest rebuttals of his sayings, showing myself modest, to be sure, in carrying out my plan to expose and refute them. Accordingly, what must be examined before anything else is the nature and extent of this foundation of his—so firm, so solid and (may I say it?) as hard as steel. Once this has been carefully and accurately examined, we can more easily observe and clearly understand the kind and quantity of other items piled on top of these truly flimsy foundations—not full of rock and steel but sandy and ready to crumble.[59]

45

46 Ac primum quam falsum sit illud et quam ab ipsa rei veritate abhorreat quod de *heu* et *ha*, duabus naturalibus interiectionibus, ad claram quandam et manifestam humanae miseriae expressionem refert, veneranda sacrae scripturae verba plane et aperte declarant. Moyses enim, Divino Spiritu afflatus, in principia *Geneseos* ita inquit: Et vocavit Adam nomen uxoris suae Evam eo quod mater esset cunctorum viventium. Itaque huiusmodi *Evae* cognomine propterea appellata fuit quoniam mater et origo et principium esset omnium hominum qui ab ea, veluti a primaeva radice, propagandi et oriundi erant—quemadmodum ex sacris textus Latini verbis evidenter ostenditur, licet in Hebraico idiomate evidentius appareat.

Nam propheta ille maximus in praeallegato libro, cunctarum rerum originem progressumque describens, inter cetera sic ait: et vocavit nomen uxoris suae *Ava*.[41] Et causam talis appellationis assignare et demonstrare volens, statim intulit: quoniam mater omnium viventium futura erat—hoc est *cunctorum hominum* qui ob humanae naturae excellentiam et (ut Graeci expressius dicunt) ob antonomasiam, *viventes* merito appellari merebantur: qui quidem *viventes* hoc Hebraico nomine nuncupantur. Sed pro eo Hebraice ubique posito Hieronymus noster—omnium sacrorum tam Graecorum quam Latinorum interpretum accuratissimus—*Evam* euphoniae causa semper expressit.

47 Huic simile illud alterum[42] quod de *viragine* dicit quando ipsam ante peccatum *viraginem* et post peccatum *Evam* appelari meruisse confirmat. Quod pariter quemadmodum et primum falsum esse demonstrabitur, praesertim si propria eiusdem prophetae verba paulo diligentius et accuratius considerabuntur. Quae talia sunt: Dixitque Adam, hoc—nunc os ex ossibus meis et caro de carne mea—haec vocabitur virago quoniam de viro sumpta est.

First, the worshipful words of sacred Scripture show with com-   46
plete clarity how false it is, and how inconsistent with the real
facts, to relate *oh* and *ah*, two normal interjections, to some obvious and transparent expression of human misery. Moses, inspired
by the Holy Spirit, says this at the beginning of Genesis: and
Adam called the name of his wife Eva because she would be the
mother of all the living. Thus, the reason for naming her *Eva* in
this way is because she was to be the mother, origin and beginning
of all the humans who would come forth and spread from her, as
from their original root—just as the sacred words of the Latin
text plainly show, though this is plainer to see in the Hebrew language.

For in the book under discussion, that greatest of prophets,
while describing the origin and development of all things, added
this to what he says: and he called the name of his wife *Ava*. Then,
wishing to assign a cause for this designation and explain it, he
immediately brought this in: because she was going to be the
mother of all the living—meaning *all humans* who, because human
nature is superior, and (as the Greeks say more explicitly) by antonomasia, deserve to be called *the living*: and they are indeed
named *the living* by this Hebrew name. But wherever it occurs in
Hebrew, our Jerome—the most accurate of all Greek and Latin
translators of sacred texts—always uses *Eva* for the sake of euphony.[60]

Like this is Innocent's other point about *heroine*, when he as-   47
serts that before sinning she should have been called *he-roine* and
Eva after sinning. This will be shown to be just as false as his first
claim, especially if the same prophet's own words are examined
with a little more care and precision. His words go like this: and
Adam said, this one—now bone of my bones and flesh of my
flesh—this one will be called a heroine because she was taken
from a man.

Quod, etsi in Latino sermone manifeste intelligatur, Hebraice tamen manifestius et evidentius apparet, ubi ita exprimitur: haec vocabitur *ischa* quoniam de *isch*[43] — quod nomen Latine interpretatum *virum* significat — sumpta est. Hieronymus vero, ut ethimologiam verbi in sua, quoad fieri poterat, translatione efficacius servaret, pro *hisca* Hebraice posito *viraginem* a *viro* derivatam[44] posuit. Haec dicta[45] Iosephus primo *Antiquitatis iudaicae* his verbis vera esse confirmat, sic enim inquit: *ischa* Hebraica[46] lingua mulier appellatur, nomen vero mulieris illius erat *Eva*, quae significat omnium viventium matrem.

48   Quas ob res, si Innocentius noster in principiis et in fundamentis suis luce clarius aberrasse deprehenditur, ut supra probatum et demonstratum est, quid in reliquis, quae super praedictis erroribus fundata fuisse cernimus, eum fecisse existimabimus? Non est enim verisimile eum in progressu operis sui vera sensisse — quem in principia ab ipsa rei veritate longe aberrasse[47] intelligimus. Atqui in hos tantos ac tam manifestos errores nunquam incidisset nisi Hebraicarum litterarum omnino expers fuisset.

49   Sed qualia sint singula quaeque sua parumper videamus ac plura eius capitula de singularibus hominum calamitatibus confutandi causa breviter in medium adducamus. Quippe de nuditate, de fructibus hominum et arborum, de incommoditate senectutis, de brevitate vitae, de labore mortalium, de variis hominum studiis, de diversis anxietatibus ac de ceteris huiusmodi quae, ne longiores simus, brevitatis causa praetermittimus, multa et dicit et sentit.

50   Verum ut in hac nostra confutatione ordine quodam incedamus ab initio, de nuditate hominis incipientes[48] pauca dicemus, de qua ipse loquens sic inquit: nudus egreditur et nudus regreditur, pauper accedit et pauper recedit. Ad quod nos decoris et pulchritudinis causa homines ita nasci oportuisse respondemus. Primo namque, si variis diversisque pellibus instar brutorum cooperti et

Although the meaning is plain in the Latin language, in Hebrew it is even plainer and clearer, where this is written: she will be called *isshah* because from *ish*—the word translated into Latin means *male person*—was she taken. But Jerome, doing his best to preserve the word's etymology more effectively in his translation, used *he-roine* for *isshah* in Hebrew, deriving it from *he-man*. In the first book of his *Jewish Antiquities*, Josephus confirms that these statements are correct for the words involved, writing this: a woman is called *isshah* in the Hebrew tongue, but that woman's name was *Eva*, which means mother of all the living.[61]

So if we have seen that our Innocent went astray in his starting points and foundations—as shown in the foregoing and confirmed, just as surely as night follows day—what shall we think he has done in the rest, that we know to be based on those very confusions? For it is unlikely that he perceived the truth as his work went forward—this person whom we know to have strayed far from the true facts when he started. Yet he would never have slipped into confusions so great and so obvious had he not been utterly ignorant of the Hebrew language.[62] 48

But let me take a quick look to examine the mistaken details and then briefly, in order to refute them, call into question his several chapters about each human calamity. In fact, he has views and very much to say about nakedness, about the fruit borne by humans and trees, about the troubles of old age, the shortness of life, the various efforts that people make, their different anxieties and other such topics that I omit for the sake of brevity—in order not to go on too long.[63] 49

But to proceed with this refutation of mine in some order, I shall start by making a few initial points about man's nakedness, about which Innocent has this to say: naked he comes out and naked he goes back, starting poor and leaving poor. My answer is that it was fitting for humans to be born like this—for the sake of grace and beauty. To begin, if we were born dressed and covered 50

induti nasceremur, quam turpis et quam foedus esset aspectus ille satis dici explicarive non posset. Ob excellentiam quoque complexionis nostrae, quae ex deliciis humani seminis procedebat, aliter contingere et evenire non poterat. Sed quando aliter fieri potuisset, profecto natura humanum corpus — ceterorum omnium operum suorum pulcherrimum ac nimirum formosissimum opificium ab ea mirabiliter fabrefactum — nunquam alieno indumento abscondisset ne forte pulchritudines suas incongruis et abiectis velaminibus cooperiret.

51   Aliter etiam — si voluissemus — de naturali quodam omnium nascentium hominum vestimento respondere valebamus. Quod propterea facere noluimus quoniam ipsum in eodem loco hoc naturale indumentum quo omnes nascimur satis his verbis vituperasse legimus, sic enim subiungit: si quis autem indutus egreditur, attendat quale proferat indumentum, turpe dictu, turpius auditu, turpissimum visu, foedam pelliculam sanguine cruentatam. Quod nos de *secundina* (sic enim pellicula illa cum qua infantes nascuntur a medicis appellatur) ipsum intellexisse non iniuria interpretamur, quam ex necessitate materiae unusquisque inter nascendum ferre ac paulo post in lucem editus deponere naturali lege compellitur.

52   Quid de hominum et arborum fructibus dicemus? Quos ipse ad invicem comparare volens, paulo post praedictam nuditatem huiusmodi comparationem aggressus ita inquit:

Herbas et arbores investiga. Illae de se producunt flores, frondes et fructus, et tu de te lendes, pediculos et lumbricos. Illae de se fundunt oleum, vinum et balsamum, et tu de te sputa, urinam et stercus. Illae de se spirant suavitatem odoris, et tu de te reddis abominationem fetoris.

like animals with pelts of different kinds, it would be impossible to say just how filthy and repulsive a sight this would be or to describe it. Also, because of the excellence of our constitution, originating from fine human sperm, the result could not possibly have been different. Had things been different, however, Nature would never have used some strange garment to conceal the human body — this miracle wrought by her, a supremely handsome work beyond any doubt, the loveliest of all her different productions — since she would not want its beauties covered with ill-fitting, hand-me-down veils.[64]

I could have made a different reply, had I wished, about what kind of birthday suit all humans wear for the occasion. The reason I would rather not respond is that it suffices to read Innocent, in the same passage, where he has denounced this birthing outfit in which we are all born, using these words: if one of them comes out clothed, notice what clothing he wears — filthy to mention, filthier to hear about, filthiest of all to see, a loathsome membrane stained with blood. It would be correct to interpret this as meaning the *afterbirth* (the word used by physicians for the membrane that babies are born with), which, by physical necessity, clothes each infant during birth and must, by a law of nature, be taken off, right after seeing the light of day.[65]

What about people, trees and the fruit they produce? Wishing to compare them with one another, Innocent began such a comparison shortly after the passage on nakedness, saying this:

> Observe the plants and trees. From themselves they produce flowers, foliage and fruit, and from yourself you get nits, lice and tapeworms. They exude oil, wine and gum from themselves, while your discharges are spit, piss and shit. They breathe a smell of sweetness out of themselves, but from yourselves you exhale a detestable stench.

Et sic in reliqua huiusmodi spurcitiis foeditatibusque referta procedens late copioseque prosequitur: quae decoris honestatisque gratia in praesentiarum omittamus.

53   His tam pulchris ac tam formosis praedicti Summi Pontificis obiectionibus istam ipsam suam fructuum comparationem absurdam esse et videri responderi potest. Nam proprius cuiuslibet arboris fructus vere dicitur is[49] quem arbor illa suapte natura producit. At proprii hominis fructus non sunt foeda illa et superflua spurcitiarum et foeditatum genera superius allegata. Sed potius multiplices intelligendi et agendi operationes humani fructus habentur et sunt ad quas homo sicut arbor ad fructificandum naturaliter nascitur.

Et quanquam natura superflua illa in homine non intendat, sed ex necessaria quadam cibi et potus repletione proveniant, mirabile tamen — ac paene incredibile dictu — est quantum pleraque illorum quae in homine superflua dicuntur ad plura rerum genera conferre videantur, ceu de sputis, de urinis, et de stercoribus ac de capillis a phisicis scribitur. Quippe ieiuni hominis sputum venenosis serpentum morsibus optalmiisque medetur, eius vero urina ad laxandum ventrem et ad conservationem visus mirabiliter confert; humanarum aurium sordes naribus illinitae quibuscunque dormire nequeuntibus somnum provocare videntur. Ad fertilitatem agrorum humanum stercus — hominisque capilli, quorum ne unum quidem periturum ex evangelica lectione didicimus — ceteris omnibus stercorandi generibus copiosius et abundantius conducit.

54   Quid ad incommoda senectutis et ad brevitatem vitae respondebimus? Profecto quemadmodum ceteris superioribus fecimus, ita istis oportuna responsa nobis non defutura iure existimamus et credimus. Nam si, in primordio conditionis humanae, prisci illi maiores nostri ita longaevi extitisse comperiuntur ut usque ad nongentos circiter annos pervenerint, ceu Innocentius ad comparationem et ad detestationem huius praesentis vitae nostrae — quam dicit esse brevissimam — nonnullas rationes adducere et allegare

And then he follows up with passages crammed full of such dirt and defilement; for the sake of decency and decorum, let me leave them out now.[66]

A possible reply to the supreme pontiff's complaints — so well crafted and finely formed — is that this comparison of his, about fruits, is visibly absurd. For the fruit correctly described as belonging to any tree is the one that the tree produces by its own nature. But the fruits that belong to mankind are not the kinds alleged in the foregoing — those detestable leftovers of dirt and defilement. Instead, the fruits that are human and held to be so are the many acts of thinking and doing for which man is born, like a tree bearing such fruit naturally.

Even though Nature does not intend these things to be surplus in humans, but they arise because filling up with food and drink is inevitable, yet it is astonishing — almost incredible to say — that things judged to be leftovers in man contribute so much in so many ways: this is exactly how scientists describe saliva, urine, excrement and hair. Saliva from a person fasting treats eye disease and toxic snakebite, and such a person's urine is wonderfully good for loosening the bowels and preserving vision. Dirt from human ears spread on the nostrils seems to bring out drowsiness in those unable to sleep. Using human dung on farms produces more and richer fertility than other kinds of fertilizing — also human hair, for reading the Gospel teaches us that not even a single hair shall perish.[67]

What to say about the troubles of old age and the brevity of life? My belief and reckoning, to be sure, is that I shall not lack ready answers to these questions, just as I have replied to earlier queries. For if those ancient ancestors of ours, in mankind's primordial state, are found to have lived lives so long that they reached about nine hundred years, while we see Innocent giving various reasons and citations in order to make his comparison and heap scorn on our present lives — which he calls very short — the

53

54

videtur, profecto Deus eo tempore rebus humanis propterea recte
consuluisse ac sapienter providisse perhibetur, quoniam aliter nec
genus humanum in hac parva et praesentanea[50] temporis brevitate
propagari neque urbes aedificari neque scientiae et artes adinveniri
potuissent. Sed postquam praedicta omnia quae hominibus necessaria erant per diuturnitatem temporis adinventa in lucem pro-
diere et demum perfecta et completa in medium evasere, humana
vita paulatim decrescens in hanc postremo quasi brevitatem perve-
nit quam nunc videmus.

55   Quod Iosephus in praedicto *Antiquitatis iudaicae* libro manifeste
confirmare videtur, quando Deum religiosis illis primaevis maioribus nostris tam longam ac tam diuturnam vitam ab initio conces-
sisse et condonasse tradit. Et non multo post de Tharae, Abrahae
patris, morte disserens, cum ipsum quinque supra ducentos aetatis
annos vixisse dixisset, statim in hunc modum subiecit: Recideba-
tur enim iam vita hominum fiebatque paulatim brevior usque ad
generationem Moysi, post quem terminus vitae positus est centum
viginti annorum — quoniam ad conservationem et ad salutem humani generis post multas plurimarum urbium aedificationes, post
plerasque utilium artium adinventiones ac post humani generis
propagationem, nequaquam necessarium erat ut homines diuturni-
nioris et longioris vitae efficerentur quam nunc communiter vi-
vant.

Satis enim ad nostra propria intelligendi et agendi officia et ad
bene beateque vivendum, superque satis et olim vivebamus et nunc
vivimus, quemadmodum Seneca in libro *De brevitate vitae*, illam
celebrem et pervulgatam de longitudine artis et de vivendi pauci-
56   tate exclamationem refellens, plane et aperte demonstrat. Ad senectutis incommoda illa supra obiecta cum ante actae et senilis
vitae voluptatibus et oblectationibus conferenda et comparanda
fore praedicamus. Quod si fieret, certe multo plures ac maiores

236

correct finding is that God provided wisely in that era for human activities and took good care of them. Otherwise, considering how fleeting the brief time is that we now have, there could have been no propagating the human race, no cities built nor any arts and sciences discovered. But later, after time passed and all the things needed by humans had come to light, these became common once they were finished and complete, and then human life, ever shorter and shorter, finally became what we see now—which is brief enough.[68]

We note that Josephus plainly affirms this view in the book previously mentioned on *Jewish Antiquities*, when he reports that God permitted a life so long and lasting from the beginning, granting it to those primordial ancestors of ours because of their piety. Not much after this, talking about the death of Terah, Abraham's father, whom he described as living to the age of two hundred and five, Josephus adds this right away: For the life of humans was now cut back and gradually became shorter until Moses was born, and after him the limit of life was set at one hundred and twenty years—the reason being, once many cities had been built, various useful crafts invented and the human race propagated, that it was not at all necessary for mankind's preservation and well-being for people to have longer and more lasting lives than they now commonly live.[69]

To do our own duties of knowing and acting and to live well and happily, both the lives we now have and those we used to live are enough and more than enough, as Seneca clearly shows in his book *On the Brevity of Life*, where he rejects that famous and much-repeated utterance about the art being long and life short. Let me say that the old person's troubles mentioned before should be set beside the pleasures of old age and also compared with the delights of the life already lived. Were this done, I believe, a fair

55

56

voluptates quam molestias hominibus quondam in praesen-
tiarumque viventibus provenisse ac provenire non iniuria existimamus et credimus.

57   De labore mortalium idem dicere ac respondere possumus quod
de incommodis senectutis nuper responderamus. Multo enim
plures oblectationes quam labores ex humanis operationibus, agen-
tibus et operantibus nobis, propterea provenire censemus quoniam, si singulas quasque hominis operationes diligenter et accurate consideraverimus, profecto sicut nos semper inter agendum
aliquantulum laboramus, ita pariter ac vehementius etiam in quacunque nostra operatione oblectamur.

Homines enim inter vivendum necessario oblectari oportere
celebrata Aristotelis sententia est. Quinimmo Philosophus ipse, in
decimo *Ethicorum* de voluptate disserens, eam ab hominis operatione nequaquam seiungi et separari posse confirmat et probat,
et—quod admirabilius est—voluptatem humanae vitae usque
adeo annexam et coniunctam esse profitetur ut ab ea nullatenus
segregari seiungive possit. Haec enim eius verba sunt: Quod autem[51] per singulos sensus fiat voluptas manifestum est, dicimus
enim visiones et auditiones voluptatem afferre. Et paulo post, cum
voluptatem ab omnibus expeti probavisset, ita inquit: Sed utrum
propter voluptatem vivere expetimus vel propter vitam voluptatem
relinquamus ad praesens, coniugata enim ista videntur esse nec
separationem recipere, nam sine operatione non fit voluptas, et
omnem operationem voluptas perficit.

Unde fit ut homo in continua eius vita a principio nativitatis
suae usque in finem semper et omni quidem tempore oblectetur.
Quod si sic est, profecto plures voluptates quam labores esse
constat, quemadmodum supra paulo latius et uberius dixisse et
explicasse meminimus.

58   De variis hominum studiis diversisque eorum anxietatibus eodem modo respondendum esse censemus, ne forte—in rebus tam
claris ac tam manifestis—prolixiores simus quam materiae de qua

calculation would be that much greater — and many more — pleasures than pains certainly used to be mankind's lot and still are at present.[70]

About mortal toil I can say the same, giving the same answer given about the troubles of old age. In my view, human actions — for us as the people who see to them and get them done — provide more delight by far than toil for this reason, that if we reflect carefully and accurately about each one of these activities, just as we always do indeed toil a little to get them done, so just the same do we take delight, even stronger delight, in any activity of ours.[71]

Aristotle's famous claim, in fact, is that people must have enjoyment as they live. Discussing pleasure in the tenth book of the *Ethics*, the Philosopher affirms and proves that it can by no means be separated or divided from a person's activity, and — what is more striking — he maintains that pleasure is so conjoined and linked with human life that there is no way at all to divide and set it apart. For these are his words: pleasure is produced for every sense, obviously, for we say that sights and sounds bring pleasure. A little farther on, after showing that pleasure is sought by all, he has this to say: but we can leave out for now whether we seek life for pleasure's sake or pleasure for the sake of life, for the two are seen to be joined and will not accept being separated, since without activity no pleasure occurs, and pleasure completes every activity.[72]

The upshot is that through the whole course of a person's life, from the first instant of birth until the end, there is always enjoyment at every moment. But if this is so, the clear consequence is more pleasure than hardship, as I recall explaining just before at greater length and describing in more detail.

I think it best to answer in the same way about the various things that people attempt and their different worries about them, and thus — in matters so plain and obvious — to avoid going on

agitur qualitates et conditiones requirere et exigere videantur, praesertim cum et cuncta superius allegata, et cetera omnia quae noviter de humanis calamitatibus dici et allegari possent, ex novissima
corporum nostrorum resurrectione faciliter diluantur atque abun-
danter et copiose confutentur.

Quando enim resurgemus, profecto tunc defuncta corpora sine
aliqua labe, sine aliqua corruptione, sine aliqua imbecillitate, sine
aliqua denique deformitate renovata gloriosissime resumemus,
quae non modo cunctarum infirmitatum, aegritudinum, et ceterarum omnium incommoditatum quibus nunc abundare et undique
affluere quotidie experimur penitus et omnino expertia, sed etiam
totis singularum pulchritudinum ornamentis referta appare-
bunt—quemadmodum per plures et admirabiles glorificatorum
corporum conditiones paucis deinceps demonstrabimus.

59   Quarum prima est perpetua et aeterna absque aliqua infirmitate
sanitas—quae nullis morborum generibus aliquatenus impediri
prohiberive poterit, de qua Psalmista pluribus locis et maxime eo
carmine sensisse videtur quando dixit: lauda, anima mea, dominum, qui sanat infirmitates tuas.

Secunda, iuventus sine senectute. Non enim tantum homini
haec sua et perpetua corporis incolumitas prodesset nisi quaedam
continuae iuventutis beatitudo concomitaretur, nec etiam plurimum proficeret si ille qui semper sanus esset multorum tamen
annorum gravitate depressus, aliquo sustentationis baculo indigeret.

Cuncti enim in perfecta et completa triginta dumtaxat annorum aetate resurgemus. Nam Apostolus ita inquit: . . . donec oc-
curramus omnes in unitatem fidei et agnitionis Filii Dei,[52] in
virum perfectum, in mensuram aetatis plenitudinis Christi. Qui,
quamvis trigesimo tertio aetatis suae anno pateretur, quoniam nihilominus trigesimo ex eremo, ubi diutius contemplandi et medi-
tandi gratia latuerat, in lucem venerat et mundo manifestus appa-
ruerat, eapropter[53] triginta annorum aetate resurgemus. Nec solum

longer than the topic seems to demand, given its nature and circumstances, especially since all the charges already made, along with all the remaining statements about human disasters that might produce new charges, are easily resolved by the final resurrection of our bodies and hence fully and thoroughly refuted.[73]

For when we rise again, then we shall certainly get our dead bodies back fully glorified and renewed, with no stain, no rot, no weakness and no ugliness: not only will they be completely and absolutely free of sickness, sorrow and all the other ills that we now feel flooding in everywhere and overflowing every day, they will also look perfectly lovely and beautiful in every way — as I shall show by lining up a few points about the several astonishing features of glorified bodies.[74]

Of these the first is perpetual and eternal health without any 59 illness — health that no type of disease can in any way halt or hinder, which the Psalmist seems to have in mind in several passages, especially in the verse where he said this: praise the Lord, my soul, who heals your sicknesses.[75]

The second is youth without aging. For the perpetual soundness of body that a person has would not do him so much good were it not supported by the blessing of continuing youth, nor would it be so helpful if someone always healthy were still to sink beneath the weight of many years, needing some crutch to hold him up.

All of us shall rise, in fact, at the full and perfect age of thirty years. As the Apostle says: . . . until we all reach acceptance of God's Son and the unity of faith — as a mature man, measured by Christ's full age. Although he suffered in his thirty-third year, still, since it was in his thirtieth that he came out of the desert, where he had long hidden to think and pray, and showed himself to the world, this is why we shall rise with an age of thirty years. Rising,

ea Christi aetate sed etiam in statura corporis sui, mirabile dictu, resurgentes adstabimus, ceu suis verbis testatur Apostolus quando ita inquit: praedestinavit conformes fieri imaginis Filii sui.

60   Tertia, libertas corporum assequetur. Corpora enim nostra, quae nunc tot necessitatibus, tot oneribus, tot peccati corruptionibus opprimuntur, tunc levia et subtilia et ab omni labe libera nitidaque efficientur. Quarta est pulchritudo sine macula. Si enim omnis corporis pulchritudo est congruentia partium cum quadam coloris suavitate, profecto ibi erit perfecta et completa pulchritudo ubi nulla partium, ut ita dixerim, incongruentia fieri poterit et ubi quoque admirabilis quaedam divini coloris suavitas, necessario intercidens, omnia condecorabit. Nam ita in sacris litteris scriptum esse constat: fulgebunt iusti sicut Sol in regno Patris sui.

61   Quinta, accedet impassibilitas et immortalitas. Ibi namque habitantes neque ab aestibus neque ab algoribus neque a fame neque a siti neque a senectute neque ab ullis denique laboribus vexabuntur. Sexta, requies sine intermissione proveniet. Ibi enim totus homo semper et omni quidem tempore conquiescet. Septima, perpetuum et aeternum absque ullo maerore gaudium concomitabitur. Nam Deus omnem lacrimam ab oculis sanctorum suorum ita absterget itaque emundabit ut nusquam neque ullo unquam tempore appareat. Quippe neque dolor amplius sentietur, neque clamor et lamentatio ulterius audietur, quae prima una cum hac vita mortali et saeculari penitus et omnino abierunt et usquequaque evanuerunt.

62   Cum ergo per ea quae dicta sunt omnia quae huic nostro laudabili de dignitate et excellentia hominis proposito obiici posse videbantur, hactenus, ut potuimus, satis abundeque confutarimus, restat ut de beatorum praemiis et gaudiis simul atque de damnatorum hominum poenis ac doloribus aliqua memoratu digna in medium adducamus.

we shall stand up there not only at Christ's age but also, amazing to say, with the size of his body, just as the Apostle's statement testifies: he predestined them to conform to his Son's image.[76]

The third to follow is freedom for our bodies: though now they 60 are crushed by so many needs, burdens and sinful infections, then they shall be made to shine—light, delicate and altogether free of stain. The fourth is spotless beauty. For if all bodily beauty is a matching of parts and a certain sweetness of color, surely the beauty will be complete and perfect where no mismatch (so to speak) of parts can occur and where the astonishing sweetness of divine color that must emerge will adorn them all. For so it is written in the plain words of Scripture: the just shall gleam like the Sun in their Father's kingdom.[77]

The fifth to come is immortality without suffering. For bodies 61 dwelling there shall be distressed neither by heat nor cold nor hunger nor thirst nor old age nor any other hardships. The sixth to appear is rest without interruption. For the whole person shall always find repose there at every moment. The seventh to join the group is perpetual and eternal joy without any sorrow. For God shall cleanse the eyes of his saints and wash away every tear so that no weeping shall ever be seen there again. No more pain shall be felt, in fact, no more screaming and wailing heard: along with this mortal and worldly life, these shall all vanish, entirely and immediately, and shall disappear everywhere.[78]

Therefore, since what I have said up to now has fully and suffi- 62 ciently refuted—as much as I could—every objection against my case on behalf of man's precious value and excellence, what remains is to make some points worth remembering about the rewards and joys of the blessed, and likewise about the pains and punishments of the damned.

63   Sanctorum gaudia plura ac magna et paene infinita esse nemo vel sacris litteris mediocriter doctus ignorat. Primo namque gloriosissimo et suavissimo divinae maiestatis aspectu perfruentur; quippe, ut ait Paulus Apostolus: nunc videmus per speculum in aenigmate, tunc autem facie ad faciem. Et Iohannes Evangelista: cum apparuerit, inquit, similes ei erimus, quoniam videbimus eum sicuti est. Quod et Mathaeus—in illo celebrato et pervulgato Domini Nostri sermone quem solis apostolis a turbis segregatis in monte habuit—his verbis plane et aperte confirmat: beati mundo corde quoniam ipsi Deum videbunt. Et sexcenta insuper alia huiusmodi divinarum scripturarum praeconia commemorare et allegare possemus ex quibus iustos in patria Deum videre assereremus, sed nimiam longitudinem veriti de industria vitavimus, praesertim cum res ipsa ita clara et manifesta sit ut de ea iure dubitari et ambigi non possit.

64   Ceterum illud quaeri solet utrum Deus corporeis oculis vel mente sola vel utroque potius in paradiso a sanctis hominibus videatur. De quo quidem varias doctissimorum et sanctissimorum virorum sententias fuisse legimus. Sed quomodocunque videatur, satis superque satis est ut beati illud splendidum omnium divinarum et humanarum rerum speculum spectaculumque intueantur in qua quidem *beatifica*, ut sic dixerim, visione quanta letitiae magnitudo futura sit nec satis dici nec excogitari potest. Si enim gemmarum, si stellarum, si pulchrorum et formosorum hominum aspectus nos apprime delectat, quid in omnipotentis Dei intuitione faciemus? Profecto usque adeo oblectabimur ut perpetuo et sine intermissione atque immense infiniteque laetemur.

De hac admirabili et incredibili laetitia quae nobis ex divina visione proventura est nemo mirabitur qui in Deo omnia, quaecunque et ubicunque sunt, ita relucere consideraverit ut omnibus intuentibus meridiana—ceu dicitur—luce clarius et evidentius

No one who has learned even a little from the sacred writings is   63
unaware that the many joys of the saints are great and nearly limitless. To begin, they shall enjoy the sweetest and most glorious
sight of all, the divine majesty. Indeed, as Paul the Apostle says,
now we see obscurely in a mirror, but then face to face. Also John
the Evangelist: When he appears, he says, we shall be like him, for
we shall see him as he is. And Matthew—in the famous and well-
known sermon that our Lord preached to the apostles alone on
the mount, apart from the crowds—clearly confirms this in these
plain words: blessed are the pure in heart because they shall see
God. And there are six hundred more such proclamations that I
might mention and cite from sacred Scripture in order to assert
that the just see God in their homeland, but I fear saying too
much and have tried intentionally to avoid this, especially since the
clear fact is so obvious that there can be no real doubt or indeci-
sion about it.[79]

Otherwise, the usual question is whether the saints in paradise   64
see God with the body's eyes or the mind alone or both. The fact,
as I have read, is that the saintliest and most learned people have
made a variety of statements about this. Yet, however one sees
God, it is enough and more than enough for the blessed to gaze at
that shining sight which reflects all things divine and human in a
vision which, to speak its name, surely is *beatific,* and one cannot
think or say how much bliss this will hold. For if we get such immense pleasure from seeing gems and stars or fair and shapely
people, what shall we make of gazing on God Almighty? Surely
our delight will be such that our joy will be immense and infinite,
perpetual and uninterrupted.[80]

The wonderful and unbelievable happiness that will come to us
from seeing God will surprise no one who has considered this:
that in God all things, whatever and wherever they are, produce
such a blaze that to everyone looking they seem clearer and more
visible than by the light of noon—just as it says. For we gather

patere videantur. Nam a beato Gregorio sacris litteris scriptum legimus: quid est quod non videat qui videntem omnia videt?

65   Quid plura de hac tam immensa et tam infinita laetitia dicemus cum istam divinam visionem totam beatae vitae mercedem et versa vice eius privationem miserorum et damnatorum hominum poenam fore Catholici doctores dogmatibus suis manifestissime expresserint? Quando deinde claritatem, subtilitatem, agilitatem, impassibilitatem, decorem et immortalitatem—praeclaras quasdam et admirabiles illas glorificatorum corporum conditiones, praecipuas eorum dotes et singularia privilegia—conspicabuntur, supra modum atque incredibiliter exhilarescent.

66   Beatorum namque corpora usque adeo lucida erunt ut nihil sit in rebus humanis quod tanto et tam immenso eorum splendori conferri et comparari possit. Proinde et Esaias propheta et Mathaeus evangelista, hanc tam egregiam et tam singularem glorificatorum corporum claritatem per aliqua corporalium rerum exempla exprimere volentes, nec ex omnibus quicquam Sole lucidius invenirent, nimirum quantum potuerunt, solari splendori equipararunt. Alter namque: fulgebunt, inquit, iusti sicut Sol in conspectu Dei; alter vero in transfiguratione Christi super montem[54] Tabor apparente verba haec posuit: resplenduit facies eius sicut Sol.

67   Usque adeo quoque subtilia videbuntur ut neque ostia neque parietes neque muri neque moenia neque aliqua alia adamantina impedimenta obstare ac resistere valebunt, ut uno momento quocunque voluerint praetergredi et penetrare nequiverint. Quod Christus tunc vel maxime indicavit quando post resurrectionem suam, ianuis clausis ingressus, in medio discipulorum manifestus apparuit. Usque adeo insuper agilia ostendentur, ut nulla gravitate ad pergendum quocunque concupiverint aliquatenus impediantur. Quod celebrato illo Christi exemplo evidentissime declaratur quando periclitantibus[55] discipulis opitulaturus per mare Galilee siccis pedibus inambulans hinc inde perrexit.

from St Gregory that this was written in the holy texts: what does he not see who sees the One who sees everything?[81]

What more to say about a happiness so immense and bound- 65
less? In their doctrines the Catholic teachers have quite explicitly described the divine vision that will reward a blessed life completely, whereas, on the other hand, the pitiful damned will be punished by being deprived of it. When the blessed get sight of the brightness, delicacy, agility, lack of suffering, beauty, and immortality — those celebrated and amazing features of glorified bodies which are their outstanding gifts and special privileges — their bliss shall grow beyond measure and belief.[82]

In fact, the bodies of the blessed will be so full of light that 66
there is nothing comparable in human experience that can be related to a brilliance so immense. Hence both Isaiah the prophet and the evangelist Matthew, wishing to describe this brightness of glorified bodies, so singular and exceptional, with examples of physical things, could do no better than to equate it with the shining Sun, since nothing they found was more full of light. So one of them said that the just will gleam like the Sun in the sight of God, while the other used these words about Christ's transfiguration upon Mount Tabor: his face shone like the Sun.[83]

So delicate will these bodies be, as we shall see, that neither 67
doors nor partitions nor walls nor obstacles nor any other steely barriers will be strong enough to halt them or stand in their way — none that they cannot penetrate and pass through at any moment they choose. Christ gave the best evidence of this after his resurrection by making himself visible amid his disciples, after entering with the doors closed. Glorified bodies will show themselves so nimble that nothing heavy will prevent them from going wherever they wish. Here the most evident demonstration was Christ's famous example, when he proceeded to walk with dry feet across the Sea of Galilee to help the disciples in their peril.[84]

68   Postremo impassibilia et formosa atque immortalia demonstrabuntur quando nullo elementorum pondere gravabuntur, quando nulla turpitudine deformabuntur, quando nulla denique aegritudine debilitabuntur, quando praeterea infinitam beatorum canentium societatem et maximam quandam sanctorum amicorum multitudinem intuebuntur, admodum laetabuntur. Si enim amicitia in rebus humanis, ubi tot suspiciones, tot fraudes, et talia ac tanta pericula quotidie imminere cernuntur, ita suavis et dulcis est, quantum suavitatis ac dulcedinis in illa divina et mutua ac vicissitudinaria caritate fore arbitrabimur, ubi erit sine aliquo dolo atque ullo discrimine summa tranquillitas?

Quando ulterius caelestem illam Ierusalem civitatem inhabitantes propriis oculis videbunt, apprime exultabunt. Cuius quidem fundamenta, e duodecim[56] candidissimarum gemmarum generibus iacta, moenia circumcirca ex iaspide structa, portas pariter duodecim singulas e singulis margaritis et unionibus confectas, Iohannes Evangelista in fine libri Apocalipsis suae ex angelica revelatione fuisse testatur, ac reliqua huiusmodi magnificentiis excellentiisque referta late copioseque complectitur. Ad extremum quando se in perpetua felicitate beatos, damnatos vero in aeternis poenis mansuros contemplabuntur, profecto maximis et infinitis iubilationibus replebuntur.

69   Huiusmodi beatorum gaudiis totidem vel plura etiam miserorum hominum tormenta consonabunt. Nam primo miserabiles illi divina visione privabuntur, cuius quidem carentia *damni poena* a modernis theologis appellatur. Ac talis et tanta habetur ut—secundum celebratas Chrisostomi et Augustini sententias—quicunque a caelesti patria exulantes, cum huiusmodi videndi Dei conditionibus, apud inferos quam alibi uspiam esse mallent ubi Deum videre et conspicere non possent.

70   Ad hanc talem et tantam damni poenam infiniti et vere intollerabiles ignis, sulphuris, fetoris, vermium, frigoris et ceterorum talium perpetuorum tormentorum cruciatus accedunt quae quidem

Finally, these bodies will be shown to be handsome and free   68
from suffering and also immortal because no weight of matter will
drag them down, no deformity will mar them, nor finally will sickness weaken them as, in great happiness, they look upon an endless company of the blessed chanting and a huge multitude of
sainted friends. Now if friendship is so sweet and pleasant in human affairs, where we see daily threats of so much distrust, deceit
and danger, how much pleasure and sweetness will there be — shall
we suppose — in trading love back and forth with God, where the
ultimate serenity will be without distinction or deception?[85]

When at last the saints dwell in the heavenly Jerusalem and see
that city with their own eyes, their exulting will be boundless.
From an angel's revelation, at the end of his book of the Apocalypse, John the Evangelist testifies that its foundations have been
built of twelve types of the most dazzling gems, its ramparts piled
all around with jasper, equaled by twelve gates each constructed of
both kinds of pearl, and John includes a rich and extensive account
of the other things, surpassingly magnificent, that fill the city up.
Finally, when the blessed see themselves in perpetual happiness,
while observing that the damned will go on being punished forever, they will surely be full, beyond measure, of the greatest jubilation.[86]

As many or even worse torments for the people suffering will   69
match these joys of the blessed. Primarily, those wretched souls
will be deprived of the divine vision: modern theologians call this
deficit the *penalty of loss*. They consider it so painful — according to
famous statements by Chrysostom and Augustine — that exiles
from the heavenly homeland would rather be in Hell, provided
they would have this view of God, than any other place where
they could not catch sight of God and see him.[87]

On top of this penalty of loss, as great as it is, come limitless   70
and truly unbearable tortures of fire, sulfur, stench, worms,
freezing and the rest of the perpetual torments that the same

poena sensus ab eisdem theologis appellari et nuncupari consuevit.[57]
Haec duo nimirum maximi quidem et continui damnatorum la-
mentantium, stridentium et eiulantium, gemitus, ploratus et ulu-
latus concomitabuntur.

Quid de horrido ac terribili illo infinitorum hominum pluribus
intollerabilibus tormentorum generibus cruciatorum mutuo et vi-
cissitudinario conspectu dicemus, quae quidem ita taetra et horri-
bilia sunt ut ea nostra fugiat cogitatio et reformidet oratio? Postremo quantum cruciabuntur quando sese perpetuo miseros, sine
aliqua futurae liberationis spe, continuis cruciatibus consepultos,
imaginabuntur, beatos vero versa vice infinitis et sempiternis gaudiis repletos satiatosque semper exultaturos et iubilaturos cogita-
bunt!

71   Quapropter, ut tandem aliquando finem dicendi faciamus et ultimas demum huic nostro operi manus imponamus, cum primo
quanta et quam miranda sit humani corporis dignitas, quanta deinde esset animi sui celsitudo ac sublimitas, quanta praeterea et
quam praeclara ipsius hominis ex duabus praedictis partibus compositi excellentia foret, tribus superioribus libris satis abunde satisque copiose explicaverimus. Postremo, cum hoc quarto cuncta
quae commemoratis sententiis nostris maxime adversari et repugnare putabantur hactenus diluisse et confutasse meminerimus, reliquum est ut ad diligentem quandam et accuratam divinorum
mandatorum observationem praesentes et posteros parumper ex-
hortemur, per quam dumtaxat in caelestem illam et aeternam patriam ascendere valeamus.

72   Itaque non modo Maiestatem Tuam, Serenissime Princeps, ut
ad te tandem aliquando quasi longo quodam postliminio rever-
tamur, sed quoscunque etiam alios ad quorum manus haec nostra
scripta forte pervenerint, humiliter et suppliciter deprecamur quatenus cuncta quaeque divina mandata observare et exequi velitis.
Quod si quisque pro virili sua efficere et operari curaverit nimirum

theologians usually call *penalties of sense*. These two punishments will certainly be accompanied by deep groaning and constant wailing and howling from the damned as they weep, moan and shriek.[88]

And what can I say about the horrid, terrifying sight that countless humans have of one another, tormented by so many unbearable types of torture, so horrifying and repulsive that my thoughts flee and my speech shrinks from them? Finally, how great their anguish as they picture themselves in perpetual misery, with no hope of relief to come, buried together under constant torture, while they think contrariwise of the blessed, filled full of eternal and numberless joys, always exulting in jubilation![89]

So now let me finally bring my account to an end and at last give 71 this work of mine a conclusion, having started in the three preceding books with a full and satisfactory explanation of the worth of man's body and how admirable it is, next how exalted the loftiness of his soul and then besides how splendid the excellence of the human composed of those two parts. Last of all, since I have recorded in this fourth book all the points that resolve and refute the main arguments thought to oppose and contradict my own stated views, what remains is briefly to urge those present, and those to come, toward a careful and exact observance of God's commandments, our only way to rise to that heavenly and eternal home.

Therefore, Fairest Prince, while coming back after so long and 72 returning to you, I humbly and meekly beg Your Majesty, and any others who may come upon these writings of mine, to choose to follow every single one of God's commandments and fulfill them all. Whoever does his utmost to act on the commandments and put them into practice will certainly get temporal privileges here as

et temporalia haec privilegia et perpetua utriusque vitae praemia consequetur, proinde cunctis accuratis caelestium praeceptorum observatoribus proculdubio contigerit ut—statim a principio nativitatis suae—fortunati semper et felices ac beati fuisse atque esse et fore in aeternum videantur.

73   Quocirca et rogamus et obsecramus omnes huius qualiscunque operis lectores ut ad hanc nostram brevem et amatoriam exhortatiunculam ceteris posthabitis diligenter attendant, et ea operentur et faciant quae nos his ipsis breviter persuadere conabimur.

O homines—vel o viri potius, quinimmo o reges et principes et imperatores—postquam in tanta et tam immensa dignitate et excellentia constituti et ordinati estis ut omnia quaecunque in mundo, sive in terris, sive in mari et aquis, sive in aere, sive in aethere, sive in caelis facta sunt vestro imperio dicionique subdita et subiecta esse, per ea quae supra scripsimus, nullatenus dubitetis: sit vobis cura virtutis. Hanc, calcatis et suppeditatis vitiis, totis animi et corporis viribus diligite. Hanc amate, hanc observate, hanc, quaesumus, apprehendite, hanc capessite, hanc complectimini ut per continuas et assiduas eius ipsius operationes non solum felices et beati videamini sed ut etiam immortali Deo quasi similes efficiamini.

Vestra enim intelligendi et agendi officia cum omnipotenti Deo communia habentur et sunt. Unde, si vobis per acquisitionem et usum virtutis tranquillae immortalitatis beatitudo provenerit, nimirum in patria aeterno illi Principi quasi similes apparebitis. Nam semper intelligendo et agendo ac contemplando, quae propria solius Dei officia creduntur—in perpetua et aeterna beatitudine, una et simplici voluptate, instar sui—cum continuis exultationibus et cum sempiternis iubilationibus et cantibus gaudebitis.[58]

74   Haec igitur habuimus quae ad te, Serenissime Princeps, de dignitate atque excellentia hominis in praesentiarum scriberemus. Ac cuncta superius a nobis late copioseque explicata totiens vel

well as rewards that last, both for this life and the next, with the undoubted result that all who keep heaven's rules carefully seem always — right from the moment of birth — to be those who have been fortunate, are happy and will be blessed for eternity.

This is why I beg and beseech all readers of this work, such as it is, to set other things aside and pay close attention to this short and friendly little plea of mine — that they may take action to do as I shall try to persuade them in the few words that follow. 73

My fellow humans — no, you brave men, rather, you kings, princes and generals — you have been created with such immense value and appointed to a rank so high that no doubt at all remains, given what I have written, about this: all there is in this universe, whether on land or sea or in the waters, whether in the air or the aether or the heavens, has been made subject to your command and put under your control: attend to virtue, then. With vices pressed upon you in abundance, cherish virtue with all your strength of mind and body. Love virtue and preserve it, I beg you, grasp, seize and embrace it so that by putting virtue in action, constantly and ceaselessly, you may not only be seen as fortunate and happy but also become almost like the immortal God.

In fact, your roles of knowing and acting are recognized as shared with Almighty God. Then, if by acquiring and practicing virtue you receive the blessing of serene immortality, your appearance, when you return home, will surely be like that of the eternal Prince. For with constant rejoicing and endless, jubilant song — in bliss perpetual and eternal, with pleasure unique and simple like God's own — you will always rejoice in understanding, acting and contemplation, which properly are considered God's roles alone.[90]

And so, Fairest Prince, what I have for you is this present writing of mine about man's worth and excellence. Whenever I turn my eyes and thoughts back to the singular and wonderful gifts of 74

maxime vera esse sentimus quotiens in singulares illas et admirabiles personae tuae dotes et pretiosa privilegia oculos mentemque convertimus. Tunc enim, quando singula quaeque tua humanae naturae beneficia diligenter et accurate consideramus, tale profecto corpus talemque animum ex praecipuis quibusdam et egregiis utriusque partis conditionibus abs te haberi et possideri intelligimus, qualia singillatim hactenus explicasse meminimus. Ex quibus tam excellentibus et tam praestantibus membris ac muneribus, inter se mirabiliter compactis et simul in unum convenientibus, talem profecto ac tantam Alfonsi regis personam in lucem prodiisse conspeximus ut non communi et trita naturae lege natus sed potius ab omnipotenti Deo institutus et electus esse videaris.

your person and to your own esteemed privileges, I sense that what I have just explained at some length is absolutely correct. For then, reflecting carefully and exactly on each and every bounty of the human nature that you have, I realize that you do indeed possess such a body and such a mind, and that you get them from the special and outstanding features of both those parts, as I recall detailing them one by one. From parts so excellent and capabilities so outstanding, wonderfully put together and joined in a unity, I have clearly seen that King Alfonso's person was born to such greatness as, plainly, no common and familiar law of nature produced. Instead, it was Almighty God who chose and appointed you.

APPENDIX I

ANTONIO DA BARGA

On Mankind's Worth and the Excellence of Human Life

Antonio da Barga, the monk called prior of Monte Oliveto in   1
Naples, sends greetings to Bartolomeo Facio, his most beloved son
in Christ, for health and happiness now, salvation and eternal
glory in the end.

A man called Innocent, once supreme pontiff of the Roman   2
Church, wrote a little book in splendid language to deal fully and
extensively with human misery and man's vileness: starting with
conception, he did not stop talking about man's miseries and un-
happiness until he sent this perfect wretch to hell. Moreover, this
bishop of blessed memory was quite right to title his book *On
Human Misery*.

In this work, the same happily remembered pope promised to   3
write a companion volume which, since it was to take the opposite
view, would have been titled *On the Worth and Excellence of Human
Life*. But he never did this. Nor from bygone times do I find any
treatment of this exceptional topic by earlier poets, theologians or
orators. This same Innocent, I believe — once appointed to rule
the Church when the Lord gave the house of Israel a gladiator
against the Church's enemies and a watchman, like David's tower
overlooking Damascus — this Innocent became so completely busy
that there was no way for him to keep the promise he had made.

For this reason, my son most beloved — among my other sons   4
in Christ, the very dearest — with every trust in your love and affection, neither ordering nor compelling but gently beseeching and
humbly urging, I ask that you might wish to follow through with

the same book promised so long ago by that supreme pontiff, the purpose being to encourage me, to console and benefit yourself and, in the future, teach eternal salvation to all the faithful in Christ. So I send you this very same book—not finished, however, just a bit of a brief sketch with various headings and distinctions.

5   As you know, beloved son, with the end of Lent now upon us, I have been weakened and worn out by many fasts, vigils and observances of the *Rule,* while busy against my will—alas!—with outside affairs in defense of our monastery. After all this, I still find no rest. Instead, while keeping the seasonal fast and with Easter coming, I am forced by obedience and the needs of my Order to hurry off as quickly as possible to our general chapter soon to be held near the city of Siena. Fettered by all these obligations, then, I cannot give due care and attention to the project that I have mentioned.

6   Yet I am really delighted, dearest son, to find you so skilled in the art of oratory. You are not just placed high in that art among other orators, you take first place after Cicero, I dare say, in expressing Ciceronian eloquence. Such a son brings me no shame, only pride. So whatever you find poorly sketched by me is yours to correct, adjust, expand, embellish and finish since your gift of talent from above is so outstanding—knowledge great enough in itself to make someone excel who behaves well. For this I send endless praise to the Creator of all, the God who has honored my son with so excellent a gift.

7   Come then, best beloved, gird your soul with courage and have no fear of undertaking so noble a project, trusting in the Lord who bestows everything good and makes the newborn fluent in speech. Full of all goodness, merciful and bountiful in giving, he will not deny you anything you humbly ask that might praise his most blessed name and win merit and salvation. But I want you to send

this book to me without delay when—with thanks for the Almighty's help—you have brought it to completion.

A book entitled *On Mankind's Worth and the Excellence of Human Life.* 8

Before anything else, you must explain why God made humans 9 both bodily and nonbodily. Except through understanding, no one can share in God's blessedness—considered fuller the more it is understood. So he made one creation capable of reasoning in order to *understand* the Greatest Good, by understanding to *love* it, by loving to *possess* it and by possessing to *enjoy* it. And he divided this creation so that one part—angels, namely—would remain in their own purity, not joined to a body, while the other part—souls, in other words—would be joined to bodies. The reasoning creation was divided into unbodily and bodily, the angels being unbodily, while the bodily is called man, consisting of human flesh and a soul that reasons. The soul was in a state of reasoning because the goodness of God, as its first cause, produced it.

And so, if someone asks why a human or an angel was created, 10 the answer can be quick: because of God's goodness, as Augustine writes in his book *On Christian Teaching.* Because God is good, we exist, and we are good inasmuch as we exist. And if someone asks for the purpose behind a reasoning creation, the answer is to praise God, serve him and enjoy him—for the sake of the creation, not God's. For God, who is perfect and full of the ultimate goodness, cannot become more or less. Therefore, you must connect the fact that God made a reasoning creation with the Creator's goodness and the benefit of the creation.

Hence, when the question is why or for what a creature was 11 made to reason, you can answer very quickly that it was because of God's goodness and the creature's own benefit. For a creature, certainly it is beneficial to serve God and enjoy him. So they say that an angel or a human was made not because the Creator and

supremely blessed God needed another's assistance. He needs no favors from us, only to be served and enjoyed — the God whose service is kingly power.

12   But just as man was made for God — made to serve him, that is — so the world was made for man or to serve man. Man was put in between, then, in order to serve and be served, so that all of this would revert to man's good, both the submission paid to him and what he pays. For God wanted man to serve him in such a way that the human serving God, not God himself, would be helped by the serving, but he wanted the world to serve man and for man to be helped by that service too.

13   It was all for man's good, then, both what he was made for and what was made for him. All things are ours, as the Apostle says — higher, equal and lower. The higher, like God and the Trinity, are ours entirely to enjoy. The equal are ours to share life with — the angels. Although they are above us now, in the future they will be our equals in knowledge and enjoyment. And they are ours now because they exist for our benefit. In this way, a master's property is said to be the household's not by right of mastery but because of whom it benefits. Also, in certain passages of scripture, angels are said to serve us because they are sent to minister to us for our sake.

14   At the same time, people sometimes find that man was made to make up for the fall of the angels. You should not interpret this to mean that no human would have been made had no angel sinned but that this reason, among others, also plays a part. So the higher and the equal are ours — and the lower as well because they were made to serve us.

15   A common question asks why the soul was joined to a body since it would seem to have higher standing had it remained bodiless. You can answer this way: because God willed it so, and the cause of his willing is not to be sought.

But a second answer is possible: because God wanted soul 16
joined with body in order for their union in man to give a new
example of the blessed union between God and spirit, where God
is seen face to face and loved with the whole heart. For a creature
might think this: except by seeing spirit, the best creation of all,
joined to flesh—flesh low enough to be made of earth—and
joined by a love so great that spirit could not be pushed far
enough to abandon the flesh, then, except for that, the creature
could not be joined to his Creator by coming close enough to
know and love God with his whole mind. The Apostle shows this
when he says that we want not to be stripped of the body but for
the body to be clothed over, indicating that a created spirit is
joined by a love beyond description to an uncreated spirit.

Thus, as an example of the future fellowship to be achieved 17
between God and the reasoning spirit in its glorified state, God
connected the soul with bodily coverings and earthly dwellings.
He gave muddy matter the power to live and feel so that man
would know—since God could join natures as unlike as body and
soul in a single alliance and so great a friendship—that it would
not be at all impossible for him to raise a reasoning creature, so far
beneath God, up from its lowliness to share in God's glory.

Therefore, while showing how a reasoning spirit was lowered in 18
part to commune with an earthly body, then, lest spirit seem sunk
too far, God's providence added that later on the spirit would be
lifted up with that same body, when glorified, to commune with
those who had continued in their purity. What was diminished in
the spirit at the creation, because the Creator so arranged it, would
later return to the spirit, when glorified, through the same God's
grace.

While arranging different outcomes for reasoning spirits by his 19
own willed choice, God the Creator established a dwelling above
in heaven for those whom he left in their purity. And on earth

below he set up a habitation for those whom he joined to earthly bodies, imposing on both a rule of obedience—for the former not to fall from where they were, for the latter not to rise from where they were to where they were not. So God made man with two kinds of substance, fashioning a body from earth but making a soul from nothing. Souls were also joined to bodies so that, by serving God in bodies, souls would earn a greater crown.

20   About man's rank this is what you should say. After everything had been created and arranged, man was made last of all as the master and proprietor set above them all. Then comes this: Seeing that it was good, God said let us make a human in our image and likeness, and let him be over the fish of the sea, the birds in the sky and the beasts of the whole land. Man's great excellence is shown where God says *let us make*, indicating one act by three persons. For this statement comes from the Father's person to the Son and the Holy Spirit, not to the angels, as some suppose, since God's image and likeness and that of the angels are not one and the same.

21   Man's great excellence is also shown where God says *in our image and likeness*. So you need to explain what in man is God's image and likeness. In this passage, image and likeness is understood either as uncreated, the essence of the Trinity, the basis on which man was made, or else as created—in which man was made and also the image and likeness created along with man. Bede seems to have been thinking of the uncreated image which is God when he says that the single image is not of God and angels but of three persons, so that the text there addresses those persons, not angels.

22   But *image* is not said strictly of itself because it is said in relation to another whose likeness it bears and which it was made to represent—like an image of Caesar that carried his likeness and somehow represented him. But calling an image after what it is made for is not to speak strictly about the image, just as that image is, strictly speaking, a copied example taken from something

else, while the exemplar is that from which it is taken. Sometimes, however, one is used mistakenly for the other. So the usage is not quite strict when *image* is taken for the Trinity's essence, assuming that the word *image* has that meaning in this passage.

A different interpretation: in regard to man's mind, by which he 23 surpasses unreasoning things, he was made in God's image and likeness—in the image regarding memory, intellect and will, but in the likeness regarding innocence and justice, which exist naturally in the reasoning mind. Or else they treat image along with awareness of virtue but likeness along with love of virtue. Or they treat image along with everything else and likeness with essence because it is immortal and indivisible. Hence Augustine in his book *On the Soul's Quantity:* The soul was made like God because he made it immortal and indestructible. Image also belongs to form, then, and likeness to nature. So regarding his soul, man was made in the image and likeness of the whole Trinity, not of the Father, Son and Holy Spirit.

Also regarding the soul, they say that a human is God's image 24 because an image of God is in him, just as an image is both the surface and the picture on it, though it is because of the picture on it that the surface too is called an image. So also, because of the Trinity's greatness, we also use the word *image* for what this image is in.

For this reason, man is said to be both the *image* and *in the im-* 25 *age,* while the Son is the image but not in the image because he was born, not created, equal and in no way dissimilar. Man was created by God, not begotten, not fully equal but approaching this by a certain similarity.

Hence Augustine in book 7 *On the Trinity.* This is what *Genesis* 26 reads: let us make man in our image and likeness. He said *let us make* and *our* in the plural, which can only mean that relations are involved. Hence, we are meant to read *Father, Son and Holy Spirit—* in the image of the Father, Son and Holy Spirit so that man may

be an image of God. But because that image was not made entirely equal—not being born of God but created by him—therefore it says *image* because man is in the image and not exactly on a par, though he approaches somewhat by similarity. The Son is the image, however, though not in the image because he is equal to the Father. Man is said to be *in the image*, then, because of an inexact likeness, and it says *our* so that we can understand man as an image of the Trinity but not equal to the Trinity as the Father is to the Son.

27   Notice that it says in what way man is like God—namely, regarding the soul. But even in the body there is a certain property that indicates this because man's stature is erect, whereby the body fits with a reasoning soul by standing straight toward heaven.

28   In the book and in your conclusions you should repeat this often: Be aware of your rank, you human; the heavens have been prepared for you, and you must not sink down into the ground nor change from a citizen of heaven into some beast. Because man did not realize when he was held in honor, he has been compared to unfeeling beasts of burden and likened to them.

29   Also, you should say this about man's worth—namely, about the soul's immortality according to Plato and the theologians. So you should talk about intellect, memory, and will according to the pagans and the theologians.

30   Also, you should say this about man's worth—in particular, about the making of man and the handsomeness of his parts that Lactantius writes about.

31   Also, Jerome says this about man's worth: great is the worth of souls so that from the moment of birth each one has an angel appointed to watch over it. Paul also witnesses to the Hebrews: are they all not ministering spirits sent to minister for those who receive the inheritance of salvation?

32   Also, about man's worth: angels have their assignments in provinces and territories to watch over humans and instruct them, and

their princes especially provide for what must be done, as we read that an angel gave Pharaoh a revelation about a famine to come for seven years and the necessary provisioning. And in Daniel we read about revelations made to Nebuchadnezzar and the vision of future kingdoms — the kingdoms of the Persians and Medes and of the Greeks and Romans. The great Dionysius also says that generally all such revelations happen with angels as mediators.

Also, humans are to be taken up among the orders of angels to 33 be their equals, as John says in the Apocalypse: a human is the angel's measure. And Gregory: sometimes humility in humans leads to equality with angels.

Also, in Christ our nature was taken up into godhood and in 34 Christ the man — to whom every knee bends in Heaven, on earth and in Hell — is God and revered by angels.

Also, the Lord said to Peter and his successors: whatever you 35 bind on earth shall be bound also in heaven, and whatever you unbind on earth shall also be unbound in heaven, and I will give you the keys to the kingdom of heaven.

Also, humans shall come with the judge at the end of the world 36 to judge the world and the evil angels. Also that the judge himself will be Christ in the form of a human, like both God and the man in whom the whole of divinity dwells in a bodily way.

Also, God allowed humans, not angels, to prepare the body of 37 Christ and took a human, not angels, up into divinity: there is greater worth in a human, therefore, than in an angel.

Also, we often read in the lives of the Fathers and the deeds of 38 the saints that angels delivered food and such things to humans, healed them, attended their funeral services and accompanied their souls to heaven.

Also, humans were often permitted to raise the dead, expel demons and heal all kinds of weariness. 39

Also, we often read that certain people commanded the Sun to 40 stand still and that it stood still for two days, as it says in Joshua

and in the Book of Kings when Hezekiah made the Sun go backward.

41   Also, Moses commanded the sea to dry up, and the waters came upon them right and left like a wall until the people of God passed through.

42   Also, some moved mountains by prayer, and with a command others made large lakes dry up and turned them into fields with growing plants.

43   Also, we read that while Saint Benedict was at Monte Cassino in the body, he appeared in the spirit to his followers in Terracina, outlining for them all the jobs required to build a monastery.

44   Also, about human excellence you should say that God loved man so much that he chose to join the human with the divine, choosing to suffer and die for man in Christ as far as humanity is concerned.

45   And although man's excellence makes him incomparably more outstanding than other created things, and while he is better able to keep close to real beatitude and is capable of enjoying all such blessings, yet there will be twelve blessings in which he himself, wholly human, will abound forever, once the tribulations of the present age have passed: health without illness, . . . youth without aging, . . . fullness without disgust, . . . freedom of the body, . . . beauty without bad feeling, . . . immortality and no suffering, . . . plenty without fail, . . . peace without turmoil, . . . rest without toil, . . . knowledge without ignorance, . . . the glory and honor that all the elect show to one another, . . . and joy without sadness. Then God will wash every tear from the eyes of his saints, with no more wailing nor grief because the earlier times will have passed away.

46   The six joys of the elect. We should know that joy consists mainly of six things for the elect: namely, seeing and knowing the most holy Trinity, a delightful location, the company of saints, bodies glorified, Hell and the world. . . .

In the fifth joy, about Hell, the elect will feel three joys. They 47
will rejoice first because, by the mercy of the Redeemer, they
themselves have avoided such punishments and eternal damnation; second because they will see God's enemies severely tormented; . . . third because, once gathered at the portal of eternal
salvation, they will no longer fear any more sinning. . . . In the
sixth joy, about the world, God's elect will feel two joys. First, they
are now freed from the world's misery and dangers, . . . second
they will have vanquished the world and its miseries with help
from God's grace. . . .

Because we cannot speak fully about God and the blessed life 48
while located in this frail body, because we are strangers to God
while in the body — and even the very angels fall short of him —
because no angel nor patriarch nor prophet nor apostle nor any
other saint can fully explain the essence and mystery of the most
holy Trinity, which according to Augustine is known only to itself,
still — in the afterthought that comes next below — I will say something briefly to indicate what such a thing is like.

Next comes a description of the first heaven — the first, for one 49
must recognize that the heavens are three. The first heaven is
called starry, . . . the second heaven is called crystalline or watery,
. . . the third heaven is called empyrean. . . .

APPENDIX II

BARTOLOMEO FACIO

On Human Excellence and Distinction

For Pope Pius the Second

I recently set out to write about human excellence, Most Blessed 149.1
Father, for I had gathered that the Innocent Fiéschi who was once
supreme pontiff, and clearly a very learned man, promised to write
on this topic in a book where he dealt with mankind's afflictions.
This might have happened, though—as things worked out—papal business prevented him from keeping his promise. But now,
since I have been very anxious to publish something in your name
that would testify to Your Holiness, and hence to everyone, about
my special reverence and devotion to you, I have decided that this
topic is the one most worthy of your patronage. For what could
one write about that is weightier and more important than the human rank and distinction that make mankind almost the equal
even of angels? Besides, what subject could better suit Your Excel-
lency who, by God's goodness and your own distinguished talent,
have attained the world's highest rank?

As I turned my thoughts to the many different subjects re- 2
corded in literature, I could think of almost nothing else to write
about that actually seemed worthy of a Pontiff's majesty. For in
all the fields of higher learning, what is left that someone has
not dealt with extensively? Accordingly, do we not see that some
people—desiring glory and indeed eloquent and eminent—apply
themselves to translating works by Greeks in order to attract and
amuse readers with novel material? Far from finding fault with

their decision, I think it quite praiseworthy. For this is how they avoid the sin of idleness, nourish their thoughts and bring us knowledge of much that we do not know. But more about this elsewhere.

3   I would like you to accept this small effort, best and Most Holy Father, as a little taste of my studies, such as they are. But if you reject it, I hope you will accept other things from me later, if I have time to write—especially if it is something you want, as I understand, and I can produce, so I believe. Enough of that: let me develop my topic.

4   In my view, the best thing to do when discussing mankind's distinction is to give a brief account of why God made man. This seems to have no small bearing on human rank and honor, about which people actually differ in their views—so I find.

150.5   The Platonists, considered great authorities by pagan philosophers, think that the reason why God made humans was to inhabit this earthly globe that he divided from the waters, also to gaze at the heavens and—amazed by the world's order and regularity—to imitate it in their lives and deeds. But this reason seems hardly solid enough. For if God created humans to inhabit the world, then evidently the world would not have been made for the sake of humans: instead, they would have been made because of the world.

6   The Stoics said more plausibly that humans were born to benefit humans: this too seems not quite right, however, though they came closer to the truth than the Platonists. If God created man on that basis, no one would deny, of course, that it would serve the general welfare, enabling one person to help and defend another as much as possible. But this reason is also not strong enough to produce a human.

7   Lactantius followed the Platonists up to a point, so it seems to me, concluding that just as God made the world for mankind's

sake, so he made man for his own sake, in order for him to look on the works that God produced, talk about them and wonder at the Craftsman's wisdom. The main point of all this is for humans to revere and worship God — he says — so that from God's works they might perceive the excellence of God's majesty. Important evidence that God made them for his own sake is that he fashioned the human body to be tall in stature, as if lifted up by God's hand to know and attend to him.

But Augustine thinks that God made humans out of his 8 boundless goodness — not primarily for his own sake, in other words, but for theirs because, he says, almighty God is good, needing no favors or service from them since he is abundantly and perfectly happy. But Augustine asserts that he made man equipped with thought and reason so that man might know, love, possess and then likewise enjoy that greatest good which is both God himself and also *in* God. Man's greatest advantage lies in devoting and surrendering himself to God, for whom ruling is giving help. What we do is actually beneficial not for God but for ourselves since nothing can add to divinity and make God more perfect. Hence, the whole product of human deeds returns to the very humans who do them, not to the God whom we honor and worship by doing them.

God actually wanted us to benefit ourselves, making our deeds 9 helpful to us, not to God. But he made the world benefit us so that we might get from it what we need to live, while showing at the same time that he created all that we see — so beautiful, so various, so amazing — for the sake of humanity. All things are ours, in fact, according to Paul: the highest, equal and least. The highest are ours to observe and enjoy, and of that kind are God and the Trinity. The equal are ours to rejoice with, of which kind are the angels: even though we are below them in this life, we shall be their peers and equals when we depart for heaven, free and

clear of earthly cares and entirely dedicated to gazing on divinity and knowing it. The least are ours to use as things needed and helpful for life.

151.10 However, we read in sacred Scripture that God created humans so that, for a time, their race would fill the celestial places vacated by angels expelled from heaven for conspiring with Lucifer. But I prefer Augustine's view. Could God not have created other angels right away to replace those who were ejected? Doing that would surely have been simpler. Then there would have been no need — since this was for man's sake — to make the Sun, the Moon and the other heavenly bodies, to create elements, to adorn the land with such a variety of crops, to fill it with such a multitude of animals and then clothe souls themselves with bodies. Forget about the work since God does no work when he creates: for he spoke, and they were made; he gives a command, and they are created. Why would God have needed to produce all this, such huge variety, if there were another, quicker way — with no time passing, not an instant — to fill empty posts in heaven?

11 We may trust, then, that God made humans because of his infinite and ineffable goodness (as already stated) rather than to fill places in heaven. The more correct view, then, assigns man's creation to God's kindly will — not to any need, since absolutely none occurs in him. But on this point enough has been said. If we want to examine man's value and look deeper, I think we must ask what gifts God gave him and also which ones other animals lack. As I see it, mankind's whole distinction lies in these gifts. Surely this is something remarkable and worth knowing for humans, so that they will neither devise nor do anything at all unworthy of them once they have understood their worth.

12 The facts are nearly numberless that show the singular and exceptional effect on man of divine love. One of these — absolutely undebatable — stands out in humans: that God made man in his image and likeness. What greater, more exceptional or more divine

gift could God have given man than to make him in his own image and likeness, giving him a soul equipped with mind, reason and immortality?

With this mind, in fact, we perceive, judge, understand and remember: these too belong to God and, except that he allows it, they could never flow down into human souls. None of the elements can have this power — even fire and air, which are by nature lighter and purer; earth and water are less plausible. Lacking life and sense, these can be broken up and taken apart so that people can use them to make hidden powers known, to build cities, design shelter and clothing, establish laws, observe the turning heavens and motions of the cycling stars, devise medicine and so many more arts and sciences and especially philosophy, which teaches and directs us in right living, which instructs us first to worship God and then urges us to every virtuous deed.

And the memory we use to grasp so many things that are different and difficult cannot arise from these elements. For if I may leave Carneades out as well as Metrodorus and certain others whose memory, they say, was amazing, how much has been remembered by the jurists, philosophers, logicians and their followers? These things persuade me that a power so great and complex can only be divine.

But truly, to see that our soul was made to resemble the Trinity, no better argument can be proposed than that the result was immortality, seeing that this alone, more than anything else, makes the soul closer to God, its parent and origin. Clearly now, the human soul is far, far inferior to God in wisdom, thought, knowledge and the rest, whereas in being immortal it is quite like God and nearly equal. For when someone has lived a good life and left the body, after the filth picked up by touching the body has first been purged and set aside, the liberated soul next seeks heaven, there to lead a blessed and everlasting life with the choirs of saints and angels and the Trinity itself.

13

152.14

15

16   I think it reasonable to give a fuller account of why I believe this, especially since settling this one point makes it easier to settle other issues about the soul's divinity. I believe that a brief review of the topic is in order — the position not only of our theologians but of ancient philosophers as well, especially those who have said that the souls of humans are divine and immortal. For surely we see that the rest of the philosophers, like plagues infecting the human race, are to be excluded from our debate.

17   Some say that Pherecydes of Syros was the first person known to state the immortality of souls — not only sharing that belief with Pythagoras, his student, but also spreading it about. And Plato, following Pythagoras, not only continued in that view but also produced many arguments to explain why he held it. Aristotle, in the book that he published about the souls of animals, says that the intellect — or intellective soul — is separable from the body, as the perpetual is from the destructible. The *Book of Causes*, however — whether it was written by Aristotle or, as some prefer, by Proclus — states that every intelligence, in keeping with its substance, endures and is indestructible. Cicero reckons that the soul is immortal mainly because there is no animal but the human that has any knowledge of God or practices religion: this fact alone makes it clear, then, that in this way we desire what will belong to us.

153.18   What do our people say — and Paul especially, that special light of our wisdom and religion? He states that our debt is to the spirit, not the flesh, so that we may live by desiring it. For he affirms that they are dead who have lived by sensing and desiring the flesh, while they will live who have held the wanton flesh in check.

19   But Lactantius declares that human souls have perpetual life with these arguments: just as sound, voice and wind are not seen by us, and yet we perceive that they exist from their strength and effects, so we can observe God through his works with our mental

vision even though our eyes cannot see him. Furthermore, there is great evidence of the soul's divinity in the virtue given to man alone of all the animals: surely humans would never expose themselves to so much hardship and danger for virtue's sake — because virtue itself is what they need — unless they thought that through virtue they would rise to the real life that is immortal.

Augustine confirms that by its nature a soul equipped with   20
reason cannot die because it is not subject to destruction. And he uses the words of Plato and Porphyry to make this case for immortality: Plato says that souls will return again to their bodies after separating from them, but Porphyry says they will never go back to bodies so vile; plainly, then, if souls are to return to bodies but not to vile bodies, they will go back to bodies that are glorious.

However, when Jerome — that man of godlike brilliance — de-   21
fines the soul, he says that this is man's life, motion and sense; it provides the body with intellect and equips it with immortality; it is also invisible and always self-moving in its place. Because this force animates the body, he calls it soul; because it is aware, he calls it spirit; because it feels, sense; because it knows, mind; because it understands, thought; because it makes distinctions, reason; because it decides, will; because it recalls, memory.

On this same topic of immortality, Gregory too has spoken,   22
asking this: what tongue or what intellect is enough to capture how great the joys are of that supernal city? With the gift of perpetual indestructibility, there are many other things to rejoice in, but chiefly this — not to be troubled by the fear of death.

Moreover, there are not just declarations but also various rea-   154.23
sons for supporting immortality in some way. First we see that nature leads all humans to seek happiness. This desire would seem pointless unless people could sometimes attain happiness. If the soul were to perish, however, how could it become happy? It must be immortal in order to succeed, with the evident result that the human soul is immortal.

24   Aristotle agrees with this. According to him, everything destructible breaks down into what it was made or born from. But nothing that exists breaks down into nothing or perishes entirely. Being destroyed is not being reduced to nothing, in fact, but returning to a source. Now when a body is destroyed, since it is part of the earth, it breaks down into earth, while things made of air break down into air, and likewise the two other kinds into elements suiting their nature. But if the soul, created from nothing, were destroyed, then necessarily it would be changed back into nothing by the wisest of craftsmen. Yet there is no way for the soul to return to nothing since nothing is not a natural principle of production. And the soul is not a composite of matter. So plainly it follows that the soul is immortal.

25   Since God is the best and most just, it certainly seems right and fitting for him to take account of good and evil people and to afflict the latter with punishments while repaying the former with rewards for their good deeds. Otherwise God himself would scarcely be thought just—a sinful thought to have about the Highest. For if evil people get their reward in this life from power, influence and riches, then, if death ends everything, what payment or reward will there be for good people who ignore these things in order to attain heavenly life? How mad and foolish it would be to suffer death and the harshest torments instead, if there were no other life after the soul leaves the body and this were seen as the recompense for religion and piety. Would we not be more miserable than other people, as Paul says, if our only hope were for this life?

26   But now I feel I have said rather enough about the immortality of souls, making it quite clear, I believe, not only that the soul does not die when it leaves the body but that it moves on to an everlasting celestial life, if it has lived piously and chastely while in the body—not on its own merits, to be sure, since these are not great, but by the immense goodness of God himself.

To return to where I was before digressing, the distinguished 155.27
master of the *Sentences* rules that man was made in God's image
and likeness, so it must be granted, as I said, that man was given
the mind by which he surpasses all the animals that lack reason.
And he thinks that wisdom, memory and love relate to the image,
while the innocence and justice that assuredly exist in the divine
mind relate to the likeness. Or else by image the rest are to be
understood and by likeness the nature because the soul is immortal and cannot be divided or taken apart at all.

And he confirms this from what Augustine wrote in his book 28
On the Quantity of the Soul, stating that the soul must be described
as made in God's image and likeness because it is immortal and
indestructible and because that likeness actually pertains to nature
and image pertains to form. Man was made in the image and likeness not just of the Father or the Son or the Holy Spirit but of the
whole Trinity: the correct statement, then, is that man, regarding
his soul, is *near to* God's image.

Strictly speaking, in fact, we say that God's image is *in* God's 29
son, our Lord Jesus Christ—born of God, not made, equal to the
Father in eternity, greatness and power and in no way dissimilar.
But man was made by God, not born of him nor just like him nor
equal, seeing that our image is neither coeternal with God nor of
the same substance as God but extremely remote from that divine
nature. Therefore, man was described as *made near to God's image*,
not as *God's image*, though this can be said in a loose way. Let me
set this aside, however.

How much does it say about man's surpassing value that when 30
God made him he said *let us* make him? The apparent meaning, in
fact, is that three persons—not just the Father—joined together
to create man. For it is evident that the order to create other living
things has only one source. For it is written that *God saw that it was
good*, and so on, which cannot be connected with the choirs of
angels, as some suppose. For image and likeness are not one and

the same in God and angels since in greatness and power angels are not at all equal to God.

31   Therefore, our most exalted God wanted the Trinity to be present in the creation that he created in his image and likeness, or surely God said this to express a sense of utmost resolution since this creature was to be made the greatest thing alive—lord and master of all on earth. In fact, God wanted and commanded him to rule all the animals that feed on land and in the sea and sky. For he says this: let him also rule the fish in the sea, the birds in the sky and the whole earth—immense authority, to be sure.

32   But this was given to man so he might understand that in his life and deeds he must repay the great benefits conferred on him by the Creator, must acknowledge their author, worship and venerate him with his whole mind and heart, must follow his commandments with the utmost promptness and diligence, must strive for virtue, attend to grace and honor and do no wrong that in any deed or thought might offend him from whom he received so much power.

156.33   A splendid fact matches this exceptional human excellence: since God decided to make man more beautiful than all other animals, he gave his body a stature much unlike that of others in form and figure, one capable of reason and speech to fit a soul of so noble a lineage. For he determined that brute animals would have faces looking at the ground in order to observe the earth from which they were produced, while humans would be tall and erect, with their eyes turning toward the heaven whence they came. And plainly he did this on the best possible plan and a very wise one. For God wanted those animals concerned with immortality to lift their faces to heaven and its creator, gazing at the place where one day they would go. This is why he made man only with feet for walking and support. And he gave him a tongue, perhaps the most wonderful gift—except for wisdom—given to mortals because it

expresses the mind's thoughts and words conceived within, by whose use especially we differ so very much from beasts, for they are without speech, as they are without reason and thought.

And this also must be regarded as of the greatest value in man, showing as clear as day God's unbelievable love for humans: that God sent an angel to watch over him, to guide his steps, to urge him to what is good, right and honest, to excite and inspire him to be mindful and attentive to heaven, piety, religion and the love of wisdom. Do we not see that doing this is normal with good parents who have the means to commit their children to teachers who guide their steps, informing and instructing them to deeds of virtue, so that they do not go wrong or make mistakes. That an angel was given to man to lead and support him is quite clear from Paul's words, for he says this about angels: Are they not all ministering spirits, sent to minister for the sake of those who will receive the inheritance of salvation? 34

But we read in Tobias that Raphael — one of the seven always stationed with God to hear his orders and follow them — guided Tobias on earth and accompanied him on a journey when he was sent by his father, whose name was the same, to Gabellus in Media because the father thought he was owed ten talents of silver. Raphael not only showed Tobias the route and saved him from a sea monster that they encountered but also drove a demon away from the wife that he took on the journey. And the angel went back with him, after roasting the liver of the fish they had caught for the eyes of Tobias the father, and when Raphael gave it to Tobias the sight returned to his eyes, and at last, according to all witnesses, the angel vanished from their sight. 35

We read in the book of Daniel, which Jerome claims was translated by Theodotion, that an angel led Habakkuk to Daniel after ordering him to bring a meal to this servant of God who had been thrown into a den of lions because of the malicious Babylonians. 157.36

For it is written: the Lord took him by the top of his head and carried him by the hair of his head, and by the force of his spirit he put him in Babylon above the lions' den, crying out to Habakkuk and saying this: take up the meal as God has commanded you and serve it to Daniel.

37   And because Lot was a servant of God who carefully kept his commandments and did everything to keep himself free from that wicked pleasure, we read that three angels freed him and his family from the burning of his land, standing by to guide them until they escaped the danger from that terrible flame and fire. I might cite many such examples except that I think it redundant since many may be found in the holy books.

38   We also read, in fact, that the rulers of a place and its districts have been assigned to angels for protection, especially to Gabriel and Michael, from which we can judge how much almighty God cared about the salvation of the human race. Especially in the book that records the lives of the saints, we often read that some holy men used to get food from angels at set times, also that they completely cured some whose bodies were troubled by bad health, that they were heard conducting the rites for the dead at their funerals, and finally, when the ceremonies were over, that they were seen bearing their souls to heaven.

39   What a great demonstration of man's superiority it is that God granted many holy men the power to rouse some of the dead to life, to drive demons quickly out of human bodies and cleanse them of sicknesses. God gave this gift first to Elias and certain other pious people, and then our Lord Jesus Christ showed that the gift was also in him, and later he confirmed it in the apostles and saints, as he says according to the Evangelist: whatever you seek from the Father in my name, he will give you; also, in my name they shall cast out demons, pick up snakes and so on, along with other sayings. What more than this can have been given to angels? This gift was surely the greatest, for the power belongs to

God's Majesty. I leave out countless other miracles done by saints by God's might and word. For we read in sacred history that sight was restored to the blind, straight posture to the lame and health to those impaired by leprosy and others troubled by illness.

Furthermore, this human excellence was not to be thought   158.40 trivial inasmuch as the power that God granted and gave was so great that one person could either make another share in the life of Heaven or banish him forever to Hell. For Christ, our God, wanted the supreme pontiffs — those whom we honor as his vicars on earth — to have this power. To Peter, the first one appointed to rule the Most Holy Roman Church, he said this: I give you the keys of the kingdom of heaven, and whatever you bind on earth, it will also be bound in heaven, and whatever you release on earth, it will also be released in heaven. To this day, the authority has been transmitted in turn to Peter's successors for the salvation of many mortals who would have been hurled down to Hell because of the filth and sin they lived in had they not found forgiveness for their crimes from a pontiff or his vicar.

But let me say what great glory belongs to man because, when   41 God decided to redeem the human race, damned for the arrogance of its first parent, he chose to have his only Son descend to earth from his heavenly home to enter the womb of the Most Holy Virgin, to take on this lowly mortal body, to become vulnerable to thirst, hunger, cold and other hardships and — still more astonishing — to suffer death on the cross. And what a death, so slavish and unseemly! How great is God's goodness! How beyond words his kindness! What a singular and extraordinary gift! Can any other be conceived or described that would declare God's immense goodness or his love for mankind more plainly than that he deigned to join divinity with humanity, and that his Son — the same as God and Our Lord — should not only become human but also, just for man's sake, undergo abuse and death?

42 What good would it do for man to have come into this life and enjoy it along with these human benefits if, after body and soul are parted, what he gets is everlasting death and misery? How can this life have been happy for one who thinks that after dying he will always be in darkness and distress? Therefore, I would be perfectly correct to prefer this favor to all of them that God has indeed granted to man. He would never have conferred it on him except that he loved man more than all his creatures on earth and ranked him higher.

43 Nor do I think I should be silent about this power that was divinely granted to man so that while sacrificing to God, and saying a few words, he might bring it about for the substance of bread to pass into the substance of the body of Our Lord, Jesus Christ, which was nailed to a cross for the sake of our salvation. Nowhere do we read that God gave this power to any of the angels or supernal spirits.

159.44 Nor should I skip this either, for it is the most outstanding gift, compared to the others: that on the terrible day when Christ our God will rouse the souls of the dead to take back their bodies for judgment, he decreed that he would consult the apostles as his colleagues. For he says: Amen I say to you that whoever has followed me to be reborn, you will also sit on twelve seats to judge the twelve tribes of Israel when the Son of Man comes to sit on his throne in majesty. I actually think that this was the greatest gift of all that God provided to humans, when this person — not just his servant but also his creation from nothing — was set up as his peer in judgment. For if we observe no one in this life choosing to put himself on the same level of power and authority with his servant, how much should we make of what God, the head and creator of them all, deigned to do? Then who can honor these gifts with praises worthy of the God who gave them? Who can weigh their great benefits fairly? Who can give enough thanks?

I could also mention certain other things that seem to accrue to 45
man's value. However, though God in fact provided them for this
mortal life, I fear I might seem too concerned with them if I were
to pursue each one or some of them. For there are many of this
kind, as everyone knows. So I think it better to move on to what
God has arranged after the course of this present life for a person
who has lived justly and in keeping with divine laws.

Because I have talked about many of them in the book I wrote 46
about life's happiness, I shall have less to say now. In that book
you can recognize those that apply here. They are such that they
demonstrate human worth far more fully than all the rest that I
have shown to be given by God in this life. These gifts continue,
while the others last scarcely a generation.

Nor would those goods that I have described previously as hu- 47
man seem of much value if the soul, after leaving the body, were to
roam here and there without rest, wandering and unsure, with no
fixed place assigned to it, until finally it would wear out and stop.
For how could such things make anyone happy who knew that all
his goods would perish along with his short and uncertain life?
For he would seem not much better than the beasts if he differed
from them only in the present life. Nor would his worth be anything so great if nothing worthy remained after death that seemed
related to his original worth.

This part that I have still to finish is actually harder, then, for 48
I shall discuss things removed from our sight and sense that human thought and reason cannot grasp well. Nor can anyone un-
equipped with divine wisdom know or judge them correctly. These
things, as Augustine says, I have barely seen with my eyes, yet
what I can report as a reliable witness is what I have seen. But this
will have the force of secure testimony, in fact, for people who are
Christians not only in name but in fact. Those who correctly believe whatever the prophets or apostles or teachers of our religion's

faith have passed down — they never doubt that the happiness of souls is real after death.

49   Not to say more than the topic demands, however, let me press on with what I started.

160.50   So I shall not talk about the perpetual health of the blessed who can never again fall ill nor need any drug or remedy or prescription. I shall not talk about their perpetual youth, always flowering at the same age, exactly as Christ, the best teacher, undertook to teach his disciples, according to Paul, that their youth would remain and they would never grow old. I shall not talk about all the abundance that never causes any distaste for the blessed. I shall not talk about their most ample freedom that will be free of every need and burden. I shall not talk about their appearance in bodies where no ugliness at all, no blemish may be found. I shall not talk about the perpetual peace that will prevail in the city of God, where no clatter of arms, no alarm of war may be heard. I shall not talk about the completely honorable and advantageous repose that no toil, no additional business will disturb. I shall not talk about the love and mutual accord in which the blessed embrace and hold one another. For I have dealt with these rather extensively in the work that I mentioned before. But I shall describe, if I can, what joys the souls of the blessed feel after they journey to heaven.

51   For when I think about the soul, and when I come to the kinds of not inconsiderable joy in that divine city and assembly, of these I rightly say that the first is the sight of God, an ability given us by God as a reward for faith. For just as angels see God in keeping with the wisdom divinely given to them, so the souls of the blessed will see, in keeping with their capacity and limits. But this is what the Apostle says: we know in part and we prophesy in part until completion comes, and now we see dimly through a mirror but then face to face. The apostle John also talks about this, say-

ing: when he appears, we shall be like him because we shall see him just as he is.

But a frequent question is whether we shall look upon God 52 with the eyes of the body or the mind. It must not be doubted that our eyes will do their job, and with those eyes glorified (as the theologians say) or our glorified bodies we shall see, but there is less doubt that we shall also look on God with eyes closed.

For if the prophet Elisha—when he had gone away to accept a 53 gift from Naaman, whose leprosy he had taken away—could see his servant with his own spirit, then how much better should the body see spiritual things with that same spirit when the body is completely pure and rid of every earthly stain, since the strength of our eyes will be such that we may even see unbodily things through them? Surely the mind's vision will be far sharper and clearer.

For Job says this to God: with the hearing of my ear I used to 161.54 hear you, and now my eye sees you because I have despised myself and withered away, regarding myself as earth and ashes. Does anyone doubt that this Job saw God with the eyes of his mind and spirit, even though Augustine seems to take this as also about the body's eyes? They shall see the King in his glory, says Isaiah. But if this was a prediction about Christ seated in divine majesty, it can also be applied correctly to the eyes of the body. But if this is about God, in my view it should be referred to the mind's eyes, which is easy to decide from Paul's statement: but we, gazing on God's glory when he reveals his face, are transformed into the same image, from glory into glory, as by the spirit of God. And we should not take the Psalmist's famous line in any other way: come near to God and be enlightened, and your faces shall show no shame. For we go to God through faith, which beyond doubt belongs to the heart and soul, not the body. But if it is the mind that sees while we are in this mortal life (for the eye is the tool and

instrument by which the mind tells all those things apart), who would deny that it is likelier that we shall look on the divine majesty with the spirit's eyes rather than the body's?

55   Yet Augustine sometimes seems to lean to the view that we shall also see God with the body's eyes, saying: either we shall see God through the body's eyes because there is something excellent and mind-like in us whereby we can understand an unbodily and divine nature, or—and this is easier to understand—we shall know and view God by turns as each of us sees him in one another and in himself, in the new heaven and the new earth, in every person both through all bodies and in every body, wherever we direct the eyes of the spiritual body. Yes, and he also claims that we shall see the thoughts of others, fulfilling what the Apostle said: judge nothing before the time, until the Lord comes to light up what hides in darkness and reveal the heart's thoughts, and then God shall praise each one.

56   In any case, whether we see with the heart's eyes or the body's or both, we shall assuredly see God. What more authoritative witness to this fact than Christ, the light of truth and fount of wisdom, who, as the Evangelist left it in writing, said this: blessed are the pure of heart, for they shall see God? Who then can conceive of such a magnitude of joy, much less describe it—which we shall get from the sight of God, so sweet and joyous? From all the things that enter the mind, can anything more desirable or joyous be desired?

162.57   For if the sight of heaven and the stars delights us intensely, recalling the beauty lying within and more to be admired, how much better will be our delight in looking upon God, the best and most expert Creator of all those things, in whom indeed lies everything by which the souls of the blessed are evidently delighted? Besides, by so much study of those human and scientific subjects, what do we learn? If desire for knowledge of that Wisdom—the head of all, for whose benefit we strive to attain knowledge of the

divine — draws us to such studies in this life, how much more does the sight and knowledge of that most noble and divine nature ravish us away to it? Finally, if these earthly and mortal things — gold, silver, gems, images and others considered splendid and magnificent — attract humans to them by their beauty and hold them, how much more must we believe that looking at divine things, in no way comparable to others, should attract and hold us?

On this point Augustine's view seems correct: that those shut out of Paradise would rather be in Hell forever — provided they could see God — than anywhere else where they had to do without seeing God. Chrysostom plainly confirms this, judging exclusion from the divine vision a harsher punishment than being sent to Hell. The Psalmist also testifies to this when he says show your face, and we shall be saved. For all our bliss is contained in viewing and seeing God.

58

Furthermore, what joy we shall have as we look at Christ our Lord, the Son of God, in human form and figure, presiding over the choirs of angels as we look upon divinity and humanity conjoined in him! For if we are very eager to see a father we have not seen for a long time when he returns from abroad, how great will be that future joy that we shall get from seeing him who is the parent common to all? To save and snatch us away from eternal torment, he himself did not refuse to undergo a final torment. And certainly it will also delight us immeasurably when we shall see that Most Blessed and Holy Virgin — our advocate and protector, who carried our salvation in her womb — and, together with her, John the Baptist, the apostles and martyrs crowded around Christ our Savior among the ranks of angels with whom we shall spend all eternity. But enough has been said about what relates to seeing God.

59

For the blessed shall also find the most ardent joy in the renewal or, as others say, the glorification of bodies which, by God's plan and power, they shall take up again in wondrous wholeness.

60

The dead shall rise, says Isaiah, and those who were in their graves shall rise, and all who are in the earth shall be made glad. But this renewal has been set up in four kinds: brightness, fineness, quickness and invulnerability.

163.61   Our bodies will shine so brightly that nothing at all human can compare to their splendor: when Isaiah wanted to express their gleaming, in fact, and had nothing to equal it, he proposed an analogy with the Sun since the eyes discern nothing brighter. The just, he says, will gleam like the Sun in the Lord's sight. On the Mount called Tabor, Christ our God displayed this brightness that the bodies of the blessed will have to three apostles. Within sight of them, he appeared in a human form far more august and divine, and the Evangelist says that his face shone like the Sun. He said *like the Sun*, as I explained, because he could think of no other likeness to express the great gleaming.

62   Their bodies shall have such fineness that no doors nor any walls can stand in their way and that they cannot pass through in an instant, whenever they want. Christ also made this bodily fineness or refinement known (I will not delay for many examples) when he went in to his disciples through closed doors after his resurrection. Christ, before death was inflicted on him, also showed clearly the quickness that bodies will have when he walked on the Sea of Galilee with dry feet in order to save the endangered disciples from death. His doing this means that the blessed, after getting their bodies back, can not only move across seas and rivers without using a boat but also fly around in the air without the help of wings and without getting tired.

63   That the bodies of the blessed will be unable to suffer injury seems obvious (I consider it too picky for anyone to debate this) since by putting aside the heaviness and filth of the elements, they will be unable to be touched at all. The throng of citizens in that divine and eternal city will also be a special joy for the blessed, which John mentions in the *Apocalypse*, saying: I saw a great crowd

that no one could count. Life's worries plainly take nothing at all away from this happiness. The blessed take delight from seeing not just one another but also the angels, and not only angels but also the ranks into which God, the wisest and fairest of all, has divided them, and these apply just the same to the blessed in keeping with the merits of their lives. For all are not assigned to one and the same rank; some have a higher level than others. Yet there is no envy from lower to higher or from peer to peer, for all will be content with the place allotted them by divine justice.

Yes: the accord among them will be so great that each one will find scarcely less joy in another's honor and glory than in his own, which is the essence of real and absolutely lasting friendship. For what else is friendship but having the same will and the same mind, joined by mutual love, in all things human and divine? If friendship is the sweetest thing in this mortal life, where it is prey to so many risks and yet not broken by them, how much sweeter will be the celestial friendship that is untroubled and can in no way be destroyed. For none of the desire that has brought ruin and disaster to many great friendships can intrude into that divine city to draw the souls of the blessed away from their mutual love and unity. For all the thoughts of the blessed will be about praising God and their shared joy. Nor will any of them, as I said, want to surpass another in the level of their rank. 164.64

The next addition to their joy is the beauty and splendor of this celestial city. For plainly the appearance of the city where they dwell serves much for their happiness. This place they call the *empyrean* heaven because its splendor is fiery. This crystalline heaven of the fixed stars is surrounded by the heaven lying around it that some call the First Movable, others the Firmament. For while there are seven spheres between the Moon to the First Movable that are all driven by the strong force of the Firmament, this empyrean and crystalline heaven that I have described they suppose unmoved because the place of God and the blessed is there, 65

even though God himself exists wholly in heaven and earth and everywhere. For it is written: I fill heaven and earth, as if to say that no place is empty of me, wherefore heaven is preeminently God's place alone. My throne is heaven, says Isaiah, but earth is my footstool.

66   But they claim that this empyrean heaven far outshines the others in beauty and luster, about which it may not be unfitting to mention briefly what John recorded in his *Apocalypse*. For this is the heavenly Jerusalem whose foundations he describes as laid with twelve types of glittering jewels. He says it has twelve gates, each made with a pearl of its own, and the walls in their whole course are of jasper. There is no temple in it because almighty God, with the Lamb whom we understand to be Christ, serves as the temple for those who inhabit this city. Nor will there be any Sun or Moon in this city because God's light and brilliance will light it up, and its lamp will be the Lamb, so that the nations will walk in the light of the Lamb and the kings of the earth will bring him glory.

165.67   Tobias spoke about that very city in this way: I shall be blessed if any of my seed are left to see Jerusalem shining. Its gates will be built of sapphire and emerald, and the whole circuit of its walls of precious stone, and with clean, bright stone all its avenues will be covered, and through its streets they will sing hallelujah.

68   Since this city is so beautiful and splendid, then, it is the right place for God almighty, our Lord Jesus Christ and the whole gathering of the blessed. For because of God's endless and inconceivable greatness that heaven and earth cannot contain, there we shall see him, even though he exists everywhere, as I have said. Although the blessed are located in this city, God will not limit them to this place, just as Thomas Aquinas stated. In fact, they may come and go as they wish: for if they did not have this power to leave the place for a while when they wanted, they could not be called *blessed* since their freedom would seem to be taken away.

I would not dare to deny that a statement by a man so wise and   69
holy is correct. But if those in heaven can see everything mentally
and in the spirit, as surely they can if they see God, why do they
need to move about in heaven and seek the earth or see anything
more delightful? What could be more delightful than heaven and
God? Are they sated and need to refuse? How could they have too
much of a place or community where the blessed assemble —
choirs of angels and archangels, the Holy Spirit, Christ and God
almighty?

Since God permits it, says Thomas, they will also have the   70
power to enter the earthly globe where we live, and they will not
be blocked by the solidity of the heavens (of which Job says: perhaps you and God fashioned the heavens, which are very solid like
brass) from flying in an instant down to earth and then up to
heaven again. For then the earth will be purged, cleansed and
emptied of everything corruptible. After God delivers his sentence,
driving the damned out into eternal torment, this whole earthly
globe will burn up, as we read it was once covered by a deluge of
waters. When things burn up, all destructible qualities of the elements that make up human bodies will be eliminated. But those
that are fit and suited to immortal bodies will remain and survive,
so that a world purified by renewal may, by a renovation of the
flesh, be a match for human nature.

About this renewal John speaks in this way: I have seen a new   71
heaven and a new earth, for the first heaven and the first earth
have gone away, and the sea no longer exists. So perhaps one
should not be amazed if the blessed sometimes descend from
heaven to an earth cleared and cleansed by God, with no winds
blowing, no rains and no storms. For the motions and turnings of
the heavens will cease.

But every thought of the blessed will be to join together and   166.72
praise God, to give thanks for kindnesses received, so many and so
great, and they will even be able to do this in words spoken by the

tongue, as Augustine says. Otherwise their bodies would hardly seem to be real if they had no use of the tongue. And the divine gift of wisdom to these citizens will be so great that the mind can imagine nothing at all that could cause their judgment to fail. For if they were ignorant about something, their happiness would certainly not seem complete: no one who is ignorant can be happy since there is still something to seek. But if they recognize God, what will they not know? Therefore, they recognize one another and recognize the angels, with whom they will be made fellow citizens and equals by their merits in life with the concurrence of divine grace.

73   Nor will they need anyone to judge. All the different languages will be clear and known to them so that there will be no call for the job of translator among them. And the exultation of the blessed will be nothing ordinary since they will realize how very great are the troubles, how numberless the dangers, how various the disasters from which they have been rescued — those for whom this completely wretched life that we so highly desire is a waste. All of them, just like sailors reaching port unharmed after surviving a bad storm at sea, will also rejoice that when the pleasures of the present life and the lures of earthly things have been overcome — though very few mortals can withstand them — they have gained admittance to heaven.

74   They shall rejoice no less because they will be freed, God willing, from the punishments inflicted on the wicked, both soul and body, which no passage of time will bring to an end. Nor indeed will they feel sad that the damned are tormented in Hell, even their relatives, because they will love — with a love stronger than for their own kin — the divine justice that decrees rewards and punishments for everyone according to the merits of their lives. Seeing the revenge, says God's prophet, a just person will rejoice and wash his hands in the blood of sinners.

Finally they will rejoice that never again will they fear falling 75
into the sins for which God would expel them from Heaven, for
our most beneficent God, since he wants them to be completely
happy, will strengthen them in their endeavor, aided by the Holy
Spirit, to let no lust for sin penetrate their hearts, which are completely clean and clear. Augustine has discussed this at length, and,
in the other work that I mentioned just before, I have said enough
about it. Augustine also confirmed that the other angels who did
not agree with Lucifer were like humans when, as it is written, he
fell from Heaven, and dragged a third of the stars — meaning that
many angels — from the skies.

But because we come to know such things by faith more than 167.76
reason, no mortal can describe them nor even any of the angels
who are closer to God and not weighed down by any of the body's
heaviness or contagion. For we are reporting things unseen — like
the blind. So let me bring an end to this discussion.

I think I have shown quite well that man's value and excellence 77
is very great and admirable because of what divine providence
has bestowed on his soul and body both, first in this troubled
and mortal life, then in the celestial one. For his soul has been
equipped with thought, wisdom, immortality and memory and
with a very beautiful and becoming body, and then he was en-
trusted to the care of angels. From God he got the power to rouse
dead people to life, to consecrate the Lord's body and to sit in
judgment, along with Christ Our Lord, on that most fearful day.
Christ, Our Lord and God, endured dying on the cross for his
sake. And at last, after turning aside earthly enticements and the
torments of Hell, he will experience those most coveted joys of the
divine city — seeing divinity with a renewed body, I mean, in the
most joyous company of the blessed and in that celestial sphere of
unbelievable beauty and splendor. Who will deny that comparing
him to angels is correct?

78 But it is a short argument and a true precept that leads to this place of joys and eternal happiness. For God teaches us and says: if you want to enter into life, keep the commandments — although this cannot be done by a human without God's help. For he says: without me you can do nothing. And this is confirmed plainly by this saying of the prophet: he crowns you with mercy and compassion. For our merits are hardly of such weight that in justice they could give us eternal life, which is why Augustine's famous saying often gets praise: I believe no one can achieve salvation unless God helps. Beyond doubt, however, the sum of all the commandments amounts to loving God and one's neighbor, for love is the fullness of the law, as the Apostle says, and Christ confirms this in the Gospel. On those commandments depend all the laws and the prophets: one seeks heaven only on this path.

79 At the end of this work, however, which I have brought to completion with God's help, I am ready to shout this in a clear voice: Humans with their stupid ideas! Their blind hearts!

80 Forgetting their own excellence and worth, they run eagerly after these frail and fleeting things. Some have embraced pleasure and given themselves to the belly, sleep and idleness, thinking that all human happiness lies there. Others are preoccupied with amassing riches, which they will keep for a very short time, since an early death sometimes snatches them away to leave their wealth in the middle of life, as they seek nothing but money and, to get it, spare no fraud or plunder or robbery. Others are more desirous of the honors where they think all human value lies, and to procure them they respect no limit nor moderation.

168.81 Glory has led others to put control and power first in all human affairs; they think they will become like God by having the right of life and death over people. Others have no fear of seizing control by carnage, betrayal and every kind of injustice, crushing the liberty of another land — and sometimes their own — by the utmost wickedness. Not ashamed to take the name *tyrant*, they are

gripped by this error, thinking they may break human and divine laws in order to rule.

How much better it would be to embrace divine things and, 82 while we are still in this life, think about them and become used to them, so that before we reach that other life, we would recognize them all as if we had seen them before and understood them. Better not to make so much of these mortal things whose main results for the human race have been inequality and envy. In fact, since our situation of being born and dying makes us private persons equal to kings, we are unequal only in the midst of life, which is very short and uncertain. Likewise, it seems we are already desirous of the eternal rank that we shall attain in that city.

Not all who go into battle are crowned by the commander, only 83 those who fight bravely and hard against the enemy, who take risks, who undertake harsh and difficult tasks, who are the first to climb the walls and rush into the enemy's camp. So also not all who keep the Christian faith are held worthy of this prize of rank that is so exceptional and so divine, but only those who take arms against these human traps and powers to show themselves purified of them and unconquered. After the present life has run its course, let us hope we may succeed.

Note on Sources, Texts, and Translations

Manetti names only six authorities more than a few times: Aristotle, Augustine, Cicero, Innocent III, Lactantius, and Plato. Among named sources, Cicero and Lactantius are the most prominent; Aristotle and Augustine are both more visible than Plato. Manetti's Cicero wrote *On the Nature of the Gods*, the *Tusculan Disputations*, and other philosophical works; he is not the orator, the rhetorician, or the author of lively letters. *On God's Workmanship* by Lactantius dominates the first book, but his *Elements of Divinity* replaces it in the other three. Innocent III (standing in for Cardinal Lotario) appears seven times, though not until the fourth book shreds his tract on human misery. Although the "Master of the *Sentences*" enters only once, Peter Lombard had shaped much of what Facio and Antonio da Barga said about *dignitas*, and their statements were Manetti's starting points — with only Facio acknowledged.

Appendices I and II of this volume provide provisional translations, without Latin texts or annotation, of these short works by Antonio and Facio. The Latin texts on which these translations are based are indicated in the Abbreviations and the Bibliography. Manetti's book cannot be understood without them: he completed a project that Antonio initiated and passed on to Facio. Paul Kristeller first edited Antonio's Latin text from the single surviving manuscript. To my knowledge, it has never been translated. Nor has Facio's treatise, which lacks a modern edition and has been printed only once.[1] Cardinal Lotario's text, by contrast, was enormously popular and was printed in Latin and in various European vernaculars dozens of times, beginning in the fifteenth century.

Facio, though not Manetti, cites Thomas Aquinas on the glorified body, and Manetti knew related material independently, suggesting that Thomas may have helped him elsewhere on philosophical theology. He is not professedly Thomist, however, though Thomas's works are as good a guide as any other scholastic's to his broad (though not deep or partisan) awareness of contemporary doctrine. Since biblical theology was crucial

for him, Thomas's *Commentary on the Sentences* may have been more valuable than either *Summa*. Yet he mentions only one Christian theologian later than Peter Lombard—Albert the Great, and him only twice, like Avicenna. The theological expertise that Manetti bothers to certify with names is more patristic than medieval: Ambrose, Chrysostom, pseudo-Dionysius, Jerome, all overshadowed by Lactantius and Augustine. He takes a good deal of information from a medieval physician, Mondino de Luzzi, who remains offstage.

Most names from ancient Greece and Rome are merely decorative, usually repeated from Cicero. Some references—not many—to the elder Pliny, Seneca, and Vergil may be direct. A few words by Lucretius and some citations of Varro certainly come from Lactantius. Besides Aristotle and Plato, the only Greek writer who shows up in person is Josephus, and Aristotle stands taller than Plato.

Manetti's presentation is orderly, repetitive, rigid, and dull: the pleonasms are annoying; outlining and signposting are incessant, though not always successful. Sentences are frequently longer and more convoluted (I hope) than their versions in this translation. The vocabulary, by and large, is the normal classicizing Latin of the period. I have not tried to maintain consistency of terminology, for two reasons: Manetti's writing is not exact or technical, and his pleonastic Latin would show up as too grand and wordy in English. While keeping close track of the *dignitas, excellentia,* and *praestantia* cluster, I have found no single way to render *dignitas*: compare "rank" in 3.56–57, for example, with "worth" in 1.53.

When Manetti uses a source, he does not always say so, nor does a name attached to his words guarantee an exact or even a close quotation of the authority named: for those reasons, I have avoided quotation marks, both single and double, using italics to indicate the use/mention, distinction, or—less often—emphasis. Sources cited in my notes, which err on the side of inclusion, sometimes suggest context, background, or an explanation rather than indicating that Manetti used them.[2]

I began with the critical Latin text (marking it as *L*) published by Elizabeth R. Leonard in 1975, and I have not checked the manuscripts that she collated.[3] Her sigla, also mine, are:

A   London, Library of Major J. R. Abbey, MS 3212 (sold at
       Sotheby's in 1974)

B   Vatican City, Biblioteca Apostolica Vaticana, Pal. lat. 1604

C   Florence, Biblioteca Mediceo-Laurenziana, San Marco 456

D   Vatican City, Biblioteca Apostolica Vaticana, Urb. lat. 5

E   London, British Museum, Harl. 2593

F   London, British Museum, Harl. 2523

b   *editio princeps*, ed. Johann Alexander Brassicanus (Basel:
       Cratander, 1532)

According to Leonard all seven witnesses are independently related to
the lost archetype, so that in principle all could contain correct readings.

Notes to my Latin text indicate departures from *L*. Most adjustments
favor the first printed edition, *b*, whose readings I have trusted more than
L does. As a consequence, *L's* choices respond more conservatively than
mine to the manuscripts, though the differences have had few meaningful
results for translating. The first full vernacular translation known to me
is Hartmut Leppin's German — without a Latin text — of 1990. Giuseppe
Marcellino has just finished a splendid Italian version and has kindly allowed me to see it before publication. I have checked my version against
Marcellino's, and I have also compared partial English renderings by
Bernard Murchland and others.[4]

NOTES

1. See Bibliography for both editions.

2. For examples, see *MDE* 4.13, 40, 64.

3. See Bibliography.

4. See Bibliography for Murchland and Leppin.

Notes to the Texts

❧❦❧

BOOK I

1. AD ALFONSUM CLARISSIMUM ET GLORIOSISSIMUM ARAGO-
NUM REGEM IANNOTII MANETTI PRAEFATIO INCIPIT FELICI-
TER *L*

2. vel maxime *L*: maxime *b*

3. *sic b*: suae *L*

4. AD EUNDEM EIUSDEM DE DIGNITATE ET EXCELLENTIA
HOMINIS LIBER PRIMUS INCIPIT FELICITER *L*

5. *sic b*: edon *L*

6. *sic b*: homines *L*

7. *sic b*: indagari *L*

8. ea qua eductus sit spiritus eademque *L*, *Nat. D.*

9. id muturi *b*, *Nat. D.*: immutari *L*

10. cocta *BCD*, *Nat. D.*: concocta *A(L)*: coacta *EF*: tracta *b*

11. is quo alimur *b*, *Nat. D.*: ipse quo aluntur *L*

12. *sic b*, *Nat. D.*: partes *L*

13. *sic b*, *Nat. D.*: coactusque *L*

14. tum *om. L*

15. coagitatione *L*, *ex cogitatione corr. B¹*: cogitatione *F*: contagione
Nat. D.

16. *sic b*, *Nat. D.*: ad iecorem *L*

17. *sic b*, *Nat. D.*: intelliguntur *L*

18. *sic b*: nimios *L*

19. *sic b*, *Nat. D.*: fluentia *L*

20. *sic b, Nat. D.*: Quod *L*

21. *sic C, Nat. D.*: ne delerent *L*

22. *sic EFb, Nat. D.*: et ex excelsis *L*

23. *sic b, Nat. D.*: directus *L*

24. *sic b, Nat. D.*: abiectae *L*

25. leve *Nat. D.*

26. *emended*: arte et tangendi *L*: arte et tangendi *om. F, but inserted by F²*: et ⟨quadam ex⟩ parte tangendi *emended by Plasberg in Nat. D.*

27. *sic b, Nat. D.*: dederit *L*

28. *om. L*

29. *corrected following Nat. D.*: verborum *L*

30. *sic b, Opif.*: Deus *om. L*

31. quod cum *b, Opif.*: et tamen *L*

32. *sic b, Opif.*: *om. L*

33. noluit *emended following Opif.*: uoluit *L*

34. *sic b*: et spargi *om. L, Opif.*

35. angusti oris vasa *emended following Opif.*: angustiora *L*; angustiora vasa *b*

36. *sic b*: se ipsa *L*

37. *sic b, Opif.*: usus *L*

38. inest *L*

39. *sic b, Opif.*: ordine stantibus saeptum *L*: ordinem *EF*

40. *sic b, Opif.*: oriens *L*

41. *sic b, Opif.*: levis *L*

42. duos *L*

43. ad *L*

44. partes *L*

45. in ipso *b*: ipso *L*

46. *sic b*: actus *L*

47. *corrected following Opif.*: labiorum L

48. *sic b, Opif.*: labia L

49. *sic b, Opif.*: levi L

50. *sic b, Opif.*: quae L

51. *sic b, Opif.*: si *om.* L

52. igitur pollicis nomen *b*: igiture etiam nomen pollicis L

53. *sic b, Opif.*: fuisset e tribus L

54. *sic b, Opif.*: altero L

55. *sic b, Opif.*: sic L

56. *corrected from Opif.*: uteri L

57. *sic b, Opif.*: venientis L

58. *corrected from Opif.*: iter patet L; colles L] *Opif.*

59. *corrected from Opif.*: colles L

60. *sic b, Opif.*: nondum L

61. *sic b, Opif.*: pulsibus suis *om.* L

62. *corrected from Opif.*: ne qui *b*(L): ne cui *AD*: necui *BCEF*

63. *sic b*: semina L: seminium *Opif.*

64. *sic b, Opif.*: *om.* L

65. *sic b, Opif.*: genitalium L

66. *sic b, Opif.*: efficeret L

67. *sic b*: *Opif.*: et quidem L

68. *corrected following Opif.*: et manu L: et in manu *b*

69. *sic b*: recta L

70. instructu *b*

71. *sic b*: deformitatibus L

72. *L adds* humano *after* corpore: *omitted by EFb*

73. *sic b*: spondiles L

74. *sic b*: esse videatur L

· NOTES TO THE TEXTS ·

75. *corrected*: labde *L*

76. *corrected*: spatulis *L*

77. *sic b*: *om. L*

78. *sic b*: complecteretur *L*

79. *corrected*: passilari *L*

80. *corrected*: nuncupatur *L*

81. ad necessitatem *b*: necessitate *L*

82. extrinsicarum scilicet *b*: ad extrinsecarum *L*

83. *sic b*: traditur *L*

84. *corrected*: videtur *L*

85. *sic b*: ab extrinseco *L*

86. ut *b*: quin *L*

87. *sic b*: vulgatioribus *L*

88. *added (a conjecture)*: *om. L*

89. *corrected*: tribus *L*

90. *sic EFb*: esse *L*

91. *corrected from the Vulgate of Genesis 7:11*: quingentorum *L*

92. *sic b*: satis superque satis *L*

93. *corrected from Augustine, Civ. 21.8*: idissimiles *L*

94. *sic b*: appareret *L*

95. *corrected from Augustine, Civ. 1.13*: tertia *L*

96. *sic b*: certis *L*

BOOK II

1. *sic b*: umquam *om. L*

2. *sic b*: solida *L*

3. *sic b*: percepimus *L*

4. *sic b*: unicum *L*

5. *sic EFb*: memoretur *L*

304

6. *sic* EF: facit L

7. cepi L

8. ενδελεχιαν b

9. in totum b: inde in totum L

10. *sic* b: enim in *om.* L

11. *sic* b: est L

12. *sic* b: quod L

13. *The quotation varies at several points from modern texts of Cicero; cf. the same text at MDE 4.31.*

14. *a conjecture*: mediantibus L

15. *sic* b: videbantur L

16. *sic litteris graecis* b: usiam L: ousiam *corr.* F³

17. *sic* b: et aperte et L

18. *sic* b: *om.* L

19. *sic* b: definitionis suae L: suae *om.* Eb

20. *sic* b: modum L

21. *sic* b: faciamus inquit *transp.* L

22. *sic* b: dicimus

23. *sic* b: nomine L

24. *sic* b: eius ipsius L

25. *sic* b: sanctis L

26. theoidem L

27. *sic* EFb: eiusdem L

28. *corrected from Augustine, Gen. litt. 7.43*: rationalis L

29. *sic* b: extinguerentur L

30. *corrected (cf. MDE 4.14.39)*: Teombrotum L

31. *corrected (cf. MDE 2.12)*: protoplausto L

32. *sic* b: audimus L

33. *sic* b: *om.* L

34. *sic* b: *om.* L

35. quoniam *EFb*: quorum L

36. *sic EFb*: accedemus L

37. *sic* b: comparari L

38. *corrected from Valerius Maximus 8.11 ext. 4*: Indorum L

39. *corrected following Valerius Maximus*: conspectibus L

40. *sic* b: pharmachiis L

41. *sic* b *and Lactantius, Div. inst. 2.5.18*: efficeret L

42. *sic* b: suos L

43. *corrected following Cicero, Tusc. 1.59*: Theodorus . . . Carneades L

44. *sic* b: *om.* L

45. *sic* b: existimamus L

BOOK III

1. *sic* b: in hoc L

2. *sic* b: prosequemur L

3. *sic* b: hominis L

4. *sic* b: pariter ac L

5. *sic* b: habuerit L

6. *sic* b: construamus L

7. *sic* b: reperirive et L

8. *sic* b *(cf. Cicero, Tusc. 1.68)*: *om.* L

9. *sic* b: vocant Graeci *transp.* L

10. *sic Cb*: cum L

11. *sic Fb*: animatis quoque L

12. *sic EFb*: nobis maxime L

13. *sic* b: quae sibi ipsi ea L: quae sibi ea EF

14. *sic* b: *om.* L

15. *sic b*: domus *L*

16. *sic BCDEFb*: quaeque atque *L*

17. *sic b*: denique sunt *transp. L*

18. *sic b*: spectare et pertinere *L*

19. *sic b*: eius *L*

20. *sic EFb*: vera sapientia *L*

21. *sic b*: nostri agri, nostri campi *L*

22. *sic Eb*: quarum quidem *L*

23. *sic graecis litteris b*: proneam *L*

24. *sic b*: partim vero *L*

25. *sic EFb*: multo post *L*

26. et aperte *b*: aperteque *L*

27. ipsi Iovi *b*: ab ipso Iove *L*

28. *corrected*: septimo *L*: *canc.* A^1

29. *sic b*: plurimosque *L*

30. *corrected*: suas *L*

31. *sic b*: distinguerent *L*

32. *sic b*: testaretur *L*

33. *sic b*: peregrinaretur *L*

34. *sic b*: iusto illo *L*

35. *corrected*: Corruncanum *L*

36. *sic b*: adiungeret *L*

37. *a conjecture*: potentatibus *L*

38. *sic EFb*: *om. L*

39. *sic b (cf. Lactantius, Div. inst. 2.5.3)*: suscipiat *L*

40. *sic b*: pariter et *L*

41. *corrected*: potentatibus *L*

42. *as at MDE 2.12*: protoplaustus *L*

BOOK IV

1. *sic b*: tabe *L*

2. *sic EFb*: constructum *L*

3. *sic b*: tormines *L*

4. *sic b*: celos *L*

5. *sic b*: procedemus *L*

6. *corrected*: Terrineneum *L*: Thermaneum *b*

7. *corrected*: Cleope et Binoto *L*: Cleobe et Bitone *b*

8. *corrected*: Argiae *L*

9. *sic b*: Triphoneus *L*

10. *sic b*: *om. L*

11. *sic b*: Salomon *L*

12. *sic b*: videatur *L*

13. *corrected (cf. Ecclesiastes 4:3 and above in this paragraph)*: sunt *L*

14. *sic b*: est ait dies *L*

15. *sic EFb*: ponat *L*

16. *sic b*: iactatis *L*

17. *sic b*: sputa *L*

18. *corrected as in MDE 2.12*: protoplaustus *L*

19. *sic b*: earum molestiarum *L*

20. *sic b*: animadverterimus *L*

21. *sic b*: delectet *L*

22. *sic b*: quos *L*

23. *sic b*: *om. L*

24. *sic b*: somnis *L*

25. *sic b*: prodierant *L*

26. *sic BCEFb*: ad eloquendum *L*

27. *sic b*: communia et pervulgata corpora *L*

28. *sic b*: quo ad L

29. *sic b*: quod L

30. physicorum omnium L] *b*

31. *corrected following MDE 2.9*: Animarum L

32. *sic b (cf. MDE 2.9, Cicero ad loc.)*: om. L

33. *corrected (cf. MDE 2.7)*: enthelechiam L: endelecheia *b*, Cicero

34. *sic b*: refricamus L

35. *sic as at MDE 4.14, 39 etc.*: Teombroti L

36. *sic b, Vulgate*: domo L

37. *corrected following the Vulgate*: victa L: vita *b*

38. *sic b*: mandaverint L

39. *sic b*: nostra antea diluisse L] *b*

40. *sic b*: et ab apostolica L

41. *corrected*: Aia L: Eva *b*. *Manetti, knowing how to spell the Hebrew name, would probably have preferred the Roman character* v *to mimic the doubled* waw *in* H̲awwah, *whereas a Roman* i *would reflect* iod, *not* waw: *see MDE 4.46 and note.*

42. *sic b*: videtur *before* quod L

43. *sic b*: hisca quoniam de hisc L

44. *sic b*: derivatum L

45. *sic b*: duo L

46. *sic b*: hisca Hebraica L

47. *sic b*: abhorruisse L

48. *sic b*: inde incipientes L] *b*

49. *sic b*: is vere dicitur *transp.* L

50. *sic b*: praesentaria L

51. *corrected*: Quid autem A(L): qui autem BCDF*b*

52. et agnitionis Filii Dei *b (cf. Vulgate)*: om. L

53. *sic b*: ea propria L

54. *sic b*: monte L

55. *A (cf. Aquinas, Cat. in Matt. 14.5)*: periclitabundis L

56. *sic b*: duodecima L

57. *a conjecture*: rigoris L

58. *In b, paragraph 74 begins a new section of text labelled* Peroratio.

Notes to the Translations

ᏏᏒᏃᏏ

ABBREVIATIONS

ADE   Antonio da Barga, *On Mankind's Worth and the Excellence of Human Life*, cited from the text of P. O. Kristeller (see Bibliography). Translated in Appendix I.

DBI   *Dizionario biografico degli Italiani* (Rome, 1960–). Cited from the online edition at http://www.treccani.it/biografico/.

FEP   Bartolomeo Facio, *On Human Excellence and Distinction*. Cited according to F. Sandeo's text of 1611, 149–68. Translated in Appendix II.

Intro.   The Introduction to this book.

LDM   Lotario dei Segni, *De miseria condicionis humanae*. Cited from the edition of R. Lewis.

MDE   Giannozzo Manetti, *On Human Worth and Excellence*

MPL   *Patrologiae cursus completus, series latina*, ed. J.-P. Migne, 221 vols. (Paris, 1844–91)

Nat. D.   Cicero, *De natura deorum*

OLD   *Oxford Latin Dictionary*, ed. P. G. W. Glare (Oxford, 1982)

Opif.   Lactantius, *De opificio hominis*

SCG   Thomas Aquinas, *Summa contra Gentiles*

ST   Thomas Aquinas, *Summa theologiae*

SVF   *Stoicorum veterum fragmenta*, ed. H. F. A. von Arnim (Leipzig, 1903–24)

Abbreviations of works of classical authors follow those of *The Oxford Classical Dictionary*, 4th ed., ed. S. Hornblower, A. Spawforth, and E. Eidinow (Oxford, 2012).

BOOK I

1. *Intro.* §4 on Manetti's use of *dignitas*.

2. *MDE* pr. 6 with note; 4.73–74.

3. *Intro.* §1 on Facio and Nicholas V.

4. *Intro.* §1 for Frederick III.

5. The preface to Manetti's *Lives of Socrates and Seneca*, written in 1440, is an encomium of Alfonso. In addition to a *Vita Alphonsi Regis*, Vespasiano da Bisticci lists several orations addressed to or involving the king: Vespasiano da Bisticci, *Vite di uomini illustri del secolo XV*, ed. P. D'Ancona and E. Aeschlimann (Milan: Hoepli, 1951), 290; Manetti, *Biographical Writings*, ed. S. Baldassarri and R. Bagemihl (Cambridge, MA: Harvard University Press, 2003), ix, 165–75.

6. Genesis 2:7; Josephus, *Jewish Antiquities* 1.1.2.34; Ovid, *Met.* 1.84–86; Jerome, *Nom. hebr.* in *MPL* 23:817; Lactantius, *Div. inst.* 2.1.15–16, 10.3; Isidore of Seville, *Etym.* 11.4–5; ADE 27; FEP 150.7, 156.33: For *anthrôpos*, Lactantius (who also supplies the lines from Ovid) is thinking of an etymology like *anô* (upward) plus *opsis* (seeing). The three consonants of Adam's name appear in Hebrew words for "red" (*adom*) and "soil" (*adamah*) and also in Edom, a name of Esau, who was given a red stew by Jacob in trade for his birthright. Josephus writes in Greek, not Hebrew, that Adam's name came "from red earth" (*apo tês purras gês*).

7. Cicero, *Nat. D.* 2.134–46, 149; *Intro.* §2: Manetti's extract from Cicero extends through MDE 1.12.

8. Birdlime (*viscum*) made from mistletoe was spread on branches as a glue to trap birds: see Vergil, *G.* 1.139; Pliny the Elder, *HN* 16.248.

9. MDE 1.3 with the note; Manetti skips a passage of argumentation at Cicero, *Nat. D.* 2.147–48.

10. MDE 1.3 with the note; the long excerpt from Cicero ends here.

11. Lactantius, *Opif.* 1.12–14; FEP 150.7, 156.33; ADE 30; *Intro.* §2: Antonio, unlike Facio, calls attention to praise of the body by Lactantius, who criticizes the body's treatment by Cicero, *On the Nature of the Gods*, *On the Republic*, and *On the Laws*. Manetti's selection, continuing through MDE 1.32, comes from *Opif.* 8.1–13.8, with omissions as indicated in the notes. The usual title is *De opificio Dei* — *On God's Workmanship*; the title of only one manuscript, *De opificio corporis humani*, shows what Manetti was interested in. The rare *opificium* names the product of an *opifex*, *artifex*, or

dêmiourgos. See Lactantius, *L'Ouvrage du Dieu créateur*, ed. and trans. M. Perrin (Paris: Éditions du Cerf, 1974), 17–19, 37–39, 106; Perrin, *L'Homme antique et chrétien: L'Anthropologie de Lactance* — 250–325 (Paris: Beauchesne 1981), 29–30, 49–52.

12. *MDE* 1.10.

13. *MDE* 1.8, 14, 20, 49; 2.39–40: Lactantius sees both the body's beauty (*decus, pulchritudo*) and its functionality (*utilitas*) as providential.

14. Lactantius, *Opif.*, ed. Perrin, 40–44: After Cicero, the famously erudite Marcus Terentius Varro is the most cited authority in *De opificio*, especially for etymologies; here Lactantius connects *frons* (forehead, brow), with *foramen* (opening) and *foratus* (boring). Etymology, along with the structure of words (morphology) and sentences (syntax), was one of the divisions of Varro's twenty-five books *On the Latin Language*, of which only six survive. For *frons*, later experts on Latin etymology find no link to *foramen* or other relatives of the verb *foro* (to pierce). But Varro was not always wrong.

15. Manetti omits a few lines on the etymology of *aures*, connected with *haurio, audio*, and αὐδή, illustrated by Vergil, *Aen.* 4.359. The negative sense of *demereor* is postclassical.

16. After the comparison of vision with reflecting by a mirror, Manetti omits an extended attack by Lactantius on Epicurean and Stoic theories of vision that rejects Lucretius explicitly while tacitly following Cicero's dematerialized account in the *Tusculans*: for details, see Perrin's commentary on Lactantius, *Opif.* 8.10–12. Since the deleted material explains the placement of membranes in front of the eyeballs, the transition to the next topic, the eyeballs themselves, is forced. After this paragraph, Lactantius announces a digression — also excised by Manetti — to state objections to Arcesilaus and the Academic skeptics on the sense of vision as deceptive.

17. *MDE* 1.16 with the note on Varro: literally, "he covered (*occuluit*) them with shielding lids, whence they were called 'eyes' (*oculos*). . . . The lashes (*palpebrae*) themselves, to whose rapidity or blinking (*palpitatio*). . . ." The link between *palpebrae* and *palpitatio* is real.

18. Vergil, *Ecl.* 8.75: Lactantius, expert in the Latin classics, would have known Vergil's dictum that "God rejoices in the odd number," but he

derives the body's beauty, even in unseen places like the brain, from its bilateral symmetry.

19. Lucretius, 6.1149; Augustine, *De civ. D.* 16.43; Lactantius, *Opif.*, ed. Perrin, 330; *MDE* 1.16 with the note on Varro: Literally, "infants (*infantes*) do not start speaking (*fari*) before they have teeth." A nonspeaking (*non fans*) person is *in-fans*, though only some nonspeakers are infants. Lactantius is thinking of Varro's etymology, repeated by Augustine and others. At this point, Manetti skips a passage on the tongue, with another etymology by Varro, picking up again where Lactantius goes back to discussing the teeth.

20. *MDE* 1.16 with the note on etymology.

21. Ibid.

22. Lactantius, *Opif.*, ed. Perrin, 108; *MDE* 1.16 with the note on etymology: *Aphrona*, which appears nowhere in Perrin's text or apparatus, could be a gloss by Manetti or the scribe who made his copy of Lactantius, displaying some Greek in yet another etymology. The parts of the adjective *aphrôn* are *a-* (alpha-privative, negating what follows) and *-phrôn*, from *phrên* ("breast" or "heart"), with the psychological faculties, like mind, reason, and sense, thought to reside there.

23. *MDE* 1.29 and note.

24. Vergil, *E* 2.36–37; Pliny the Elder, *HN* 30.31 has *uva* (grape) for the uvula; *uvula* in Latin is postclassical.

25. *MDE* 1.16 with the note on etymology: Lactantius connects *nares* (nostrils) with *nare* (swim, sail), also *tolles* (tonsils) with *tollere* in the sense of "raise up." Manetti omits a passage on the anatomy of defects in speech and hearing.

26. *MDE* 1.5, 15, 26 with notes; *Intro.* §2.

27. *MDE* 1.16 with the note on etymology: Lactantius connects *planta* (sole) with *planities* (flat surface).

28. Lactantius, *Opif.* 13.1, 15.5, 16.11.

29. *MDE* 1.10, 14–15, 25: Starting with this discussion of human superiority to other animals—a theme already introduced from Cicero and Lactantius—Manetti (as indicated by Leonard's edition) takes his lead

mainly from Mondino de Luzzi's survey of anatomy, a work of the early fourteenth century, cited here in the edition of 1550 by Matteo Corti, a physician from Pavia. In crude Latin, Mondino locates man's physical distinctiveness in the "shape or location of parts, in behavior or skills and in particular parts," which are also Manetti's topics through 1.38 — including Aristotle's remark about "tools of tools": see *Doctoris Matthaei Curtii papiensis medicorum sua tempestate facile principis in Mundini anatomen explicatio* (Pavia: Moschino and Negri, 1550), 17–18, 26–27.

30. *MDE* 1.35, n. 29: Manetti follows Mondino's account of human stature as an effect of the four Aristotelian causes: material (light matter), efficient (intense heat), formal (intelligence), and final (understanding).

31. Mondino, as in *MDE* 1.35, n. 29.

32. Ibid.

33. Aristotle, *Part. an.* 687a19–21; Mondino, as in *MDE* 1.35, n. 29.

34. Mondino, as in *MDE* 1.35, n. 29; *Intro.* §00: like Aristotle, Albert the Great wrote extensively about animals; technical terms in the next two paragraphs suggest that Manetti consulted his *De animalibus* for general human anatomy.

35. *In Mundini anatomen*, 363, 373; Albert the Great, *De animal.* 1.2.1.18.

36. *In Mundini anatomen*, 373–89.

37. *In Mundini anatomen*, 29–303; *MDE* 1.29–30; *Intro.* §2.

38. *In Mundini anatomen*, 311–12.

39. Ibid.

40. *In Mundini anatomen*, 312.

41. *In Mundini anatomen*, 311–12.

42. *In Mundini anatomen*, 313; *MDE* 1.48: *Cranium* is postclassical for the whole skull or just the top part that covers the brain (*cerebrum*); the flesh (*caro*) described here lies below the top layer of skin (*cutis*) and above the bone; both the *dura mater* and the *pia mater* in modern anatomy are membranes beneath the bone, but here the outer "garment" (*panniculus*) is above the bone, and the *pia mater* just below is an inner garment under the bone.

43. *In Mundini anatomen*, 316–18.

44. *In Mundini anatomen*, 322–23; *MDE* 1.47.

45. *In Mundini anatomen*, 325–31. If the brain has only three compartments, but the internal senses are five and each compartment contains something, two can accommodate two senses each, which is why Manetti allots five "sites" (*loculi*) to five senses in a three-celled brain. For a clearer account than Mondino's, see Albert the Great, reporting on Avicenna in his *Summa de creaturis* 2.42.2.3: "Avicenna, distinguishing the soul's powers by organ, puts the common sense in the front hollow of the first cell, imagination in the back; but he puts the fantasy (*phantasia*) in the front part of the middle cell, and the estimative faculty in the back of the middle; memory and recall, however, he puts in the rear cell." Elsewhere Albert explains that in humans the "cogitative faculty" replaces the *fantasia*.

46. *In Mundini anatomen*, 342–45.

47. Aristotle, *Ph.* 252b24–28; Cicero, *Nat. D.* 1.47; Ambrose, *Hex.* 6.9.55; *In Mundini anatomen*, 26.

48. Genesis 6:15; Ambrose, *Noe*, 6–11; Augustine, *De civ. D.* 15.26.1.

49. Genesis 7:11; Augustine, *De civ. D.* 15.24: Augustine follows the biblical account, which says that "the windows of heaven were opened" when Noah had lived almost six hundred years.

50. Lactantius, *Div. inst.* 2.10.14; Augustine, *De civ. D.* 21.8.

51. Manetti announces the topic of his next book.

52. Augustine, *De civ. D.* 1.13, commenting on Genesis 49:29–33, 50:25; Tobias 2:9, 12:12–15; Matthew 26:6–14; John 19:38–42; *MDE* 4.43, 58–70; *Intro.* §2.

BOOK II

1. Cicero, *Tusc.* 1.18; Lactantius, *Opif.* 17.2; cf. *Div. inst.* 3.1.1, 13.2; *MDE* 1.13 and note on the title of *De opificio*; *Intro.* §3.

2. Lucretius 3.31–40; Cicero, *Tusc.* 1.24, 60; Pliny the Elder, *HN* 2.14; Lactantius, *Opif.* 18; Nonius Marcellus (ed. Lindsay 426); *FEP* 153.21; *Intro.* §3: Nonius Marcellus, the lexicographer, makes the usual distinction

sharply, writing that "the mind (*animus*) is what we know with, the soul (*anima*) what we live with." But Lucretius sets out to explain both "the nature of mind (*animus*) and of soul (*anima*)"—a job that Pliny thinks impossible: "whatever God is, if there is any such, . . . is all sense, all sight, all hearing, all soul (*anima*), all mind (*animus*) and all his own."

3. Augustine, *De civ. D.* 8.1–2; Albertus Magnus, *De anim.* 130–90 (ed. Borgnet); Augustine covers this list of pre-Socratics while mentioning *animus* only in connection with Anaxagoras; the doxography comes after praise for the Platonists who affirmed God's creation of the human soul (*anima*). The extensive account of authorities given by Albert in the second part of his treatise *On the Soul* is specifically about that subject.

4. Aristotle, *De an.* 403b20–5b31; Cicero, *Tusc.* 1.19–22; *Acad.* 2.118; *Nat. D.* 1.66–68; *Fin.* 2.15; *Intro.* §3: Aristotle presents versions of the soul from Alcmaeon, Anaxagoras, Critias, Democritus, Empedocles, Heraclitus, Hippon of Samos (not Hippias of Elis), Leucippus, Plato, the Pythagoreans, and Thales; Cicero does the same in the *Tusculans*, and the *Academics* also provides a doxography, but about the world, not the soul. Heraclitus is *skoteinos* (obscure) in the treatise *On Ends*.

5. Cicero, *Tusc.* 1.38, 5.10–11; *Nat. D.* 1.27; *Fin.* 2.15; ADE 29; FEP 152.15: Cicero finds Plato's thought obscure, but not his style. And he notes that when Alcmaeon of Croton (a Pythagorean philosopher of the fifth century BCE) attributed divinity to the soul (*animus*), it was not to grant immortality to mortals. But tradition linked Alcmaeon and Pherecydes of Syros, who taught in the previous century, with that doctrine. Plato's main work on that topic is the *Phaedo*, available in a medieval Latin version that was little read; Bruni made a new Latin translation in 1405; see also Aulus Gellius 2.18.1–3.

6. Cicero, *Tusc.* 1.18, 24, 38–39, where different speakers make the statements cited by Manetti.

7. Albertus, *De anim.* 1.2.3 (ed. Borgnet, 142), discusses the soul as material or immaterial, including number as a "self-moving" principle; for Pythagoras and Xenocrates, see MDE 2.5.

8. Aristotle, *De an.* 412a28–30, 12b10–12, 15b9–10; Cicero, *Tusc.* 1.22; Averroes, *Long Commentary on De anima*, 289; *Avicennae perhypatetici phi-*

losophi . . . opera: De anima (repr.: Frankfurt am Main: Minerva, 1961), 1–2; *FEP* 151.13; *MDE* 4.32: Aristotle defines the soul as the "first act (*entelecheia*) of a natural body having life potentially," while also giving other definitions.

9. Lactantius, *Opif.* 17.5; cf. Seneca, *Ep.* 58.11–14, 90.29.

10. Lactantius, *Div. inst.* 2.24, citing Cicero, *Nat. D.* 1.91; *MDE* 2.6, 10; *Intro.* §3: Only Aristotle among the ancients needs no refuting, says Manetti, who finds that Cicero follows Aristotle and that Plato is obscure.

11. Cicero, *Tusc.* 1.66, quoting from his *Consolation*, now lost; *MDE* 2.2, where Manetti refers to his promise.

12. Aristotle, *De an.* 405b8–11, 6b24–26, 9b19–10a13, 16a18–19; Cicero, *Tusc.* 1.41; *ADE* 29; *FEP* 151.13, 152.17: Cicero calls Aristotle the teacher of Aristoxenus, not of himself, as Manetti seems to have thought. Asking how the soul moves the body, Aristotle excludes moving it in space, as when one atom collides with another: "the soul seems not to move the living thing in this way, but by choosing and thinking." Noting that none of the ancients thought the soul to be made just of earth, Aristotle excludes all the elements. But he refutes his predecessors in the first book of *De anima*, not the second.

13. Aristotle, *De an.* 412a3–b9, 15b9–28, 30a10–25; Augustine, *De civ. D.* 12.2; *FEP* 154.24; *Intro.* §3: Aristotle's account of the soul is notoriously vague about immortality, but see the note on *MDE* 2.8.

14. *ADE* 19; *FEP* 155.28.

15. Exodus 33:11; LXX Wisdom 7:1, 10:1; Josephus, *Jewish Antiquities* 2.10; Philo, *Leg.* 2.67; ; Ambrose, *Hex.* 1.6; Adam is the "first-formed" in the Vulgate text of Wisdom; on Moses in Ethiopia and his Ethiopian wife, the account in Josephus, if not its allegorization by Philo, might have been known to Manetti.

16. Genesis 1:1, 26; Romans 8:13; 1 Thessalonians 5:23; Ambrose, *Hex.* 6.40–50; Augustine, *Gen. litt.* 7.22; *Trin.* 10.10–12.15; Ps.-Anselm, *Lib. medit. et orat.* in *MPL* 158:709–22A; *ADE* 23; *FEP* 151.12, 153.18; *MDE* 2.19; *Intro.* §3.

17. Aristotle, *Eth. Nic.* 1098b2–12; Ambrose, *Hex.* 6.40; Augustine, *An. orig.* 1.24; Aquinas, *ST* II.118.2; *ADE* 20–21, 23; *FEP* 155.30; *MDE* 1.1, 2.19; Johannes Quasten, *Patrology* (Allen: Christian Classics, 1986), 2:287–89, 317. What Aristotle says is more plausible, that everything *factual* accords with the truth. Tertullian, denying God's direct creation of souls in favor of the traducian view that parents beget them, attacked Apollonius of Ephesus, but he did this in a lost work about a different topic — the Montanist controversy about ecstatic prophecy.

18. Ambrose, *Hex.* 6.41; *ADE* 20–21.

19. Genesis 1:1–26; Petrus Alphonsi, *Dialog.*, in *MPL* 157:608B–12C; *Intro.* §3: Written in the twelfth century, the *Dialogues* of Petrus Alphonsi explain the plural *Elohim* as trinitarian but make no connection with the human soul.

20. Genesis 1:28, 2:7: of God's various names in the Hebrew Bible, the one too sacred to be uttered is spelled with four letters: *yod, he, waw, he* — sometimes approximated as Yahweh or Jehovah.

21. Cicero, *Tusc.* 1.65; Augustine, *Trin.* 7.10; Augustine, *Gen. litt.* 7.17; cf. Maimonides, *Guide to the Perplexed*, 1.61.

22. Plato, *Phd.* 95C; *Resp.* 501B; Cicero, *Sen.* 40; *Nat. D.* 1.76; Vergil, *Aen.* 6.730–32; Lactantius, *Opif.* 19.3 (citing Lucretius 2.991–92); *Div. inst.* 1.6.3, 2.10.4, 7.4.3; *Asclep.* 7.

23. Augustine, *Gen. litt.* 7.25, 43: The former passage is the only one in the books on the creation of man (6 and 7, not 7 and 8) that mentions *dignitas*, attributing it to the soul as a higher rank: "just as God surpasses (*praecellit*) every creature, so the soul surpasses every bodily creature in the order of nature (*dignitate naturae*)." Adam came *ex Deo*, according to Augustine, but *de nihilo*: writing *ex nihilo* would have suggested that God is nothing.

24. Remigius of Auxerre, *Expositio super Genesim*, ed. B. Van Name Edwards, Corpus Christianorum Continuatio Medievalis (Turnhout: Brepols, 1999); Peter Lombard, *Sent.* 2.16.3.5; *ADE* 23; *FEP* 153.18–22, 154.27–28; *MDE* 2.12–15, 3.54; Quasten, *Patrology*, 4:153–54, 378; G. R.

Evans, *The Thought of Gregory the Great* (Cambridge: Cambridge University Press, 1986), 87–95; Marcia Colish, *Peter Lombard* (Leiden: Brill, 1994), 1:25, 174, 322, 335, 468; *Intro.* §3: Ambrose had written his *Hexameron* by 390, just before Augustine started his unfinished literal commentary on Genesis. The *Moralia in Job* is the most influential work on the Bible by Gregory the Great (d. 604), but a contemporary anthology of his exegetical writings (*MPL* 79) starts with the creation story. *On the Orthodox Faith* by John of Damascus (d. 749) covers the same material in its second book. Remigius of Auxerre worked in the ninth century, but the Genesis commentary assigned to him by the *Patrologia Latina* (*MPL* 131) is probably an earlier work by Haimo of Auxerre (d. ca. 866); a study of Genesis actually by Remigius has recently been published.

25. Lactantius, *Div. inst.* 7.13–14

26. Cicero, *Tusc.* 1.31; *FEP* 152.13, 153.17.

27. Aristotle, *Rh.* 1369a2–4; Cicero, *Tusc.* 1.31; Augustine, *De civ. D.* 10.29; Aquinas, *ST* I–II.8.1, 46.4, 66.4; *FEP* 154.23; *Intro.* §3: Cicero sees our concern for posterity as meaningless unless it arises from a natural inclination to believe in immortality: "Since all people are concerned, and greatly so, about what will happen after death, nature herself judges tacitly in favor of the immortality of souls. . . . To beget children, propagate a name, adopt sons, take care about wills, also the funeral monuments themselves and their inscriptions — what could these mean except that we reflect on the future as well?" Augustine also sees this inclination as a natural desire: "God has implanted it in us by nature (*naturaliter indidit*) that we want (*cupiamus*) to be blessed and immortal."

28. *FEP* 153.19, 154.25.

29. Dicaearchus of Messana was a naturalist Peripatetic who taught around 300 BCE; Panaetius of Rhodes, an eclectic Stoic who came to Rome after 140, was much admired by Cicero.

30. Cicero, *Tusc.* 1.41–42; Vergil, *Aen.* 6.540–43; *Sibylline Oracles* 8.81–83; Lactantius, *Div. inst.* 7.8.7–9, 24.1.

31. Cicero, *Tusc.* 1.38–39, 51; Lactantius, *Div. inst.* 3.18.2–3; Augustine, *Trin.* 10.9.

32. Plato, *Phd.*; Aristotle, *De an.* 405a29–31; Cicero, *Sen.* 78–81, citing Xenophon, *Cyr.* 8.17–22.

33. Aristotle, *De an.* 430a10–25; *Eth. Nic.* 1111b20–23; Seneca, *Ep.* 102.26; Lactantius, *Div. inst.* 7.13.3–5; Augustine, *De civ. D.* 22.25–27; Eusebius, *Praep. evang.* 11.28; Aquinas, *Script. sent.* 2.19.1.1; FEP 153.20; *Intro.* §3: As Manetti surely knew, Aristotle's treatise *On the Soul* does not claim immortality for the individual human soul, and the *Nicomachean Ethics* calls it impossible; nonetheless, Aquinas and others invoked Aristotle's authority to support immortality. Manetti could have known about Porphyry from Augustine, Eusebius, or Facio. Lactantius quotes from the lost Greek original of the *Asclepius*. Manetti has already cited Cicero frequently on immortality, especially the first book of the *Tusculans*. Seneca writes that "the final day that you fear is like an eternal birthday." As a Stoic, however, he had no grounds for such a belief; for a sage, indifference was the right attitude to death or to the alternative.

34. Lactantius, *Div. inst.* 3.18.5–10: The work by Plato is the *Phaedo*; Cleanthes of Assos was a Stoic, like Zeno and Chrysippus; on Theombrotus see MDE 4.14, 35, 39 with notes.

35. Genesis 1:26, 5:21–24; 2 Kings 2:11–12, 4:32–35; Ambrose, *Hex.* 6.43; MDE 2.14; *Intro.* §3: Manetti, following Ambrose and Augustine, maintains that man's divine "image and likeness" belong "only to the soul and not the body," and Ambrose says that "without the soul the body is nothing." Accordingly, God's perfections, like omnipotence and omniscience, are nothing like human qualities, yet the immaterial soul can share eternity or immortality because it is not a body — not destructible. Moses states this "plainly and openly," says Manetti. But he finds immortality more explicit in the Enoch story, although the patriarch who lives long and vanishes is not said to go on forever. The tales about Elijah and Elisha are no more helpful. When a whirlwind takes Elijah up to heaven, the story says nothing about the prophet's death, neither asserting nor denying it. When Elisha restores the Shunammite woman's son to life, he does not make the boy immortal. In fact, since the Hebrew Bible has no doctrine of immortality, Manetti struggles to make a case from these parts of Scripture.

36. Isaiah 25:8, cf. 26:19; Job 14:10–14; Psalm 5:12: Job is less emphatic about resurrection than Manetti claims, but the Psalmist promises those who hope in God that they will "exult forever (*in aeternum*)"; Isaiah also has "forever (*in sempiternum*)."

37. Ezekiel 18:9, 17–28; 26:20; 31:15–17; 32:21–32; Daniel 6, 12:2: None of this comes from Jeremiah, and Manetti does not cite Daniel 12:2, which promises resurrection to many (not all) of the dead and eternal life only to some of those who will rise. The dead who gather in Sheol, or the Pit, are not said to be immortal.

38. Hosea 13:14; Joel 2:12: Manetti, a student of Hebrew, might have known that the death (*mors* in the Vulgate) addressed by Hosea is Sheol.

39. Amos 9:1–2: Uzziah, the son of Amaziah, ruled in Judah in the first half of the eighth century BCE, when Amos was active; the story of his martyrdom (not biblical) comes from the *Lives of the Prophets* (James Charlesworth, *The Old Testament Pseudepigrapha* [New York: Doubleday, 1983], 2:391), probably from the early first century CE; a Latin version was available by the seventh century. The *Lives* also tells the story of Isaiah's death by sawing, told in more detail by a somewhat later work, *The Ascension of Isaiah* (Charlesworth, *Pseudepigrapha*, 2:163–64), probably not known to Manetti.

40. Malachi 3:23–24 for the promise to send Elijah: otherwise, which passages Manetti has in mind is unclear, but see Obadiah 1:17; Jonah 2:7; Micah 4:5; Nahum 1:7–8; Habakkuk 3:17–18; Zephaniah 3:20; Haggai 2:18–19; Zechariah 9:16–17. He names these nine minor prophets in the order of their books in the Vulgate, where Maccabees 1 and 2 tell the story of the Maccabees; see also Josephus, *Jewish Antiquities* 12.6.

41. Acts 7:54–8:2, 12:1–2; Josephus, *Jewish Antiquities* 20.199–200; ADE 39; see also the *Martyrology of Usuard* in MPL 123–24.

42. Augustine, *De civ. D.* 18.52: Augustine has doubts about a count of ten persecutions, matching the plagues of Egypt, under Nero, Domitian, Trajan, Marcus Aurelius, Septimius Severus, Maximinus, Decius, Valerian, Aurelian, and (counted as a single reign) Diocletian and Maximian, with Antichrist (when he arrives) as the eleventh villain. The first five Fathers (twelve in all, like the Apostles) named by Manetti are "foreign-

ers" because they wrote in Greek, not Latin; he sees them primarily as exegetes of the Bible.

43. Cicero, *Nat. D.* 2.87–89; *Intro.* §3: Cicero, citing Accius, argues (by analogy) for natural design in the world from artificial design in human inventions, like the first ship built for Jason by Argus, one of his crew; see also Juv. 2.1–2. Europeans, well acquainted with North Africa and the Mediterranean, were sailing in the Atlantic along the coast of West Africa and among the Azores by the early fifteenth century — within Manetti's lifetime. But not everyone saw maritime adventuring as progressive: more than half a century after Manetti, Polydore Vergil's history of inventions simply transmitted Pliny's harsh words about the person who first made sails: Polydore Vergil, *On Discovery*, ed. and trans. B. Copenhaver in this I Tatti Renaissance Library (Cambridge: Harvard University Press, 2002), xiv, 392–93 (3.6.1), citing Pliny the Elder, *HN* 19.2–6.

44. Genesis 6:14–22; Pliny the Elder, *HN* 5.61; 16.20; 36.71, 75; Valerius Maximus, 8.12 ext. 2; Servius, *A.* 11.849: Philo of Eleusis designed the arsenal at Piraeus in the fourth century BCE. Manetti's "very tall tower" was probably the so-called pyramid of Romulus, or Meta Romuli, between the Vatican and the Castel Sant'Angelo, dismantled for its marble in the sixteenth century, not the Pyramid of Cestius (only partly visible in Manetti's time). See E. M. Steinby, *Lexicon Topographicum Urbis Romae* (Rome 1993–2000). According to Jerome (*Nom. hebr.*, in *MPL* 23:782), Noah's name means "respite" (*requies*), but "comforter" comes closer. Filippo Brunelleschi (1377–1446), about twenty years older than Manetti, began the cupola of Santa Maria del Fiore in 1420 and put the first stones of the lantern in place in 1445.

45. Pliny the Elder, *HN* 35.65–66, 95, 111; Valerius Maximus, 8.11 ext. 4: Giotto di Bondone lived from around 1265 to 1337.

46. Pliny the Elder, *HN* 34.54, 64; 36.15; Valerius Maximus, 8.11 ext. 4: Lorenzo Ghiberti, born in 1378 or 1381, died in 1455; he finished his first doors for the Baptistery in Florence in 1424, the second in 1452.

47. Manetti has referred to some of these authorities before, to argue for the immortality of the soul, but not on the soul's faculties and human ingenuity.

48. Cicero, *Div.* 1.111; *Tusc.* 1.63; Lactantius, *Div. inst.* 2.5.18

49. Catholic theology was sometimes more restrained than Manetti suggests: Augustine, *Mor. eccl.* 1.12.20, teaches that the human mind is like God's only as a creature's who submits for enlightenment to the Creator; Aquinas, *ST* I.12.5 develops this notion of illumination by divine grace to explain how humans see God's essence in the beatific vision: "some supernatural condition must be added to raise it to such heights . . . so that by God's grace the power of understanding grows beyond itself—a greater growth in intellectual power that we call 'illumination,' just as the intelligible object itself is called 'light' or 'enlightenment.' . . . And in keeping with this light they are called 'deiform' (*deiformes*), meaning 'like God.'" See also Manetti 2.13 with the note and *Expos. symb. apost.* 1–2, where Aquinas follows tradition to show that while "nothing is more like God than man's soul," the "likeness" established by Genesis 1:26 "refers not to the body but to the human soul," a restriction that Manetti has accepted, like Antonio da Barga: see *ADE* 27.

50. Cicero, *Tusc.* 1.59; *Acad.* 2.2; *Fin.* 5.2; *De or.* 2.299; Quintilian, *Inst.* 11.50–51; Pliny the Elder, *HN* 7.88–89; Seneca, *Ep.* 40.1, 49.1, 50.1, 72.1, 74.1, 102.29; *FEP* 152.14; *MDE* 2.46: the topic of the last letter is immortality, closing on the thought that "a noble person's presence is no less useful than his memory," on which Seneca often reflects to start his letters. Cicero, like Quintilian, attributes feats of memory to Theodectes (not Theodorus) of Phaselis, the poet and orator. Charmadas, an Academic philosopher, was the memory artist, not his teacher Carneades. Manetti attributed this skill to Speusippus by misreading the passage cited from *De finibus,* which is about the power of places, like the Academy in Athens, to evoke memories of persons, of whom Speusippus is one of three scholarchs remembered—just as the Curia Hostilia in Rome brings Scipio, Cato, and Laelius to mind.

51. Cicero, *Acad.* 2.2.

BOOK III

1. Lactantius, *Div. inst.* 3.12.1.

2. See *MDE* 3.10 for the human composite as the subject of this book.

3. Aristotle, *Pol.* 1253a1–3; Chrysippus in *SVF* 224.3–4; Cicero, *Off.* 1.7; *Acad.* 2.21; Seneca, *Ep.* 41.8; *MDE* 3.7; *Intro.* §3: What the philosophers are blind about—human immortality—goes unmentioned.

4. Cicero, *Nat. D.* 1.66–67; Seneca, *Ep.* 88.44–45; Lactantius, *Div. inst.* 1.2.1–3, 2.10.17, 7.3.1–5, citing Vergil, *Aen.* 6.726–27; but cf. 2.8.48; Lactantius, *Epit.* 70; *MDE* 2.24.

5. Lactantius, *Div. inst.* 7.4.4–8; *ADE* 12; *FEP* 150.9.

6. Lactantius, *Div. inst.* 7.4.9.

7. Lactantius, *Div. inst.* 2.10.5–12; Augustine, *De civ. D.* 18.8.

8. Cicero, *Leg.* 1.22.

9. Lactantius, *Div. inst.* 2.10.1: Manetti thinks that Lactantius and other Christian theologians had given better accounts of man's creation than pagan philosophers and poets had.

10. Lactantius, *Div. inst.* 2.10.2: Aquinas, *Script. sent.* 1.39.1.3, uses *procreare* (go on creating) of God to cover divine creations of human souls subsequent to the creation of Adam.

11. Pliny the Elder, *HN* 35.19, 65–72, 95, 111; 34.54, 64; 36.15; *MDE* 2.39–40.

12. *MDE* 1.13; *Intro.* §3: A human is "so wonderfully put together" because "God put him together in that way"—the divine miracle of composition. The sustained analysis of man's *officium* at *MDE* 3.44–50, repeating "in a little more detail" what has already been said, will explain the miracle's purpose and result. Manetti's self-deprecating words (*ieiune exiliterque*) about his project are those he used in Book 1 to express criticism of Cicero by Lactantius.

13. Cicero, *Nat. D.* 1.77; *MDE* 1.1, 8, 14–15.

14. Cicero, *Nat. D.* 1.47: *mundus* for "world," like *kosmos* in Greek but in a different register, connotes "beauty," as in *Nat. D.* 2.93.

15. Cicero, *Nat. D.* 2.95, presenting an argument from design for providential divinity in nature.

16. Cicero, *Nat. D.* 2.98–100.

17. Cicero, *Nat. D.* 2.99.

18. Cicero, *Tusc.* 1.45–46; *MDE* 2.37

19. Cicero, *Nat. D.* 1.88, 2.100, 165; *Tusc.* 1.45: Although Cicero uses *Oceanus* for the open waters beyond the straits of Gibraltar, *mediterraneus* is not his word for the smaller sea to which that passage leads; there is no *terrarum orbis*, a phrase well known to Romans, in the passage from Cicero's *Nature of the Gods* paraphrased by Manetti.

20. Cicero, *Nat. D.* 2.101–4.

21. Cicero, *Tusc.* 1.68–70, where the Greek is ἀντίχθονα, from ἀντί-χθων: The first two lines of verse that Cicero cites are by Accius, the other five unidentified, though sometimes ascribed to Ennius; *antichthôn*, referring in this case to the southern hemisphere, can also mean "counterearth," a construct of Pythagorean cosmology.

22. Cicero, *Nat. D.* 1.46–49, 75–77, 103; Pliny the Elder, *HN* 34.15: Although Cicero's study of the gods is important in other ways for Manetti, these passages attack the anthropomorphism in Epicurean religion; cf. Lactantius, *Div. inst.* 2.6.1–2, 17.6–9, and Augustine, *De civ. D.* 4.9, 31 for Christian hostility to pagan images.

23. Lactantius, *Div. inst.* 5.11.2, citing Cicero, *Rep.* 4.1; Augustine, *De civ. D.* 18.18: Manetti relies on the account of Apuleius by Augustine, who treats the author of *The Golden Ass* as the person who was transformed. But in the novel's unstable first-person narrative, the author, a clever Roman from North Africa, depicts Lucius as a naive Greek from Corinth; whether Apuleius had "Lucius" as a *praenomen* is unknown. For a study of how the text was read in the Renaissance, see Julia Haig Gaisser, *The Fortunes of Apuleius and the Golden Ass: A Study in Transmission and Reception* (Princeton, 2008).

24. Manetti alludes to the famous antiskeptical argument, that the Skeptics are inconsistent because they claim to know that there is no such thing as knowledge. See Cicero, *Acad.* 2.28. Manetti may have believed he had coined the word *nescientia* (unknowing), as it is unclassical and rarely attested even in patristic sources.

25. Cicero, *Tusc.* 1.62, discusses naming, forming social groups, and writing as outstanding cases of human invention; in *Phil.* 2.4 letter-writing is "conversation with absent friends"; see also *FEP* 156.33.

26. Lactantius, *Div. inst.* 1.18; Augustine, *De civ. D.* 7.18.

27. Cicero, *Nat. D.* 2.99, as in 3.12; *Off.* 1.152–56; *Intro.* §3.

28. Lactantius, *Div. inst.* 5.17.33: Having relied heavily on Cicero up to this point, Manetti is about to invoke Aristotle; otherwise, his distinction between oratory and dialectic amounts to little, especially since Lactantius, a self-taught theologian, is still his main guide here.

29. Aristotle, *Eth. Nic.* 1141b3–5; Lactantius, *Div. inst.* 3.30.3, 5.17.34.

30. Aristotle, *Hist. an.* 589a4–5; Cicero, *Tusc.* 3.19, 4.31; Lactantius, *Div. inst.* 6.20.2; Aquinas, *ST* I.81.2: Thomas attributes desire for food and sex to animals, but Cicero is more restrictive; Manetti's main source is Lactantius.

31. Cicero, *Nat. D.* 1.18; 2.73, 154–62; Servius on Vergil, *Aen.* 6.395: The natural world was made for mankind, demonstrating a divine providence in nature. The element of the upper sky is fire.

32. Hebrews 1:14; Cicero, *Nat. D.* 2.153; Ps.-Dionysius the Areopagite, *CH* 165C, 209C, 273C; *EH* 504A, 508D–9A, 536D; *ADE* 31; *FEP* 156.34; *Intro.* §1: In Manetti's lifetime, Ambrogio Traversari made a new translation of the theological treatises falsely attributed to Dionysius the Areopagite, which had long been read in earlier versions by John Scotus Eriugena, Grosseteste, and others. Antonio da Barga cites Dionysius in this context, but Facio does not: this detail, like others at *MDE* 4.58, 61, suggests that Manetti used Antonio's outline directly, independently of Facio.

33. Genesis 18:1–15, 21:1–8, 32:23–33; Josephus, *Jewish Antiquities* 1.12.213, 20.333: When Sarah says "God has brought me laughter," the Hebrew for "laughter" (*tsehoq*, *risus* in Latin) echoes the name *Yitshaq*. In *Yisra'el*, Jacob's new name, the first consonants of the verb "strive" (*saritha*) are less conspicuous.

34. Tobias 4–5; Daniel 3:8–29, 6:17–24; *ADE* 32; *FEP* 157.35–36: Nebuchadnezzar took Jerusalem in 597 BCE; the figure of Darius in the Daniel story is unhistorical, since the famous Persian king of that name died more than a century later.

35. Luke 1:26–38, 2:8–18; Matthew 2:13–19; Gregory of Tours, *Vitae patrum*, in *MPL* 71: 1044B, 1058D, 1066A, 1095B; *ADE* 38; *FEP* 157.38.

36. Cicero, *Nat. D.* 2.64; Augustine, *De civ. D.* 2.12.

37. Aristotle, *Eth. Nic.* 1105a7–9; Cicero, *Tusc.* 3.47–50; *Sen.* 40, cited by Lactantius, *Div. inst.* 6.20.1–5; *MDE* 3.24, 32; *Intro.* §3: Although Aristotle's morality is not ascetic, pleasure is not the highest good; moreover, some pleasures (like contemplation) are better than others, and others are best avoided. Arguing the merits of old age, Cicero takes a harder line on *voluptas*, calling it incompatible with *virtus* because it destroys *mens*, the best of all divine gifts to humans. Lactantius, without the rhetorical burden of an essay on old age, cites Cicero to underwrite a call for ceaseless Christian warfare against pleasure, even though God, in order to match the allotment of virtue, had given more pleasure to humans than to animals. Cicero's criticism of Epicurean hedonism in the *Tusculans* is more nuanced, and Manetti's message is mixed (see *MDE* 3.32): pleasure is great for humans because of God's plan; by the same design, the greatest pleasure is sexual; but the purpose of sex might be either natural and biological (propagating the species) or moral and ascetic (abstaining from a natural pleasure).

38. Lactantius, *Div. inst.* 6.23.2–3.

39. Exodus 11:10; 1 Kings 17:22; 2 Kings 13:21; Daniel 6:22; Matthew 10:8; Acts 3:1–11, 6:8, 9:37–40, 20:9–11; 1 Corinthians 12:8–10; Augustine, *In Evang. Iohan.* 49.10; Gregory of Tours, *Vitae patrum*, in *MPL* 71: 743C–44C, 748B9A; *Litaniae a sanctis patribus constitutae* in *MPL* 138: 889C–98C; *ADE* 35–37; *FEP* 157.39–40. These litanies include one that names most of the figures mentioned by Manetti and in that order: Moses, Elijah, Daniel, Peter, Paul, John, Stephen, Laurence, Gervase, and Protasius. Episcopal ordination of priests and priestly remission of sins, both promoting papal power, had gathered strength since the twelfth century. But since the royal patron of Manetti's work was a pope's rival, perhaps this is why he does not say more—like Antonio da Barga and Facio—about priestly and pontifical power.

40. Ovid, *Met.* 1.76–78; Plato, *Ti.* 27D–29A; Lactantius, *Div. inst.* 2.8.49, 64: Manetti does not ascribe creation *ex nihilo* to Ovid or to Plato, who says that while a material substrate has always existed, the universe came to be from a "maker and father" or "craftsman" who formed

NOTES TO THE TRANSLATIONS

the inchoate matter into a cosmos, in accordance with an existing model, the Forms or Ideas.

41. Genesis 1:24–28; *ADE* 20; *FEP* 155.30–31.

42. Acts 9:15; 1 Corinthians 3:22–23; *Glossa ord.* ad Rom. 8:32, in *MPL* 141:449A–B; *ADE* 13–14; *FEP* 150–51.9: According to the *Glossa ordinaria* on Romans, "all that are higher (*superiora*)—namely, God as the Trinity—are ours to see or enjoy (*videndum sive fruendum*). Those that are equal (*aequalia*)—whose equals we shall be in the future, though now we are lower (*inferiores*)—are ours with whom to share happiness (*convivendum*). Lower things are ours as well—to master (*dominandum*). And some that are higher, like the angels above and God's whole heavenly ministry, are likewise ours, though for use (*usu*) and not to master, in the way that things belonging to a master are to feed a household or for clothing and other such purposes"; and the *Glossa* on 1 Corinthians, "the world is ours if we locate its passages in God's will. Life is ours if we live modestly and with God's glory. Death is ours if we die willingly for Christ and with hope in the future. Things present are ours if we use (*utimur*) them but commit no offense, and future things are ours if we desire what have more belief in."

43. Psalm 8:4–8; Hebrews 11:5–8; *ADE* 33–34; *FEP* 149.1.

44. Aquinas, *ST* I.12.13, 93.7; I–II.82.2–3; *Intro.* §5: "There is just one cause of this corrupt state called original sin, namely the privation of original justice, which eliminates the human mind's subjection to God."

45. *MDE* 2.38

46. Genesis 18:16–22; Exodus 32:15–16, 34:29.

47. Galatians 4:4.

48. Aquinas, *ST* I.113.2, citing Jerome, *Comm. Matt.* ad 18:10; *ADE* 31; *FEP* 156.34; *Intro.* §4: Where Jesus says in Matthew's Gospel of "these little ones (*pusilli*)" that "their angels in heaven always see the Father's face," Jerome explains that "so great is the value (*magna est dignitas*) of souls that each of them, from the moment of birth, has an angel assigned as a guardian (*in custodiam*)." Matthew says nothing about *dignitas*, a word that the Vulgate New Testament never uses. Since Manetti highlights

paedagogus as transliterated from Greek, he may be thinking of a Greek theologian, like Basil, *Contra Eunom.* 3.29.656.

49. Cicero, *Nat. D.* 2.164–65, arguing that some humans have been helped not only by the divine providence that sustains the universe as a whole but also by the care shown by the gods for certain outstanding people.

50. Plato, *Ap.* 21A–D, 31C–D; *Euthyd.* 272D–E; Cicero, *Nat. D.* 2.166; Apuleius, *De deo Soc.* 14, 18–19: Plato's phrase for the numinous force that guides Socrates at crucial moments is hard to render in English—perhaps "a godlike power (*daimonion*) of some kind," which Apuleius Latinized as *daemon*; in Latin *angelus* is postclassical, used by the Vulgate where the Septuagint has *angelos*, which sometimes is simply "messenger," like *mal'ach* in Hebrew, as in Genesis 16:7.

51. Starting here and ending at *MDE* 3.50, Manetti makes his case for man's unique role (*officium*): see also 3.2, 10; *Intro.* §3.

52. Augustine, *De civ. D.* 15.17, commenting on Genesis 5:2, teaches that Adam's name, unlike Eve's, applies to the whole human race of which he is the one and only father, distinct from the rest of the species: "Adam was the father of both lines, the one whose descent belongs to the earthly city, and the other to the heavenly. . . . The meaning of this name is 'man,' but in that language, which is Hebrew, it applies to male and female in common, as it is written, 'male and female he made them, blessed them and named them Adam together [*cognominavit*, where the Vulgate is simply *vocavit* and the Septuagint restricts the name to the male],' . . . so that Adam, meaning 'human,' names them both." See also *MDE* 1.1; *Intro.* §2.

53. Aristotle, *Part. an.* 673a4–10; Peter of Spain, *Summaries*, 139: Aristotle records the biological observation that humans are the only laughing animals, but Peter of Spain, drawing on Porphyry and Boethius, makes the salient logical and metaphysical point. A *proprium proprie*, like risibility (*risibile*) or the human capacity for laughter, is the fourth and most restrictive type of property (*proprium*); such a property (1) belongs only to one species (in this case, the human); yet (2) it is not the essence of that species or part of its definition, which is *animal rationale et mortale*; and (3) it belongs naturally and necessarily both to the species and all its mem-

bers. Hence, as Peter writes, "a man is said to be risible not because he is always actually laughing but because he is suited by nature to laugh." Manetti would be correct to say that the *rationale* is part of man's essence, while risibility is not, but (following Cicero's reading of Aristotle) he seems to make this claim vaguely for *intelligentia*, not for *ratio*, and perhaps for *actio* or *operatio* as well.

54. Peter of Spain, *Summaries*, 139, on a common scholastic doctrine: "the risible is in every man, in man only and always." If humans are the *only* laughing *animalia* (living things), as Aristotle says, laughter is eliminated for God and angels, strictly speaking, who are also living. But Manetti uses *animal* here as Aristotle meant it in the *Parts of Animals*, for animals here on earth, and his account of risibility as a human *proprium* is unclear. Like God and angels, humans understand and act, but, since risibility is their *proprie proprium*, they are given to laughter, unlike God and angels. Risibility is not a *proprium* of God and angels, and yet, because humans understand and act, Manetti claims that humans are angelic and divine, even though understanding and action are not human *propria*.

55. Aristotle, *Eth. Nic.* 1097b22–98a20; Cicero, *Fin.* 2.40; cf. *MDE* 3.48 and note; *Intro.* §3.

56. Romans 1:20; Lactantius, *Div. inst.* 2.1.17, 3.9.4–11; Peter Lombard, *Sent.* 1.3.1–6; Aquinas, *Script. sent.* 1.3–4; *FEP* 153.18–19; *Intro.* §3: Manetti alludes to the verse from Romans that authorized natural theology for Peter Lombard, Aquinas, and other scholastics. *Sapientia* and *religio*, reflecting *intelligentia* and *actio*, are "inseparably connected," but the connection links "two things" with distinct functions as the poles of a practice/theory antithesis, for which see *MDE* 3.1–2, 10 and notes.

57. Aristotle, *Eth. Nic.* 1066a30–33; Aquinas, *ST* I–II.77.4 ad 1; II–II.25.4; *FEP* 154.25: Self-love, according to Manetti, is a natural instinct for self-preservation, created in Adam by God, while love of others is God's commandment given in writing to Adam's procreated descendants.

58. Lactantius, *Ira* 14.1.

59. Lactantius, *Div. inst.* 2.1.18, 5.3: Following Lactantius, Manetti sees a body/mind symmetry in mind's emulation of body — without explaining, or even asserting, any communication between them.

60. Lactantius, *Ira* 14.1–6; cf. Cicero, *Nat. D.* 2.140.

61. Lactantius, *Ira* 14.1–6, citing Cicero, *Leg.* 1.28; *Nat. D.* 2.140.

62. Lactantius, *Div. inst.* 7.5.4–5.

63. Psalm 15:2; Augustine, *Doct. chr.* 1.35; Peter Lombard, *Sent.* 2.1.3.5–4.5; *ADE* 10–11; *FEP* 150.8, 154.26.

64. Peter Lombard, *Sent.* 2.1.4.1; *ADE* 12; *FEP* 150.5–8: Before citing the passage on God's goodness from Augustine (as in *MDE* 3.53), Facio treats the Platonists and Stoics in the same way, but without mentioning the Peripatetics. For Peter Lombard, the master of the *Sentences*, see the note on *MDE* 2.19; *Intro.* §§1, 3.

65. Lactantius, *Div. inst.* 2.5.32.

66. Livy 38.57.7; Aulus Gellius 19.9.8; Suetonius, *Aug.* 40.5; *Cal.* 35.3; Augustine uses *indignabundus* once in a letter, in *MPL* 33:363; see also *Intro.* §3.

67. *MDE* 2.12; *FEP* 158.41.

68. Augustine, *Trin.* 3.22, gives other reasons, had there been no Fall, for the incarnation; one possibility supports what Manetti says: "through such great humility on God's part, human pride, which is the main obstacle to a connection with God, can be exposed as false and also remedied." Aquinas, *ST* III.1.3, recognizing that the issue was contentious, concedes that God has the power to become flesh, without reference to human sin, but he supports the opposite view because Scripture indicates that the Fall was in fact the reason. Scotus, by contrast, saw the incarnation as built into God's plan, merely human vice or virtue notwithstanding: *Ordinatio* 3.7.3 (*Opera* 14:348b). See also *Intro.* §3.

69. *FEP* 158.41; also *ADE* 34 on angels: Christ is one of three *persons* in the Trinity, and that person has two *natures*—divine and human. Human nature, in the incarnate God, is therefore divinized—according to Manetti—by the person of Christ, and mankind's is the only created nature to join with a divine nature: Christ's two natures need no joining because their sameness is perfect. The Trinity's persons and natures were a favorite puzzle for Scotus and other Franciscans, whose Christology Manetti seems to prefer to the Dominican or Thomist alternative.

BOOK IV

1. *MDE* 4.11, 15–17; *Intro.* §5: After first presenting the evidence for the misery of human life, in both body and soul, Manetti will turn to the alleged benefits of death in order to set up the main target of his book, the case made for human worthlessness by a cardinal who became pope, the Innocent III introduced at 4.4. Unlike Facio and Antonio da Barga, Manetti has not presented his whole project, only this fourth and final chapter, as a response to Innocent, but his rebuttal is strikingly aggressive.

2. Seneca, *Marc.* 11.3–4.

3. Aristotle, *Eth. Nic.* 1154b8–10; Cicero, *Tusc.* 5.3.

4. Seneca, *Helv.* 2.2; 6.7; 10.2, 6; 11.3, 6–7; Pliny the Elder, *HN* 7.1.

5. Job 4:19; *LDM* 1.1–3 (95–99); *ADE* 2–3; *FEP* 149.1.

6. *LDM* 1.4 (101).

7. Cicero, *Tusc.* 1.21; Aquinas, *Script. sent.* 2.18.2.3; *MDE* 2.4–7, 14, 24.

8. *MDE* 2.24.

9. Cicero, *Tusc.* 2.45; 4.16, 27.

10. Lactantius, *Div. inst.* 3.18.1–2, 19.19–20.

11. Cicero, *Tusc.* 1.38, 60; Vergil, *Aen.* 6.329; Lactantius, *Div. inst.* 3.19.19, 7.8.7; as in *MDE* 2.25.

12. Cicero, *Tusc.* 1.83–84.

13. Cicero, *Tusc.* 1.65, 76, 115–16; *Acad.* 2.119; [Plutarch] *Cons. ad Apoll.* 109B–D: The *Tusculans* is a dialogue between two unidentified speakers, labeled A and M. Speaker A — the "one person" mentioned by Manetti — praises the power of the *Consolation*, now lost, that Cicero had written when his daughter died. Elysius thought that Euthynous, his son, might have been poisoned, as reported by the *Consolation* attributed to Plutarch, but in that version the boy's death is simply "fated" (*moiridios*), not a gift from the Fates. Manetti compliments Cicero's eloquence by echoing what the Roman had said in his *Academics* about Aristotle's prose: *veniet flumen orationis aureum fundens Aristoteles.*

14. Pliny the Elder, *HN* 7.3–5.

15. Cicero, *Tusc.* 1.113, citing Herodotus 1.31; Lactantius, *Div. inst.* 3.18.8–12: the next seven examples, which Manetti begins to refute at *MDE* 4.19, were all used by Cicero in the first book of the *Tusculans*, not mentioned here, nor is Lactantius mentioned, who condemns some of the same suicides.

16. Cicero, *Tusc.* 1.114.

17. Cicero, *Tusc.* 1.114–15, citing Euripides, *Cresphontes*, a play that survives only in fragments, translated where Cicero cites it into Latin: cf. fr. 449.

18. Cicero, *Tusc.* 1.115: To describe this "Asiatic" custom, Manetti repeats some of the five lines of the *Cresphontes* (see the previous note) that Cicero quotes, probably misreading the title of the play as "Ctesiphon," a famous Asian city south of modern Baghdad.

19. Cicero, *Tusc.* 1.71, 74, 84, 97–100; *Off.* 1.84; Diogenes Laertius 6.94–95; Lactantius, *Div. inst.* 3.18.8, 11; Augustine, *De civ. D.* 1.22: Here Manetti omits Cicero's explanation of the suicide by Theombrotus — that he jumped after reading Plato — though he mentions it later, at 4.39, where he also cites Augustine, who gives the same name to the despairing Platonist. Diogenes Laertius lists a Theombrotus as a student of Metrocles — a Cynic, however, not a Platonist: Crates rescued the teacher from suicide. Cicero *On Duties* mentions the Cleombrotus who became king of Sparta in 380 BCE, but Ambracia was in Macedonia. After losing at Thapsus in 46, Cato the Younger killed himself rather than let Caesar take him; Lactantius says that Cato had just finished reading Plato, however, and that his motive was philosophical — not merely to thwart Caesar but to have a good reason for dying on that occasion.

20. Ecclesiastes 2:17, 3:19–21, 4:2–3, 7:2; *ADE* 28.

21. Job 7:1, 8:9, 9:25–26, 10:18–19, 14:1–2: "ships carrying fruit" follows the Vulgate.

22. Ambrose, *Bon. mort.* 3, 52–57, commenting on Job 3:2 and Romans 6:2–4; see also Job 7:1, 10:9–14, 29:13; Ecclesiastes 1:8, 2:17, 4:2–3, 6:3 and 26; Augustine, *De civ. D.* 13.2–6; *Intro.* §5.

23. *MDE* 4.4; *ADE* 2.

24. Genesis 2:23, 3:20; *LDM* 1.4–6 (101–3); *MDE* 4.4, 44, 46 with note; *Intro.* §5: at this point, Manetti makes no effort to show how the Vulgate tries to reflect the original Hebrew, but see *MDE* 4.47.

25. *LDM* 1.7–12, 22, 27 (105–13, 131–33, 137–39); *MDE* 4.52: The colorful language is Lotario's from the first book of his polemic, especially the chapters on nakedness (7), body parts (8), old age (9), effort and futility (10–12), death (22), and torment (27).

26. *LDM* 1.6 (103); *Intro.* §§3, 5: "we are all born wailing to express nature's misery," Lotario writes, claiming that suffering is the human condition on earth, but Manetti contradicts him, declaring that good deeds can bring people "joy and cheer in this world," not just happiness in the next. The "us" addressed here includes Manetti and Alfonso, as in *MDE* 4.72–73.

27. Peter Lombard, *Sent.* 2.19.1–6, commenting on Romans 8:10 and Augustine, *Gen. litt.* 6.19–25; also, for finer distinctions, Aquinas, *Script. sent.* 2.19; and *MDE* 1.1; 4.3, 43, 58–61; *Intro.* §5: This intricate analysis relies on the clearer account by Peter Lombard, whose *Sentences* Manetti has cited at *MDE* 3.55 without actually naming the author. Also without naming him, Antonio da Barga and Facio had used Peter's great commentary extensively—though not for the issues discussed here. Peter posits three states—innocence, guilt, and redemption by grace—before and after the Fall. In the original state of innocence, before the first humans sinned, immortality was certain (necessary) for their souls but only possible for their bodies: if Adam and Eve sinned, their bodies would die but otherwise would live on. In the second state of guilt, death—both spiritual and physical—was necessary: our parents had "the power to die and no power not to die." In the third state of redemption, once grace was active, death (at least the spiritual kind) was impossible for saved sinners, who had "the power not to die and no power to die." Manetti implies (but Peter does not say) that grace also makes physical death impossible for the righteous inasmuch as their bodies will be "glorified" for all eternity.

28. Aristotle, *De an.* 426b8–27a15; Aquinas, *ST* I.78.4; *Intro.* §5: Manetti lists the usual external and internal senses and faculties of the soul,

including the "common" sense that aggregates the deliverances of the "proper" senses while also discriminating among them.

29. *MDE* 4.22; *Intro.* §5.

30. Aquinas *ST* I–II.31.6, 83.4; II–II.152.2, 155.2; *Sent. de an.* 2.14.20, 21.2, 10; *Intro.* §5.

31. *MDE* 4.1–4, 9, 18, 21, 24.

32. Cicero, *Tusc.* 5.3; Job 4:19: Job was proverbially patient; *MDE* 4.3.

33. *LDM* 1.1–3 (95–99); *MDE* 4.4.

34. Cicero, *Leg.* 1.22; *Nat. D.* 2.148–49; *MDE* 1.7, 11, 36 (with Mondino), 38; 3.7.

35. *MDE* 4.20.

36. Aristotle, *Gen. an.* 727a21–30, 737b25–26; *LDM* 1.3 (97–99): Humans are the highest class of complete (or perfect) animals, according to Aristotle, those that produce not eggs but viable young resembling their parents; the more complete have more heat and moisture, less earthy matter; both semen and menstrual discharge is greater in humans than in other animals. But after Adam came from slime, says Lotario, his descendants came from unclean seed, which corrupted their flesh.

37. Aristotle, *Gen. an.* 726b1–4, 740a21–23, 766b8–23; *Part. an.* 650a30–b3.

38. *MDE* 4.18, citing Lotario.

39. *MDE* 4.5 citing Cicero, with background from Aquinas or another scholastic. For "off the branch" see *MDE* 2.14.

40. *MDE* 2.9, citing Cicero, *Tusc.* 1.66.

41. Cicero, *Tusc.* 1.22; Lucian, *Lis cons.* 10; *MDE* 2.7: In this passage from the *Tusculans*, Cicero probably wrote by mistake *endelecheia*, an ordinary word meaning "continuity," instead of *entelecheia*, a technical term for "actuality" invented by Aristotle; Lucian's joke about the confusion shows that it was well known in antiquity. Lorenzo Valla treats *entelecheia* as coined by Aristotle, while Poliziano and others debated whether Cicero was wrong to use *endelecheia*: Valla, *Dialectical Disputations*, ed. and trans. B. P. Copenhaver and L. Nauta, in this I Tatti Renaissance Library

(Cambridge, MA: Harvard University Press, 2012), 1:232 (1.16.10); for Poliziano see J. Kraye in *Rinascimento* n.s. 23 (1983): 83–84, 87–88.

42. Cicero, *Tusc.* 1.55; *Div.* 1.62; *MDE* 1.3; 2.24; 3.4, 26, 47; 4.6: The philosophers whom Cicero attacks as *plebei* and *minuti* are all those who treat the soul as merely the life of the body — not just Epicureans.

43. Cicero, *Tusc.* 1.50–51; *MDE* 4.7.

44. *MDE* 4.10–14.

45. Genesis 1:31.

46. Augustine, *De civ. D.* 12.1.

47. Lactantius, *Div. inst.* 3.18.18, 19.1; *MDE* 4.11, with note.

48. Aristotle, *Eth. Eud.* 1229b40–30a5; *Eth. Nic.* 1115b34–16a4, 1123b30–33; Cicero, *Sen.* 72–73; Aquinas, *ST* II–II.64.5, 129.5; *MDE* 4.14. Aristotle teaches that the greathearted person has all the virtues: bravery is part of magnanimity. In the *Eudemian Ethics* suicide is unmanly and weak, but in the *Nicomachaean Ethics* (Manetti's usual source for Aristotle's moral philosophy) only unjust (to the state, not oneself) and illegal. As a good Christian, however, Manetti would agree with Aquinas, for whom suicide is always sinful.

49. Plato, *Ap.* 40B–C, quoted from Cicero, *Tusc.* 1.97; Augustine, *De civ. D.* 1.22; *MDE* 2.6, 27, where the book on immortality by Plato is the *Phaedo*. Manetti cites the *Apology* in Cicero's Latin; the humanist Leonardo Bruni had translated both works by 1427, finishing the *Phaedo* in 1405.

50. Cicero, *Sest.* 60; Plutarch, *Vit. Cat.* 68.2, 66.5; Valerius Maximus, 3.2.14; Augustine, *De civ. D.* 1.23, rejecting what Plutarch implies, but does not say: that Cato's motive for killing himself was to avoid living in disgrace under Caesar. Augustine, whose treatment of Cato is more nuanced than Manetti suggests, allows that embarrassment, though not suicide, would have been reasonable.

51. *MDE* 4.15–17; *Intro.* §5; for the glorified body, see *MDE* 4.58–67.

52. Ecclesiastes 1:2, 3:19–21, 12:5–8; Psalm 39:6; Jerome, *Comm. Eccl.*, in *MPL* 23:1061–66; *MDE* 4.41; *Intro.* §5: Manetti follows the Vulgate, where the "golden bowl" (*gullah*) of the Hebrew and KJV is a "golden

band" (*vitta*). *Concionator*, a pejorative, is Jerome's rendering of *qoheleth* as "one who calls an assembly together, . . . speaking to the people and all of them generally, not to one person."

53. Ecclesiastes 4:2–3, 7:2, 9:4 and 7.

54. Ecclesiastes 12:12: The oldest manuscripts of the Septuagint, like the Codex Vaticanus from the fourth century, contain Ecclesiastes. Telling against it, however, are an apparently late date, unconventional Hebrew, signs of resonance with Greek thought, and lack of any explicit use in the New Testament: see *MDE* 4.41.

55. Job 1:20; 32–37, esp. 33:14–16; 36:11; 38:2; 41:2; 42:7–10; Ecclesiastes 2:24, 7:2, 11:9–10; Gregory the Great, *Moral.* 2.83; 4 pr., 48–53; 8.8–12, 63–64; 9.46–48; 12.1; 32.4, 10, 39, 43; 33.26; 35:8–21; 36.57; *MDE* 4.16: Job's story is a lesson in providence, according to Gregory's *Moralia in Job*, because God "tempts the elect in order to protect them all the more by his temptation." Temptation itself is providential. The doctrine is hard, however: Gregory uses troubling passages from Ecclesiastes to introduce similar problems in Job, where "the literal words sometimes contradict themselves, but . . . direct the reader to a truth"—like the transformed meanings that Manetti describes. Thus, although Elihu behaves arrogantly with Job and his friends, he says "the right things in the wrong way"—in particular that Scripture's divine secrets need interpreting.

56. Ambrose, *Bon. mort.* 5, 8, 56; *MDE* 4.17: Ambrose, not thinking of a glorified body, describes the earthly body as a "hovel" and a "prison" from whose "chains" the saved must escape.

57. *MDE* 4.1, with note.

58. *MDE* 4.18; *LDM* 1.6 (103): at this point Manetti reproduces Lotario's description of wailing infants exactly, after paraphrasing it at 4.18.

59. Dante, *Inferno*, 19.101; *Paradiso*, 11.92; *Intro.* §5: Dante excoriates popes guilty of simony, Nicholas III, Boniface VIII, and Clement V, who all ruled later than Innocent III; Dante mentions him in the *Paradiso* for authorizing the Franciscan Order, renowned for poverty.

60. Genesis 2:23, 3:20; 2 Corinthians 11:3; 1 Timothy 2:13–14; Jerome, *Qu. hebr. Gen.* ad loc.; *Nom. hebr.* s.v. *Eva*; Augustine, *Gen. litt.* 11.51; *MDE* 4.18

and note; *Intro.* §5: When Manetti says "named *the living* by this Hebrew name," the name in question is *Ḥawwah*. Antonomasia, substituting a word or phrase (like "the Philosopher") for a name (like "Aristotle"), had been applied to the Bible by Jerome and Augustine, though not explicitly in this case.

61. Genesis 2:23; Jerome, *Qu. hebr. Gen.* ad loc.; Josephus, *Jewish Antiquities* 1.1.2.36; *MDE* 4.18 with n. 24; *Intro.* §5: Lotario's mistake, according to Manetti, was not to recognize the mirroring of *'isshah* and *'ish* by *virago* and *vir*, which has nothing to do with sinning.

62. Manetti's analysis of the Hebrew text certainly improves on Innocent's, though he adds little, if anything, to what Jerome had said long before.

63. *LDM* 1.7–13 (105–15): Manetti lists the topics of the next seven chapters of Lotario's first book, following the sixth on wailing infants that he has already examined.

64. Job 1:21; Ecclesiastes 5:14; Revelation 3:17: *LDM* 1.7 (105); *MDE* 4.29; *Intro.* §5.

65. *LDM* 1.7 (105), commenting on Genesis 38:27–30; for *secundina* or *secundinae*, see Deuteronomy 28:57; also Gilbert of England, *Compendium medicinae Gilberti Anglici tam morborum universalium quam particularium nondum medicis sed et cyrurgicis utilissimum* (Lyon: Jacques Sacon and Vincenzo I de Portonariis, 1510), fol. 307v — a popular medical encyclopedia since the thirteenth century.

66. *LDM* 1.8 (105–7); *MDE* 4.18.

67. Luke 21:18; Pliny the Elder, *HN* 7.13, 15; 17.50–51; 22.65, 123; 28.35–38, 76; 31.116.

68. *LDM* 1.9 (107–9), commenting on Job 7:6; see also 7:1, 9:25–26, 14:1–2; *Intro.* §5; Lotario cites Job and other texts on the present shortness of life but gives no reasons for the longevity once enjoyed by the patriarchs. Manetti — like Josephus in the next paragraph — connects long life with the need to invent necessities that eventually became familiar, no longer requiring the extra time: the efficiency of a shorter lifespan would not make it providential, however.

69. Josephus, *Jewish Antiquities* 1.3.9.104–8, 1.6.5.152; *Intro.* §5.

70. Seneca, *Brev. vit.* 1.1–4, citing Hippocrates, *Aphor.* 1.1; *MDE* 4.54: Seneca understood that the aphorism, in context, is about the art of medicine as cumulative over many human lifetimes.

71. *LDM* 1.10 (109).

72. Aristotle, *Eth. Nic.* 1174b26–27, 1175a18–21.

73. *LDM* 1.11–13 (109–15): Lotario's eleventh chapter deals with intellectual inquiry, the twelfth with physical exploration, invention, and production, the thirteenth with assorted anxieties.

74. Augustine, *De civ. D.* 22.15–21, 29; Anselm, *Liber de simil.* 50–58; Lotario dei Segni, *Myst. evang. leg.* 4.12, in *MPL* 217: 864A–D; Aquinas, *Script. sent.* 4.49.4.5.3; *ST* III.81.3; *SCG* 4.86–88; [Aquinas], *ST Suppl.* 82–85; *ADE* 45–48; *FEP* 159–66; *MDE* 4.59–60, 65: In his inventory of the glorified body, Antonio da Barga lists twelve blessings (*beatitudines*), six joys (*gaudia*), and three levels of Heaven: starry, crystalline, and empyrean. The blessings — perfect, unspoiled, and undiminished — are (1) health, (2) youth, (3) satisfaction, (4) spatial freedom, (5) beauty, (6) immortality without suffering, (7) abundance, (8) peace, (9) rest, (10) knowledge, (11) mutual respect, and (12) joy. Facio says a little — much less than Antonio — about only seven of these: 1, 2, 5, 7, 8, 9, and 11; Manetti also describes seven, but they are different — 1, 2, 4, 5, 6, 9, and 12 — indicating that he had seen Antonio's list, not just Facio's. Antonio's joys are (1) the beatific vision, (2) the heavenly location, (3) fellowship, (4) the glorified body, (5) the sight of Hell, and (6) the sight of the world. After a lengthy account of the beatific vision, Facio names four different joys — (7) brightness, (8) delicacy, (9) agility, and (10) invulnerability — before adding (3) fellowship, the three heavens, and (5) seeing the damned in Hell. Manetti names Facio's four distinctive joys, along with beauty and immortality, as causing a seventh, which is bliss (*exhilaratio*). Such catalogs can be traced back to Augustine. Aquinas approved joys 7, 8, 9 and 10, paring down the seven in the *Book of Similitudes* associated with Anselm; Aquinas also cites Lotario (as Innocent III), who named the same four in his *Mysteries of Gospel Law and the Sacrament of the Eucharist.* By Anselm's time such lists were proliferating, inspired by

Augustine's less doctrinaire presentation; focusing on the risen body's beauty, Augustine names four defects that it cannot have: ugliness, weakness, sluggishness, and corruption, later adding immortality and preternaturally powerful eyesight as positive endowments.

75. Psalm 103:2–3; *ADE* 45; *FEP* 159.51.

76. Ephesians 4:11–16; Romans 8:29; Augustine, *De civ. D.* 22.15; *ADE* 45; *FEP* 160.51: Augustine confirms that the temporal standard was set by Christ at the age of thirty, but he denies that this refers to physical size.

77. Augustine, *De civ. D.* 22.19, citing Matthew 13:43; *ADE* 45; *FEP* 160.51: the definition of beauty is Augustine's, but see the previous note.

78. Revelation 21:4; Aquinas, *Script. sent.* 4.49.4.5.3; *ADE* 45; *FEP* 160.51; *MDE* 3.37, 4.58 with notes: The postclassical *impassibilitas*, used by Aquinas and other theologians for the inability to suffer (*patior*) — or more broadly, to be subject to any affect — is usually transliterated as "impassibility" because it is hard to translate; Aquinas writes that the glorified body "is called impassible because the soul's strength keeps it immune from all injury." Facio does not mention the twelfth blessing in Antonio's list, which is "joy without sadness" when "God will wash every tear from the eyes of his saints" — another detail suggesting that Manetti, independently of Facio, made direct use of Antonio's outline.

79. Augustine, *De civ. D.* 22.29, commenting on Matthew 5:8; 1 John 3:2; 1 Corinthians 13:12; and other biblical texts; *ADE* 46; *FEP* 160.52.

80. Augustine, *De civ. D.* 22.29; Aquinas, *ST* III.55.2; [Aquinas], *ST Suppl.* 92.2; *FEP* 160.53–57; *Intro.* §1: Augustine speculates that the eyes of the glorified body will have a role in seeing God, but Aquinas insists that such sight can only be indirect, from seeing "God in his creatures seen corporeally." Manetti seems to come down on both sides. The phrase used by Aquinas is *visio beata*.

81. Isaiah 18:4; Gregory the Great, *Moral.* 4.19.12, *ad Job* 29:4, with Psalm 19:14, Hebrews 4:3, in *MPL* 76:108A–9A: Perhaps Manetti did not intend an exact quotation of Gregory's words, which make a similar point in a different way: "Acting externally, we often fear to seem out of line in the eyes of men, while in our inner thoughts we have no fear of His at-

titude toward us—the One whom we do not see as He sees it all" (*quem videntem omnia non videmus*).

82. FEP 162.61–63.64; *MDE* 4.58 and note; the next paragraphs explain the four joys singled out by Facio and listed by Aquinas.

83. Wisdom 3:7; cf. Daniel 12:3; Matthew 13:43, 17:2; Philippians 3:21; Aquinas, *Script. sent.* 4.44.2.1.1, 4.1–2; [Aquinas], *ST Suppl.* 85.1: In the parable of the good and bad seed, not in the transfiguration story, Matthew alludes to a passage from the Wisdom of Solomon, "the just shall shine (*fulgebunt*) and flash like sparks through reeds," which Manetti attributes to Isaiah.

84. John 20:19, 26: Matthew 14:25–32; Luke 24:39; John 20:24–29; 1 Corinthians 15:44–46; Gregory the Great, *Moral.* 14.72, *ad Job* 19:26; Aquinas, *Script. sent.* 4.44.2.2.1–2, 5; 3.1; 49.2.7; *ST* III.45.1; [Aquinas], *ST Suppl.* 83.1–6; FEP 163.63, 165.69–71; *MDE* 4.58 and note: Some physical things are *subtilis*, meaning "fine" or "delicate," like Christ's body after the resurrection, when he walked through doors. Gregory describes the resurrected body as "subtler than wind and air, . . . subtle indeed by the working of a spiritual power, but palpable by its real nature." The long account of *subtilitas* given by Aquinas, citing Gregory, is less than satisfying. Although "the word is taken from the power of penetrating," a *corpus subtile* obeys the law of impenetrability, whereby two bodies are never in exactly the same place. Nor is a subtle body impalpable: hence the Gospel story of doubting Thomas, whom the risen Jesus told to "reach your finger here, and . . . put it into my side." Needing a positive description, Aquinas thinks of ordinary bodies, like the fluids whose tiny parts penetrate other physical things. The *subtilitas* of glorified bodies is different, however: their subtlety is the *effect* of the soul's mastery of the body in the glorified composite, where the composite's matter is completely subject to its form, which is the soul, and subtlety is also the *cause* of the "spirituality" that Paul attributes to the risen body. *Agilitas* and the other two *dotes* also illuminate Paul's meaning. Just as subtlety depends on the body's complete subjection to its *form*, which is the soul, agility has the same basis, since the soul is the body's *mover* as well, and the resulting *agilitas* is sensory as well as locomotive. Where Facio claims that the blessed "may come and go as they wish" and also describes their deli-

cacy, he cites Aquinas, which guarantees that Manetti had a route to Thomas's views on these issues.

85. 1 Corinthians 1:9; Revelation 7:9, 18:22; Aquinas, *ST* I.97.2; II-II, 23.1, 25.1, 9; *SCG* 3.62–64; 144.4; 4.55.13, 86.4; *De virt.* 2.2; *FEP* 163.64–64.65.

86. Revelation 21:10–21; Psalm 58:11; Aquinas, *Script. sent.* 4.50.2.4; [Aquinas], *ST Suppl.* 94.1–3; *ADE* 47; *FEP* 164.66–67, 166.74; *Intro.* §5: According to Antonio, the elect "will rejoice . . . because they will see God's enemies severely tormented," and Facio cites a Psalm about revenge in which "a just person will rejoice, washing his hands in the blood of sinners." Aquinas concludes that the blessed enjoy seeing the damned suffer because the sight increases their happiness and gratitude to God. Reason precludes pity. But it is not pain, as such, that causes their joy, which is indirect—because the blessed know they have been saved from a punishment that God's justice imposes on others.

87. Psalm 80:3; Aquinas, *ST* I-II.88.4; *De malo* 5.1.3–4, citing Chrysostom, *Hom. in Matt.* 23.9; Augustine, *Enchir.* 23.93; *Conf.* 5.4; *FEP* 162.59.

88. Psalm 11:6; Isaiah 3:24; Judges 16:21; Matthew 13:42; Luke 13:28; Revelation 21:8; Aquinas, *ST* I-II.88.4; *SCG* 4.90.6; *Cat. in Matt.* 8.3; [Aquinas], *ST Suppl.* 97.1–5.

89. Augustine, *De civ. D.* 20.22; [Aquinas], *ST Suppl.* 94.1, 97.4: Although the blessed actually see the damned suffering, the damned can only think about their lost delights in Heaven. As for Hell, "the place is dark," says Aquinas, "yet there is a certain amount of light, enough to see the things that can torment the soul. . . . The damned see their own punishment because it increases their pain."

90. Proverb 13:10; Aristotle, *Eth. Nic.* 1177a11–18, 78a9–10; Aquinas, *Comm. Job* ad 40:6; [Aquinas], *Comm. Matt.* ad 4:19; *Intro.* §5: The assessment of action and contemplation, and the relation of happiness to contemplation, is a little less austere in the *Summa theologica* than in the *Reportatio* on Thomas's Matthew commentary.

Bibliography

❧❧❧

TEXTS OF MANETTI'S *DE DIGNITATE ET EXCELLENTIA HOMINIS*

Clarissimi viri Ianocii de Manettis . . . ad inclytum Arragonum regem Alfonsum, de dignitate et excellentia hominis libri IIII. Edited by Johann Alexander Brassicanus. Basel: Andreas Cratander, 1532. Online via eRara, on the website of the Universitätsbibliothek Basel.

Giannozzo Manetti. *De dignitate et excellentia hominis.* Photoreprint of Basel, 1532 edition, with introduction, bibliography, and indexes. Prepared by Elizabeth R. Leonard. Frankfurt am Main: Minerva, 1975.

——— . *De dignitate et excellentia hominis.* Edited by Elizabeth R. Leonard. Padua: Antenore, 1975. Critical edition based on the seven known witnesses.

TEXTS OF LOTARIO DI SEGNI, ANTONIO DA BARGA, AND BARTOLOMEO FACIO

Kristeller, Paul Oskar. "Frater Antonius Bargensis and His Treatise on the Dignity of Man." In *Studies in Renaissance Thought and Letters,* 2:531–60. Rome: Storia e Letteratura, 1985. Contains the Latin text of Antonio da Barga's *De dignitate hominis et de excellentia humane vite.*

Lotario di Segni [Pope Innocent III]. *De miseria humanae condicionis.* Edited by Michele Maccarrone. Lugano: Thesaurus Mundi, 1955.

——— . *De miseria condicionis humanae.* Edited and translated by Robert E. Lewis. Athens: University of Georgia Press, 1978.

Sandeo, Felino. *De regibus Siciliae et Apuliae in queis et nominatim de Alfonso rege Arragonum epitome Felini Sandei, . . . quibus accedunt Bartholomei Faccii Genuensis de humanae vitae felicitate liber, . . . de excellentia ac praestantia hominis.* Hanover: Wechel and the Heirs of Ioannes Aubrius, 1611. Electronic file available through Münchener DigitalisierungsZentrum (Digitale Bibliothek).

345

· BIBLIOGRAPHY ·

TRANSLATIONS

Lotario di Segni. *De miseria condicionis humanae*. Edited and translated by Robert E. Lewis. Athens: University of Georgia Press, 1978.

Manetti, Giannozzo. *Über die Würde und Erhabenheit des Menschen. De dignitate et excellentia hominis*. German translation only by Hartmut Leppin. Introduction by August Buck. Hamburg: F. Meiner, 1990. Brief notes.

Two Views of Man: Pope Innocent III On the Misery of Man, Giannozzo Manetti on the Dignity of Man. Translated with an introduction by Bernard Murchland. New York: F. Ungar, 1966. Contains a translation of Books 1 and 2 of Lotario's *On the Misery of Man* and Book 4 of Manetti's *On the Dignity and Excellence of Man*.

LITERATURE

Atkins, E. M. "Cicero." In *The Cambridge History of Greek and Roman Political Thought*, edited by C. Rowe and M. Schofield, 477–516. Cambridge: Cambridge University Press, 2000.

Balsdon, J. P. V. D. "*Auctoritas, dignitas, otium*." *The Classical Quarterly* 10 (1960): 43–50.

Botley, Paul. *Latin Translation in the Renaissance: The Theory and Practice of Leonardo Bruni, Giannozzo Manetti and Desiderius Erasmus*. Cambridge: Cambridge University Press, 2004.

Dignitas et excellentia hominis: Atti del convegno internazionale di studi su Giannozzo Manetti. Edited by Stefano Baldassarri. Florence: Le Lettere, 2008.

Dröge, Christoph. *Giannozzo Manetti als Denker und Hebraist*. Frankfurt am Main: Peter Lang, 1987.

Foà, Simona. "Giannozzo Manetti." In *DBI* (2007).

Garin, Eugenio. "La *dignitas hominis* e la letteratura patristica." *Rinascimento* 4 (1938): 102–46.

Gentile, Giovanni. "Il concetto dell'uomo nel rinascimento." *Giornale storico della letteratura italiana* 67 (1916): 17–75.

Glaap, Oliver. *Untersuchungen zu Giannozzo Manettis* De dignitate et excellentia hominis: *Ein Renaissance-Humanist und sein Menschenbild*. Wiesbaden: Springer, 1994.

Grant, W. Leonard. "Cicero on the Moral Character of the Orator." *The Classical Journal* 38 (1943): 472–78.

Kristeller, Paul Oskar. "The Dignity of Man." In *Renaissance Concepts of Man*, 1–21. New York: Harper and Row, 1972. Reprinted in *Renaissance Thought and Its Sources*, edited by Michael Mooney, 169–81. New York: Columbia University Press, 1979.

——— . "The Humanist Bartolomeo Facio and His Unknown Correspondence." In Kristeller's *Studies in Renaissance Thought and Letters*, 2:265–80. Rome: Storia e letteratura, 1985.

Lugano, Placido. "De vita scriptisque Antonii Bargensis commentatio." In Antonio Da Barga, *Chronicon Montis Oliveti* (1313–1450), edited by P. Lugano, xxv–li. Florence: Cocchi e Chiti, 1901.

Paravicini Bagliani, Agostino. "Papa Innocenzo IV." In *DBI* (2004).

Pico della Mirandola, Giovanni. *Discorso sulla dignità dell'uomo*. Edited by Francesco Bausi. Parma: Ugo Guanda, 2003. Bausi's introduction, pp. vii–lxix, gives a useful overview of the literature.

Pöschl, Viktor. *Der Begriff der Würde im antiken Rom und später*. Heidelberg: Carl Winter, 1989.

Radin, Max. "Roman Concepts of Equality." *Political Science Quarterly* 38 (1923): 262–89.

Schofield, Malcolm. "The Fourth Virtue." In *Cicero's Practical Philosophy*, edited by Walter Nicgorski, 43–57. Notre Dame: University of Notre Dame Press, 2012.

Schmeisser, Martin. *"Wie ein sterblicher Gott . . ." Gianozzo Manettis Konzeptzion der Würde des Menschen und ihre Rezeption im Zeitalter der Renaissance*. Paderborn: Wilhelm Fink, 2006.

Trinkaus, Charles. *In Our Image and Likeness: Humanity and Divinity in Italian Humanist Thought*. 2 vols. Chicago: University of Chicago Press and London: Constable, 1970. Reprint, Notre Dame: University of Notre Dame Press, 1995.

Viti, Paolo. "Bartolomeo Facio." In *DBI* (1994).

Wirszubski, Chaim. "*Cum dignitate otium*: A Reconsideration." *The Journal of Roman Studies* 44 (1954): 1–13.

——. *Libertas as a Political Idea at Rome During the Late Republic and Early Principate*. Cambridge: Cambridge University Press, 1950. Repr. 1968.

Index

❧❧❧

Abraham (patriarch), 147, 157
Academics, 69, 121, 139, 313n16, 324n50
Academy (Athens), 324n50
Accius, Lucius (poet), xxv, 105, 323n43, 326n21
Achilles, 161
Adam (first man), xix, xxiv, xxviii, xxxvii, xxxix, xli, 9, 97, 161, 163, 183, 197, 201, 229, 312n6, 318n15, 319n23, 325n10, 330n52, 331n57, 335n27, 336n36
Aeschines, 109
Africa, 131; North, 323n43, 326n23
Agamades, 193
Agamemnon (king), 161
Albertus Magnus (Albert the Great), 47, 71; On Animals, 315nn34–35; On the Soul, 317n3, 317n7; Summa on the Creation, 316n45
Alcidamas, 191, 217
Alcmaeon of Croton, 71, 93, 317nn4–5
Alfonso (king of Aragon, Sicily, and Naples), xi, xii, xiii, xv, xvi, xxxvi, xliv, 312n5, 335n26; dedicatee, 3–7, 251–55
Alighieri. See Dante Alighieri
Amaziah (king of Judah), 99
Ambracia, 334n19
Ambrose (saint, bishop), xxiv, xxxvii, xxxix, xl, 87, 103, 197, 221, 225, 321n35; Hexameron, 316n47, 318–19nn15–18, 320n24, 321n35; On Noah, 316n48; On the Goodness of Death, l n71, 334n22, 338n56
Amos (prophet), 322n39
Anaxagoras, 69, 165, 185, 211, 317nn3–4
Anaximander of Miletus, 69, 185, 211
Anaximenes, 69, 185, 211
Annaeus Seneca, Lucius (Seneca the Younger), xvii, 73, 95, 109, 113, 181, 207, 321n33, 324n50; Consolation to His Mother Helvia, 181, 333n4; Letters, 318n9, 321n33, 324n50, 325nn3–4; On the Shortness of Life, 237, 340n70; To Marcia on Consolation, 333n2
Anselm of Canterbury (attrib.), Book of Similitudes, 340n74
Antichrist, 322n42
Antiochus (king of Armenia), 101
Antonio da Barga, vii, viii–xii, xiv, xv, xviii, xix, xxii, xxiv, xxxvi, xliv, xlv, xlvi, 257, 312n11, 324n49, 327n32, 328n39, 333n1, 335n27, 340n74, 341n78, 343n86; Chronicle of Monte Oliveto, vii
Antonio da Barga, On Mankind's Worth (ADE), vii; 1–4, xlvii n11; 2, 334n23; 2–3, 333n5; 2–4, xlviii n29, l n68, li n89; 2–6, xlvii n12; 5, xlvii n9; 6, xlvii n6; 9, xlvii n8;

Philo of Eleusis, 323n44
Pico della Mirandola, Gianfran-
cesco, viii, xlvi n3
Pico della Mirandola, Giovanni,
vii–viii; *Oration (on the Dignity of
Man)*, vii–viii, xxxi, xxxiii, xlvi n2
Piraeus, 323n44
Pius II (pope), xiii, 269
Plato, xxii, 69, 71, 85, 93, 95, 109,
161, 213, 221, 264, 274, 275,
317nn4–5, 318n10, 328n40,
330n50, 334n19; *Apology*, 330n50,
337n49; *Euthydemus*, 330n50;
Phaedo, 71, 317n5, 319n22, 321n32,
321n34, 337n49; *Republic*, 319n22;
Timaeus, 153, 328n40
Platonists, 171, 270, 317n3, 334n19
Plautus, Titus Maccius, 109
Pliny the Elder, xxv, 109, 181, 207,
217; *Natural History*, xlix n46, 181–
83, 193, 312n8, 314n24, 316n2,
323nn43–46, 324n50, 325n11,
326n22, 333n4, 334n14, 339n67
Plutarch, 221; *Life of Cato*, 337n50
[Plutarch], *Consolation for Apollonius*,
333n13
Polites, "a certain," 95
Poliziano (Angelo Ambrogini),
336n41
Polybius, 109
Polyclitus (sculptor), 107, 127
Porcius Cato Uticensis, Marcus
(Cato the Younger), xxxix, 95,
161, 195, 217, 219, 221, 324n50,
334n19, 337n50
Porphyry, xxvii, 95, 275, 321n33,
330n53
Porphyry's Tree, xxvii

Praxiteles (sculptor), xxv, 107, 127
pre-Socratics, 317n3
Proclus, 274
Prometheus, 123
Protasius (saint, martyr), 151,
328n39
Psalmist, xl, 97, 155, 241, 285, 287,
322n36
Ps.-Anselm, *Book of Meditations and
Prayers*, l n66, 318n16
Ps.-Dionysius the Areopagite: *Celes-
tial Hierarchy*, 327n32; *Ecclesiastical
Hierarchy*, 327n32
Ptolemy (king of Egypt), 191
Punic War: First, 161; Second, 161
Pyrrhus (king of Epirus), 113, 161
Pythagoras of Samos, 69, 71, 93,
109, 187, 221, 274
Pythagorean/Pythagoreans, 93,
317nn4–5, 326n21

Quintilian (Marcus Fabius Quinti-
lianus), 324n50; *Institutes*, 324n50

Rabanus Maurus, *Homilies on the
Major Feastdays*, xlvii n9
Raphael (archangel), 147, 279
Remigius of Auxerre, xxiv, 87,
320n24; *Commentary on Genesis*,
319n24
Roman: Church, 151, 257, 281; elo-
quence, 65; politics, xxxiii, xxxiv;
religion, xx; thought, xxxiii
Romans, 149, 265, 326n19, 326n23
Rome, xii, xvi, 5, 105, 107, 320n29;
Castel Sant'Angelo, 323n44; Cu-
ria Hostilia, 324n50; Pyramid of
Cestius, 323n44; pyramid of

Publication of this volume has been made possible by

The Myron and Sheila Gilmore Publication Fund at I Tatti
The Robert Lehman Endowment Fund
The Jean-François Malle Scholarly Programs and Publications Fund
The Andrew W. Mellon Scholarly Publications Fund
The Craig and Barbara Smyth Fund
for Scholarly Programs and Publications
The Lila Wallace–Reader's Digest Endowment Fund
The Malcolm Wiener Fund for Scholarly Programs and Publications